NATIONAL GEOGRAPHIC
TRAVELER
San Diego

NATIONAL GEOGRAPHIC

TRAVELER

San Diego

Marael Johnson and Joe Yogerst
Photography by Michael Melford

Contents

How to use this guide 6–7 About the authors & photographer 8
San Diego areas 45–234 Travelwise 235–264
Index 265–269 Credits 270-271

Page 1: Roller-coasting high over Legoland
Pages 2–3: Green palms and blue sky in the Golden Triangle
Left: Tiled dome of the California Building, Balboa Park

How to use this guide

See back flap for keys to text and map symbols

The *National Geographic Traveler* brings you the best of sunny San Diego in text, pictures, and maps. Divided into three main sections, the guide begins with an overview of the city's history and culture. Following are nine area chapters that cover the city, the far reaches of the county, and Baja California; each chapter's featured sites are treated in depth and were selected by the authors for their particular interest.

The selected areas within the city and the surrounding regions are arranged geographically. A map introduces each chapter, highlighting the featured sites. Walks and drives, plotted on their own maps, suggest routes for discovering an area. Features and sidebars give intriguing detail on history, culture, or contemporary life.

The final section, Travelwise, lists essential information for the traveler—pretrip planning, special events, getting around, and emergencies—together with a selection of hotels, restaurants, shops, and entertainment.

To the best of our knowledge, all information is accurate as of the press date. However, it's always advisable to call ahead when possible.

Color coding

Each area of the city is color coded for easy reference. Find the area you want on the map on the front flap, then look for the color flash at the top of the pages of the relevant chapter. Information in **Travelwise** is also color coded to each area.

San Diego Natural History Museum
www.sdnhm.org
Map p. 69
1788 El Prado
619-232-3821
Open daily except Thanksgiving, Christmas, & New Year's Day
$$
Bus: 7, 7A, 7B

Visitor information

Practical information for most sites is given in the side column (see key to symbols on back flap). The map reference gives the page number of the map and often the grid reference. Other details are address, telephone number, days closed, entrance charge in a range from $ (under $5) to $$$$$ (over $20), and nearest public transportation in San Diego. Other sites have information in italics and parentheses in the text.

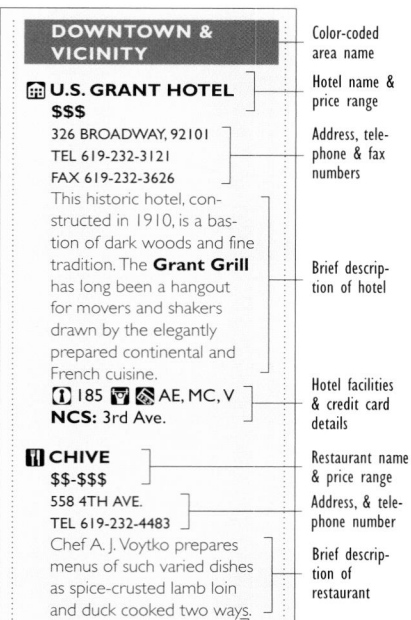

TRAVELWISE

DOWNTOWN & VICINITY — Color-coded area name

U.S. GRANT HOTEL $$$ — Hotel name & price range

326 BROADWAY, 92101
TEL 619-232-3121
FAX 619-232-3626 — Address, telephone & fax numbers

This historic hotel, constructed in 1910, is a bastion of dark woods and fine tradition. The **Grant Grill** has long been a hangout for movers and shakers drawn by the elegantly prepared continental and French cuisine. — Brief description of hotel

185 AE, MC, V NCS: 3rd Ave. — Hotel facilities & credit card details

CHIVE $$-$$$ — Restaurant name & price range

558 4TH AVE.
TEL 619-232-4483 — Address, & telephone number

Chef A. J. Voytko prepares menus of such varied dishes as spice-crusted lamb loin and duck cooked two ways. — Brief description of restaurant

D only **NCS:** F St.
2, 3, 5, 20
All major cards — Restaurant closures & credit card details

Hotel & restaurant prices

An explanation of the price bands used in entries is given in the Hotels & Restaurants section (on p. 242).

AREA MAPS

● A locator map accompanies each area map and shows the location of that area in the city.

WALKING TOURS

● An information box gives the starting and ending points, time and length of walk, and places not to be missed along the route.

EXCURSION MAPS

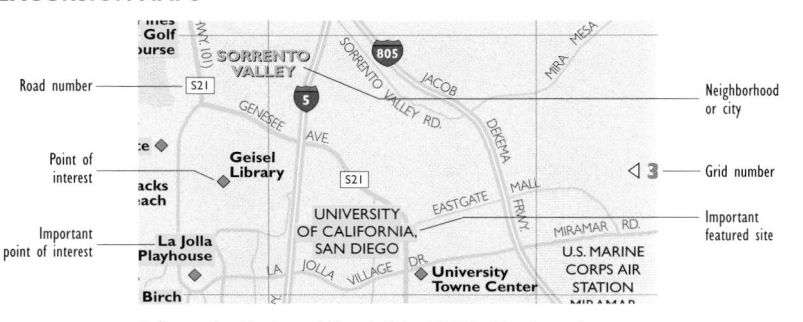

● Sites mentioned in chapters 4-10 are bolded and highlighted in yellow on the map. Other suggested places to visit are also bolded and are shown with a red diamond symbol.

NATIONAL GEOGRAPHIC

TRAVELER

San Diego

About the authors & photographer

Author **Marael Johnson** is a travel writer and editor who has been based in southern California for most of her life. She has written for numerous print and on-line publications, profiling regions as diverse as Outback Australia, Europe's Basque region, remote South Pacific islands, Central America, and Louisiana's Cajun country. Johnson has received a Lowell Thomas Award from the Society of American Travel Writers and a Benjamin Franklin Award for best guidebook from the Publisher Marketing Association. She is also the author of The National Geographic Traveler's *Los Angeles* guide.

Born and raised in San Diego, co-author **Joe Yogerst** spent 20 years wandering the globe before moving back to his hometown in 1995. His work has appeared in *The Washington Post,* the *Los Angeles Times, Islands, Travel Holiday, Vogue,* the *International Herald Tribune,* and various National Geographic publications. His four Lowell Thomas Awards include one for *Long Road South* (National Geographic Books, 1999), his account of a journey along the Pan-American Highway from Texas to Argentina.

Photographer **Michael Melford** delights in sharing his fresh perspective of destinations around the globe with fellow travelers. In addition to shooting the *New England* and *Alaska* guidebooks for the National Geographic Guides to America's Outdoors, he has published award-winning travel photography in all the top publications, among them *National Geographic Traveler, Travel and Leisure, Life, Fortune,* and *Newsweek.*

History & culture

An explosion of color over San Diego Bay

San Diego today

"AMERICA'S FINEST CITY," THE MONIKER BESTOWED BY CITY OFFICIALS SOME years ago, was less a marketing tool than a simple statement of civic pride. As the birthplace of California, San Diego has set the standard for the state's carefree and casual lifestyle. Indeed, blessed with a rich history, stunning geography, and a Mediterranean climate, San Diego is without exaggeration one of Earth's delightful cities.

IN WITH THE OLD

The Spanish heritage imparted by the early explorers and missionaries remains evident throughout the landscape. Much of the city's architecture and many of its historic sites still reflect that era. At Mission San Diego de Alcalá—dedicated by Padre Junípero Serra in 1769, the first in a chain of 21 California missions—the reconstructed chapel and other structures have served the communal and spiritual needs of generation upon generation of parishioners. The buildings continue to function as a community church today.

Indeed, San Diegans have managed to incorporate a large chunk of history in their contemporary lives. The old Mexican ranchos have slowly evolved to become parks, sporting fields, picnic grounds, and residential areas.

Need to get downtown? Commuters and sightseers alike enjoy the short, pleasant ferry trip across San Diego Bay.

moving farther north. That red-light district developed into San Diego's Gaslamp Quarter—downtown's resurrected heart and soul—which is now a historic district filled with rehabilitated buildings. Many businesses are located inside converted gambling halls and reformed whorehouses.

The quarter may bustle during the day, but come nighttime, watch out! That's when residents from all over San Diego County converge on the area to dine on fine food, listen to great music, chat at chic bars and trendy cafés, load up on purchases at colorful Horton Plaza, take in movies and theater performances, or simply soak up the energy of the San Diego street scene.

Unlike any other city of its size, San Diego's downtown core is a clean, cosmopolitan center of fun and frivolity, not some tawdry place to avoid when the sun goes down. And though the Gaslamp Quarter is considered the city's hub, it's surrounded by myriad competing sights. Short strolls lead to the Embarcadero—a waterside promenade—and to glorious San Diego Bay, where motorboats and excursion yachts bob alongside cruise ships and U.S. Navy vessels; to the newly expanded convention center (with its sail-like roof!); to the Civic Center and Concourse; and even to the courthouse and federal buildings.

Northwest of downtown's core, Little Italy (once the enclave of Italian immigrants lured to San Diego in the 1920s and '30s by its thriving tuna industry) is enjoying a little Italian renaissance of its own, booming with residential building, fine shops and galleries, and—of course—Italian eateries and ambience. At the eastern edge of the Gaslamp Quarter, the formerly decrepit warehouse district has metamorphosed into the East Village, made newly convivial by its renovated lofts and antique malls. The adjacent Ballpark District, slated to become the site of the San Diego Padres' baseball stadium, should generate exciting changes as well.

OASIS BY THE BAY

Across San Diego Bay, the town of Coronado

Old Town—the city's first European settlement—has been left relatively untouched. As a matter of fact, most of the early city has been designated a state historic park, and much of its historic ambience has endured or been recreated. Old Town may rank near the top of most visitors' must-see lists, but that doesn't deter locals intent on revisiting their roots—especially since those roots now tap into a multicultural mélange fed by such festive currents as Bazaar del Mundo, strolling mariachis, and folkloric dancers.

Early entrepreneur and developer Alonzo Horton might puff with pride if he could see his "New Town" today. After Horton persuaded residents to shift the city core to its present location by San Diego Bay, a seedier element took over the town and many locals wound up

may still be home to Naval Air Station North Island and headquarters for Pacific Fleet naval aviation, but that hardly makes it a rough-and-tumble navy town. In fact, Coronado has retained the gentility for which it was original-ly noted—as a classy seaside resort, crowned by the landmark Hotel del Coronado. Still a glamorous getaway for tourists, the hotel also attracts locals for its famed Sunday brunches and other social occasions.

The peninsula (not an island!) offers proof that one of the country's largest naval bases (and San Diego's largest employer) can coexist with tourists. It's common to see Navy SEALs training on the same beaches that welcome sunbathers, surfers, joggers, and kids building castles in the sand. The huge naval complex takes up one corner, with the Naval Amphibi-ous Base straddling the Silver Strand to Coro-nado's south, yet the residents—a mix of retired military, old-money descendants of city founders, and conservative younger com-

muters—mesh peacefully in a town filled with eclectic architecture and tidy homes, independently owned businesses, and practically no crime.

NICE & EASY

Despite the fact that San Diegans have a lot to gloat about, the locals are not haughty, but nice. They are casual, sporty, smiling, relaxed, friendly, open-minded, and seemingly allergic to controversy. Environmentally conscious,

they clean up after their dogs, never litter, and recycle everything in sight. They may even spend time picking up other peoples' trash. And why wouldn't they be in such good cheer? San Diegans are blessed with some of the country's most enviable climate and geography. Often referred to as the "Riviera of the

Not just another face in the crowd: Colorfully lifelike characters amaze and attract kids—and kids at heart—at Legoland.

United States," the city and its coastal areas have a Mediterranean climate, with very low levels of both rainfall and humidity. In summer, temperature-moderating ocean breezes clean away most pollution and cool off inland areas. Out of the east in late summer and early fall sweep the dry Santa Ana winds.

The landscape is both luscious and large. With three distinct biomes—coast, inland valleys and mountains, and deserts—San Diego County doesn't lack character. Within view

from any high locale in the city are verdant valleys, prickly desert, Baja California, ebb and flow of the Pacific Ocean, and mountain peaks—the latter often dusted with snow. Even though towering palms and perennially colorful flower beds in and around the city create a tropical atmosphere (albeit one blissfully devoid of steamy humidity), the native plant community conforms to a drier climate. Many trees and shrubs of the chaparral that extensively covers much of the county never shed a leaf. Up in the higher elevations of the Peninsular Ranges, the cooler environment offers a leafy retreat of oaks, pinyons, and Jeffrey pines.

LIFE ON THE AMERICAN RIVIERA

San Diegans spend a lot of their time outdoors. Most are health conscious and physically active, thus casually—even minimally—clothed. The adjacent Pacific Ocean plays an important role in almost everyone's life.

Without even checking the forecast, sailors can predict it's going to be another clear, dry, sunny day for sailing in San Diego.

The city's beautiful beaches, particularly those near La Jolla and in the North County, are used throughout the year by surfers and swimmers (the cooler waters of winter mandate wet suits). Except in summer, when visitors and students descend en masse for fun in the sun, San Diegans pick and choose among

favored beaches for surfside walks and jogs, to explore tide pools, toss Frisbees, play volleyball and other sports, or just take up a perch and wait for another glorious sunset to unfold. In-line skaters glide back and forth along the Mission Beach boardwalk, while skateboarders roll and twirl wherever a paved incline presents itself.

Other San Diegans are drawn to Mission Bay Park, just a short drive north from downtown. This 4,000-acre aquatic park serves as the ultimate tribute to San Diego's love of sports and the outdoors. A tidal marsh until the 1960s, the park is now a paradise for boating, swimming, fishing, waterskiing, cycling, kite flying, and a panoply of other sporty delights.

Not all of the action takes place on the water. The San Diego area features world-class golf and tennis facilities, and it hosts many prominent annual events: The PGA Tour is one, the Toshiba Tennis Classic another. Joggers and cyclists are almost as common as automobiles, and many city and country roads have special lanes reserved for those pursuits (not that any self-respecting San Diegan would dare impede these revered citizens). Even those who are unable to join the hordes outdoors head to a fitness club or yoga class to keep toned and tuned.

Most of San Diego's special events take place outside, and all are planned with a benign disregard for the weather: It will be sunny and perfect, of course. San Diegans celebrations of any stripe: love street parties, block parties, beach parties; fetes on yachts and sailboats, in coves and atop cliffs; concerts, festivals, parades, fireworks, surfing and sandcastle competitions—it's all good.

Dining and drinking beneath sun and sky provide more sedentary delights. City dwellers flock to alfresco restaurants, sidewalk cafés, waterfront bars and eateries, or—picnic baskets in hand—to beaches and parks. Fresh seafood, creative salads, and Mexican specialties are among the top sellers at most restaurants, be they tiny diners or more upmarket establishments.

Laid-back appearances and attitudes to the contrary, most San Diegans work every bit as hard as they play. At the forefront of the local economy are the naval bases and aerospace industries, which contribute to the defense of the entire country. The city is also a major center for biotech development, medical research, and high-tech enterprises: it is home to the highly regarded Salk Institute, a medical and scientific research center founded by Dr. Jonas Salk; the Scripps Institution of Oceanography, the world's oldest marine-related teaching and research facility; and the University of California at San Diego, which has spawned ten Nobel laureates, three of whom were active faculty members as of October 2002.

SEASIDE SOPHISTICATION

More than just a monument to outdoor living and topographical pyrotechnics, San Diego gently but firmly guides the way to its impressive array of museums and other cultural shrines. Most of them congregate within Balboa Park, a 1,200-acre social center and leafy retreat near downtown that locals have adopted as their own backyard. The majority of

museums here reside inside gorgeous Spanish Colonial structures left over from promotional expositions held in 1915-16 and 1935-36.

Anchoring the northwest corner of Balboa Park is the World-Famous San Diego Zoo. (So often was that hyphenated adjective deployed to describe the zoo that officials bowed to the inevitable and made it part of the site's official name.) On most days, locals and visitors can be found streaming through the grounds and buildings in equal numbers.

San Diego is also proud of its internationally renowned opera company—and, more recently, its symphony. The San Diego Symphony, having grown moribund from a lack of funds, was resuscitated in 2002 by a $120 million endowment commitment from philanthropists Joan and Irwin Jacobs (the latter is co-founder, board chairman, and CEO of Qualcomm, a homegrown technology company). The symphony stands poised to join the ranks of the country's finest orchestras.

A LIVABLE CITY

Although San Diego offers up a cornucopia of see-worthy sights, almost all of them are eminently accessible. Both the Santa Fe Depot and the Greyhound bus terminal lie within walking distance of most downtown attractions. Amtrak and the Coaster commuter trains—most of their runs adjacent to or within a short distance of the Pacific Ocean—arrive

San Diego's Mediterranean climate invites year-round alfresco dining.

In this city less than 20 miles from the international border—a city that once belonged to Mexico and that continues to be home to generations of Hispanics—Mexican culture plays a central role in day-to-day life. Food, language, architecture, and art all pay tribute to this rich heritage, bestowing upon the region a stunning combination of serenity, exuberance, and nostalgia.

and depart from the Santa Fe Depot, while the bright red San Diego trolleys thread their way through greater downtown, Mission Valley, East County, and all the way to the Mexican border. The cruise-ship terminal is located near the Little Italy trolley station (one stop north of the Santa Fe Depot), while San Diego harbor-excursion vessels and the Coronado Ferry usually stand waiting to sail just a few blocks away. San Diego International Airport at Lindbergh Field sits within the city limits,

giving arriving air passengers a harrowingly low-level aerial view of the greenery in Balboa Park as their plane passes overhead.

In a sure sign of urban vitality, more and more San Diegans are forsaking suburbia for inner-city living. Converted warehouses, high-rise condominiums, townhomes, houseboats, and—for the ambitious—fixer-uppers have become sought-after residences for everyone from hipsters to retirees. Like San Diego's visitors, they all have one thing in common:

A denizen of San Diego **Wild Animal Park** sticks its neck out for visitors.

They can't get enough of this vibrant city. Neither, apparently, can the city's sizable population of homeless people. With its mild climate, San Diego attracts a fair number of transients, but nowhere near the proportion typically seen in other large cities. Still, visitors should be aware of the situation and prepared to deal with it. Most homeless people congregate around Horton Plaza and the East Village area. Visitors can also expect to encounter panhandlers in the Gaslamp Quarter, a city brochure advises, because many social-service providers are based nearby.

Most San Diegans go downtown, day or night, without hesitation. Given the area's easygoing atmosphere and the preponderance of celebrations that take place there, you may start thinking like a local and come to see San Diego as a majorly mellow metropolis. ■

History of San Diego

A COVETED TREASURE CHEST OVERFLOWING WITH NATURAL JEWELS, SAN Diego has a multifaceted history as well. The city that is often dubbed "America's Riviera" happens to be the place where California began.

EARLY INHABITANTS

A skull found in 1929 on the seaside bluffs between Del Mar and Solana Beach reveals the presence of human life in the San Diego area at least 12,000 years ago. Little is known about "Del Mar Man" other than the fact that his clan harvested shellfish along the shore—and was eventually displaced by the equally little-known La Jollan people. Some time around 1000 B.C., the La Jollans were dislodged by the migration of a more advanced desert society called the Kumeyaay, whose language and lifestyle closely approximated those of the Mojave and Yuma.

The migratory Kumeyaay moved back and forth between the seaside and the mountains and lived together in tribal groups organized into small villages. Their huts were made of interwoven tule—a large bulrush that grows on overflowed ground in the Southwest. Although they lived throughout present-day San Diego County, the largest settlement stood near the mouth of the San Diego River, at the base of modern Presidio Hill. Each village controlled its own designated territory, with the tribal leaders overseeing land use, distributing food, and trading with other clans.

Primarily vegetarians, the Kumeyaay ground acorns into flour, then boiled the flour into a daily gruel. Animal flesh was not a dietary mainstay, yet hunting was popular. Hunters eagerly sought out snakes, rabbits, coyotes, crows, mice, frogs, and ground squirrels, but spared the creatures they considered sacred:

In 1542, explorer Juan Rodríguez Cabrillo (above) and his expeditionary forces were the first Europeans to visit San Diego.

pigeons, doves, and bears. Seafood, plentiful in local bays and marshes, was captured using nets and weirs, and occasionally via hooks and lines dropped from rafts.

The Kumeyaay fashioned tools from bone, wood, stone, and shell, produced primitive pottery, and carved local granite and sandstone into grinding bowls and food containers. Thanks to the temperate climate, clothing was rarely necessary—Kumeyaay men usually went naked except for smears of black and white paint (thought to ward off evil spirits and human enemies), while Kumeyaay women wore skirts made of animal skins or woven fibers. A relatively high number of people were adorned with tattoos rendered with cactus needles and charcoal. Healing rituals were carried out by medicine men, who had high ranking in tribal groups.

Kumeyaay land management techniques centered on the slash and burn of native sage and chaparral. Not only did this ward off potentially disastrous forest fires, it permitted plants to reseed themselves for enhanced food production.

The myths and legends of the Kumeyaay people reached their most sophisticated expression in highly developed rock-art paintings. Kumeyaay rock art abounds in San Diego's backcountry—especially the Blair Valley area of Anza-Borrego Desert State Park.

THE SPANISH ARE COMING!

Spanish explorer Juan Rodríguez Cabrillo, a veteran of the Cortés expedition that vanquished the Aztecs in Mexico, sailed into San Diego Bay on September 28, 1542. His ships dropped anchor in the lee of Point Loma, and Cabrillo made the first European landing in

San Diego's accessible coastline—typified by Swami's Beach, above—encouraged Spanish exploration in the 16th century.

what is now the state of California. It being the feast day of San Miguel Archángel, Cabrillo christened the site San Miguel and claimed the land for Spain. Though Cabrillo and his entourage went ashore and were greeted by the Kumeyaay, they remained in the newly found territory only six days before continuing north in search of the mythical Strait of Anian (the Northwest Passage).

Another 60 years passed before the Spanish returned, this time in three ships commanded by explorer Sebastián Vizcaíno. After they landed, the expedition priests said the first Roman Catholic Mass on California soil, and the site was rechristened San Diego de Alcalá to honor the 15th-century Franciscan saint whose feast day was approaching. Vizcaíno sailed off after just ten days, but his visit marked the start of Spanish interest in both San Diego and the California coast.

That interest proved fleeting, however. Although the Spanish used California harbors as stopovers on trading voyages between Europe and the Orient, they made no effort to settle the region permanently until the late 18th

century. After fighting the Seven Year War with France, the Spanish began to worry that other European countries might have their eye on relatively untouched southern California. Already well established on the east coast of North America and in the Mississippi Valley, both the English and the French did not conceal their desire to expand west across the continent. Adding to this angst were the Russians; making their way from Siberia to Alaska and southward in their search for sea-otter pelts, they were already a presence in northern California. The time had come, Spain decided, to colonize the California coast.

The Spanish launched their two-pronged colonization campaign in the first half of 1769. This immense effort, led by Captain Gaspar de Portolá (later the first governor of California), was known as the Sacred Expedition: its primary aim was to convert the region's Kumeyaay people to Christianity. The ships *San Antonio* and *San Carlos* arrived in San Diego in April, bearing an advance party that established a waterfront encampment near what is now Harbor Island. By the time

Portolá arrived on July 1 after marching across Baja (Lower) California, nearly all of the crewmen had died from scurvy.

Soon afterward, Portolá and most of his troops moved north by land to claim Monterey Bay for Spain and establish another colony. Among the small band of soldiers and missionaries who stayed behind in San Diego was 55-year-old Franciscan padre Junípero Serra, who on July 16 celebrated Mass on Presidio Hill, officially founding San Diego as the first of California's 21 missions.

The Spaniards called the native people Diegueños and placed them under the mission's jurisdiction. Some of the Indians headed for the hills. The majority—weakened by imported European diseases—reluctantly became wards of the mission. Christian conversion, however, took longer to accomplish than the Spanish had anticipated: Nearly a year would pass before the first Kumeyaay was baptized.

After Kumeyaay Indians attacked the settlement and killed a member of the expedition, a stockade, small church, and simple wood-and-brush dwellings were built around the mission at the crest of Presidio Hill. They were eventually replaced by more permanent adobe structures. The strategic hilltop fortress became the center for Spanish culture and colonization in Alta (Upper) California. The Spanish scorned the Kumeyaay's land-management skills in favor of their own techniques—planting crops and grazing livestock. However, the padres had difficulty procuring enough labor to provide food for themselves and the Spanish troops stationed at the Presidio.

Padre Luis Jayme, who stayed at the mission when Padre Serra went on to missionary work in northern California, moved Mission San Diego de Alcalá 6 miles northeast. The mission would be nearer the Kumeyaay village of Nipaguay (a sizable source of potential converts) and it would enjoy access to river water and fertile farmland. The new mission was completed in December 1774. The Presidio remained on the hilltop site to serve as the region's strategic, civil, and political center.

In 1775, hundreds of recent Indian converts, disgruntled by their new slavelike conditions, launched a midnight attack on the new mission—the only such raid on any of the California missions. Fire destroyed or damaged the church and other buildings, and Padre Jayme was one of three men killed.

This early drawing of San Diego shows the rudimentary town just months before it was incorporated as a city in March 1850.

THE MISSION ERA

Padre Serra returned from northern California to supervise San Diego de Alcalá's reconstruction. By October 1776, the new church—with a stone foundation and high adobe walls—was ready for use. Additional repairs and expansions continued through the mid-1780s.

Daily life at the mission revolved around religious discipline and strict control of nearly every aspect of neophyte life. Most days were the same—dawn Mass, education in church doctrine, fieldwork for the men and craftwork for the women, more doctrine, Spanish language instruction, supper, and bed. This patriarchal system mandated that unmarried female converts be locked in their barracks each night, while married couples were allowed to live in huts. Anyone who strayed from the rules was subject to flogging and imprisonment in stocks.

By 1797, the mission harbored 1,405 converts and encompassed 50,000 cultivated acres, plus pasturage for thousands of sheep, cattle, and horses. Although its daily routine rarely varied, San Diego de Alcalá was beset by various hardships until the early 1820s—insufficient numbers of settlers, drought, floods, and a series of earthquakes that leveled the church. The third church to stand on the site was dedicated in 1813; it featured buttress-style construction to foil future shocks.

Having established the first California missions, the Spanish then tried to strangle foreign trade and block other European settlers from gaining a toehold in the area. They did not want outsiders enticing the locals who had been coerced into the mission work force. But foreigners eventually came calling, English explorer George Vancouver paid a visit in 1793 and wasted no time in letting his British compatriots know that San Diego was not merely an excellent harbor but a haphazardly guarded one as well. In the wake of his visit, the Spanish enlarged and fortified the Presidio and constructed a fort on Point Guijarros (Cobblestones) near Point Loma. In 1800, a fur-trading brig called the *Betsy* was the first American ship to enter San Diego Bay. Word spread of profitable trade opportunities with China and the thriving market in otter pelts along the California coast; the seafaring traffic in and out of the harbor steadily grew.

UNDER THE MEXICAN FLAG

Throughout the mission period, California remained distant in both miles and spirit from the powers that controlled it—the royals in Spain and the Spanish viceroys in Mexico. By the second decade of the 19th century, independence movements had flared up in every Spanish possession in the western hemisphere except California, where the padres and their Indian converts carried on as if the world

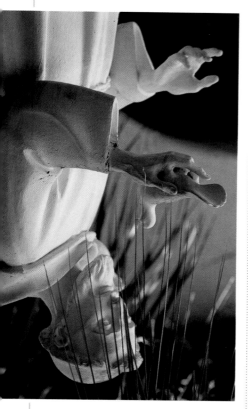

St. Francis of Assisi graces the garden of Mission San Diego de Alcalá—the first of 21 California missions established by Franciscan friars.

would never change. In 1821, Mexico gained its independence from Spain and wasted little time in stamping its authority on San Diego. The Spanish officially ceded control of the Presidio on April 20, 1822.

Remaining faithful to its original mandate, the 1816 Mission San Antonio de Pala continues to minister to the surrounding Native American community.

Under Mexican rule, the Presidio was left to crumble and the mission began to decline. Most of the Spanish troops chose to remain in San Diego rather than make their own way back to Spain. Capt. Francisco María Ruiz, former commander of the Presidio, spearheaded a move to the area below the hill. By 1829, the settlement numbered roughly 30 dwellings, most of them occupied by retired soldiers and their families.

Attempting to scale back the power of the Catholic Church, which had gained an economic and social stranglehold on Mexico during the Spanish colonial period, the new Mexican government passed the Secularization Act of 1833, which dissolved the mission system and placed church property in private hands. Local Mexican rulers and savvy new arrivals turned the mission lands into enormous—and prosperous—*ranchos* (cattle ranches).

The indigenous people didn't fare so well. They went from being subjugated labor for the missionaries to virtual slaves for the influx of wealthy dons—who dubbed themselves *Cali-*

fornios to stand out from the rest of Mexico. Unlike the insular Spanish, the Californios embraced foreign trade and had a valuable commodity as a lure. Using agricultural and animal-husbandry techniques introduced by the Spaniards, these nouveau *rancheros* excelled at cattle ranching to such a degree that San Diego became a source of highly sought-after cowhides (called "California bank notes"). San Diego became a prosperous port and a fulcrum of the international pelt trade. Cattle were herded from local ranchos to the abattoirs of La Playa village on Point Loma, where they were slaughtered. The hides were cleaned and cured in barnlike hide houses. Payment took myriad forms: guns, woolens, boots, and hardware from the U.S. Atlantic states; liquor and perfume from France; and silk goods from China.

Richard Henry Dana, a sailor who arrived from New England in 1835, vividly detailed this community and its colorful lifestyle in his 1840 book, *Two Years Before the Mast.* "Things sell, on an average, at an advance of nearly 300

Paying homage to the short-lived 1846 Bear Flag Revolt, which helped pave the way for California statehood four years later, the state's official flag proudly displays a lumbering grizzly.

percent upon Boston prices," Dana noted of life along the waterfront. Indeed, the local economy was booming.

The settlement that grew up at the base of Presidio Hill also reaped rewards from trade. Hides were responsible for port revenues totaling around $34,000 annually—many times higher than San Francisco's maritime earnings at the time. In 1834, San Diego—with a population of about 400—was officially proclaimed a *pueblo* (municipality), shedding its military status at the same time it sloughed off its crumbled Presidio. Juan María Osuna was elected the first mayor, and Old Town became a hub of social, cultural, and political life.

Despite their burgeoning prosperity, the Californios grew edgy about the Yankee traders and their ultimate intentions. Since the turn of the 19th century, the Americans had negotiated the Louisiana Purchase from France, staked a claim to the Pacific Northwest, and by 1848 wrangled Texas away from Mexico. Nor did the U.S. government make any secret of its designs on the rich lands of northern Mexico.

Though the Yankee merchants who arrived by sea were outwardly welcomed and accepted by the church and local oligarchy, fears of an overland invasion simmered beneath the surface.

YANKEE INVASION

Such jitters were soon justified. After several years of diplomatic skirmishes, President James K. Polk ordered the seizure of disputed land along the Rio Grande, precipitating war between Mexico and the United States in 1846. U.S. troops invaded Mexico. On June 14, a handful of American citizens living in California declared the territory a republic—a homegrown insurrection known as the Bear Flag Revolt. The Californios resisted mightily but proved to be no match for the U.S. forces.

The Californios did, however, inflict one major defeat on the conquering forces. Marines from the U.S. warship *Cyane* hoisted the first American flag over Old Town on July 29, 1846. A few days later, U.S. Army Col. John C. Frémont headed north to capture the Mexican pueblo of Los Angeles. The small band of

Yankees left to "hold down the fort"—in an area populated by Mexican loyalists—began to feel edgy and sought refuge on the whaler *Stonington*, anchored in San Diego Bay. As soon as they steamed offshore, the Californios raised the Mexican flag again; however, their rebellion evaporated in November with the appearance of U.S. Navy Commodore Robert Stockton at the helm of the 60-gun ship *Congress*. Without having to fire a shot, Stockton and his men raised the Stars and Stripes above Old Town once more, set to work rebuilding the long-neglected fort on Presidio Hill. They established a garrison of 100 soldiers and renamed the site Fort Stockton.

Meanwhile, Gen. Stephen W. Kearny and his troops—more than 110 dragoons dubbed the "Army of the West"—were advancing overland from Fort Leavenworth, Kansas, which they had departed on June 30. Kearny sent word of his impending arrival in San Diego to Stockton, who arranged for his own contingent to ride north, rendezvous with Kearny, and escort the reinforcements into town. After the two forces linked up in what is now northern San Diego County, Kearny learned that an encampment of armed Californios was lying in wait in the San Pasqual Valley near Escondido. On December 6, instead of heading directly to San Diego, the general set out to take the Californios by surprise.

The surprise was on Kearny. Shouting *"Viva Mexico!"* the Californios pounced on his troops, wielding their willow lances and lariats to deadly effect. Damp powder and misunderstood commands blunted the American response. The attack broke off after a brief skirmish, both sides claiming victory. The Americans, however, suffered the most casualties (19 deaths), making this the single bloodiest battle of the American invasion.

U.S. forces in San Diego were soon joined by the 350-strong Mormon Battalion, which had trekked nearly 2,000 miles overland from Illinois in the longest infantry march in military history. The Mormons may have missed the fighting, but they built the city's first brick house and conducted the area's first census under American rule. The tally: 248 residents of European descent, 483 converted Indians, 1,550 wild Indians, three Negroes, and three Sandwich Islanders.

Cut off from reinforcements in Mexico and realizing they could not overcome superior American firepower, the Californios surrendered to Frémont at Cahuenga Pass (between the San Fernando Valley and present-day Hollywood) in January 1847. The Treaty of Guadalupe Hidalgo, signed 13 months later, transferred to the United States sovereignty over California and a vast swath of what is now Arizona and New Mexico, as well as parts of other states. The U.S. border was redrawn, reaching the Pacific Coast about 20 miles south of San Diego. The Mexican era had officially come to a close.

STATEHOOD & AMERICAN INFLUENCE

In 1850, California was admitted to the United States as the 31st state. By then the state's economic and political power base had shifted to San Francisco, with its own fine harbor and its proximity to the Sierra Nevada goldfields.

San Diego receded into something of a backwater—a sleepy coastal town detached from the boom taking shape in northern California. But American influence was still evident. One of the most contentious issues was property law: The Californios battled a U.S. legal system (and would-be Yankee settlers) that sought to carve up their ranchos in much the same way the Mexican government had subdivided the mission lands 20 years before. The Kumeyaay, though dwindling in number through disease and other hardships, were marginalized even more from mainstream society; U.S. authorities relocated them to the San Pasqual Valley and the Pala area along the San Luis Rey River.

Having made a fortune in San Francisco, entrepreneur William Heath Davis arrived in San Diego during the first year of statehood looking for ways to make another quick million. Davis believed that San Diego's commercial core should be moved closer to the bay in order to take advantage of its marvelous port. He and his business partners promptly purchased 160 acres of waterfront land for around $2,300. A new community—located on the same site as San Diego's present downtown—was laid out with streets, prefabricated houses, and a wharf.

The only thing missing was people to populate the place. Though prescient in determining the area that would eventually become downtown San Diego, Davis could not persuade enough Old Town dwellers to pull up their roots. Within two years construction had come to a halt, the population had dwindled, and the new waterfront community—derided by locals as "Davis's Folly"—had to acknowledge its status as a ghost town. Many of the houses were moved or razed for firewood.

The mission style of early Spanish settlers continues to influence the architecture of the San Diego area.

The completion of the Point Loma Lighthouse in the mid-1850s signaled San Diego's rebirth as a major West Coast port. The 1860s bore witness to the city's increased stature. Geographically isolated from the conflict and obsessed with their own affairs, San Diegans seemed barely to notice the Civil War raging on the other side of the continent. (During it, President Abraham Lincoln returned the long-derelict Mission San Diego de Alcala to the Catholic Church.)

Finally, in April 1867 entrepreneur Alonzo Erastus Horton rode a paddle-wheel steamer into San Diego Bay. His arrival altered the city's fortunes indelibly. Horton had already earned (and lost) a fortune in San Francisco, so he was scouting out new investment opportunities. Like Davis, he believed that San Diego must be closer to the water if it was to prosper. For just $265, Horton purchased 960 acres and promised a waterfront lot to anyone who would build on it. Some parcels were handed

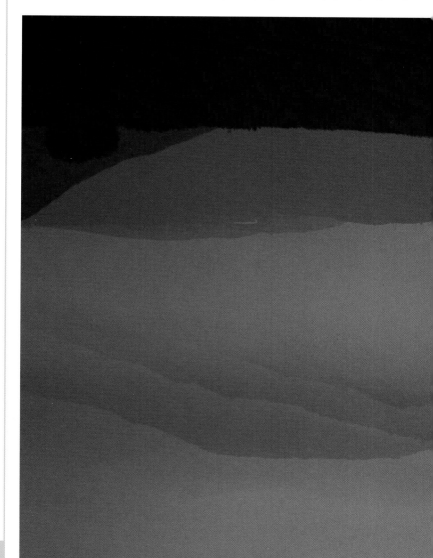

out free; others brought $10 or so. A development called Horton's Addition soon rose just blocks from the ill-fated Davis's Folly. Within a few years, the neighborhood—which included a wharf, a hotel, and a plaza—had drawn enough residents and commerce away from Old Town to be deemed the heart of the city. The combined Davis-Horton land area became known as New Town, and Horton would later be dubbed the "father of San Diego." By the end of the decade, the *San Diego*

Though mountains east of San Diego caused the transcontinental railway's diversion to Los Angeles, the rail line (and its attendant prosperity) eventually reached the infant city.

Union had been founded. Later it would merge with the *Evening Tribune*, and today the *San Diego Union-Tribune* remains the city's major newspaper. A courthouse was under construction, and San Diego's population had swelled to 2,300.

GOLD RUSH & GILDED AGE

In 1870, when placer gold was discovered in the Cuyamaca and Laguna Mountains of northeast San Diego County, hundreds of miners rushed south from digs in the northern part of the state. Five years later, San Diego's gold rush was over. By then, however, the infusion of wealth had given the city economy the boost it sorely needed: San Diego mines produced gold worth about two million dollars.

The area's first whaling station had been established in 1859, and the years 1870 to 1874 turned out to be very profitable ones for the industry. Whalers from New England established an oil-rendering depot at Ballast Point (previously known as Point Guijarros) and harpooned tens of thousands of California gray whales in San Diego Bay and offshore during the animals' annual migration between the Bering Strait and Baja California.

Any doubts about the success of Horton's creation evaporated in 1872, when Old Town suffered a devastating fire and most of its merchants relocated to Horton's up-and-coming New Town. The original settlement (and Presidio Hill) languished.

By the end of 1885 the transcontinental railroad had arrived in San Diego, prompting the construction of a new passenger-and-freight depot along New Town's waterfront. A rising tide of clipper ships and steamers began to call on the city, which now evolved into a major center for commerce and transport.

A few years earlier, local inventor and daredevil John J. Montgomery had begun experimenting with gliders launched from local mesas. These were the world's first controlled flights in heavier-than-air machines—precursors to an aviation industry that would dominate San Diego half a century later.

San Diego was expanding horizontally as well. During the land boom of 1886–88, land speculators and developers broke ground on such future seaside suburbs as Ocean Beach, La Jolla, and Del Mar. Lots were sold and then resold, sometimes fetching 100 times their original price.

San Diego underwent phenomenal growth during this boom. The city population shot from 5,000 in 1885 to 40,000 in 1887 (the height of the expansion), and much of San Diego's urban armature was put in place: Elec-

tric lights were installed over the downtown streets in 1887; telephone lines were strung and trolley tracks were laid out; fire and police departments were established.

The boom ended almost as fast as it had begun. Subdivision lots became practically worthless, leaving investors disillusioned and destitute. By 1890, the population of San Diego had sunk to a paltry 16,000.

An influx of sailors, meanwhile, was spurring the growth of a seedy waterfront area, as well as the region called the Stingaree—a decrepit red-light district riddled with saloons and brothels where the almost equally boisterous Gaslamp Quarter now stands. Having made a name for himself at the OK Corral, legendary lawman Wyatt Earp moved to San Diego and opened three gambling halls.

Though the gold was all panned out, local prospectors began to uncover exquisite crystals and gems—tourmalines, garnets, kunzite, beryl, and quartz—in the rugged hills and canyons around Julian and Ramona in the San

Land speculation in the 1880s encouraged the growth of communities such as Del Mar.

Diego backcountry, as well as in the San Luis Rey Valley east of Oceanside. Experts determined that the specimens were of exceptional cutting quality, earmarking San Diego as the center of the West Coast lapidary industry. Gem mining would take off in earnest midway through the decade of the 1900s, with the Himalaya tourmaline mine in the Mesa Grande area near Julian distinguishing itself as the region's most productive.

Across the bay, a jewel of another sort—the landmark Hotel del Coronado—rose from the ground in 1888. Envisioned by financiers Elisha S. Babcock, Jr., and Hampton L. Story as the perfect site for a resort, the Victorian gingerbread castle—the world's first electrically lighted hotel—has been celebrated ever since. The hotel soon came under the control of sugar magnate John D. Spreckels, who saw great potential in this sleepy southern California city. Capitalizing on a weak municipal government and a laissez-faire attitude among the local populace, Spreckels dominated San

Diego's economic and civic life from the end of the 1890s until the 1920s. He liberally spread his cash around, subsidizing the city's water company, an electric utility, and a railroad line to Arizona. Spreckels owned a bank, a hotel, a lumber business, and the passenger ferries that plied San Diego Bay. He funded construction of the Mission Beach Amusement Park and the majestic Spreckels Theater. Self-serving his economic activity may have been, yet it was John Spreckels who prepared San Diego to become a modern metropolis.

EARLY 20TH CENTURY

As the 20th century dawned, the city's population numbered approximately 18,000. Downtown consisted of a few hundred buildings. Tourism—thanks in part to the Hotel del Coronado—was growing steadily. The harbor bustled with regional trade.

San Diego State University had been founded in 1897 as the State Normal School for Teachers. In 1902 the Park Improvement Committee commissioned landscaping plans for City Park (later renamed Balboa Park), a 1,400-acre plot that had been set aside in perpetuity back in 1868. George W. Marston—civic leader, businessman, philanthropist—funded the beautification project to the tune of $10,000. A year later, in 1903, the Marine Biological Association of San Diego—precursor of the esteemed Scripps Institution of Oceanography—established its first laboratory in the Hotel del Coronado's boathouse, courtesy of the owners.

San Diego had also taken its first steps toward becoming a modern military bastion. With the outbreak of the Spanish-American War in 1898, the U.S. Navy decided that a permanent presence in San Diego would be a good way to flex American muscle in the Pacific. The U.S.S. *Pinta,* which had been assigned there before the war, became the first of hundreds of naval vessels to call San Diego their home port. The navy occupied Coronado's northern shore, erecting a camp that would evolve over the next half-century into an aircraft-carrier base and a naval air station. And shortly before and during the first decade of the new century, Fort Rosecrans at the tip of Point Loma acquired powerful new long-range guns.

With its dry climate and largely cloudless skies, San Diego was ideal for aviation. The world's first seaplane—a Curtiss biplane fitted with floats—took off from San Diego Bay in 1911, just eight years after the Wright brothers had made history at Kitty Hawk. Many milestones followed: the world's first aerial photograph (1912), the first air-to-ground radio broadcast (1912), the first night flight (1913), and the first midair refueling (1923).

EXPOSITIONS & WORLD WARS

San Diego planned the Panama-California Exposition of 1915–16 as a way to celebrate the opening of the Panama Canal. As the first U.S. port of call on the West Coast, the city anticipated substantial economic benefits from the canal's completion. The exposition would proclaim to the world that viable, prosperous San Diego had arrived as a city.

Situated within the lush confines of Balboa Park, the expo's grounds, architecture, and exhibits all succeeded in dazzling fairgoers. Elegant Spanish Colonial structures designed for the event included the California Building (with its landmark multicolored tile dome) and the Cabrillo Bridge; both are still in use today.

The two-year fair boosted both local tourism and the city's self-esteem. It and drew numerous dignitaries, including three past or future U.S. presidents: Theodore Roosevelt, William Taft, and Franklin Delano Roosevelt.

Left behind when the show was over was a small group of exotic animals, This coterie of creatures inspired exposition surgeon Dr. Harry Wegeforth to found the San Diego Zoo, which has since grown to world renown. (Almost as a footnote, the canal's opening failed to deliver financial gains in line with the city's expectations.)

After the armistice ending World War I was signed in Europe, trends evident in the prewar years intensified. In 1923, two events stamped San Diego as "Navy Town" for decades to come: The city was designated the headquarters of the U.S. Pacific Fleet, and the Naval Training Center opened on Point Loma.

Aviation, meanwhile, continued to prosper. T. Claude Ryan, a former Army Air Corps ace, purchased a fleet of surplus biplanes in 1925 and inaugurated regular runs between San Diego and Los Angeles. In the event, Ryan Airlines became the country's first scheduled passenger service of any kind.

Ryan's reputation as an aircraft modifier spread across the country and caught the eye of a young pilot with daring dreams—Charles Lindbergh. In 1927, Lindbergh asked Ryan to design, build, and outfit a monoplane for super-long-distance flight. The result—built within 60 days for just over $10,000—was a sleek silver aircraft, the *Spirit of St. Louis.* After test-flying it above the mudflats between downtown San Diego and Point Loma at the end of April, Lindbergh felt confident enough to attempt a bolder feat: In May of that year he flew fly the plane from New York to Paris—the world's first transatlantic solo flight.

A placard trumpets the 1915-16 Panama-California Exposition, held in Balboa Park.

San Diego managed to shrug off the effects of the Great Depression. The city had its share of soup kitchens and bankruptcies, but it weathered the 1930s better than the rest of the country thanks to a thriving aviation industry and the influx of even more military dollars.

The tuna industry also flourished. Offshore tuna fishing had begun in the mid-1920s, and the 1929 advent of the long-distance tuna clipper had enable San Diego's tuna fleet to travel as much as 5,000 miles before returning to port. Five canneries had sprung up on Point Loma by 1935, and San Diego had become the tuna capital of the world.

The 1930s also saw a zoo expansion, the building of a new fairgrounds, and the opening of a Thoroughbred race track in Del Mar

(funded by FDR's relief programs). San Diego even managed to stage another world's fair—the California-Pacific International Exposition of 1935. It included such offbeat attractions as a village full of midgets and a nudist colony that could be scrutinized from bleacher seats.

With its huge Navy population, San Diego was stunned even more than most communities by the Japanese attack on Pearl Harbor on December 7, 1941. Paranoia swept the city, with rumors swirling that San Diego Bay was next on Japan's list of targets. Submarine nets were strung across the harbor mouth. Barrage balloons floated over the city and its military installations to deter attacking aircraft. The bunkers on Point Loma were reinforced with even more concrete and steel.

Once the threat of immediate invasion had been dispelled, San Diego transformed itself into a focal point of the war effort. Thousands of green troops drilled on the obstacle courses and parade grounds of the U.S. Naval Training Center and the Marine Corps Recruit Depot. Battleships and cruisers were outfitted in slips and dry docks in the bay.

Local aviation switched to a war footing as well. Leading the charge was Reuben H. Fleet's Consolidated Aircraft (later Consolidated Vultee), which had relocated from Buffalo, New York, in 1935. During the four years that America was at war, the company worked around the clock to turn out thousands of B-24 Liberator bombers and PBY Catalina seaplanes.

POSTWAR PROSPERITY

San Diego could have reverted to its breezy seaside ways after the war, but several factors kept the city booming. Foremost was the continued presence of the military; the war economy was winding down in the rest of the country, but San Diego remained a naval town. By the 1950s it was the world's largest military seaport.

San Diego's temperate climate, endless beaches, and other natural attractions continued to entice visitors from around the globe. To expand the tourism industry, local voters approved a two-million-dollar bond drive in

Baseball fans throng the San Diego Padres' home opener in April 2002.

1945 to refashion swampy Mission Bay into a huge aquatic playground. Later on, millions of tons of sand were dredged and dumped to create two artificial islets in San Diego Bay: Shelter Island around 1950 and Harbor Island in the early 1960s.

The city itself was expanding too. Postwar prosperity fueled a housing boom, and California's growing addiction to the automobile fanned it. San Diego's first freeway—a four-lane, 7-mile stretch from downtown to Mission Valley via Cabrillo Canyon in Balboa Park—was built in 1948. By 1950, San Diego's population had reached 334,387—a 20-fold increase in 50 years, the fastest growth of any major U.S. city during that period.

As the 1950s waned, civic pride surged when the Salk Institute and the University of California at San Diego (UCSD) established themselves on the bluffs above La Jolla. In 1963—a halcyon year for downtown expansion—the first modern skyscraper rose above the waterfront at 707 Broadway, and city leaders broke ground on a state-of-the-art civic center and municipal theater. A year later, the marine theme park known as SeaWorld opened on the shores of Mission Bay. New interstate highways, meanwhile, were linking the city to Los Angeles, Phoenix, and Las Vegas.

The city's self-image was boosted even more by the arrival of major-league sports teams—the Chargers of the National Football League and the Padres of major-league baseball, both ensconced in a brand-new stadium in Mission Valley that was dedicated in 1967. San Diegans also took pride that the Atlas missile carrying the first lunar astronauts had been manufactured in San Diego. By 1970 San Diego's population had hit 700,000, making it the country's 14th-largest city.

Another economic boom was ushered in by the Vietnam war. President Richard M. Nixon then tapped the city to host the Republican Party's national convention in 1972, but the lack of public floor space at the time forced an 11th-hour shift in venue to Miami instead.

INTO THE NEW MILLENNIUM

In 1975 the municipal government formed a body called the Centre City Development Corporation (CCDC) and charged it with renovating and revitalizing derelict downtown

areas. Several CCDC projects—Seaport Village, Horton Plaza, the Gaslamp Quarter—came to fruition in the early 1980s. The jewel in this crown was the dramatic 1989 waterfront Convention Center with its billowing, sail-like roof. In 1996, the center welcomed the city's long-sought-after Republican National Convention.

The 1980s saw the local economy begin to evolve from its traditional reliance on aviation and the military toward new fields such as computers, biotech, and telecommunications. Much of the growth centered in an area near La Jolla called the Golden Triangle—an ultra-modern urban sprawl located roughly at the foot of Mount Soledad and east of UCSD.

The high-tech boom continued into the early 1990s, drawing even more transplants from across the United States—and, increasingly, from overseas as well. San Diego's proximity to Mexico turned the city into both a conduit and a community for Hispanic immigrants from south of the border. The number of Asian residents also swelled, along with newcomers from the Philippines, Vietnam, India, and China—all drawn by San Diego's climate and seemingly infinite job opportunities. By the start of the 21st century, the population explosion had pushed the number of city residents to 1.25 million (seventh-largest in the U.S.) and the number of county residents to nearly 3 million. San Diegans had vowed

that their beloved city would "never become another Los Angeles," but decades of unhampered growth had started to yield dubious dividends: smog, bumper-to-bumper traffic, overburdened schools. As the new millennium gains steam, the major issue facing San Diego is how to manage growth without manacling the economy.

Despite these growing pains, San Diego remains a rewarding place to live and an exciting place to visit. Few can quibble with its self-appointed status as "America's Finest City." ■

Built in the 1980s, the creatively designed Horton Plaza retail and entertainment complex breathed new life into downtown.

The arts

BY THE LATE 1800S, SAN DIEGO'S CULTURAL LIFE CONSISTED LARGELY OF military bands marching through Horton Plaza and waterfront saloons filled with drunken sailors. What a difference a century makes! Over the next hundred years, the city evolved into a nucleus of arts and entertainment—the birthplace and workplace for some of the greatest performers and artists of our time.

DRAMA

San Diego thrives on drama more than any other art form. Since the 1930s, the city has gained a worldwide reputation for both the quality and the variety of its stage productions. Many fine stage actors, directors, and playwrights have honed their craft here, transforming modest local productions into Broadway hits and Tony Award winners.

Foremost among local theaters is the renowned Old Globe Theatre in Balboa Park. A replica of William Shakespeare's London playhouse, the theater was originally constructed for the 1935 California-Pacific International Exposition. Like many of the expo buildings, it was scheduled for demolition, but earnest theater devotees raised $10,000 to purchase the building and transform it into a permanent theater. After arson destroyed the Old Globe in 1978, its patrons rallied once again: They raised the funds necessary to rebuild the mock-Elizabethan structure as part of a three-theater complex called the Globe Theatres. Queen Elizabeth II unveiled a bust of Shakespeare outside the Old Globe during her 1983 visit to San Diego.

As the name suggests, the Old Globe's stock-in-trade is Shakespeare—especially a popular summer series of the Bard's works that kicked off with *Twelfth Night* in 1949. But the complex has been a venue for all sorts of stage productions, from Thornton Wilder's *Skin of Our Teeth* in 1984 to Harold Pinter's *Betrayal* in 2002. In 1984 the Old Globe captured a Tony Award for distinguished achievement in and continued dedication to the regional theater industry.

Balboa Park's other stage is the Starlight Bowl, likewise built for the 1935 expo and transformed into a permanent venue about a decade later. The accent here is on musical theater, with summer offerings ranging from Gilbert and Sullivan's *Mikado* to Rodgers and Hammerstein's *South Pacific*. The Starlight occupies a unique (or at least distinctive) perch in American musical theater by virtue of its location: Sited in an outdoor amphitheater directly beneath the flight path for the San Diego airport just a few miles away, actors freeze in mid-performance until the noise of approaching passenger jets dissipates, then continue their lines or tunes where they left off.

Another world-renowned stage is the La Jolla Playhouse, founded in 1947 by Gregory Peck, Mel Ferrer, and Dorothy McGuire as a place where Hollywood actors could dabble in legitimate theater—as well as a little San Diego sunshine and sand—between movie shoots. For nearly 18 years, the trio produced a variety of plays in the auditorium of the La Jolla High School. These productions starred some of the greatest entertainers of the era: Vincent Price, James Mason, Olivia De Havilland, Ginger Rogers, and Groucho Marx.

Declining interest forced the La Jolla Playhouse to close its doors in 1964. As it had done before (and would do again) for the Old Globe, the local citizenry rode to the rescue. After years of campaigning and fund-raising, the La Jolla Playhouse was revived in 1983 on the campus of the University of California, San Diego. The city's theater community has not looked back since then. The playhouse quickly evolved into one of America's premier regional theaters, known for its innovative productions of classics and new works. From *Big River* to *Thoroughly Modern Millie,* the theater has sent a number of homegrown productions to Broadway, where they have garnered big-league accolades. Athol Fugard and Stephen Sondheim are among the renowned playwrights who have been in residence at the playhouse, helping the company land a Tony

A *Lion King* character wows crowds at the World-Famous San Diego Zoo.

Award in 1993 as the country's outstanding regional theater.

MOVIES & TELEVISION

San Diego has been a cradle for budding Hollywood talent and a backdrop for numerous films and television series—with Balboa Park being perennially popular as a shooting location—since the early 1910s.

An impressive number of Hollywood stars were born or raised in San Diego. Gregory Peck attended San Diego High School before winning an Oscar in 1962 for his brilliant portrayal of Alabama defense attorney Atticus Finch in *To Kill a Mockingbird*. Cliff Robertson was likewise a standout at La Jolla High before his Oscar-winning performance in *Charly* (1968) as a mentally retarded man who briefly becomes a genius. Another La Jolla High alum was '60s sex symbol Raquel Welch, crowned "Fairest of the Fair" at the San Diego County Fair in 1958. Victor Buono, who graduated from St. Augustine High School near Balboa Park, starred in more than 20 Old Globe productions before his 1962 Oscar nomination for *What Ever Happened to Baby Jane?* A rebellious San Diego lad named Dennis Hopper went on to silver-screen fame after his breakthrough performance as outlaw biker Billy in the cult classic *Easy Rider* (1969). Other well-known film and television actors who cut their teeth in San Diego include silent-film legend

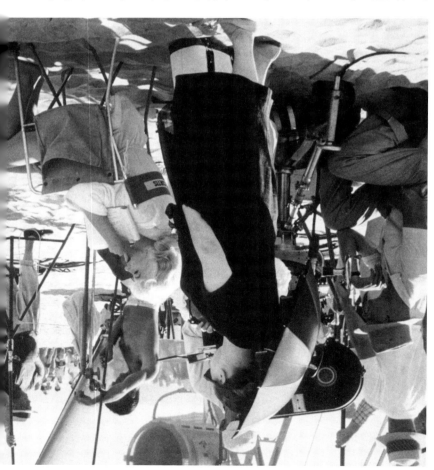

On location at the Hotel del Coronado, Tony Curtis models his gams for Marilyn Monroe between takes of *Some Like It Hot*.

1970s; it was written and directed by the city's own Cameron Crowe.

At least nine movies have been filmed at the Hotel del Coronado. The first, shot in 1901 and titled *The Knights of Pythias Camp,* is thought to be a documentary of the hotel. Later offerings included one of the greatest in Hollywood history: Billy Wilder's farcical *Some Like It Hot* (1959), starring Jack Lemmon, Tony Curtis, and Marilyn Monroe. Warren Beatty and Goldie Hawn used the hotel as the centerpiece of *$* (1971). Shirley MacLaine, James Coburn, and Susan Sarandon frolicked through the grounds in *Loving Couples* (1980).

Not surprisingly, San Diego's reputation as "Navy Town" has attracted a steady stream of movie productions with military themes. San Diego will always be remembered as the shooting location of *Top Gun,* in which Tom Cruise strove to become a fighter jock at Miramar Naval Air Station, some 15 miles north of the city. One of the Francis the Talking Mule pictures *(Francis in the Navy,* 1955) was filmed at the U.S. Navy Amphibious Training Base in Coronado. And battle-weary Clint Eastwood drilled untested troops at Camp Pendleton, about 40 miles north of the city, for the 1984 film *Heartbreak Ridge.*

San Diego has also provided the scenic backdrop for a number of long-running TV series, among them *Manhunt* and *Simon and Simon.* The murder-mystery series *Silk Stalkings* frequently flaunted the mansions of La Jolla and the broad lawns of Mission Bay.

MUSIC

From early pop idols Bing Crosby and Liberace to opera diva Beverly Sills and 1960s rock band Iron Butterfly, San Diego's musical heritage is eclectic to say the least.

The San Diego Symphony staged its first concert in 1910 at the U.S. Grant Hotel. By 1927 the company had moved to new digs at the ornate Spreckels Theater, hiring Nino Marcelli as conductor and resident composer. Nowadays the group performs at the Copley Symphony Hall downtown (whose French rococo-style interior is a restored version of

Harold Lloyd, comedians (and, briefly, roommates) Whoopi Goldberg and Ted Danson, *Blazing Saddles* star Cleavon Little, and Academy Award winner Robert Duvall.

Given its mild climate and its nearness to the major studios, San Diego has always been ideal for location shoots. One of Hollywood's first big productions—1915's *Fatty and Mabel at the San Diego Exposition*—depicted the fictional misadventures of Roscoe "Fatty" Arbuckle and Mabel Normand at the California-Panama Exposition in Balboa Park. Recent films with a local angle include *Almost Famous* (2000), an autobiographical comedy about the musical and emotional coming-of-age of a 15-year-old San Diego rock journalist in the

the old moviehouse Fox Theater) and at the California Center for the Arts in Escondido.

The symphony stages its main season from October through May, plus a 10-week summer pops season that runs from July through September. Though plagued by funding problems in the past, the symphony was guaranteed a harmonious future when philanthropists Joan and Irwin Jacobs endowed the group to the tune of $120 million in 2002.

Not until 1965 did the city get its own resident opera troupe. Like so many other local cultural institutions, however, the San Diego Opera Company (SDOC) quickly earned a reputation for fine productions and top international stars. Both Joan Sutherland and Placido Domingo have headlined SDOC productions over the years. The company's most consistent draw was Beverly Sills; she appeared in eight shows, including Verdi's *La Traviata* and Strauss's *Die Fledermaus*. The SDOC stages five operas at the Civic Theater downtown each year, with its main season running from January to May. The company's Recital Series features star performers from around the globe, among them Luciano Pavarotti, Kiri Te Kanawa, and José Carreras.

San Diego's pop-music heritage is all over the charts. Through much of the 1940s and '50s, Bing Crosby lived and composed at a sprawling Thoroughbred horse ranch in upscale Rancho Santa Fe. His brother Bob Crosby founded a local Dixieland jazz band called the Bob Cats. Liberace's stay was much briefer: a two-year stint playing piano (1949-50) at the Hotel del Coronado.

San Francisco may have fueled the psychedelic music scene in California, but the hoopla did not bypass San Diego. In June 1968 a local group, Iron Butterfly, released a 17-minute, 5-second hard-rock instrumental that rode the *Billboard* charts for 140 weeks and became the first platinum album in history, eventually selling more than 25 million copies. Though the track bore the mystically Indian title of "In-a-Gadda-Da-Vida," it actually had its origin in lead singer Doug Ingle's drunken slurring of the words "In the Garden of Eden." Gary Puckett & the Union Gap ("Young Girl," "Lady Willpower") hailed from San Diego as well. Sitar maestro Ravi Shankar—who had such a profound effect on the Beatles and other groups—retired to Encinitas in San Diego's North County, where his teenage daugh-

Left: Musicians from the Buena Vista Social Club play regular gigs in San Diego.
Above: A performance of *H.M.S. Pinafore* at Balboa Park's Casa del Prado.

LITERATURE

San Diego's most popular and best-known author is without a doubt the late Theodor S. Geisel (aka Dr. Seuss; see p. 180). But the city has inspired many other bards over the years. Life along the rough-and-tumble Point Loma waterfront of the 1830s—populated as it was by boisterous whalers, hide tanners, and fishermen—stirred young seaman Richard Henry Dana to write *Two Years Before the Mast* (1840), which became a classic of early California coastal life. Nearly 50 years later, the wretched state of local Native American tribes moved Helen Hunt Jackson to write *Ramona* (1884), a runaway bestseller that spurred a nationwide movement for better treatment of Indians.

The Wonderful Wizard of Oz author L. Frank Baum (the "L" stood for Lyman) win-tered in Coronado from 1904 to 1910. Several of his books—among them *The Sea Fairies*

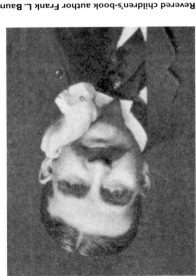

Revered children's-book author Frank L. Baum (left), creator of *The Wonderful Wizard of Oz* (right), found inspiration in the ocean views and otherworldly landscape of La Jolla.

(1911) and *Sky Island* (1912)—contain descriptions that match the La Jolla landscape. Since the Baum boom, the San Diego area has cultivated many masters of children's literature. Newbery Medal winners who have called the region home include Marguerite Henry (*Misty of Chincoteague*, 1947), Scott O'Dell (*Island of the Blue Dolphins*, 1960), and Sid Fleischman (*The Whipping Boy*, 1986).

Potboilers and detective novels are another homegrown specialty of the local literary landscape. In the 1930s, *San Diego Sun* reporter Max Miller wrote several best-selling books about the underbelly of San Diego life, including a collection of loosely related nonfiction stories called *I Cover the Waterfront* and the novel *Harbor of the Sun* (1940). After rising to prominence as a screenwriter in Hollywood with films including *Double Indemnity* (1944) and *The Blue Dahlia* (1946), hardboiled detective novelist (and genre pioneer) Raymond Chandler retired to La Jolla in 1949. There he lived, wrote, and drank away the final decade of his life. *Playback* (1958), one of Chandler's last books, was set in the fictitious California coastal city of Esmeralda. Spend any time at all in this area and you will quickly recognize La Jolla as Esmeralda's real-life counterpart. ■

ter Anoushka is now an Indian music prodigy. Other local pop stars include Eddie Vedder (lead singer for Pearl Jam and former security guard at La Jolla's La Valencia Hotel) and sultry folk singer Jewel, who lived out of a van parked on various San Diego streets before hitting it big in the 1990s.

With the bay glistening as an exquisite backdrop, downtown San Diego combines its enviable location with laid-back ambience and a cool splash of urban hip.

Downtown & vicinity

Commerce as art at Horton Plaza

Downtown & vicinity

SAN DIEGO IS JUSTIFIABLY PROUD OF ITS URBAN CORE, WHICH HAS EVOLVED into a favored destination for visitors and locals alike. Snazzy high-rises, chic lofts, hip clubs and restaurants, and a wonderfully preserved historic district filled with Victorian buildings share a relatively compact space with government buildings, a new convention center, the sprawl of construction, and a gentle bay where commuter ferries and private yachts ply the waters alongside cruise ships and naval vessels.

Downtown's survival has historically been a hit-or-miss proposition. The waterfront area lay relatively dormant until 1867, when a bearded developer named Alonzo Horton blew into town from San Francisco and dubbed as "New Town" the 965 waterfront acres he had just snapped up at auction for $265. This was the opening salvo in Horton's carefully engineered campaign to relocate San Diego's city center from its original Old Town site to this more lucrative location.

By the late 1880s, the transcontinental railroad had arrived, and oceangoing traffic (freighters and fishing boats, for the most part) was on the increase. The city's newfound prosperity attracted a host of marginal entrepreneurs as well: Prostitutes and gamblers—among the latter, gambling-hall manager Wyatt Earp—set up shop in the area south of Market Street, which decayed into the red-light district known as the Stingaree. (You

could be stung just as memorably there, it was said, as you could by the stingrays swimming in San Diego Bay.) During World War II, further local color was contributed by the presence of brawling sailors.

By then, legitimate businesses and more genteel residents had long since migrated to areas of the city north of Market Street. Indeed, San Diego's downtown languished unlamented until the mid-1970s, when enterprising developers joined forces to produce what you see today: a showstopper of a major city.

The 16-block Gaslamp Quarter continues to shine as the centerpiece of downtown. Sporadic restoration of the area's venerable Victorian buildings got started around 1974; six years later the entire district was placed on the National Register of Historic Places. The fanciful Horton Plaza retail and entertainment complex, facing Broadway, fills a

Palms frame a classic view of downtown, anchored by Broadway's 34-story America Plaza.

seven-block area. On and off Broadway, which runs west to meet the bay, historic grandes dames such as the Spreckels Theatre and Copley Symphony Hall stand out amid functional government buildings and chic hotels and residences.

Presiding over Kettner Boulevard, the Santa Fe Depot looks just as it did in 1915, while in bold counterpoint across the street rises the avant-garde Museum of Contemporary Art

San Diego. To the north, savvy new merchants and shops are enlivening the bedrock Italian community of Little Italy.

Across the tracks, the eminently strollable Embarcadero stretches along the waterfront from the Maritime Museum past piers and landings to delightfully ticky-tacky Seaport Village. The convention center lies just a few steps southeast of there, with the East Village and Ballpark District just beyond. ∎

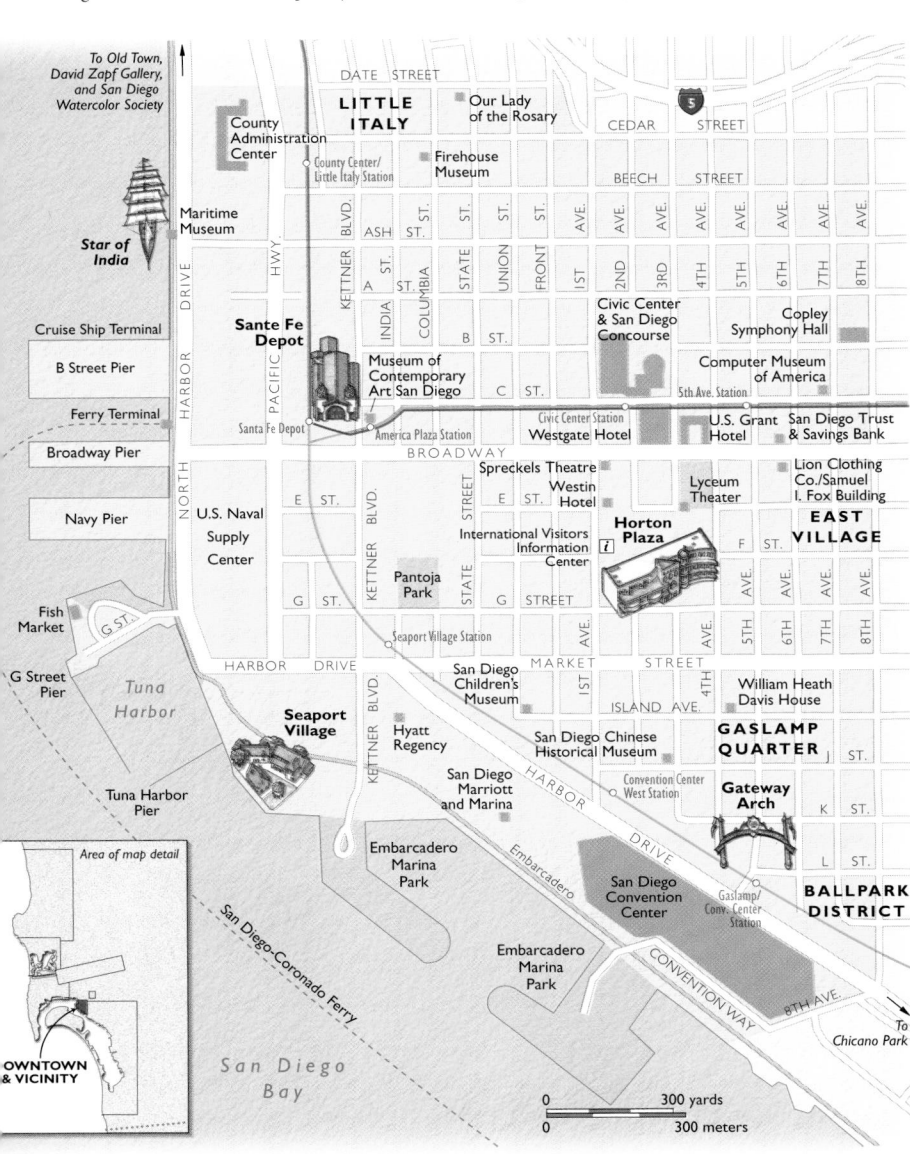

Gaslamp Quarter

QUAINT AND ROMANTIC BY DAY, THE 16-BLOCK GASLAMP Quarter rocks by night—particularly on weekends, when locals and out-of-towners jam the streets to converge on this epicenter of urban ultra-cool. Those seeking a glimpse of San Diego's past can find that as well, in the historic houses that dot the quarter.

Gaslamp Quarter Historical Foundation

- www.gaslampquarter.org
- Map p. 47
- 410 Island Ave.
- 619-233-4692
- Closed Mon., walking tours depart Sat., 11 a.m.
- $$ (walking tour)
- Blue or orange line trolley; Bus: 1, 3, 4, 5, 16, 25

Though 19th-century developer Alonzo Horton would barely recognize his New Town today, he might revel in its distinction as a national historic district. Even as it undergoes continued revitalization, the area—roughly circumscribed by Broadway, Harbor Drive, and Fourth and Sixth Avenues—embodies Horton's vision of San Diego as a grand waterfront city. Starting on the day in 1869 when Horton finished building a $50,000 wharf at the end of Fifth Avenue, the street served as downtown's main thoroughfare. But then, as legitimate businesses moved north of Broadway to distance themselves from the area's wharves and warehouses, the street gave way to sleaze. In the late 1800s, the lamps that cast their light on the quarter's wooden sidewalks also illuminated seedy saloons, brothels,

On Fifth Avenue, there's a whole lotta neon glowin' on.

opium dens, and gambling halls—at least three of them, legend has it, operated by consummate Wild West lawman Wyatt Earp. Dubbed the "Stingaree" to acknowledge the artistry of local scamsters, the area was something of a no-man's land. By the 1960s the area had deteriorated still further, becoming a classic postwar skid row. Though some civic officials advocated the wrecking ball cure (and though some buildings fell to same), local preservationists were galvanized into action by developers intent on starting anew. Their outcry coalesced in the form of the Gaslamp Quarter Association, created in 1974 to protect the historic district from further depredations. By 1980, the Gaslamp Quarter had been decreed a national historic district. Today, the Centre City Development Corporation and other watchdog agencies keep a tight rein on development and building rehabilitation.

It's easy to tour the Gaslamp on foot. Red bricks have replaced the wooden sidewalks, and wrought-iron streetlights in 19th-century designs now light the way. With the exception of the occasional tattoo parlor or adult bookstore, Fifth Avenue has shed its Stingaree pedigree. Trendy bistros offering sidewalk dining line the street, punctuated by hip clubs, eclectic shops, movie theaters, and historic buildings with decorative facades.

The sleek San Diego Trolley whisks riders to the Gateway Arch at Fifth Avenue, across from the convention center. You can pick up maps for self-guided walking tours at any tourist information center; two-hour guided tours depart from the 1850 **William Heath Davis House** *(410 Island Ave., 619-233-4692)* on Saturdays. The Davis House—downtown's oldest surviving wooden structure—serves as the headquarters for the Gaslamp Quarter Historical Foundation.

Davis, a San Franciscan like Horton after him, had a grand vision of San Diego as a glittering seaport. Unlike Horton, his timing was less than perfect. He spent $2,304 on 160 acres filled with cactus and brush, then erected eight to ten prefabricated saltbox houses he imported from Maine via Cape Horn. Though Davis never lived in his eponymous house, the two-story dwelling is a perfectly preserved example of period New England architecture. The surrounding park, dotted with old cobblestones, is a popular gathering spot for locals.

Now a museum, Davis House re-creates the city's Victorian era while explaining how Davis and Horton developed San Diego. The Military Room—originally built as

Asian-Pacific Historic District

Overlapping both the history and the geography of the Gaslamp Quarter, the Asian-Pacific Historic District—bounded by Market and J Streets and Second and Sixth Avenues—honors the Asian community's role in the growth of San Diego.

The thematic district was established in 1987. It highlights Asian influences on the city during the Victorian era. Arriving fresh from the gold rush in the 1850s, for example, Chinese workers played a key part in the city's fishing industry for several decades. Other settlers became merchants, worked in construction, or operated borderline businesses in the Stingaree.

Although the size of the Asian community was once limited by the Chinese Exclusions Act of 1882, San Diego's Chinese-American population now numbers about 55,000.

At the San Diego Chinese Historical Museum *(404 3rd Ave., 619-338-9888, closed Mon.),* visitors can view historical artifacts (including opium pipes and ivory dice) and unwind in the Asian garden. ∎

housing for soldiers—features pre-Civil War uniforms and artifacts. From 1873 to 1881, when San Diego opened its own facility, the home was operated as the County Hospital; this story is told on the upper level.

Dozens of historic Victorian-era structures dot the streets within the Gaslamp Quarter. Some now house shops and businesses; others have been converted to hotels or residences. ∎

Horton Plaza

Horton Plaza

✉ Map p. 47

Bounded by
Broadway, G St., &
1st & 4th Aves.

☎ 619-238-1596

Open daily

Blue or orange line
trolley; most down-
town buses

Avant-garde Horton Plaza: a magnet for visitors, a catalyst for development

DREAMED UP BY DEVELOPER ERNEST HAHN AND BROUGHT to life by architect Jon Jerde, phantasmagoric Horton Plaza (known officially as Westfield Shoppingtown Horton Plaza) became a symbol of downtown San Diego's promising future as soon as it opened its doors for business in 1985.

A five-story fantasyland forms the interior of this seven-block retail and entertainment complex. Kaleidoscopic colors, abstract shapes, and teasing shadows lead to levels-within-levels where cupolas, gargoyles, and striking views loom at every turn. The atmosphere is so festive you may forget you're in a mall.

In addition to a 14-screen multiplex, the various levels house more than 140 stores and restaurants. Anchoring Horton Plaza is the four-sided 1907 Jessop Clock, a landmark in its prominent position on the lower level. The top-story food court dishes up everything from Mexican and Mongolian to corn dogs and gigantic cinnamon rolls. Musicians, flower carts, and outdoor vendors add to the gala atmosphere. Retailers include the usual spectrum of upscale names as well as numerous independent jewelers, salons, and other specialty shops. **Thomas Cook Foreign Exchange** *(800-287-7362)*, on Level 3, trades most currencies; tourists from overseas can also seek assistance at the **International Visitor's Center** *(619-236-1212)* along First Avenue.

Two obelisks grace the plaza's northern edge along Broadway Circle. One, set within a seascape, stands before the **Westin Hotel.** The other, a bright mosaic, marks the foyer of the subterranean **Lyceum Theater** *(619-235-8025)*. Home to the **San Diego Repertory Theatre,** which was founded in 1976, the Lyceum presents both innovative and traditional works in its 550-seat **Lyceum Stage** or its 220-seat **Space.** The **Arts Tix Booth** *(619-497-5000)*, near the theater steps, sells half-price same-day tickets for concerts and theatrical performances throughout San Diego County.

The one bright note in other-wise down-at-the-heels **Horton Plaza Park,** wedged between Broadway and the front entrance to Horton Plaza, is a 1909 Irving Gill fountain. Its illuminated cascades and Greek-inspired elements mark the spot that Alonzo Horton had designated for entertainment purposes in 1870. ■

On & off Broadway

DOWNTOWN'S MAJOR ARTERY IS NORMALLY THRONGED with businesspeople, shoppers, visitors, loafers and panhandlers, and—on weekdays—government workers and attorneys and their clients trotting in and out of court facilities (and the attached jail). Historic redbrick buildings are more prevalent at the street's eastern edge; nearer the bay, contemporary structures are on the rise.

John D. Spreckels commissioned the 1912 neo-Baroque **Spreckels Theatre** *(121 Broadway),* just northwest of Horton Plaza. A superior concert venue, the 1,466-seat theater is rich with exuberant ornamentation and subtle detailing; check out its elegant marble lobby.

Two blocks east of Horton Plaza, at the northwest corner of Broadway and Sixth Avenue, stands the splendid 1928 **San Diego Trust & Savings Bank.** Designed by William Templeton Johnson, the building now houses an elegant Courtyard by Marriott hotel. Decorative touches include the painted coffer ceiling in the dramatic lobby,

as well as the old bronze teller wickets, or grilled windows, that line the reception area.

Architect Johnson was likewise responsible for the 1929 **Lion Clothing Co.** building across the street at 531 Broadway. Known today as the Samuel I. Fox building, it still boasts walnut window frames, 16-foot-high ceilings, an overhanging tile roof, and other grace notes from yesteryear.

Two blocks north of Broadway, at 750 B Street, you'll find the lush, acoustically divine **Copley Symphony Hall.** Originally dubbed the Fox Theater, it is now owned by the San Diego Symphony. The

On & off Broadway

🅰 Map p. 47
🚊 Blue or orange line trolley; most downtown buses

Irving Gill's 1909 fountain commemorates the entertainment zone designated by Alonzo Horton in 1870.

A solitary stroller finds serenity amid the bustling business and entertainment district.

Harlem of the West

From the 1890s until the early 1920s, San Diego was home to a large and active African-American community, which came to be known as the "Harlem of the West." Black-owned enterprises included hotels, restaurants, and businesses spread out through today's East Village, Ballpark District, and Gaslamp Quarter.

The 1924 Douglas Hotel on Market Street—torn down in 1985—served as the community's cultural center, hosting such entertainers as Billie Holiday, Nat King Cole, Duke Ellington, and the Mills Brothers. The Black Historical Society of San Diego (619-685-7215), founded in 1999, is dedicated to preserving the area's remaining historic properties—among them the 1893 Cleremont Hotel, the 1912 Ideal Hotel, and the 1942 Harlem Locker Club. ■

Spanish-Rococo Renaissance hall started its performance life as a venue for vaudeville acts and talkies in 1929. It became the symphony's home in 1984, underwent an overhaul in 2002, and now seats 2,250.

Chugging up and down C Street, one block north of Broadway, are those distinctive, bright red trolleys that have become a distinctive emblem of San Diego. Between First and Second Avenues, the 1960s-era **Civic Center** and the **San Diego Concourse** are home to the **Civic Theatre,** the **San Diego Opera,** and various outdoor craft shows and fairs.

Local hotels near Broadway range from decrepit to regal. The nostalgic **U.S. Grant Hotel** (*326 Broadway*), across from Horton Plaza, was built by Ulysses S. Grant, Jr., and dedicated in 1910 to his President-father. It exudes Old World charm and a prestigious clientele. The neighboring **Westgate Hotel** (*1055 Second Ave.*) boasts a grandiose re-creation of the anteroom at Versailles. ■

Museum of Contemporary Art San Diego

INCORPORATED WITHIN THE AMERICA PLAZA SITE, OPPOSITE the trolley station and across Kettner Boulevard from the Santa Fe Depot, this downtown branch of La Jolla's Museum of Contemporary Art (MCA) came to life in 1993—a happy coincidence when the main museum closed for renovations before opening again in 1996. Although perhaps not quite as sophisticated as MCA La Jolla, this compact museum has nonetheless filled a cultural need in San Diego's urban core.

Commuters awaiting their trolleys at the transit center next door have grown accustomed to the ceaseless bludgeoning of midair performed 24 hours a day by the towering sculpture out front, American artist Jonathan Borofsky's 18-foot-high "Hammering Man at 3,110,527." If that doesn't pass the time until the next train, they can always contemplate the provocative "Is that art?" exhibits in the museum's storefront gallery, whose pointed corner meets the busy intersection of Broadway and Kettner Boulevard.

The two-level museum presents changing exhibitions of painting, sculpture, and multimedia. Works from the permanent collection occasionally share the spotlight. MCA also hosts lectures, workshops, family activities, and other special events—some of which enable members of the public to observe (or even interact with) featured artists at work.

At press time, MCA's plan to expand into the Santa Fe Depot baggage building across the street awaited the City Council's blessing. The move would convert the historic 18,000-square-foot facility into a museum annex with added gallery and studio space. ∎

Museum of Contemporary Art San Diego
www.mcasandiego.org

- Map p. 47
- 1001 Kettner Blvd.
- 858-454-3541
- Closed Wed.
- Blue or orange line trolley; most downtown buses; Coaster train or Amtrak to Santa Fe Depot

Jonathan Borofsky's kinetic masterpiece, "Hammering Man at 3,110,527" (1988), greets commuters and art lovers.

The smart new face of San Diego is captured in "Coming Together" by Niki de Saint Phalle.

A walk downtown

A stroll through the hurly-burly of San Diego's downtown lets you take in the city's colorful mix of 19th-century history, ongoing urban development, and breezy waterfront ambience. The following loop allows lots of flexibility.

Begin beneath the tiled double domes of the wonderful 1915 **Santa Fe Depot** ❶ (*1050 Kettner Blvd.*), the Spanish Colonial-style railway station (see p. 57) that is still used by Amtrak, Coaster commuter trains, and the San Diego Trolley. Walk toward the water along Broadway, crossing the trolley and train tracks to reach the World War II-era **Broadway Pier**, where Navy ships occasionally dock. As you face the pier, the departure point for harbor excursions and the Coronado ferry will be to your right; walk out onto the pier to visit the Pearl Harbor plaque, shaded by a coral tree and a New Zealand Christmas tree.

Turn left onto the **Embarcadero** walking path ❷ (it's marked "Bike Lane" at first) along North Harbor Drive. To the right beckons the

bay and its seagoing vessels under a flock of swooping gulls. The next landing south on your walk is **Tuna Pier:** once the unloading site of the local fishing fleet, it now hosts the Fish Market restaurant complex.

Stroll through **Seaport Village** ❸, a collection of gift shops and a food court with a maritime theme. Artists and street entertainers—mimes, jugglers, and others—frequent this area. Adults and kids alike will thrill to riding the glass-enclosed **Broadway Flying Horses Carousel,** a circa 1900 Looff merry-go-round.

Continue along the waterfront, with its commanding view of the Coronado Bay Bridge. At Embarcadero Marina Park, bear left and wander past the **San Diego Marriott**

54 DOWNTOWN & VICINITY

START

Museum of Contemporary Art San Diego ❶ ❽

Civic Center and San Diego Concourse

B ST.

U.S. Grant Hotel ❼

C ST.

B Street Pier

Sante Fe Depot ❶

HARBOR DRIVE

Santa Fe Depot

America Plaza Station

Civic Center Station

5th Ave. Station

Historic Louis Bank of Commerce

Broadway Pier

BROADWAY

Westgate Hotel

Horton Plaza Park

E ST.

San Diego Hardware

Nesmith-Greeley Bldg.

Navy Pier

Embarcadero

E ST.

KETTNER BLVD.

STATE ST.

E ST.

FRONT AVE.

1ST AVE.

Geo. J. Keating Bldg.

Marston Bldg.

U.S. NAVAL SUPPLY CENTER

PACIFIC HWY

F ST.

F ST.

UNION ST.

ℹ️ ❻

Horton Plaza

4TH AVE.

5TH AVE.

6TH AVE.

7TH AVE.

8TH AVE.

Fish Market

Tuna Pier

G ST.

Pantoja Park

G ST.

William Heath Davis House

Lincoln Hotel Manila Café (Bocca Restaurant)

N. HARBOR DRIVE

HARBOR DR.

MARKET ST.

❺

Tuna Harbor

Seaport Village Station

ASIAN-PACIFIC HISTORIC DISTRICT

ISLAND AVE.

Royal Thai Cuisine

San Diego-Coronado Ferry

Hyatt Regency

J ST.

GASLAMP QUARTER

Seaport Village ❸

San Diego Marriott and Marina

Convention Center West Station

K ST.

Gateway Arch

San Diego Convention Center ❹

HARBOR DRIVE

Gaslamp/Convention Center Station

San Diego Bay

Embarcardero Marina Park

0 ——— 300 yards
0 ——— 300 meters

🅰️ See area map p. 47

▶ Santa Fe Depot, 1050 Kettner Blvd.

↔ 4 miles

🕐 3 hours

▶ Museum of Contemporary Art

NOT TO BE MISSED

- Embarcadero waterfront
- San Diego Hardware
- Horton Plaza

and Marina (you'll pass three sets of public restrooms on your left) to reach the shiplike **San Diego Convention Center ❹.** Climb the outside stairs and cut through the convention center on its Upper Level, stopping to marvel at the 90,000-square-foot interior expanse of its sail-vaulted pavilion. Emerging from the convention center, turn right on Harbor Drive and cross at the corner of Fifth Avenue, where the **Gateway Arch** welcomes you to the Gaslamp Quarter—the "historic heart of San Diego," the former site of the Stingaree, and the current hub of urban chic.

Passengers await trains and trolleys inside the Spanish-Colonial-style Santa Fe Depot.

Shops and galleries purvey unique wares in San Diego's Little Italy neighborhood.

Proceed north on Fifth Avenue to the **Royal Thai Cuisine Restaurant** *(465-467 5th Ave.)*; this Asian-Pacific historic site has been serving Asian cuisine since it was built in 1912. Other nearby examples of Asian-style architecture include the 1930 **Manila Café** (now the Bocca Restaurant) at 515 Fifth Avenue and the run-down 1913 **Lincoln Hotel** at 536 opposite.

Backtrack slightly to Island Avenue and turn right (west) to reach San Diego's oldest surviving wooden structure, the 1850 **William Heath Davis House** 5 *(410 Island Ave.)*. Here you can tour the house and pick up a map of the 16-block historic district and its overlapping Asian-Pacific Historic District. Return to Fifth Avenue and hang a left to hit F Street, where a landmark brownstone—the 1890 **Geo. J. Keating Building**—has served as a shooting location for movies and TV shows (fictional detectives Simon and Simon did business here). The white-turreted 1881 **Marston Building** sits opposite.

As you follow Fifth Avenue to Broadway, you'll pass the 1888 **Nesmith-Greeley Building** *(825 5th Ave.; note the storefront spelling "Greely")* and the gold-balconied 1888 **Historic Louis Bank of Commerce** *(835 5th Ave.)*. Next door to the Midnight Adult Book & Video Center, don't miss a trip

to **San Diego Hardware** *(840 5th Ave.)*, in operation since 1892. The store offers a walk back in time on wooden floors through a superior selection of decorative hardware. Turn left on Broadway. At the corner of Fourth Avenue, somewhat seedy **Horton Plaza Park**—with its 1909 Irving Gill fountain—marks the area that Alonzo Horton named an entertainment zone in 1870. Just behind the park is the architecturally extravagant **Horton Plaza** 6 retail and entertainment complex (see p. 50).

Across the street from Horton park, the **U.S. Grant Hotel** 7 *(326 Broadway)*, dedicated in 1910 to President Ulysses S. Grant, is a bastion of old-fashioned elegance. Its venerable **Grant Grill** has served Harry Truman and Albert Einstein and continues to charm dignitaries. Make your way through the ornately decorated **Westgate Hotel** *(1055 2nd Ave.)* to C Street, then hop a San Diego Trolley and ride it six blocks west, passing the **Civic Center** and the **San Diego Concourse** on the north side of the street. Get off beneath the steel-and-glass canopy at **America Plaza**, a sleek high-rise at the end of C Street housing the downtown branch of the **Museum of Contemporary Art San Diego** 8 *(see p. 53)*. Just across the street is your start point, the Santa Fe Depot. ■

Santa Fe Depot

OPENED IN 1915, THE SANTA FE RAILWAY DEPOT WAS BUILT TO commemorate the completion of the Panama Canal in 1914 and San Diego's ensuing celebration of it, the 1915-16 Panama-California Exposition. The distinctive Spanish Colonial-style train station was designed by San Francisco architects John Bakewell and Arthur Brown, Jr. It continues to serve Amtrak riders, tour buses bound for Mexico, and Coaster and trolley commuter traffic. Locals thwarted a 1971 attempt to level the building; 12 years later, a sensitive refurbishment restored the depot to its original magnificence.

Santa Fe Depot
- Map p. 47
- 1050 Kettner Blvd.
- Blue or orange line trolley; most downtown buses; Coaster and Amtrak trains

The depot's crowning glory also happens to be its most striking exterior detail: Rising from a red tile roof are twin towers capped by blue and yellow glazed tiles, laid in a zigzag pattern and bearing the Santa Fe Railroad's distinctive cross-inside-a-circle emblem. (These domes would be emulated 20 years later in those gracing Balboa Park's Museum of Man.)

The depot itself—106 feet wide and 650 feet long—is built of wood, brick, tile, and cement. It features wide arches supported by Tuscan columns and graced by baroque cornices. Connected to the depot's north end via arches and a trackside arcade is the baggage building—a potential future annex for contemporary art (see p. 53).

Passengers gather in the vast 170-by-55-foot waiting room, resplendent with bronze-and-glass chandeliers (six Santa Fe crosses top each globe), glazed-tile wainscoting, a Native American frieze, and polished oak benches. Ticket counters are located at one end of the room, a concession stand at the other. The old trolley car terminal —torn down in 1954 and turned into a parking lot—has been reborn as a junction for the San Diego Trolley. Arrayed on the east side of the waiting room are tour-bus offices, a travel information booth, and the business office for the **San Diego Railroad Museum** *(Campo, CA; 619-595-3031).* ■

With public transport alive and well in San Diego, the Spanish Colonial Santa Fe Depot is a pleasant place to await a train or trolley.

Little Italy

Though energized by urban renewal, Littly Italy retains its ethnic traditions.

SETTLED IN THE 1920s BY ITALIAN IMMIGRANTS TO SAN Diego, Little Italy has come to harbor a diverse mix of people while remaining the cultural and religious epicenter of the city's Italian population. The district stretches from Ash Street to Laurel and from Front Street to Pacific Highway.

West Coast numbers. But what really devastated the neighborhood was the construction of Interstate 5—the main Los Angeles–San Diego freeway. Buildings, streets, and any other obstacles to "progress" were demolished to make way for the thoroughfare, completed in 1962.

In the 1990s, business and property owners in the area joined forces to create a Business Improvement District managed by the Little Italy Association. Together they embarked on a course of urban renewal that has resulted in a dynamic neighborhood with a vibrant blend of homes, offices, galleries, antique shops, and *ristorantes* galore: mainstay pizza grottoes, casual cappuccino bars, hip *osterie*.

The **2400 Kettner Boulevard** building houses the respected **David Zapf Gallery** (*619-232-5004*) and numerous artists' studios, many open to the public. Another showcase worth a stop is the **San Diego Watercolor Society** (*2100 Kettner Blvd.*).

Sitting serenely at the corner of State and Date Streets, **Our Lady of the Rosary Church** has served as Little Italy's spiritual heart since its consecration in 1925. The whitewashed, single-nave church houses an impressive art collection including statuary, stained glass, and ceiling and wall paintings by Venetian painter Fausto Tasca.

For the full-on Little Italy experience, attend Festa, held in October. It celebrates the area's heritage with entertainment, exhibits, and no shortage of food and drink. ■

Little Italy
www.littleitalysd.com

- Map p. 47
- 1830 Columbia St.
- 619-233-3898
- Blue line trolley; Bus: 2, 5, 16, 30, 34, 50, 150, 810, 820

Enticed by the waterfront and the ocean beyond, immigrant fishermen and their families planted roots and cultivated a tightly knit enclave. After toiling tirelessly to make San Diego the star of the global tuna industry, they were hit hard by the decline of that fish's

The Embarcadero's winding paths and broad lawns allow room to roam on two legs or four.

San Diego Bay & the Embarcadero

ARCING PAST THE AIRPORT AND SWEEPING DOWNTOWN, San Diego Bay overflows with postcard images: billowing sails, funky houseboats, chic yachts, wallowing excursion craft, awesome Navy ships. All share a lovely harbor that has welcomed visitors from around the world for centuries.

San Diego's waterfront **Embarca-dero**—a walkway built mainly on landfill—dates from the 1800s. Today its manicured expanses and smooth paths beckon visitors to run, walk, or just lounge on the grass. Passengers arriving by ship will find it's an easy stroll to reach the **Maritime Museum** and its array of historic vessels; a choice of seafood restaurants by the bay; and the delightfully informal shopping and alfresco dining on tap at **Seaport Village.** Just a few blocks inland await the blandishments of **Little Italy, Horton Plaza,** and the **Gaslamp Quarter.**

Major cruise lines schedule San Diego as both a port of call and a point of departure, dropping and weighing anchor at the pastel-colored **B Street Terminal** just south of the Maritime Museum. Housed within the cavernous pier building are a cruise information area, a gift shop, and a small bar.

Harbor cruises, whale-watching excursions, dining yachts, and the San Diego-Coronado Ferry all depart from the north arm of **Broadway Pier.** Just a few blocks south of that landmark, the **Navy Pier** now hosts the retired U.S.S. *Midway*, as well as summer-pops performances by the San Diego Symphony that culminate in patriotic fireworks. Commercial fishermen still gather at **Tuna Harbor** *(G St. & the Embarcadero)*, adding a splash of local color if not quite equaling the salty scene prevalent during the tuna industry's boom years.

The **Port of San Diego** monitors the busy vessel traffic at cruise and cargo terminals, shipyards, and mooring sites around the bay. It also manages recreational boating, sport fishing, and marinas. The Port even wields power in hotel construction and installations of public art. ∎

San Diego Bay & the Embarcadero
www.portofsandiego.org

Map p. 47

Blue line trolley; Bus: 2, 4, 15, 20, 22, 23, 29, 40, 70, 115, 210, 901, 902, 903, 932, 992

San Diego celebrates

Inward migration—the tendency of city residents to descend upon the urban core—is among San Diego's most appealing features. Unlike that of most other megalopoli, the downtown area gains population during off-peak hours.

The city center is an ideal place to party for a host of reasons: It's vital and relatively clean, attractions proliferate, and the climate is superb year-round. Block parties—a San Diego specialty—put entire sections of town off-limits to traffic. Given the predictable lack of rain, all events are outdoors. Honeymooners, resident families, and visiting conventioneers share the streets—and the fun.

On the weekend after Labor Day, **Street Scene** *(www.street-scene.com)* takes over more than 15 blocks of the Gaslamp Quarter. This annual three-day music festival, brings in the *crème de la crème* of both touring musicians and local groups. Every musical style from progressive jazz, rock-and-roll, and cryin' blues to heavy metal, reggae, and ska beats down upon the town. Some stages are open only to adults; others cater to families. The net effect is a good time for all ages and tastes. Spontaneous entertainment pops up on various makeshift stages as well, while beer gardens and food booths provide sustenance to musicians and listeners alike.

Even though Street Scene doesn't kick off the calendar, it is one of the most eagerly awaited celebrations of the year. Other major block-party events include the St. Patrick's Day's **ShamROCK**, an adults-only event billed as the largest such celebration west of the Mississippi River. The streets are "paved" in astro-turf green, matching the copious quantities of green brew and Irish whiskey served up by beer gardens and pubs.

San Diego's version of **Mardi Gras** in the Gaslamp Quarter may not quite rival the revelry of the Big Easy's French Quarter, but the city's Fat Tuesday celebration (the last Tuesday before Lent) rocks nonetheless with lively processions, bands, food and drink, and plenty of chances to catch those infamous hurled beads. Jazz takes over the town on Memorial Day

weekend for the **KiFM Jazz Festival,** a fete that hosts hot jazz musicians on street stages as well as in neighboring clubs and restaurants.

The people take back the streets—or at least the sidewalks—for **ArtWalk,** a two-day spring event in Little Italy. Visual and performing artists from all over town gather to share their creative processes with bystanders browsing open studios and public stages.

Locals work up an appetite for June's **Taste of the Gaslamp,** which encourages participants to take a self-guided grazing tour of the finest restaurants in the quarter.

Everyone loves a parade, and San Diego excels at staging them. Marching bands and floats thread the downtown thoroughfares for **Martin Luther King Day,** the **Easter Bonnet Parade,** the month-long **Fleet Week** in October, and the **Holiday Bowl** late in December.

Nor is the action limited to landlubbers: In early December, cruise over to the Embarcadero to witness the dazzling procession of pleasure craft that make up the **San Diego Bay Parade of Lights.** ∎

Left: St. Patrick's Day celebrants strut their shamrocks. Below: A saxophonist heats up the streets at an outdoor jazz festival.

Maritime Museum

FOUNDED IN 1948 TO PRESERVE AND HONOR THE LOCAL seafaring heritage, the Maritime Museum blossomed with the 1958 acquisition of the *Star of India*, the world's oldest sailing ship that still puts out to sea. Anchored alongside are the historic steamers *Berkeley* and *Medea*. Exhibits and programs aboard all three vessels tell the story of the city's long relationship with the sea.

Maritime Museum

www.sdmaritime.com

[A] Map p. 47

✉ 1306 N. Harbor Dr.

☎ 619-234-9153

$ $$

🚊 Blue line trolley;
Bus: 2, 4, 15, 20, 22,
23, 29, 40, 70, 115,
210, 901, 902, 903,
932, 992

A single admission allows entry to all three ships, where you can run your hand over the polished woods, peer into authentically decorated cabins, and view permanent displays and changing exhibits. As you breathe the salty sea air, consider that these centuries-old decks have weathered wars, mutinies, and cargoes of everything from Indian jute and Alaskan salmon to steerage-class emigrants and wealthy stateroom passengers.

The centerpiece of the Maritime Museum is a 278-foot, 1,318-ton merchant ship named the **Star of India**. Launched in 1863 as the *Euterpe* at Britain's Isle of Man, the *Star* has been anointed by *Guinness World Records* as the world's oldest active sailing ship. The fully rigged ship, bristling with 100-foot-high masts, was one of the earliest iron-hulled vessels ever built. Although the original *Euterpe* was scheduled to make six voyages on the trade

The *Star of India* (above), world's oldest active ship, is also the star of the Maritime Museum.

route from England to India, it got off to a miserable start, suffering a mutiny, a mid-ocean collision, a cyclone, and the captain's death and burial at sea.

In 1901 the Alaska Packers of San Francisco bought the *Euterpe*, rigged it down to a bark, renamed it the *Star of India*, and sent it to work the salmon fisheries of the Bering Sea. After its retirement, San Diego historians bought the ship in 1927 and moored it in the bay. Designated a national historic landmark in 1966, the *Star* and its tall wooden masts and billowing sails have become an iconic fixture of San Diego Bay. The craft still takes to the sea on special occasions.

The propeller-driven ferry **Berkeley** was launched in 1898, when it entered service as a steamer for the Southern Pacific Railroad. Until 1958, the 1,884-ton boat shuttled railroad passengers and commuters between San Francisco and Oakland. During the 1906 earthquake and fire, the boat heroically carried residents to safety across the bay. Acquired by the Maritime Museum in 1973, the *Berkeley* retains many of its original lavish fittings.

On the *Berkeley's* main deck, check out the exhibits on local naval history, oceanography, and the fishing industry, as well as models of early ships. Descend the steep staircase into the engine room for a close-up view of the rare triple-expansion steam engine. Then climb to the upper deck's former

Two young visitors turn a ventilator shaft into a sound tunnel on the steam yacht Medea.

A builder of model ships demonstrates his craft aboard the Berkeley.

passenger lounge, which is still fitted with polished benches and a stained-glass clerestory. (In Victorian times, the upper deck was designated "ladies only"; men were relegated to the main deck, where they used baggage carts for seats.)

One of the few steam yachts still in existence worldwide, the 143-ton **Medea** was built in Scotland and launched in 1904. The vessel's elegant timbers—English oak and imported teak—belie its speedy (51-day) construction. The Medea's original owner, William Macalister Hall, used the yacht for hunting trips and other social outings, but it also saw service in both world wars. Back in private ownership in 1946, the Medea changed hands until 1973, when a wealthy American donated the restored craft to the Maritime Museum.

In addition to its permanent displays (most aboard the Berkeley), the Maritime Museum welcomes exhibits in a wide variety of media. Recent shows have included the maritime paintings of the 17th-century Dutch masters; maritime paintings; ship models; and a light-hearted look at pirate paraphernalia from movie props to Blackbeard's skull. The Berkeley also houses a gift shop and research library.

In summer the museum hosts

Movies Before the Mast—
nautically themed films projected on the Star of India's billowy white sails. A snack bar serves clam chow-

der, popcorn, cappuccino and hot chocolate, and moviegoers are free to explore the ship at intermission. Ticket reservations are recommended.

Maritime Museum vessels also serve as venues for concerts and special events. In addition, they take part in such annual celebrations as July's Sea Chantey Festival, October's Fleet Week, and December's Parade of Lights. ■

COATLICUE, DIOSA DE LA TIERRA · EARTH GODDESS

More places to visit downtown

CHICANO PARK
Beneath the San Diego side of the Coronado Bay Bridge, spread out on National Avenue between Crosby and Dewey Streets in Barrio Logan (heart of the city's Mexican-American community) is Chicano Park. Since 1973, local artists have painted the bridge's support pylons with scores of murals depicting the historic and cultural struggles of Chicanos, creating this unusual open-air "museum." ⚠ Map p. 47 ✉ Logan Heights 🚋 Orange line trolley; Bus: 4, 11, 29

COMPUTER MUSEUM OF AMERICA
Relocated downtown in 2001, San Diego's Computer Museum continues to garner plaudits from geeks and Luddites alike. In partnership with the nonprofit Coleman Foundation, the museum presents a permanent collection of such obsolete hardware as the Hollerith manual card punch, an IBM wiring board, a Royal Precision vacuum-tube computer, an Apple *LISA,* and a bulky Sperry calculator. Additional draws include the Computer Hall of Fame, a look at computerized photography, and the exhibit "A History of Home Computing."

Unveiled in 2002, the "Secrets, Lies, and Teletypes" exhibit explores the historical development of cryptology and code breaking, including the contribution of the Navajo code talkers and the refinement of equipment used to transmit classified information in wartime. The computer archive preserves how-to manuals and magazines from the 1950s through the present. There's no parking, but the trolley stops just a block away. www.computer-museum.org ⚠ Map p. 47 ✉ 640 C St. ☎ 619-235-8222. 🕐 Closed Mon. 💲 $ 🚋 Blue or orange line trolley; most downtown buses

COUNTY ADMINISTRATION CENTER
One of the country's finest public buildings, this elegant 1936 Spanish Colonial complex (wedged between the Maritime Museum

The murals at Chicano Park are created by local artists expressing cultural themes.

and Little Italy) was constructed with WPA funding and dedicated by President Franklin Roosevelt. Near the front (harbor) entrance stands Donal Hord's treasured "Guardian of Water" sculpture of a pioneer woman hefting a water jug. Visitors can wander the ten-story building during business hours; the fourth-floor cafeteria, likewise open to the public, provides a peerless view of the bay. ⚠ Map p. 47 ✉ 1600 Pacific Hwy. ☎ 619-531-5197 🕐 Open weekdays 🚋 Blue line trolley; Bus: 23, 34

EAST VILLAGE & BALLPARK DISTRICT
This once-decrepit area east of the city's historic core has undergone a facelift even more profound than that of the Gaslamp Quarter. The 26 blocks bounded by Market Street, Interstate 5, Harbor Drive, and Sixth Avenue were once a badlands mix of cutting-edge artists and street people. Then the area picked up its "East Village" moniker, and a whirlwind of classy construction ensued.

One impetus for the activity was San Diego Padres Ballpark, proposed future home of the city's baseball team. Buoyed by the promise of a visitor influx, the area saw a burst of improvements: Warehouses and flophouses were reborn as trendy lofts, while new hotels and offices seemed to sprout from the ground. Already home to the New School of Architecture and San Diego City College, the area braced for explosive residential growth.

After kicking off in May 2000, however, ballpark construction ground to a halt six months later amid financing headaches, allegations of corruption, and community opposition. Though the park was forced to move its opening date from 2002 to 2004, related projects—a 33-story hotel, a 500,000-square-foot library, the creation of a neighborhood park—have all forged ahead. ⚠ Map p. 47 🚋 Orange line trolley; Bus: 1, 4, 11, 29, 901

EMBARCADERO MARINA PARK
Reaching out from Seaport Village like asymmetrical crab claws, the park's two arms embrace Embarcadero Marina. The northern arm is a broad, grassy expanse that lures kite-fliers,

A vendor displays handicrafts at her kiosk near Chicano Park.

picnickers, and street entertainers. Here you'll find Donal Hord's "Morning Statue" sculpture, paying homage to the local fishermen. The southern arm, reached via the walkway stretching past the Marriott Hotel and the San Diego Convention Center, presents outdoor concerts in summer. Performances range from rhythm and blues to rock-and-roll to jazz. Audiences usually bring their own lawn chairs and blankets; if you decide to join the fun, you may want to pack a picnic as well. Some concerts feature a fireworks finale. Map p. 47 Orange line trolley; Bus: 7, 7A, 7B

FIREHOUSE MUSEUM

A working firehouse of the 1940s and 1950s, this museum occupies the San Diego Fire Department's old Station 6 in the Little Italy neighborhood. Artifacts pay tribute to the history of firefighting. Exhibits include a hand-drawn fire engine and memorabilia such as old fire extinguishers and alarm boxes. Map p. 47 1572 Columbia St. 619-232-3473 Open Thurs.-Fri. 10 a.m.-2 p.m., weekends 10 a.m.-4 p.m. $ Blue line trolley; Bus: 5, 16

SAN DIEGO CHILDREN'S MUSEUM

Across from the convention center, this museum offers 25,000 square feet of interactive thrills for young children. Art stations invite kids to participate in improvisational theater, create art projects, and take part in educational workshops. Creative areas are undeniably that: There's a paintable 1952 Dodge truck, a play theater, an art studio, and a small house where rain seems to fall on the roof. Also on tap: music, yoga for kids, storytelling, and programs for toddlers. www.sdchildrensmuseum.org Map p. 47 200 W. Island Ave. 619-233-5437 Closed Mon. $$ Orange line trolley; Bus: 4

SEAPORT VILLAGE

Set on 14 acres of prime waterfront property connecting the harbor to the convention center, Seaport Village offers a calmer alternative to Horton Plaza—which it predates by several years. Bayside shopping, dining, and entertainment are the order of the day (or evening).

The village consists of three plazas built in Old Monterey, Victorian San Francisco, and traditional Mexican styles. The cobblestone walk and old-fashioned paths are popular strolling spots, primarily for tourists. Souvenir hunters can pick from a range of goods—nautical gewgaws, sportswear, artwork, music boxes, rubber stamps—along with gift shops specializing in cats, big dogs, or southpaws.

Atmospheric seafood restaurants are complemented by bay-front eateries and sidewalk food stands. Prepare yourself for a couple of nostalgic surprises: a 45-foot-tall reproduction of Washington State's Mukilteo Lighthouse, and the restored circa 1900 Broadway Flying Horses Carousel. www.seaportvillage.com Map p. 47 W. Harbor Dr. at Pacific Hwy. 619-235-4014. $ (carousel) Orange line trolley; Bus: 7, 7A, 7B

VILLA MONTEZUMA

The San Diego Historical Society restored this highly decorative 1887 mansion—the former home of pianist, novelist, and spiritualist Jesse Shepard—east of Interstate 5 on the fringe of downtown. Docents lead tours of the frilly, fascinating structure, replete with such architectural embellishments as tiled fireplaces and stained-glass windows depicting Beethoven, Mozart, Shakespeare, and Sappho. www.sandiegohistory.org Map p. 47 1925 K St. 619-239-2211 Open Fri.-Sun. $$ Orange line trolley; Bus: 932 ■

Lush, green, and close to downtown, Balboa Park—home to fabulous gardens, major museums, and an internationally acclaimed zoo—is the uncontested cultural heart of the city.

Balboa Park & around

Black rhino, World-Famous San Diego Zoo

Balboa Park & around

SPRAWLING OVER 1,200 ACRES SMACK-DAB IN THE MIDDLE OF THE CITY, Balboa Park is an oasis for local residents and a mecca for out-of-towners. The park plays host to 15 museums, the World-Famous San Diego Zoo, and a panoply of theaters, gardens, recreational areas, and spontaneous street performances. It all adds up to one of the most inviting—and welcoming—urban expanses in the country.

site landscaping that visitors see today. In 1910, Balboa Park—known as City Park until then—was renamed for Vasco Núñez de Balboa, the first European to sight the Pacific Ocean from the west coast of the Americas.

The Spanish Colonial buildings that now house more than a dozen fine museums were originally constructed for the 1915-16 Panama-California Exposition—which, in turn, was held to celebrate the 1914 opening of the Panama Canal. Primarily designed by New York architect Bertram Goodhue, most of the structures were intended to be only temporary venues for exposition exhibits. So captivating did they turn out to be, however, that exposition managers left them in place, then renovated them with more durable materials.

Another burst of construction followed for the 1935-36 California-Pacific International Exposition, which continued the Spanish theme while adding architectural details inspired by the Mayan temples that had been discovered and excavated in the early 1900s. Most of the museums flank El Prado; the zoo, botanical gardens, organ pavilion, and myriad other attractions are scattered nearby. Open areas are designated for picnics, concerts, and athletic pursuits that run the gamut from croquet to tackle football. At the park's northwest edge looms a splendid example of American Craftsman-era architecture and decor: Built in 1905, it was once the home of business tycoon George Marston.

Nearby neighborhoods reflect San Diego's trademark diversity. To the west, Middletown harbors the India Street Art Colony. To the northwest, bustling Hillcrest—the heart of San Diego's gay community—draws tourists of all persuasions to its artsy shops and hip eateries. Farther north, Adams Avenue runs east into lovely, low-key Kensington, which has cafés, an art-house cinema, and streets lined with intriguing dwelling places. ■

San Diego's early community leaders—among them foresighted developer Alonzo Horton—designated 1,400 acres for a city park in 1868. Covered in chaparral, the site remained a barren expanse of sunburned mesas and arroyos until 1892, when pioneering horticulturist Kate Sessions (see pp. 96-97) established a nursery in the park. Sessions planted thousands of trees and shrubs, creating much of the exqui-

Beautiful Spanish platateresque buildings line El Prado, the axis of Balboa Park.

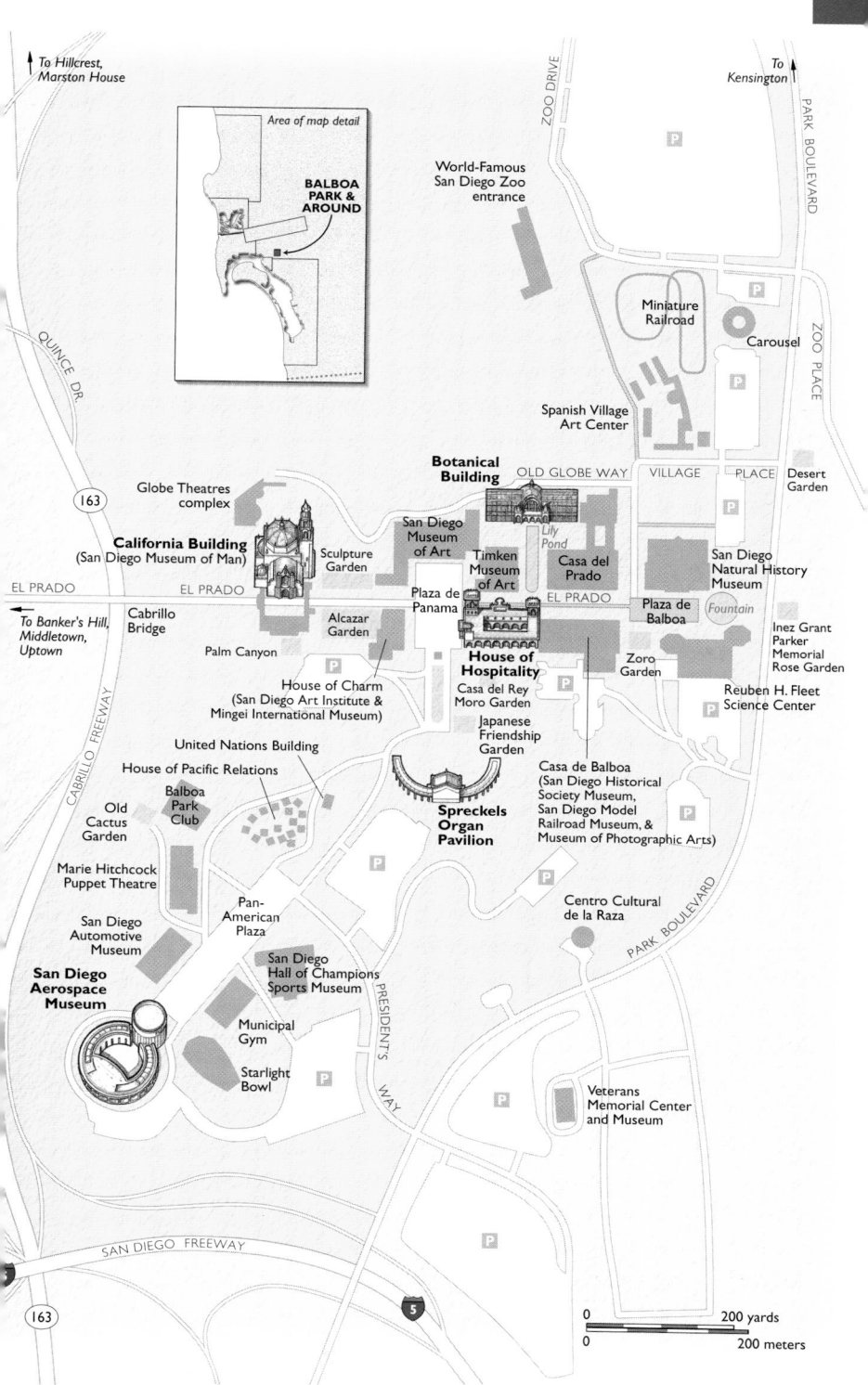

To Hillcrest,
Marston House

To
Kensington

Area of map detail

**BALBOA
PARK &
AROUND**

PARK BOULEVARD

ZOO DRIVE

World-Famous
San Diego Zoo
entrance

QUINCE DR

Miniature
Railroad

Carousel

ZOO PLACE

Spanish Village
Art Center

Globe Theatres
complex

163

**Botanical
Building**

OLD GLOBE WAY   VILLAGE   PLACE   Desert
Garden

California Building
(San Diego Museum of Man)

Sculpture
Garden

San Diego
Museum
of Art

Timken
Museum
of Art

**Casa del
Prado**

Lily
Pond

San Diego
Natural History
Museum

EL PRADO   EL PRADO

Plaza de
Panama

EL PRADO

Plaza de
Balboa

Fountain

Cabrillo
Bridge

To Banker's Hill,
Middletown,
Uptown

Alcazar
Garden

Inez Grant
Parker
Memorial
Rose Garden

Palm Canyon

**House of
Hospitality**

Zoro
Garden

Reuben H. Fleet
Science Center

CABRILLO FREEWAY

House of Charm
(San Diego Art Institute &
Mingei International Museum)

Casa del Rey
Moro Garden

United Nations Building

Japanese
Friendship
Garden

House of Pacific Relations

Casa de Balboa
(San Diego Historical
Society Museum,
San Diego Model
Railroad Museum, &
Museum of Photographic Arts)

Old
Cactus
Garden

Balboa
Park
Club

**Spreckels
Organ
Pavilion**

Marie Hitchcock
Puppet Theatre

Pan-
American
Plaza

Centro Cultural
de la Raza

PARK BOULEVARD

San Diego
Automotive
Museum

**San Diego
Aerospace
Museum**

San Diego
Hall of Champions
Sports Museum

PRESIDENT'S WAY

Municipal
Gym

Starlight
Bowl

Veterans
Memorial Center
and Museum

SAN DIEGO FREEWAY

163

5

0   200 yards

0   200 meters

World-Famous
San Diego Zoo

World-Famous
San Diego Zoo

www.sandiegozoo.org

🅰 Map p. 69

✉ Park Blvd. and
Zoo Pl.

☎ 619-234-3153

🕐 Open daily

💲 $$$$

🚌 Bus: 7, 7A, 7B

SO GLOBALLY ACCLAIMED IS SAN DIEGO'S ZOO THAT IN THE early 1970s it added the label "world famous" to its official title. Situated on a prime parcel of 100 acres in the northwest corner of Balboa Park, the zoo provides refuge for 4,000 rare and endangered animals representing more than 800 species and subspecies.

The grounds qualify as an accredited botanical garden, tended by expert horticulturists. Here grows a profusion of more than 6,500 species of exotic plants—everything from palms, fig trees, and coral trees to cycads, acacias, and prized orchids. The eucalyptus, bamboo, and hibiscus play much more than ornamental roles: They furnish dietary supplements for many of the animals.

A denizen of Fla-mingo Lagoon eyes zoo visitors.

It may indeed be world famous now, but the San Diego Zoo had a humble genesis. After the 1915-16 Panama-California Exposition closed on January 1, 1917, a small collection of animals that had been displayed during the show remained on the park grounds. Local surgeon Harry Wegeforth and a group of friends resolved to care for the animals while keeping them on the premises for the continuing pleasure of residents and other visi-

tors. On October 2, 1916, Wegeforth and associates incorporated themselves as the not-for-profit Zoological Society of San Diego.

The society has grown a bit since then. Now boasting more than 500 million members, it welcomes 3 million visitors each year; the world's largest zoological membership association, it oversees not only the zoo but also San Diego's Wild Animal Park (see pp. 205-207). The World-Famous San Diego Zoo has occupied its present site since 1922.

Among the zoo's rare occupants are Australian koalas, New Guinea tree kangaroos, giant pandas from China, pygmy chimpanzees from central Africa, Komodo dragons from Indonesia, Vietnamese clouded leopards, Arctic polar bears, and bird species that include Tahitian blue lories, Micronesian kingfishers, Steller's sea eagles, and the kagu of New Caledonia. There's also a full complement of the classic "charismatic megavertebrates": tigers, bears, gorillas, lions, elephants, giraffes, and hippos.

The animal exhibits dot easily traversed loops that spread out in various directions from the entrance (see zoo map, pp. 72–73). Although your choice of routes will probably hinge on the age of your party, perennially popular habitats include Ituri Forest, Polar Bear Plunge, Gorilla Tropics, Tiger River, Sun Bear Forest, Reptile Mesa, Owens RainForest Aviary, Scripps Aviary, the koala exhibit, and the Children's Zoo.

On entering, you'll be face-to-face with **Flamingo Lagoon,** where the graceful pink birds put most visitors in a cheerful mood. To the left, the **Camera Den and Information Booth** offers rental strollers, wheelchairs, photo gear, brochures, and plenty of free advice. (Here's some now: Wait to purchase any souvenirs until you're about to leave the zoo.)

Guided bus tours depart every few minutes from the right side of Flamingo Lagoon. The vehicles are open-air, double-decker buses; the duration is about 40 narrated minutes; and the coverage is approximately 75 percent of the zoo. Bus-tour tickets also allow you to hop on and off the zoo's Express buses—convenient ways to get around and linger at favorite areas.

Seated in open-air gondolas 180 feet above the ground, passengers can ride the **Skyfari Aerial Tramway** for treetop views of Polar Bear Plunge, Ituri Forest, and Gorilla Tropics. Food and drinks, restrooms, telephones, and benches to soothe your weary soles abound throughout the zoo; two fine restaurants offer more substantial fare. Turn left at the zoo entrance and you'll find a number of attractions just ahead. Squeals signal your arrival at the **Reptile House,** home to slinky creatures of every ilk—and, specifically, the world's largest collection of Fiji Island iguanas. To see gharials (crocodile relatives from India) and Galápagos tortoises, follow the signs to **Reptile Mesa.** At the end of this main-entry pathway, the **Children's Zoo** delights all ages with its 30 exhibits; these include an animal nursery

A Borneo orangutan chows down on a tasty branch.

and a petting paddock, where kids can get up close with domestic goats, sheep, and pot-bellied pigs.

Along this same stretch, to the right of the main entrance and information booth, is the **koala exhibit.** You'll know you're getting near it when you hear the oohs and aahs of visitors watching the cuddly marsupials (not bears) sleep the day away. Other denizens from down under hover nearby, among them Tasmanian devils, tree kangaroos, and wallabies.

LIONS, LANGURS, & BEARS

From here it's an easy stroll to visit the zebras, camels, giraffes, pigs, and sheep that live around **Horn & Hoof Mesa.** Another loop leads to **Elephant Mesa.** For more action, follow the crowd heading up **Bear Canyon.** Along this route you'll meet lions, bears, and rhino aplenty, not to mention our distant cousins the orangutans, swinging on ropes or seemingly lost in contemplation.

The world's smallest and most aggressive bears—Malayan sun bears—reside in (you guessed it) **Sun Bear Forest,** a plot filled with waterfalls and lush vegetation. Perhaps mellowed by the San Diego climate, they content themselves with frolicking and climbing trees. Just beyond are the **Douc langurs,** endangered primates from Southeast Asia.

At the convergence of Bear, Bongo, and Cat Canyons sits the **SBC Pacific Bell Giant Panda Research Station.** It was at this facility in 1999 that the panda Bai Yun gave birth to Hua Mei, the first U.S.-born panda to survive longer than four days. Hua Mei has since been returned to China, but her mother remains in place (along with a male companion, Shi Shi) as one of the zoo's most popular residents.

The panda station encompasses more than 52,000 square feet— enough room for large exhibit areas, private exercise yards, indoor shelters, a birthing den, an interpretive center, and an outdoor classroom. Elevated walkways afford excellent vantage points on the enclosure; one area even offers a rare peek inside the birthing den. Topping it all off, the zoo's 24-hour **Panda Cam** enables viewers to watch live images online.

The first right turn after the flamingo exhibit leads to **Gorilla Tropics.** En route you'll encounter the walk-through **Scripps Aviary,** where more than 200 birds indigenous to Africa flutter about an enclosure that is 90 feet tall and 150 feet long. Simulated thunder and rain add atmosphere as you view such vivid species as the gold-breasted starling and the blue-naped mousebird.

The sonic ambience continues into the newly remodeled

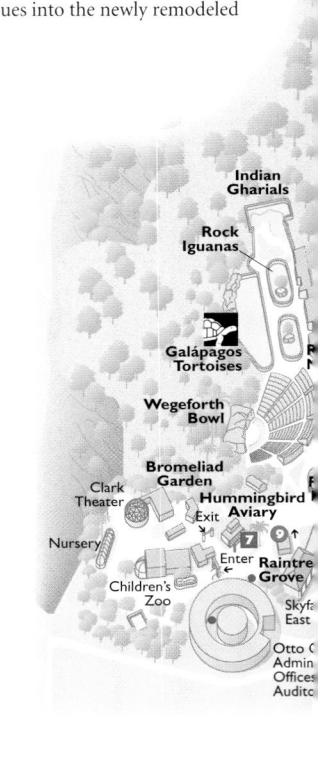

Indian Gharials

Rock Iguanas

Galápagos Tortoises

Wegeforth Bowl

Bromeliad Garden

Clark Theater

Hummingbird Aviary

Nursery

Exit

Enter

Children's Zoo

Raintree Grove

Skyfari East

Otto Center Admin Offices Audito

2.5-acre Gorilla Tropics and its 8,000-square-foot enclosure for western lowland gorillas. At viewing sta-tions sprinkled through the site, visitors stand rapt as the apes enact their oddly familiar daily routine, which usually consists of gorilla parents stoically watching gorilla kids at play.

Also residing in this section of the zoo are the bonobos, recognizable by the distinctive part down the center of their heads. Thought to be the most intelligent primates on Earth (after a select few humans), bonobos are smaller than common chimps. Their 6,000-square-foot enclosure is fitted with

Guest Services

1. Security Offices/ Lost & Found
2. First Aid (also private facilities for nursing mothers)
3. Strollers/Wheelchairs/ Motorized Scooter Rentals
4. Checks & Credit Cards
5. ATM
6. Lockers
7. Guests with Disabilities
8. Rest Rooms
9. Rest Rooms with Disabled Access
10. Public Phones
   Express Bus Stops
   Bus Tour Route

Shopping

1. San Diego Zoo Store
2. Kids' Store
3. Cinnamon Tree
4. Treehouse Trader
5. Panda Shop
6. Sydney's Shoppe
7. Arctic Trader
8. Camera Den
9. Zoofari Photos
10. Ituri Forest Outpost

Dining

1. Flamingo Café
2. Canyon Café
3. Treehouse Café
4. Sydney's Grill
5. Albert's Restaurant
6. Safari Kitchen
7. Children's Zoo Cupboard
8. Lagoon Terrace
9. Raintree Grill
10. Safari Snacks

Recycling Locations: ● Cans and Plastic   ● Glass   ● Maps
· · · · Least steep path to giant pandas and canyons (Shorter but steeper pathways are available.)

0   100 feet
0   30 meters

Polar Bear Plunge
Skyfari West
HORN & HOOF MESA
Pigs
Takins
Takins
Pigs
PANDA CANYON
Ituri Forest
The Treehouse
Pacific Bell SBC Giant Panda Research Station
Panda Discovery Center
Wings of Australasia
Speedramp #1 Up
Takins
Speedramp #2 Up
Hornbills
Zebras
Horn & Hoof Mesa
HORN & HOOF MESA
Hunte Amphitheater
Gorilla Tropics
Scripps Aviary
Parker Aviary
Owens RainForest Aviary
Future location of Heart-of-the-Zoo III
Fern Canyon
Sun Bear Forest
Lion-Tailed Macaques
Cats
CAT CANYON
Mhorr Gazelles
Giraffes
Pigs
HORN & HOOF MESA
Rhinos
Small Carnivores
Pigs
Bongos
Tapirs
Kiwi Trail
Elephant Mesa
Rhinos
Sheep & Goats
Meerkats
Tiger River entrance
Bus Tour Loading
BEAR CANYON
Bears
Lions
Meerkats
Kiwi House
Duikers
Bird Exhibit
Kangaroos/ Wallabies
Bats
Entrance
Membership Booth
Bus Tour Unloading
Rondavel Meeting Room
Warner Administration Center
Francois' Langurs
Koala Exhibit
Camels
African Kopje
P

twisted palms that they use for climbing and play.

Across from Gorilla Tropics is the 65-foot-high **Owens Rain-Forest Aviary,** a walk-through avian environment. The multitier structure guides visitors along a winding path that rises into the forest canopy; there they share space with more than 200 exotically colorful birds, representing 60 species from Southeast Asia and Australia. Designed to re-create a Southeast Asian jungle, the aviary is filled with waterfalls, ponds, and ferns, flowers, and other foliage native to the region.

INTO THE RAIN FOREST

The pathway called **Tiger River,** whose access point lies between the information booth and the aerial-tram station near the zoo entrance, snakes through a misty Asian rain forest where exotic plants surround ten tiger-filled enclosures. At home on the grassy hillside, the majestic cats blend to near-invisibility among such natural elements as waterfalls, rocks, and logs. The riverbanks also harbor Malaysian tapirs, Burmese pythons, Argus pheasants, Chinese water dragons, and gavials, or narrow-snouted crocodiles.

Wander up the road to **Ituri Forest,** the zoo's newest exhibit. Evocative of a central African jungle, this four-acre patch transports visitors to a dense rain forest filled with species of bamboo and other authentic African plants. The animal attractions here include okapis, forest buffalo, spotted-necked otters, hippopotamuses, and variegated monkeys and birds. As special features, the exhibit offers information about the Mbuti people who inhabit this environment in Africa, a replicated Mbuti camp, and underwater viewing windows that invite close-up views

of the hippos and otters.

Access Bongo Canyon from either Ituri Forest or Bear Canyon. A somewhat steep incline ushers you into the **Birds of Prey Aviary** and the opportunity to visit eagles and condors. Around the bend, **Polar Bear Plunge** surprises almost everyone for its success in converting two acres of Mediterranean-like San Diego into an arctic environment where polar bears feel at home. Surrounding the 130,000-gallon plunge pool are exhibits featuring Arctic tundra, northern birds, native plants, Siberian reindeer, and Pallas cats. An underwater viewing room allows visitors and bears to ogle one another. Zoobies can also catch the playful action online by tuning in to **Polar Cam** at the zoo's website.

Near the panda station is **Hunte Amphitheatre** in Cat Canyon, the place to be for daily performances by trained exotic animals. Shows take place at noon and 2 p.m. *(more frequently in summer).* Additional events held throughout the year include "Orchid Odyssey" (third Friday of each month), when the public is admitted to the heavenly Orchid House, and "Jungle Bells," a holiday celebration in December.

From June through August, the zoo stays open until 10 p.m. *(last admission 9 p.m.),* allowing visitors to experience some beastly nocturnal scents, sounds, and scenes. There's also musical entertainment, storytelling, and magic shows.

The World-Famous San Diego Zoo is immersed in animal conservation and research worldwide. The zoo's research branch—the Center for Reproduction of Endangered Species—has been pivotal in habitat protection, fighting to secure proper care for threatened creatures now and in the future. ∎

Opposite: An elephant turns tail on a tour bus.

The Lily Pond, in front of the Botanical Building, is picture-perfect for wedding photos.

A walk through Balboa Park

Balboa Park is vast—filled with so many attractions they can't possibly be seen in a single day. Even long-time residents have yet to explore every nook and cranny. Museum exhibits change often, as do theater productions and concert programs, making the grounds and gardens a year-round spectacle. If you're pressed for time, pick and choose among your favorites; otherwise, schedule several days to cover more territory (wear sturdy walking shoes!). An alternative is to catch the free tram that stops at various points throughout the park, allowing visitors to hop on and off.

The park's main attractions lie in the area bounded by Sixth Avenue, Park Boulevard, Interstate 5, and Upas Street.

Enter the park's western edge on Laurel Street. (Arrive early enough and you may find parking on Balboa Drive, the first right.) Walk east across **Balboa Park West,** a broad grassland thronged with picnicking families, Frisbee throwers, lawn bowlers, runners, exhibitionist sun worshipers, street people, and dog walkers. Most of the latter will be headed down the hill to your right for Nate's Point, an area devoted to dogs and their owners.

Cross busy Calif. 163 and its wide canyon on the **Cabrillo Bridge ❶** (also known as the Laurel Street Bridge). This approach provided a dramatic entrance for fairgoers to the 1915-16 Panama-California Exposition; among the first to cross it on April 12, 1914 (the day it opened) had been Franklin D.

Roosevelt, then Assistant Secretary of the Navy. Balboa Park's official gateway, the archway at the east end—adorned by reclining male and female figures pouring water from jugs—signifies the Panama Canal's link of the Pacific with the Atlantic Ocean. As you pass beneath the arch and enter the park, you'll find yourself on **El Prado,** the main east-west artery.

On the left, the 1915 Spanish Colonial-style **California Building ❷** immediately strikes most visitors. Presided over by its landmark 200-foot-tall California Tower—topped by a caravel wind vane and a 100-bell carillon that chimes the quarter-hour—this was one of the most ornate constructions for the early exposition. Among the impressive architectural elements is the gleaming dome covered in yellow, blue, and white ceramic tiles, and the decorative facade that incorporates life-size sculptures of early San Diego historical figures.

Housed within, the **San Diego Museum of Man** (also established in 1915) offers outstanding archaeology and anthropology displays. The Tudor-style **Globe Theatres** complex, in Copley Plaza behind the museum, is home to the renowned 1935 **Old Globe Theatre** and two other stages.

As you continue along El Prado, gardens pop up on both sides of the street. The **Sculpture Garden,** on the left, is part of the San Diego Museum of Art, enabling all who pass by a glimpse of works by artists such as Henry Moore and Alexander Calder. On the right, stroll through **Alcazar Garden** (behind the Art Institute) for its seasonal blooms and tile fountains, modeled after the grounds at Spain's Alcazar Castle.

East of the garden, the Spanish-style **House of Charm**—a 1990s copy of the original 1915 building—is home to the **San Diego Art Institute,** a showcase for local artists, and the **Mingei International Museum,** which exhibits colorful folk arts and

crafts from around the world. The House of Charm's northeast corner meets **Plaza de Panama,** the focal point of the park, marked by Anna Hyatt Huntington's 23-foot-tall equestrian sculpture of **El Cid Compeador,** in place since 1930.

Centerpiece of the plaza, with its magnificent Spanish Renaissance-style facade, is the

🗺	See area map page 69
►	Cabrillo Bridge
⬌	3 miles
⏱	2.5 hours
►	World-Famous San Diego Zoo

NOT TO BE MISSED

- California Tower
- Mingei International Museum
- San Diego Museum of Art
- Botanical Building
- San Diego Natural History Museum

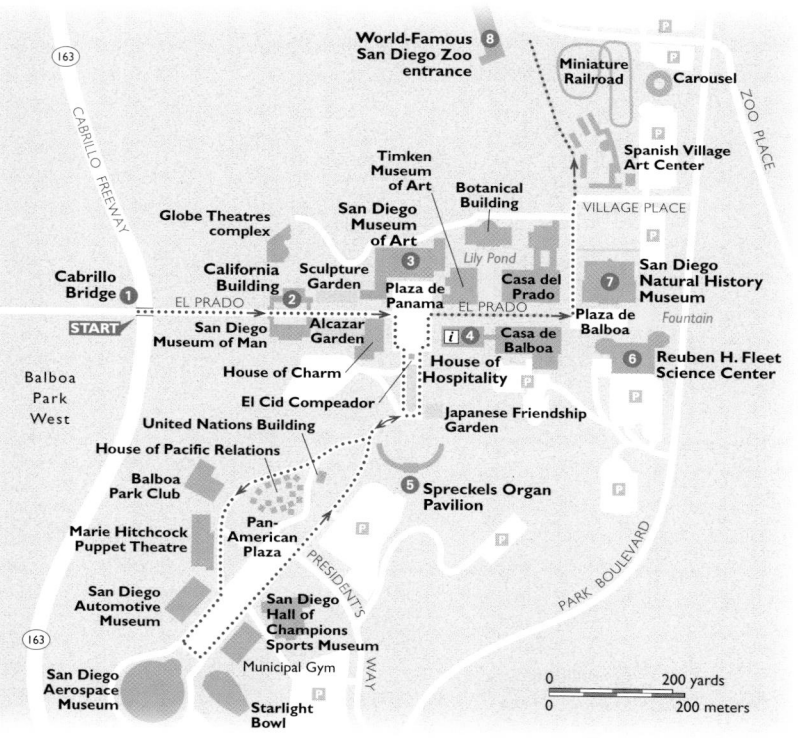

The House of Hospitality, on El Prado, houses the park visitor center. Many tours start here.

San Diego Museum of Art ❸. Fine collections of Italian Renaissance, Spanish baroque, and Asian works, as well as important traveling exhibits, make this a top West Coast art museum. At the east edge of the plaza, the circa-1960s **Timken Art Gallery** displays a private collection of American and European master paintings, and an extraordinary selection of Russian icons. The **Balboa Park Visitors Center** *(619-239-0512, www.balboapark.org)* is located in the **House of Hospitality ❹,** at the plaza's southeastern edge. Aside from providing information and selling maps, this is the departure point for various park tours. Also inside

is **Prado Restaurant,** a popular lunch and dinner spot with dramatic decor and contemporary cuisine. Behind this building, the **Japanese Friendship Garden** affords a peaceful place to relax and reflect in a Zen-like environment. Traditional tea ceremonies are held in the teahouse.

Facing south from the plaza, the **Spreckels Organ Pavilion ❺** (donated by sugar magnate John Spreckels for the 1915–16 expo) is home to the world's largest outdoor pipe organ. The 2,400-seat pavilion welcomes listeners to free Sunday afternoon and summer evening concerts. Walk counterclockwise around the Organ Pavilion to reach the

Plaza de Panama's night-lit fountain frames the Museum of Man's California Tower.

United Nations Building, the start of the **Pan-American Plaza** and a lengthy loop of sights. The 17 cottages, south of the United Nations Building, make up the **House of Pacific Relations.** Dating from the first expo, each continues to represent the cultures of various nations. The **Balboa Park Club** and **Marie Hitchcock Puppet Theatre** reside just west of the cottages. Wandering southward you'll pass the **San Diego Automotive Museum,** with its collection of vintage vehicles, and the circular **San Diego Aerospace Museum,** distinguished by the Blackbird A-12 spy plane. Returning northbound, you'll pass the **Starlight Bowl,** where summer musicals are performed, and the **San Diego Hall of Champions Sports Museum,** which recognizes local athletes.

Return to Plaza de Panama and El Prado —now a pedestrian-only walkway as it travels east. Street mimes and musicians often play to visitors who lounge around the languid koi-filled **Lily Pond,** across from the visitor center. More than 500 types of tropical and subtropical plants fill the redwood-lathed **Botanical Building,** behind the pond. Back on El Prado, lovely **Casa del Prado** is a venue used by various community performance groups. Across the way, **Casa de Balboa** is home to such popular attractions as the highly respected **Museum of Photographic Arts,** enlightening **San Diego Historical Society Museum,** and the captivating **San Diego Model Railroad Museum.**

An enormous fountain greets you at **Plaza de Balboa** on the park's eastern edge. To your right, the **Reuben H. Fleet Science Center** ❻ offers hands-on exhibits and an IMAX Theater with exciting films. To the left, the renovated 1933 **San Diego Natural History Museum** ❼ offers impressive displays focusing mainly on southern California and Baja California, and geared to all ages.

Behind the museum, the **Spanish Village Art Center,** constructed in the style of an ancient Spanish village for the 1935-36 expo, is an inviting ramble of studios and galleries—many with on-site artists who invite you to watch as they work.

Leaving Spanish Village, two attractions loom for kids and kids at heart—a 1910 **carousel,** complete with brass rings to grab, and a half-mile **miniature railroad** powered by a small version of a General Motors F-3 locomotive. Those intriguing sounds from beyond the lush eucalyptus groves mean you've reached the entrance to the **World-Famous San Diego Zoo** ❽. ■

San Diego Natural History Museum

San Diego Natural History Museum
www.sdnhm.org
Map p. 69
1788 El Prado
619-232-3821
$$
Bus: 7, 7A, 7B

A lifelike mountain lion draws the scrutiny of two wary museum visitors.

SPUN OUT OF THE SAN DIEGO SOCIETY OF NATURAL History—a fledgling group founded in 1874 by amateur naturalists—this museum is now a powerhouse of accomplished professionals. They have turned it into a world-class scientific and educational facility devoted to preserving our natural heritage.

The first exhibits were set up in a downtown hotel room in 1912. Later on, they were shuttled among various sites in Balboa Park, finally, in 1933, they settled into their present home. Situated on the north side of Plaza de Balboa, across from the Reuben H. Fleet Science Center, the original building was designed by local architect William Templeton Johnson.

In 2001, a major renovation and expansion more than doubled the museum's floor space, to 150,000 square feet. A new glass-enclosed entrance facing north (in front of the Moreton Bay fig tree) provides a dramatic welcome for visitors. Among the other improvements were an expansive atrium for public events, a multimedia theater, and updated facilities for both the Envi-

ronmental Science Education Center and the Biodiversity Research Center of the Californias.

The natural history museum focuses on the biological and geological evolution and diversity of southern and Baja California. Its holdings consist of more than 7.5 million specimens, from fossils to plants and animals. "Natural Treasures: Past and Present," which opened in 2001 to celebrate the newly remodeled facility, invites visitors to explore an assemblage of plants, fossils, rocks, and animals (some of which had never been displayed before) from southern California and Baja California. Treasures from the past—ranging from the Pleistocene epoch (about 1.8 million to 10,000 years ago) to the Cretaceous period (about 144 to 65 million years ago)—feature such showstoppers as a saber-toothed cat, a fossilized walrus, and a mosasaur. Treasures from the present highlight a squeal-provoking posse of live animals: a California mountain lion, a rattlesnake, velvet ants, iron-clad beetles, and a giant desert hairy scorpion.

Some 20,000 square feet of new permanent exhibits will be constructed and installed through 2006, all of them focusing on the regions of southern California and Baja California. **"Fossil Mysteries"**—an exploration of the region's prehistory from dinosaurs to the Ice Age—will feature a variety of hands-on and interactive experiences: These bid visitors to compare their speed and strength with those of prehistoric animals; to manipulate animal skeletons and touch real fossils; and to track how changes in coastlines and tectonic plates may have affected the sites of their own home towns over the eons.

Regional habitats—replete with walk-through dioramas, live plants and animals, and tactile features—will breathe life into the planned **"Habitat Journey"** exhibit. Here visitors will be able to undertake a virtual voyage from ocean bottom to mountaintops, exploring coastlines, caves, and blooming deserts along the way. Living plants and animals will take up residence in the **Discovery Room,** where visitors of all ages will be encouraged to learn about nature by experiencing it through touch-and-feel objects.

Temporary exhibitions often venture above and beyond the museum's tightly focused regional boundaries. Recent shows have included "Epidemic! The Natural History of Disease"; "Monarca" (an explanation of monarch butterfly migration); and "Bears: Imagina-

tion and Reality," which investigated the relationship between bears and people.

Ocean Oasis—a journey through Baja California and the Sea of Cortés—is screened daily on the natural history museum's giant-screen theater. This fascinating trek lets viewers glide alongside migrating whales, fly over palm-studded oases and snowcapped mountains, and dive undersea to explore rare marine life.

Nature walks and field trips geared to a wide spectrum of issues within the natural world are staged throughout the year for all ages and abilities. Day trips, overnights, and longer explorations *(call 619-255-0203 for information)* encompass a trove of adventures, from bird-watching and kayaking to rugged backcountry hikes. The Canyoneers—a group of museum volunteers proficient at recognizing and describing local plants and animals—lead interpretive walks within San Diego County's natural areas.

On Sundays, "Ms. Frizzle"—the wild-haired science teacher of *Magic School Bus* fame—leads kids on fun and interactive science adventures. The museum also offers a long list of educational and community outreach programs. ■

Snakes alive! Naturally, the museum takes a hands-on approach to learning.

Reuben H. Fleet
Science Center

VISITORS ALLEGEDLY DEVOID OF SCIENTIFIC PROPENSITIES soon find out otherwise at this hands-on, please-touch repository of knowledge and learning. It houses a world of gizmos, gadgets, and educational experiments, all just waiting to be activated.

Reuben H. Fleet Science Center

www.rhfleet.org

- Map p. 69
- 1875 El Prado
- 619-238-1233
- $$
- Bus: 7, 7A, 7B

It may look like a beachball to you, but to her it's a lesson in atmospheric dynamics.

Presiding over the south side of Plaza de Balboa, this pseudo-Spanish Colonial building opened in 1973. The funds that enabled the science center to be built were donated by Army Major Reuben Hollis Fleet, who earned his wings in 1917, led the first unit to fly a load of U.S. mail in 1918, and founded the Consolidated Aircraft company in 1923. His namesake legacy has proved so popular with San Diego visitors that in 1998 it underwent an expansion doubling its exhibit space.

Exhibits are housed in five gallery areas. **ExploraZone 3,** in the Main Gallery, features more than 35 interactive displays and experiments, providing diversion for budding scientists of all ages. Forming cloud rings with a mist generator, getting square wheels to roll smoothly, and spinning a brightly colored orb that models planetary atmospheres are among the fun but educational components here. The popular **SciTours**—a motion-based simulator ride—takes passengers on space missions throughout the day.

In the new **Virtual Zone,** you may be called upon to save Earth from an impending meteorite impact in **"Meteor Storm"** or to navigate mazelike environments of advertising messages in **"Smoke and Mirrors."**

TechnoVation, on the second level, showcases the sort of cutting-edge techniques and scientific breakthroughs that are being pioneered by San Diego companies on a daily basis. Other exhibits teach the principles of signal communications, DNA analysis, and facial-feature recognition. The Rotunda Gallery is reserved primarily for traveling exhibits.

Viewers get a visceral feel for the action in the 1973 **IMAX Dome Theater** (the world's first IMAX venue), where cinematic adventures in science and nature delve into caves or journey into space. **Planetarium** shows are held on the first Wednesday of each month. ∎

San Diego Historical Society Museum

Though the San Diego Historical Society dates back to 1928, it did not realize its dream of setting up this museum (in the Casa de Balboa) until 1989. The first-floor exhibits focus on all facets of San Diego history, particularly the period after the Mexican-American War when California became the 31st U.S. state. Some exhibits—"Weird San Diego," for one—depart the predictable path of history for a jaunt into the city's eccentric past.

The museum's 100-seat theater hosts public lectures, educational programs, and workshops. Research archives housed in the basement comprise books, biographies, maps, sketches, manuscripts, and a massive collection of historic photos. The images of Balboa Park's early expositions are especially intriguing. ∎

San Diego Historical Society Museum
www.sandiegohistory.org
🅰 Map p. 69
✉ 1649 El Prado
☎ 619-232-6203
🕐 Closed Mon.
💲 $
🚌 Bus: 7, 7A, 7B

Model Railroad Museum

A volunteer in training carefully engineers a working display of a model railroad.

Considered the world's largest of its kind, this paradise for train buffs is mesmerizing for all. Since the San Diego Model Railroad Museum opened in 1982, more than two million visitors have come to ogle the extravagant model exhibits as they realistically chug, screech, and whistle about the 24,000-square-foot space. Massive yet minutely detailed model layouts allow thrilling close-ups of the historic Cabrillo Southwestern, San Diego & Arizona Eastern, and Pacific Desert lines, as well as the challenging Tehachapi Pass. Each has been set up by separate railroad clubs whose members volunteer to design, construct, and operate their particular exhibit.

In the **Toy Train Gallery,** children (and adults) are encouraged to try their hand on the throttles that maneuver circa-1950s Lionel trains. Other rare Lionel and American Flyer cars are also on display. Additional highlights include a working semaphore, crossing signal, centralized tower control, prototype artifacts, and a large relief map of San Diego County. Diehard rail enthusiasts show up on Tuesday and Friday evenings, when visitors are allowed to watch the various clubs fine-tune their exhibits. ∎

San Diego Model Railroad Museum
www.sdmodelrailroadm
.com
🅰 Map p. 69
✉ 1649 El Prado
☎ 619-696-0199
🕐 Closed Mon.
💲 $
🚌 Bus: 7, 7A, 7B

Museum of Photographic Arts

ONE OF THE PREEMINENT INSTITUTIONS OF ITS KIND, THE Museum of Photographic Arts—MoPA, to fans and habitués—has earned a sterling reputation throughout the world for its collection, presentation, and conservation of the photographic arts.

MoPA opened its permanent headquarters—donated by the City of San Diego—in 1983, inside Balboa Park's Casa de Balboa. Under the auspices of director Arthur Ollman, the museum quickly became the talk of the town (and of photography lovers far and wide), drawing thousands of visitors during its first year of operation.

Thanks to a millennial renovation that doubled its gallery space, MoPA now boasts movable walls and flexible lighting; an elegant special events area; a 228-seat theater that screens American movie classics, art films, and contemporary films on Thursday, Friday, and Saturday evenings; and the Mandell Weiss Learning Center, remarkable for its world-class research library dedicated to the photographic arts. Photography lectures and

workshops are also part of MoPA's offerings.

Complementing the museum's extensive permanent collection are approximately six changing exhibitions per year. Always captivating, often provocative, these address the long and rich history of the medium, from 19th-century daguerreotypes to 21st-century photojournalism. Upcoming shows include photos by William Henry Fox Talbot, the father of modern photography, and portraits by Pulitzer Prize-winner Eddie Adams.

MoPA has produced seven traveling exhibits that have been shown at museums throughout the world. The first of these, a 1986 retrospective of portrait photographer Arnold Newman, earned MoPA an international reputation for high-quality presentation. ∎

A museum-goer appears lost before "Found," an exhibit by Nigel Poor in MoPA's entrance hall.

Timken Museum of Art

THOUGH IT IS DWARFED BY THE ADJACENT SAN DIEGO Museum of Art, the Timken Museum of Art—often referred to as the "jewel box of Balboa Park"—is a perfect showcase for its distinguished Putnam Foundation Collection.

Sisters Anne R. and Amy Putnam—nieces of an East Coast banking and manufacturing tycoon—were prominent patrons of San Diego's Fine Arts Society, which became the San Diego Museum of Art in 1978. Starting in the 1940s, the art-loving siblings steadily acquired the works of European masters. After their deaths, the Putnam Foundation was established to continue their collecting.

With construction funding provided by the Timken family (former residents of San Diego), the museum opened in 1965 as a permanent home for the Putnam Foundation Collection. The holdings have since grown to include 113 European and American paintings, as well as Russian icons from 1300 to 1900.

The Timken Museum is outwardly distinctive, too. Rather than displaying the Spanish Renaissance style typical of many other buildings in Balboa Park, it was constructed with sleek, modern lines. Built primarily of elegant materials—think bronze and travertine—the museum was designed with guidance from art-world titans such as the directors of the National Gallery of Art in Washington, D.C., and the Metropolitan Museum of Art in New York. Care was lavished on quality lighting: The galleries are suffused with natural light, which enters through skylights fitted with special filters. Inside the building, six galleries surround a rotunda hung with gorgeous 16th-century French tapestries and adorned with a late

Timken Museum of Art
http://gort.ucsd.edu/sj/timken
- Map p. 69
- 1500 El Prado
- 619-239-5548
- Closed Mon., legal holidays, & Sept.
- Bus: 7, 7A, 7B

The Timken's "Portrait of Marguerite de Sève" was painted in 1729 by French portraitist Nicolas de Largillierre.

casting of Giambologna's "Mercury." Within the galleries themselves, visitors are treated to an eye-popping assortment of five centuries' worth of masterpiece paintings, from the early Renaissance through the 19th century. Their creators include such illustrious artists as Rembrandt, Rubens, Bruegel the Elder, Veronese, Veneto, Boucher, John Singleton Copley, and a 2001 addition by painter Raphaelle Peale of the Philadelphia school. One gallery, its walls covered with rich velvet fabrics, elicits gasps for its dramatic collection of rare Russian icons.

In addition to its permanent collection, the Timken presents twice-yearly special exhibits, afternoon and evening lectures, educational programs for students and adults, and an art camp for youngsters. A three-month building-wide makeover should be completed by early 2003. ■

San Diego Museum of Art

San Diego Museum of Art
www.sdmart.org
- Map p. 69
- 1450 El Prado
- 619-232-7931
- Closed Mon.
- $$
- Bus: 7, 7A, 7B

Inspired by the popularity of art exhibits held at the 1915-16 Panama-California Exposition, community leader Appleton Bridges agreed in 1922 to fund a permanent facility to house the municipal art collection of the emerging city. Around the same time, the San Diego Art Guild and the Friends of Art merged, forming the Fine Arts Society that would operate the new museum.

Opened as the Fine Arts Gallery of San Diego in 1926 (when ownership was transferred to the city), the museum has undergone numerous changes. For the 1935-36 California-Pacific International Exposition, for example, the gallery bestowed upon itself a lofty title—the Palace of Fine Arts—befitting such a grand event. In World War II, the U.S. Navy pressed the facility into service as a hospital ward.

Two major expansions—one in 1966 that added the west wing, a second in 1974 that added the east wing—more than doubled the exhibition space. In 1978, the Board of Trustees changed the gallery's name to the San Diego Museum of Art, launching the modern growth of its collections. Since then the facility has been the beneficiary of some major-league donations and bequests. It regularly displays important traveling exhibits; and as of 2002 it boasted annual visitorship of more than 400,000.

Not a man to take chances with his money, financier Bridges hired San Diego's leading architect, William Templeton Johnson, to

design the new art gallery. Johnson followed the lead of the 1915-16 expo's Spanish Colonial design, but he also employed the filigree-happy plateresque style so strongly reminiscent of 16th-century Spanish architecture. The result was the magnificently ornate edifice that greets visitors today.

SPRUNG FROM RELATIVELY HUMBLE BEGINNINGS AS THE Fine Arts Gallery of San Diego, the San Diego Museum of Art—standing majestically at the northern edge of the Plaza de Panama—is a repository for more than 11,000 objects of art. Experts consider it one of the finest museums on the West Coast.

Opposite, top:
The variety of mediums on display at the San Diego Museum of Art cover prehistory to the present.

- Special Exhibit
- American Art
- Asian Art
- European Art
- Contemporary Art
- European Old Masters
- Maxwell & Muriel Gluck Gallery
- South Asian / Edwin Binney III Gallery

Sculpture Garden

Courtyard and café

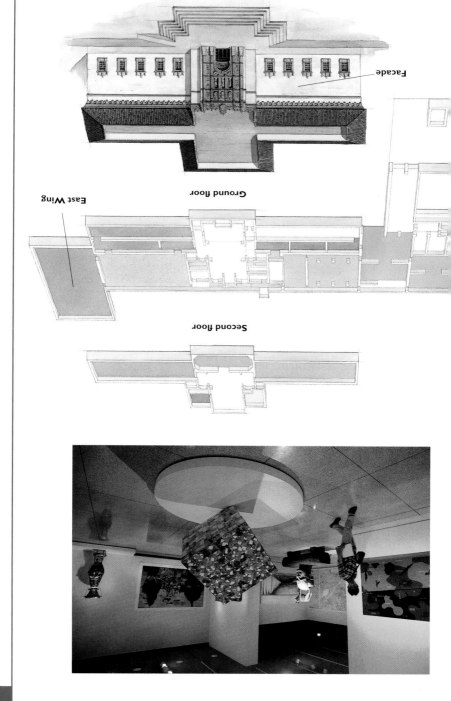

Facade

Ground floor

East Wing

Second floor

Borrowing motifs from the Cathedral of Valladolid and the University of Salamanca, the facade features life-size sculptures of the Spanish painters Murillo, Ribera, and Velázquez, each ensconced in its own recessed niche. Inlaid above the front doors is a huge seashell carved in stone—the traditional emblem of San Diego (St. James) and now the museum logo as well.

Inside there's a strong flavor of Spain as well. Thanks to funding provided during the museum's early years by sisters Anne and Amy Putnam, the collection includes Goya's "Marques de Sofraga," Sánchez Cotán's "Quince, Cabbage, Melon and Cucumber," and El Greco's "St. Peter Penitent." The Putnam sisters also admired the Italian Renaissance and northern European schools, helping the museum procure works by Veronese, Bernardo Bellotto, Guardi, and Giorgione, not to mention Rubens, Hals, van Dyck, and van Ruisdael. It was a French painter, however—Adolphe-William Bougureau—who created the museum's most popular work, "The Young Shepherdess."

1994 saw the installation of a different type of IMAGE, the **Interactive Multimedia Art Gallery Explorer.** This computerized data-retrieval system enables visitors to access the museum's collections via touch screen.

In 2000 the museum embarked on a building-wide renovation project, notably a stunning restoration of the rotunda as it appeared at the 1926 ribbon-cutting ceremony. The rotunda walls were repainted their original glowing ochre, the upstairs galleries were reinstalled, the front desk was moved to the center of the main lobby, and the layout of the museum store was reconfigured.

Few would say no to a buying spree celebrating their 75th birthday, and neither did the museum in 2001, when it added more than 100 works of art. Among the standouts was Jusepe de Rubera's "Penitent Magdalene," one of his earliest documented works (and the first Old Master painting to be acquired in more than a decade).

Today the permanent collections of the San Diego Museum of Art hold more than 11,000 paintings, drawings, sculptures, artifacts, and other art objects spanning 5000 B.C. to A.D. 2003. There are representative works by all the major French Impressionists, as well as works by modern masters Modigliani, Matisse, and Dufy. Other donors have contributed works by Toulouse-Lautrec and such fine Latin American entries as Diego Rivera's "Girl in a White Dress" and Rufino Tamayo's "Somnambulist."

The museum has also built up outstanding collections of American, Asian, and Indian art. The latter two are remarkable in both quality and extent—thousands of objects ranging from ancient Buddhist sculptures to Japanese woodblock prints. Most impressive is the 1,400-piece set of Indian miniature paintings, the largest outside India; donated in 1991 by Edwin Binney III, the collection can be sampled in a new upstairs gallery.

Recent artistic directions include the museum's venture into contemporary art with the establishment of a curatorial department devoted to the genre. You'll find earlier entries in the field populating the Sculpture Garden at the museum's west edge, filled with works by Henry Moore, Louise Nevelson, Alexander Calder, and other 20th-century artists.

The San Diego art museum has high ambitions for its traveling shows as well, one of which will bring "Degas in Bronze: The Complete Sculptures" to the site from June to late September 2003. ■

Opposite: In the museum's Sculpture Garden, opportunities abound for artistic interaction.

Botanical Building & other gardens

THOUGH MOST OF BALBOA PARK'S 1,200 LUSH ACRES SEEM transplanted from Eden, the park's defined gardens truly qualify as horticultural paradises. North of the natural history museum you'll find Balboa Park's landmark **Moreton Bay fig tree.** Planted some time before 1915, the fig now stretches 60 feet high, its twisting branches and gnarled roots spreading out some 120 feet.

BOTANICAL BUILDING

When it was built as a garden display for the 1915-16 expo, the Botanical Building was the world's largest wood-lath structure. It measures 75 feet wide and 250 feet long, and is crowned by an enormous central dome 60 feet high. Sitting east of the art museum and set back from El Prado pedestrian walkway, the redwood-lathed building admits streaming shafts of sunlight onto more than 2,000 permanent tropical and subtropical plants, as well as a forest of changing seasonal blooms. The winter poinsettias and spring tulips are especially brilliant. All plants are carefully labeled, inviting gardeners to stalk the building (get it?) in search of ideas for their own homes and nurseries. Benches set among moss-covered fountains and trickling waterfalls encourage rest and reflection.

Koi flit among the lotuses and water lilies floating about the large **Lily Pond,** which stretches from the Botanical Building toward El Prado. During World War II, the Lily Pond and a smaller companion pool provided swimming and hydrotherapy to sailors recuperating

Botanical Building
- 🅰 Map p. 69
- 🕐 Closed Thurs.

Japanese Friendship Garden
- 🅰 Map p. 69
- ✉ 2215 Pan-American Way
- ☎ 619-232-2780
- 🕐 Closed Mon, except in summer
- 💲 $

Exquisite water lilies grace the pond in front of the Botanical Building.

Reinforcing the authenticity of the Japanese Friendship Garden, koi ply the serene waters of its pond.

in a makeshift ward nearby. Today the pond is a magnet for weekend and summertime mimes, jugglers, and musicians (one guy plays guitar with his feet). Best of all, it's an opportunity for weary tourists to lie back and kick off their shoes.

OTHER GARDENS

Across from the Museum of Man, the formal **Alcazar Garden**—modeled after landscaping at Alcazar Castle in Seville, Spain—features impossibly vivid seasonal blooms framed by boxwood hedges. Linger among the benches and ornate Moorish-tile fountains here and you're likely to see a wedding party posing for photographs or overhear the backstage gossip of between-scenes actors from the nearby Globe Theatres.

South of the House of Charm, more than 450 palm trees (including early-1900s Mexican fan palms) form an oasis in the two-acre **Palm Canyon.**

The tidy design of the **Japanese Friendship Garden,** northeast of the Spreckels Organ Pavilion, translates into tranquility: Paths wind among bamboo stands, a koi pond, and a 60-foot-long *fuji-dana* (wisteria arbor), a balm from the sensory overload of Balboa Park. Traditional tea ceremonies

are performed in the teahouse. Large cactuses and other succulents (as well as exotic Australian and African protea plants) thrive in the **Old Cactus Garden** near the Balboa Park Club.

Moorish gardens of southern Spain are re-created in the **Casa del Rey Moro Garden,** behind the House of Hospitality.

Butterflies are free—to flutter about the **Zoro Garden,** that is. This sunken grotto between Casa de Balboa and the science center has been planted with every necessity for the cycles of a butterfly's life. California lilac, sunflower, passion vine, and milkweed provide sustenance during the caterpillar stage; the nectar of pincushion flower, verbena, lantana, and butterfly bush nourishes the adults. A footbridge across Park Boulevard leads to the **Inez Grant Parker Memorial Rose Garden,** where 2,400 bushes bristle with 180 varieties of roses. The peak season is April and May, though many bloom from March through December.

Nearby, the surprisingly ethereal 2.5-acre **Desert Garden** shows off more than 1,000 cactuses and other succulents and desert plants from around the world. Look here for blooms even in winter. ■

Old Globe Theatre

THOUGH JUST ONE PART OF THE THREE-STAGE GLOBE Theatres complex, San Diego's Old Globe Theatre has remained the heart and soul of the city's thespian scene since its inception.

Old Globe Theatre
www.theglobetheatres.org
- Map p. 69
- 1363 Old Globe Way
- 619-239-2001 (box office)
- Tours Sat.–Sun., or by appt.
- Tours $
- Bus: 7, 7A, 7B

Fashioned after England's Globe Theatre, which stood on the banks of the Thames in Elizabethan times, this structure was originally slated as temporary space for the 1935-36 exposition. But high praise for the Old Globe Players—notably their 40-minute renditions of the Bard's works, dubbed Streamlined Shakespeare—led to the creation of a permanent playhouse.

In 1937, the Old Globe inaugurated its first regular season with John Van Druten's *The Distaff Side*. Cast member Craig Noel made his stage debut in that performance—and never left. Within two years, he was a director; Noel stayed on for six decades, producing more than 500 works. Under his stewardship, the Old Globe grew from an obscure community theater into a resident professional company and earned a Tony Award for outstanding regional theater in 1984. Actors such as Dennis Hopper and Marion Ross got their start here, so it's no surprise that aspiring ones clamor for roles in each new production.

Modeled on its 17th-century English antecedent, the Old Globe Theatre has been the pride and joy of San Diego since the 1935-36 expo.

Two fires—both cases of arson—dealt tragic blows in the 1970s, but the spirited theater rebuilt and even expanded. Today it is one of the country's most prolific theaters, staging 14 shows per year (many of which make their way to Broadway) and drawing some 250,000 playgoers in the process. In-house costumers, set builders, and wigmakers create the lavish trappings seen on stage.

The centerpiece Old Globe Theatre, with an adaptable seating configuration for about 600, stages classic works and extravagant productions. In 1968, the Old Falstaff Tavern was converted into the 225-seat **Cassius Carter Centre Stage,** an intimate theater-in-the-round where the action takes place within arm's length of the audience. Completing the complex is the 625-seat **Lowell Davies Festival Theatre,** whose canyonside setting makes for a backdrop of eucalyptus trees. Plays are staged from July to mid-October, with Shakespeare the classic summer fare. ∎

San Diego Museum of Man

WITHIN THE PALATIAL SPANISH COLONIAL CALIFORNIA Building—designed by Bertram Goodhue and constructed for the 1915-16 Panama-California Exposition—San Diego's anthropology museum tells fascinating tales about a favorite topic: ourselves.

Visitors will find some of the city's greatest treasures within these hallowed walls—many of them from the original 1915-16 expo display. More than 78,000 objects depict mankind's journey through the ages, with a focus on the fascinating cultures of the U.S. Southwest, Mexico, South America, and ancient Egypt.

Most visitors are immediately struck by the huge Maya monuments standing in the main floor's rotunda. These rare replicas from the ruins at Quiriguá, Guatemala—an important center of the ancient Maya world—were produced for

the 1915-16 expo; studying these stelae has helped epigraphers crack the Mayan code, or system of writing. (Although the originals have lost much of their detailing to erosion, these precise copies have gracefully survived the passage of time.) Both types of monuments—the tall stelae with human figures and the shorter blocks shaped like animals—are carved from solid stone. Both feature columns of hieroglyphics.

On the East Wing's second level are two exhibits—"Mummies of the World" and "Egypt"—that feature artifacts more than 3,000

San Diego Museum of Man
www.museumofman.org
⬜ Map p. 69
✉ 1350 El Prado
☎ 619-239-2001
💲 $$
🚌 Bus: 7, 7A, 7B

The towering California Building houses an anthropology museum dedicated to explaining the mysteries of mankind.

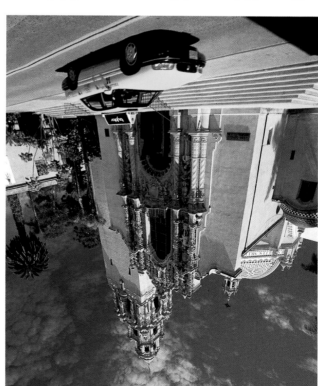

years old. These include such intriguing items as sacred amulets, falcon shrines, mummified falcons, coffin and mummy masks, and mummified human remains from Egypt and South America.

On the East Balcony, the traditional lifestyle of the Kumeyaay—San Diego's native people—springs to life through displays of their pottery and basketry, their dress and adornment, their ceremonies and food-gathering methods. The center balcony is filled with changing exhibits devoted to the cultural

An elaborately carved copy of a Maya stela has pride of place in the museum's rotunda.

and environmental diversity of indigenous peoples from the Southwest. Native arts receive special focus because they have long reflected the various groups' strong sense of pride. Normally sharing this balcony space is a provocative lineup of temporary shows featuring such items as Zuni fetishes, voodoo arts, skeletal remains, and even torture devices.

The museum's major new exhibit, "**Footsteps through Time,**" examines four million years of human evolution. The only one of its kind on the West Coast, the 7,000-square-foot show encom-

passes five galleries on the upper West Wing, as well as a 350-square-foot outdoor archaeological dig in an area previously off-limits to the public. Integrating the talents of various scientists with ties to the museum, the exhibit updates what we know about human evolution before examining the likely future impact of cloning and gene selection. Brain- and gene-mapping, artificial intelligence, and other cutting-edge technologies are addressed in the exhibit's "lab." Additional galleries feature touchable casts and environmental dioramas, as well as a "time tunnel" that conducts visitors on a heady journey documenting technological breakthroughs from early tools to mankind's first steps on the moon.

Established to help young visitors better understand the museum's exhibits, the **Children's Discovery Center** affords an interactive, sensory-based approach to the various facets of anthropological and archaeological research. "Discover Egypt," the current display, transports youngsters to that faraway time and place where they barter in an Egyptian market, navigate a small boat on the Nile, dress as pharaohs, and decipher messages written in hieroglyphics. Wooden blocks serve to highlight the dynamics of pyramid building, while the Egyptian god Anubis explains the mummification process. The last gallery is a hands-on re-creation of an archaeological site in El Amarna, Egypt. Here kids can sift sand for treasure, follow maps, and learn how to date historical artifacts.

The Museum of Man frequently features rotating shows as a complement to its permanent exhibits. Demonstrations of traditional tortilla making and Oaxacan spinning and weaving, for example, are regular events; they take place Wednesdays through Sundays. ■

Mingei International Museum

DEDICATED TO PROMOTING THE UNDERSTANDING OF ART produced by people the world over, this unique and much-loved museum vaults seemingly insuperable geographic boundaries with its enticing exhibitions from every corner of the globe.

Founder and director Martha Longenecker, an art professor at San Diego State University, became intrigued with the *mingei* concept while studying in Japan. Coined by scholar Soetsu Yanagi, *mingei* is a combination of two Japanese words that means "art of the people." This transcultural commonality refers to the direct simplicity and creative joy reflected through handmade and useful items that satisfy the human spirit; it extends to people living during all time periods and in all places throughout the world.

After its 1978 opening in a storefront at the suburban University Towne Centre shopping mall, Mingei International quickly became a sought-after attraction. The premiere exhibit, of world folk toys, was followed by displays of wearable art, Denzel carousel animals, regional Mexican crafts, and the ritual arts of India.

In 1996, the museum made the leap from its shopping-center origins to a sumptuously designed exhibit space in Balboa Park's House of Charm, facing the Plaza de Panama. Totaling 41,000 square feet, this roomier facility encompasses six galleries, a theater, a multimedia education center, an international art reference library, and a fine museum store.

In the 21st century the Mingei has made a name for itself on the strength of its sensationally colorful changing exhibits, many of which display items gleaned from the museum's growing permanent collection of 13,000 objects from 100 countries. The museum often presents traveling exhibitions.

Don't miss the dining table donated by artist Niki de Saint Phalle, whose distinctively colorful sculptures adorn many of San Diego's public spaces. A product of the Nakashima Workshop, it is the longest dining table the workshop ever made; woodworker and furniture designer George Nakashima himself hand-carved the 18 chairs that surround it. ■

A whimsical Niki de Saint Phalle sculpture near the Mingei's entrance is a beacon for climbing children.

Mingei International Museum

www.mingei.org

Ⓐ Map p. 69
✉ 1439 El Prado
☎ 619-239-0003
Ⓒ Closed Mon.
$ $

Kate Sessions

Balboa Park owes much of its Edenic luxuriance to horticulturist extraordinaire Katherine Olivia Sessions. Born in San Francisco in 1857, Sessions was one of that era's few college-educated women; perhaps even more remarkable, she graduated from the University of California, Berkeley with a degree in science. ("The Natural Sciences as a Field for Women's Labor" was the title of her graduation essay.) If gardening was a labor for Sessions, it was one of love: She once referred to the flowers she cultivated as "my children."

In 1884, when Kate Sessions was offered a teaching position in San Diego, she returned to the city and joined with friends to purchase a local nursery. Soon after that she ventured out on her own, establishing a nursery in Coronado as well as a flower shop in downtown San Diego.

By 1892, Sessions had set her sights on Balboa Park, then known as City Park. In exchange for planting 100 trees each year within the park—and another 300 elsewhere in San Diego—she leased 36 acres in the northwest corner of the parcel as her own private domain. This was a signal accomplishment for Sessions, and she attacked the task with her trademark zeal. She planted and tended hundreds of palms, eucalyptus, silky oak, Monterey cypress, and other trees—notably the jacaranda and Brazilian pepper trees that she is credited with popularizing. Within ten years, City Park had metamorphosed into a horticultural paradise filled with thousands of shrubs, beds hosting floral parades, stands of trees, and leafy arbors (another Sessions signature).

Sessions, meanwhile, had begun writing for *California Garden* and other publications, and her pioneering plant introductions were earning encomia from highbrow botanical circles. Hired to apply her landscaping techniques to elegant homes dotting the San Diego area, Sessions left her green-thumb prints from Coronado to La Jolla. At the same time, she inspired local residents and schoolchildren to start gardening themselves.

Sessions forged a tight bond with philanthropist and civic leader George Marston. She was also instrumental in guaranteeing that

Balboa Park would always be accessible to the community. Despite having more than fulfilled her end of the bargain, she continued her park plantings for years, adding so many trees, shrubs, and flowers that she came to be known as "the mother of Balboa Park."

In 1903 Sessions relocated her nursery to Mission Hills, where her planting frenzy proceeded unabated.

A decade later she relocated again, this time to Pacific Beach, where Kate Sessions Park pays tribute to the extraordinary woman who is responsible for creating and preserving so much of San Diego's natural beauty.

In 1939, a year before her death, Sessions received the American Genetic Association's Frank N. Meyer Memorial Medal for her distinguished service to American horticulture. Her Mission Hills nursery remains open for business today. ■

Evoking its real-life subject (opposite page, top), a bronze of Kate Sessions (above) welcomes visitors to the Sixth Avenue entrance of Balboa Park. Cherry blossoms keep her legacy alive.

Starlight Bowl

www.starlighttheatre.org
- Map p. 69
- End of Pan-American Plaza
- 619-544-7827 (box office)
- Closed Mon.
- $$$–$$$$$
- Bus: 7, 7A, 7B

The Starlight Bowl has undergone three major renovations since it was constructed for the 1935-36 expo, but it remains one of San Diego's finest venues for outdoor entertainment. Home to the San Diego Civic Light Opera Association—one of the country's oldest continuously producing musical theater companies—the Starlight **Musical Theatre** (founded in 1945) presents a pleasurable summer series to the appreciative patrons who pack the bowl's 4,000 seats. Over the decades, the musical offerings have included everything from Gilbert and Sullivan operettas and classical favorites to contemporary Broadway smashes such as *A Chorus Line* and *Phantom of the Opera*.

At most performances, a repertorial quirk becomes evident as soon as the first jet flies overhead on its landing approach to nearby San Diego International Airport. Rather than fruitlessly trying to make themselves heard above the whine and roar of the jet engines, the actors simply freeze in mid-line. Once the plane has passed, they pick up where they left off.

To ensure artistic integrity, only actors belonging to the Equity Association (a professional union) can land leading roles. The orchestra's musicians and stage crew are likewise affiliated with professional unions. Visiting musicians—from rock stars to symphony artists—often use the arena during the theater's "off" time. ■

Spreckels Organ Pavilion

The Spreckels Organ Pavilion seats 2,400 at free concerts staged year-round.

Spreckels Organ Pavilion
- Map p. 69
- 2211 Pan-American Way
- 619-702-8138
- Concerts Sun. 2-3 p.m.
- Bus: 7, 7A, 7B

On any given Sunday, tones ranging from festive to funeral ring forth from the Spreckels Organ, the largest outdoor pipe organ in the world. Nestled inside a vaulted cocoon on a raised stage, the 4,518-pipe Austin Organ Company masterpiece—its pipes ranging from the size of a pencil to 32 feet tall—was donated to the city in 1914 by sugar magnates John D. and Adolph Spreckels.

The Spreckels brothers attached but a single condition to their gift: San Diego must designate an official organist. That position has been held by Carol Williams since October of 2001.

As tradition dictates, today's audiences sit on white metal benches in the semicircular pavilion (graced by Corinthian colonnades and pillared walkways) to enjoy free year-round concerts. Every Monday night from mid-June through August, the pavilion hosts another installment of its free Summer International Organ Festival, which belts out everything from military marches to Broadway hits. ■

San Diego Automotive Museum

LOS ANGELES IS NOT THE ONLY CAR-CRAZY METROPOLIS on the West Coast. San Diegans are justifiably proud of this museum, which pays homage to all things automotive.

Though housed in a 1935-36 expo building, the San Diego Automotive Museum did not open to the public until 1988. By then, local automotive enthusiasts had spent eight years working toward its fruition. The building's previous roles (including wartime service as a U.S. Navy barracks) earned it a spot on the National Register of Historic Places — an unusual distinction for any such showcase of classic cars and vintage motorcycles.

More than 80 lovingly restored vehicles lead visitors through the growth of an industry that created the defining icon of 20th-century American culture. There's a 1924 Ford Model T that has been modified into a speedster, as well as a 420-horsepower 1966 Bizzarini (one of only three ever produced

with this body style). Horseless carriages, farm trucks, family sedans, 1950s cruisers, "movie-star mobiles," and sleek racers share floor space with vintage motorcycles (among the latter, a 1912 Flying Merkle). Rotating exhibitions have shown off Cadillacs, convertibles, woodies, and low riders.

"Motorcycles in the Park," a gathering of scores of bikes from around the world—among them modified street bikes, choppers, crotch rockets, and vintage motorcycles—is presented every February. The **Racing Hall of Fame** honors racing legends from all over the globe. The public is welcome to use the museum's research library, stocked with vintage photos, rare magazines, and repair manuals dating from 1901. ∎

San Diego Automotive Museum

www.sdautomuseum.org
/exhibit.html

📍 Map p. 69
✉ 2080 Pan-American Plaza
☎ 619-231-2886
💲 $$
🚌 Bus: 7, 7A, 7B

Living room: An impeccably restored 1956 Dodge Royal Lancer

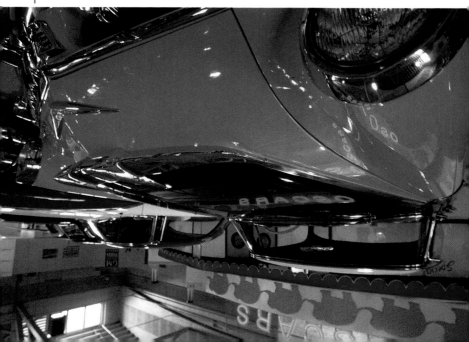

San Diego Aerospace Museum

**San Diego
Aerospace
Museum**

www.aerospacemuseum.org

🗺 Map p. 69

✉ 2001 Pan-American
Plaza

☎ 619-234-8291

💲 $$

🚌 Bus: 7, 7A, 7B

ANCHORING THE SOUTH END OF PAN-AMERICAN PLAZA, San Diego's sleek, circular, streamline-moderne aerospace museum —built as a showcase for Ford Motor Co. products in 1935—resembles something that landed from outer space. Don't be fooled; it's really an earthbound edifice tracing the history of leaving the planet.

Given its deep connections to the aviation industry, it's no surprise that San Diego boasts such a high-flying aerospace museum. The collection—more than 65 air- and spacecraft from the U.S. and abroad—ushers visitors from the dawn of powered flight to the jet age to our spotty modern record of space exploration.

High-tech and hush-hush, the early 1960s titanium Blackbird A-12 spy plane (predecessor to the better-known SR-71) that perches outside the museum was disavowed by the U.S. military until the 1990s. The entrance rotunda offers two other gems: a full-size replica of Charles Lindbergh's *Spirit of St. Louis* (the original was built in San

Diego) and a reproduction of the U.S. Navy's first plane, the 1911 Curtiss A-1 Triad hydroplane.

As you pass through the turnstiles, the **International Aerospace Hall of Fame** marks the beginning of the main exhibits, its walls hung with oil portraits of such aviation legends as Lindbergh, the Wright brothers, Amelia Earhart, Chuck Yeager, and Neil Armstrong. The exhibits progress in chronological order, tracing aerospace development from hot-air balloons and gliders to a copy of the Wright Flyer that soared above the sands of Kitty Hawk. A newer display memorializes the Korean War with a MiG-15 and its chief aerial rival, the F-86 Sabre. ■

A twin-engine PBY-5A Catalina flying boat seems frozen midair in the museum's Edwin D. McKellan Pavilion of Flight.

San Diego Hall of Champions Sports Museum

Hoop dreams take the shape of sculpted players outside the sports museum.

AN ACTIVE CITY WHOSE CITIZENRY IS IMBUED WITH a mania for physical fitness and outdoor sports, San Diego has always held athletic prowess in high esteem. That admiration has been institutionalized in this museum, dedicated exclusively to San Diego sports.

Having moved into a remodeled site—the Federal Building on Pan-American Plaza—in 1999, this one-time mini-museum has hit the big leagues: Its exhibition space now encompasses a gleaming 70,000 square feet, making the sports museum a worthy neighbor to Balboa Park's other cultural institutions. A commitment to honor excellence in sports and encourage the development of budding athletes remains the museum's underlying approach. Stimulating interactive displays covering more than 40 sports convey inspiring stories, memorable events, and fascinating profiles of San Diego athletes past and present. In July 2002, the long-awaited baseball exhibit—showcasing San Diego's history of the sport at all levels, from Little League and collegiate all the way up to the National League Padres—took up permanent residence on the main level. The baseball exhibit also features hands-on activities for kids and adults. A companion piece, the football display, traces the history of the San Diego Chargers but also looks at on local high school, college, and semipro ball.

Traveling exhibits are mounted regularly. Recent shows have celebrated San Diegans featured on the cover of *Sports Illustrated* magazine (including memorabilia owned or used by many of the cover subjects) as well as the contributions made by San Diegans to such regional sports as surfing, street luge, beach

volleyball, skateboarding, triathlon, and disabled athletics.

The museum's pièce de résistance is the **Breitbard Hall of Fame**—the highest honor that can be conferred upon a local sports figure. Housed on the upper level, plaques pay tribute to 99 (as of press time) Hall of Famers representing sports of every stripe, from archery to yachting. Renowned inductees (and therefore lauded locals) include baseball player Ted Williams, swimmer Florence Chadwick, and sailor Dennis Conner. ■

San Diego Hall of Champions Sports Museum
www.sandiegosports.org
🅰 Map p. 69
✉ 2131 Pan-American Plaza
☎ 619-234-2544
💲 $$
🚌 Bus: 7, 7A, 7B

Marston House

GEORGE MARSTON WAS MANY THINGS: PHILANTHROPIST, founder of the San Diego Historical Society, owner of the prestigious department store on Fifth Avenue that bore his name. He and his wife, Anna, also occupied one of the city's most treasured homes.

Marston House

www.sandiegohistory.org

[W] Map p. 69

[⊠] 3525 7th Ave.

[☎] 619-298-3142

[⏱] Open Fri.–Sun.

[$] $

[🚌] Bus: 1, 7A, 7B

Designed by local architects Irving Gill and William Hebbard, the 1905 Marston House immediately became an exemplar of the era's American Craftsman movement. Within a few short years, many other local homes would come to embody the same simple elegance.

The 1905 Marston House typifies the American Crafts-man movement. The earliest plantings were put in place by Marston friend Kate Sessions.

Marston was a garden-variety overachiever. He created Presidio Park and Anza-Borrego Desert State Park, sponsored San Diego's first urban plan, and immersed himself in the early development of Balboa Park by personally financing Samuel Parson's plan for the park. His daughter Mary inherited the family home and deeded it to the city in 1974. In 1988, shortly after her death at the age of 107, Marston House was declared a museum. Most of the original furnishings and art objects have been dispersed, but the San Diego Historical Soci-

ety—devoted to preserving the lega-cy of its founder and his illustrious home—has restored and refurnished the 16-room dwelling. The period decor includes Stickley pieces, Tiffany lamps, and wainscoting throughout the main floor. Historical exhibits include a display of local Native American basketry. Gardeners will gravitate to the romantic, formal English garden de-signed by Hale Walker, John Nolen, George Cooke, and William Temple-ton Johnson in 1927. The house's first landscaping was the 1906 hand-iwork of horticultural consultant Kate Sessions (see pp. 96–97), whom Marston exalted "Queen Mother of the Whole Floral Kingdom." You'll see a creeping fig, a false acacia tree, and a Moreton Bay chestnut, as well as California poppies and Queen Elizabeth roses.

OTHER SEVENTH AVENUE HOMES

Other American Craftsman homes pop up here and there in the neigh-borhood (these are private resi-dences, but you're welcome to study them from the sidewalk). The house occupied by Marston's sister at 3565 Seventh Avenue—another Irving Gill design—represents the Midwest Prairie Style, distinguished by its emphasis on horizontal lines. Gill also drew up the plans for son Ar-thur Marston's residence at 3575 Seventh Avenue.

Gill and Hebbard pooled their architectural talents to build four other signature homes on Seventh Avenue: 3526, 3560, 3574, and 3578. ∎

A free tram leaves the House of Hospitality en route to other sites of interest in Balboa Park.

More places to visit around Balboa Park

BALBOA PARK CAROUSEL

This 1910 merry-go-round was delivered to the park in 1922. Unless you're too busy marveling at the hand-painted murals and hand-carved animals, you can grab for the brass ring—one of the world's few carousels still offering that enticement.
🅰 Map p. 69 ✉ 1889 Zoo Pl. 🕐 Open daily late June–Labor Day, weekends in winter 💲 $

CENTRO CULTURAL DE LA RAZA

Hispanic, Mexican, and Native American artists have used this converted World War II-era water tank as an art center since the 1970s. Vibrant murals—most illustrating contemporary social concerns or themes from Mexican history—adorn the circular exterior walls. Inside there is gallery and studio space for local artists, as well as a theater for plays and concerts. www.centroraza.com 🅰 Map p. 69 ✉ 2004 Park Blvd. ☎ 619-235-6135 🕐 Open Thurs.–Sun. 💲 Donation

HOUSE OF PACIFIC RELATIONS

Built for the 1915-16 expo, this "house" is actually a cluster of small stucco cottages representing more than 30 nations. It is devoted to promoting goodwill, cultural exchange, and understanding among people of diverse backgrounds. Each cottage, decorated with the arts and crafts of its particular country, is hosted by a native of the country.

Open houses are held on Sunday afternoons. From March through October representatives sporting traditional national garb take turns presenting outdoor music and folk dancing. Countries represented include Argentina, Ecuador, Scotland, Israel, Sweden, France, Hungary, Ukraine, Japan, and China. 🅰 Map p. 69 ✉ 2160 Pan-American Rd. W ☎ 619-234-0739 🕐 Open Sun.; performances at 2 p.m. 💲 Free

SAN DIEGO ART INSTITUTE

Juried exhibitions of works by established and emerging artists change every six weeks in this 10,000-square-foot gallery inside the House of Charm. Media of every ilk—oil, acrylic, and watercolor painting; photography; sculpture; pen and ink; collage and assemblage—give the public insight into the local art scene. The David Fleet Young Artists Gallery displays work by students in San Diego-area schools. The gallery store offers handmade gifts and jewelry. www.sandiego-art.org 🅰 Map p. 69 ✉ 1439 El Prado ☎ 619-236-0011 🕐 Closed Mon. 💲 Donation

SPANISH VILLAGE ART CENTER

Constructed north of the natural history museum for the 1935–36 expo, quaint Spanish Village is meant to capture the ambience of a town square in Spain. Within three tile-

UPTOWN NEIGHBORHOODS

Within a short distance of Balboa Park is a refreshing hodgepodge of neighborhoods meshing the old-money establishment with an effervescent gay scene.

An exodus from the city center in the late 19th and early 20th centuries led many San Diegans to relocate in **Banker's Hill,** west of Balboa Park. This fashionable magnet for financiers (hence its name) boasts bay views and stately mansions. Among the latter is the 1889 Queen Anne **Long-Waterman House** *(2408 1st Ave.),* adorned with gables, tower, wraparound porch, and bay and dormer windows. The 375-foot-long 1912 **Spruce Street Suspension Bridge** *(between Front & Brant Sts.),* spanning a 70-foot-deep canyon, is a neighborhood icon. Residential **Mid-dletown** *(N & E of I-5)* is distinguished by its **India Street Art Colony,** a 1970s-era enclave of cafés, pubs, and import shops.

Another high-society mecca in the late 1800s was **Mission Hills** *(N of Middletown & S of I-8).* Overlooking San Diego Bay and hovering above Old Town, this area still has wildlife-filled canyons and parklands embracing homes in every architectural style: Italian Renaissance, Mission Revival, Craftsman, and Victorian (many of the latter designed by architects Irving Gill and William Templeton Johnson). It was here in 1910 that Kate Sessions opened her **Mission Hills Nursery** *(1525 Fort Stockton Dr., 619-295-2808).*

The heart of San Diego's gay community is **Hillcrest,** north and west of Balboa Park. Its lively atmosphere, unique shops, plush cinema, chic restaurants, and casual coffee houses make it a gathering spot for San Diegans of all persuasions and professions. Fifth and University Avenues intersect at the district's hub. Follow Park Boulevard north a good dozen blocks or so to reach **Adams Avenue.** The stretch running through Kensington, is filled with offbeat antiques stores interspersed with neighborhood shops and cafés. Kensington's **Ken Cinema** *(4061 Adams Ave., 619-283-5909)* is a one-screen phenomenon with ever-changing art-house films. The residential area around the cinema is an intriguing assortment of well-tended older homes. ■

VETERANS MEMORIAL CENTER AND MUSEUM

Across Park Boulevard from the park proper, this former U.S. Naval Hospital chapel now houses a museum dedicated to veterans of all service branches including the Merchant Marine. Displays commemorate conflicts dating back to the Civil War, with military memorabilia, documents, and historical artifacts highlighting the roles played and battles fought. Public programs promote awareness of veterans' contributions; tours are offered daily.

A Map p. 69 ☒ 2115 Park Blvd. ☏ 619-239-2300 ⊕ Closed Sun.–Mon. **$** Donation

Donal Hord's "Woman of Tehuantepec" tops a fountain in the House of Hospitality courtyard.

roofed buildings, 37 rooms have been set aside as gallery-studios where artisans demonstrate works-in-progress for onlookers. Much of the original art—painting, sculpture, blown glass, woodcarvings, pottery, lapidary items—is also for sale. Art shows with food and entertainment are occasionally held on the flower-filled flagstone patio.

www.spanishvillageart.com **A** Map p. 69 ☒ 1770 Village Pl. ☏ 619-233-9050 ⊕ Open daily **$** Free

Just across San Diego Bay from the boom and bustle of downtown, Coronado coaxes travelers to a tranquil oasis that locals have labeled "the village."

Coronado & the Silver Strand

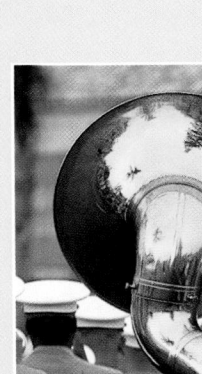

No tubby tubas here: A Marine band marches in Coronado's Fourth of July parade.

Coronado & the Silver Strand

The pier at Imperial Beach sallies out to sea, giving boardwalkers a view of Baja California.

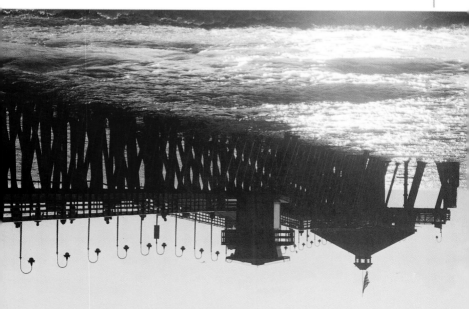

THOUGH "VILLAGE" IS A BIT MISLEADING (CORONADO'S POPULATION OF 28,000 is inflated by thousands of annual visitors), this self-contained community has an undeniably small-town ambience. This seems unlikely when you learn that Coronado shares its 5.3 square miles with one of the U.S. Navy's largest aerospace-industrial complexes, yet the city has succeeded at integrating a formidable military presence with a graceful seaside resort.

Architecturally distinctive low-key houses and stately old mansions along tree-lined streets are complemented by genteel shops and businesses, 18 public parks, abundant recreational facilities, historic buildings, dedicated bicycle paths, and 28 miles of fine beaches. Visitors—as in the past—usually gravitate toward the Hotel del Coronado, the landmark Victorian resort that has been a magnet for Presidents, dignitaries, movie stars, and sophisticates since the turn of the 20th century.

Two other world-class resorts, dozens of excellent restaurants, and two respected theater groups round out the attractions that lure both out-of-towners and San Diegans from across the bay. With its primary approaches via bridge or ferryboat, it's common but incorrect to call Coronado an island. The community actually occupies the thumb tip in the mitten cradling San Diego Bay; it is attached to the mainland by the long, narrow sand spit called the Silver Strand.

Coronado's residents might welcome island status. This conglomeration of military retirees, suburbanites, and old-money gentry is fiercely protective of its wholesome village lifestyle. The community tends to outdo even the resident U.S. Navy as a local watchdog.

Coronado's modern habitation goes back to the 1880s, when wealthy businessmen Elisha Babcock, Jr., and Hampton Story convinced themselves the scenic plot would make the perfect spot for a hunting and fishing resort. They purchased the peninsula, sold off lots, laid out streets and a water pipeline, and constructed the showpiece Hotel del Coronado. The resort started losing money almost as soon as it opened its doors for business. John D. Spreckels acquired Story's interest in the property in 1889; a year later, he assumed complete control.

By World War I, the Naval Air Station was fully established on North Island; during World War II the U.S. Naval Amphibious Base was set up on the Silver Strand, sandwiching the village between them. Nonetheless, local residents and the Navy—a more vital presence than ever—enjoy a healthy coexistence.

Beyond the Naval Amphibious Base, the Silver Strand runs south to Imperial Beach and the South Bay. This slim stretch of highway provides access to beaches, bay, and sea all the way to its end near the Mexican border. ∎

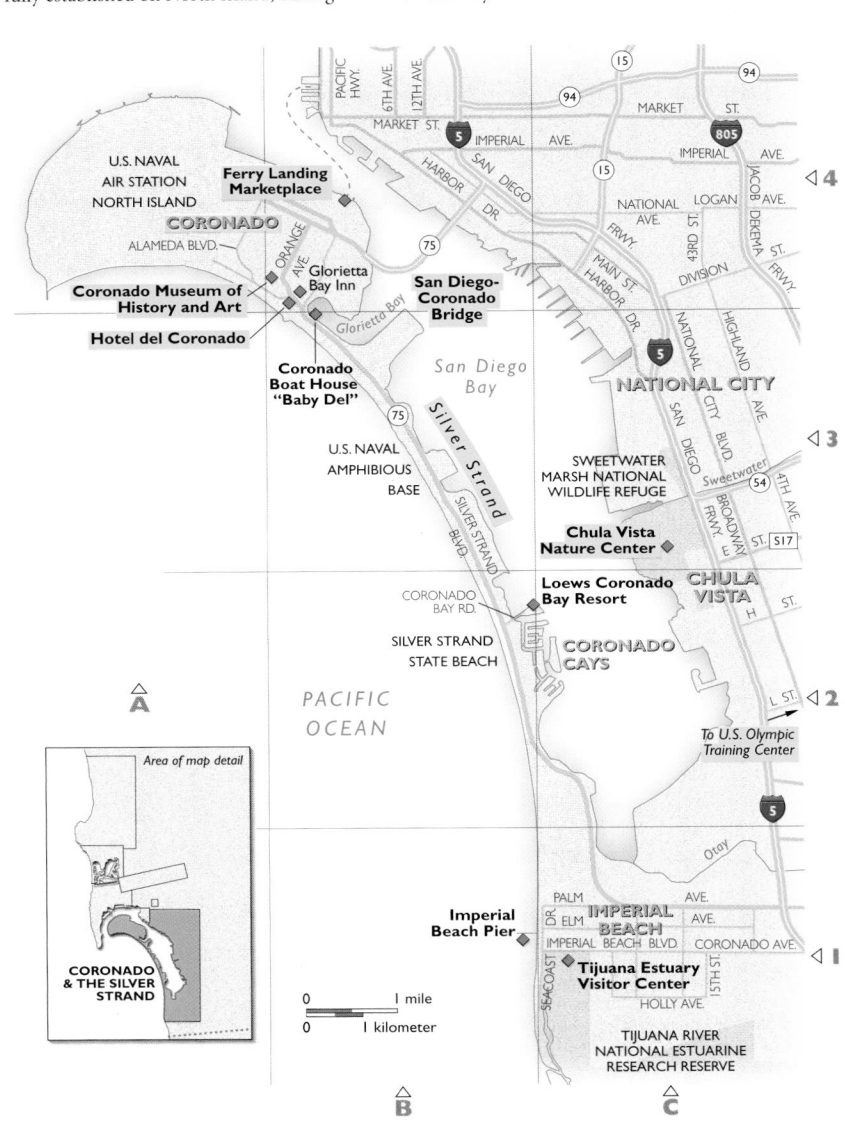

San Diego-Coronado Bridge

**San Diego-
Coronado
Bridge**
🚇 107 B4
🚌 Bus: 901

THE 1969 OPENING OF THE 2.12-MILE SAN DIEGO-Coronado Bridge brought major changes to the once-remote "village" across the bay (formerly accessible only by ferry or the lengthy Silver Strand route). Residents considered the span a mixed blessing. While some blanched at the uptick in traffic and visitors, others hailed its easy access to the city and the boost it gave to local business.

Dedicated on August 2, 1969, by California Governor Ronald Reagan, the bridge was inaugurated by hundreds of exuberant cyclists and runners whose kinetic camaraderie not only celebrated the new crossing but tested its earthquake preparedness.

Built in two years for less than 50 million dollars, the bridge—running from I-5 on the city side to Coronado—became the first structural conquest of San Diego Bay. Recipient of the American Institute of Steel Construction's Most Beautiful Bridge Award in 1970, the span is an area icon, noted for its distinctive curve and spectacular all-encompassing views. Between San Diego and Coronado, the bridge's

4.67-percent grade and 90-degree curve create a 200-foot clearance—high enough that aircraft carriers can pass beneath. Submerged 54-inch piles—driven 100 feet deep in the floor of the bay—support the 30 concrete piers, each in the graceful shape of a mission arch.

Approximately 77,000 vehicles cross the bridge daily, using two lanes going in each direction; a center lane serves alternately as a safety median and a peak-hour reversible byway. As drivers will discover, the barrier railing is low enough (34 inches) to provide idyllic views of colorful watercraft, sober-sided naval vessels, the deep-blue bay, and the skylines of both San Diego and Coronado. ■

Of palm trees and pylons: Against a backdrop of the Coronado bridge, cyclists pedal through Bayview Park at the north end of the Coronado peninsula.

Hotel del Coronado

Hotel del Coronado
www.hoteldel.com
🚗 107 B4
✉ 1500 Orange Ave.
☎ 619-435-6611
🚌 Bus: 901

A tower on the sand apes the real McCoy on land.

ONE OF SAN DIEGO'S MOST TREASURED ICONS—AND A national historic landmark—the celebrated Hotel del Coronado on the Pacific Coast has remained the epitome of Victorian elegance and grandeur. Often used as a movie location, the ornate Queen-Anne castle is recognized throughout the world.

Known simply as "The Del" to locals, the illustrious property has drawn a stellar crowd of Presidents, foreign dignitaries, celebrities, and well-heeled sophisticates for more than a century. A three-year, $55-million restoration and preservation project, completed in 2001, promises to extend The Del legend.

Although original owners Elisha Babcock, Jr., and Hampton Story promoted the property as a hunting and fishing resort, The Del was destined for other pleasures and purposes. When the developers went broke, sugar baron Claus Spreckels (son of sugar baron John D. Spreckels) transformed The Del into a chic seaside haven for a glamorous clientele. In those early years the hotel became a de rigueur stop on the railway circuit. Wealthy patrons from the East Coast would travel cross-country in private rail cars hitched to transcontinental trains, rolling to a halt at the hotel's on-site spur track.

World War I changed the composition of the client base. While Easterners stayed home, Hollywood types and their retinues took up the slack, turning the resort into a rollicking party palace. The hotel flourished during the Roaring '20s, and the military kept it afloat during the Great Depression and World War II (Navy personnel were billeted in some of the rooms).

The postwar years—when traditional tourism was forsaken for car trips to national parks—brought a slump in the hotel's fortunes. Nonetheless, in 1958 director Billy Wilder chose the hotel as a setting for the film *Some Like It Hot*, starring Marilyn Monroe, Tony Curtis, and Jack Lemmon, thereby keeping it securely on the map. By the late 1960s, historic structures were enjoying a resurgence of national attention, and The Del emerged revamped and once again revered.

Resembling something from a fairy tale—and indeed often likened to architectural gingerbread—the 31-acre beachfront gem seems beset by uncontrollable growths in its red-and-white facade: conical towers, tall cupolas, turrets, and dormer windows. Designed by James and Merritt Reid, the splendid 380-room building was erected in just 11 months by craftsmen and laborers from San Francisco. Built entirely of wood, the hotel consists of thousands of board feet of redwood, cedar, oak, pine, hemlock, fir, and mahogany. The resplendent lobby evokes the air of a country manor.

Location and ambience were not the only inducements for early visitors. They were also drawn by such cutting-edge technology as electric lighting in the rooms, an elevator (the lobby's Otis birdcage is still operable), telephones, and bathrooms with running water.

An uncontested jewel is the 13,500-square-foot **Crown Room;** its 31-foot-tall arched sugar-pine ceiling is held together with wooden pegs but not a single nail. *The Wonderful Wizard of Oz* author L. Frank Baum is credited with designing the Crown Room

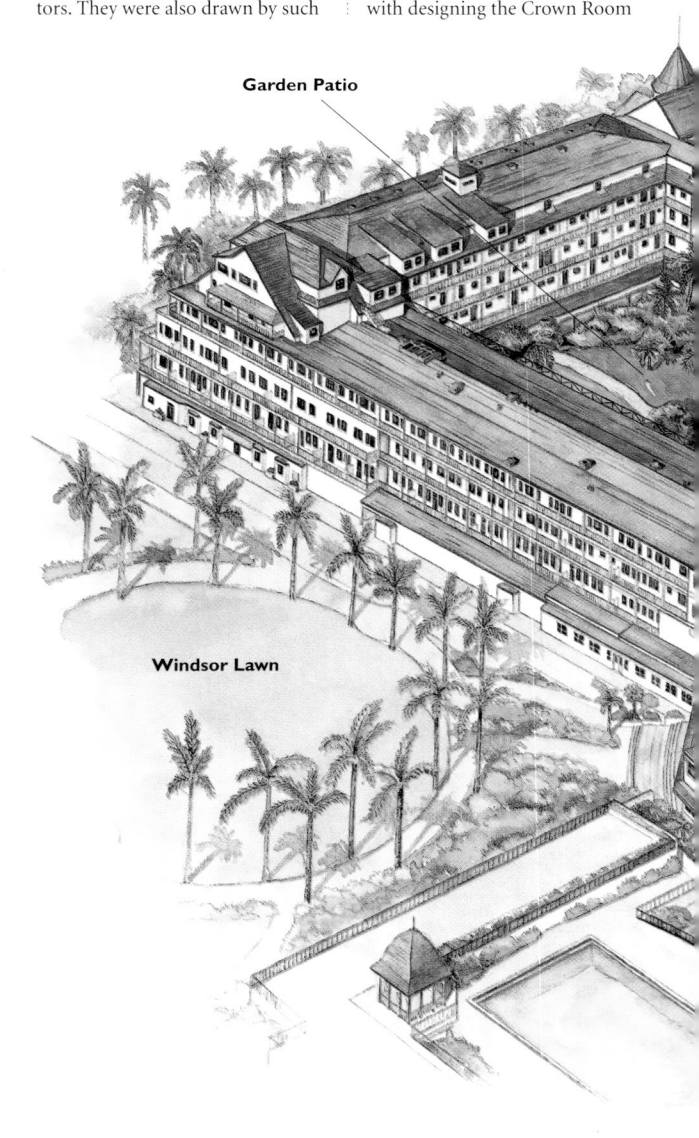

Garden Patio

Windsor Lawn

chandeliers. This may also have been the fateful spot where the visiting Duke of Windsor first met Coronado socialite Wallis Simpson, for whom he would abdicate the throne of England in 1936.

Although the seven-story tower and **Grande Hall** (a convention center) added in 1963 has its share of detractors, the 2001 restoration project was tasteful, meticulous, and faithful to The Del's historic integrity. Victorian rooms were redesigned

(and are finally air-conditioned), venues were added for oceanfront dining, and the fitness center was enlarged. The Crown Room ceiling was taken apart plank by plank, reinforced, and reinstalled.

Today the **Babcock & Story Bar** honors the hotel's founders. The **Windsor Lawn** extends seaward from the resort, reaffirming its link to the beach. Take a quick sunbath on one of its benches, or walk around it to visit the ocean. ■

Grande Hall

Crown Room

Entrance

Ballroom

A walk around Coronado

Where else could you find "surfer moms" but in the relaxingly retro village of Coronado?

A stroll through this laid-back, time-warped village is a relaxing circuit of historic hotels and houses, distinctive shops, heavenly beaches, down-home dining, and easy living.

Begin at the legendary **Hotel del Coronado** ❶ (*1500 Orange Ave.*), where you may want to unobtrusively poke your nose into the exquisite public areas of this Victorian castle, restored in 2001. The floor of the lobby's second-story balcony, for example, cants at a crazy angle, giving you an idea of how long (more than 115 years) this magnificent wedding cake of a hotel has been around.

Historically, you'll be retracing some venerable footsteps: Among the notables who have stayed here are Presidents Benjamin Harrison and William H. Taft, journalist Joseph Pulitzer, writers Henry James and Upton Sinclair, Diamond Jim Brady, Wyatt Earp, and actors Lucille Ball and Desi Arnaz. Photos of other actor guests—as well as stills from other movies shot on location here—are displayed outside the Grande Hall.

Walk around the new **Windsor Lawn** and down to the expansive public beach to dip your toe in the Pacific or watch an A-6 Intruder make its landing approach to neighboring Naval Air Station North Island.

Next, cross Orange Avenue to the 1908 **Glorietta Bay Inn** ❷ (*1630 Glorietta Blvd., 619-435-3101*), the former residence of Hotel del Coronado owner John D. Spreckels. The mansion, situated on three acres overlooking the bay, is now part of a hotel complex. Take a peek inside the horseshoe-shaped Music Room, then admire the fine woodwork, the marble staircase and floors, and the lovely gardens of this local landmark. If your timing's right catch one of the docent-led walking tours that leave from the inn (*Tues., Thurs., & Sat. at 11 a.m.*).

Return to Orange Avenue and walk north to two landmarks built in 1917, the **Bank of Coronado** (*1190 Orange Ave.*) and **Lamb's Players Theatre** (*1142 Orange Ave.*). Cross the street and pop in to **Bay Books** ❸ (*1029 Orange Ave., 619-435-0070*) to sample their wondrous array of literature and travel books. The peaceful reading room invites browsers. Crossing Orange Avenue once more, you'll reach the Coronado Historical Association's **Museum of History and Art** ❹ (*1100*

Orange Ave., 619/437-8788), housed inside the 1910 Bank of Commerce and Trust Building. Inside, three themed galleries shed light on the city's early history, The Del, and the local military presence. The museum also houses the Coronado Visitor Center; ask here for dining and lodging recommendations, sign up for other walking tours, or simply pick up a free town map.

Take an acute left on Park Place and walk oceanward to reach Star Park **5**, the hub for five spokes lined with mansions and historic houses. Walk clockwise around the circle to see the 1896 **Meade House** (1101 Star Park Cir.), a writing retreat for The Wonderful Wizard of Oz author L. Frank Baum. (Don't try to visit the interior, though—it's a private residence.) Continue clockwise around Star Park Circle, then turn left on Loma Avenue (the second time you encounter it) to **Ocean Boulevard 6**, where lavish mansions from Coronado's early days face the windswept beach and its sandy dunes. Unparalleled views of Point Loma, great sunsets, and sightings of migrating whales on their spring or fall journey make this a favorite San Diego seascape. Surfers prefer North Beach; just beyond that, pet owners can let their dogs frolic on the northernmost stretch of sand before finding their progress blocked by the Naval Air Station North Island. After taking a long, leisurely stroll along the beach, return to the Hotel del Coronado.

As a somewhat more energetic alternative, retrace your steps up Loma Avenue to Orange Avenue via Star Circle. As Orange Avenue heads north, you'll find one-of-a-kind shops selling clothing, antiques, original art, and gourmet foods. Quell hunger pangs with an inexpensive burger at a favorite local hangout, **Clayton's Coffee Shop 7** (979 Orange Ave., 619-435-5425). Inside this 1950s-style diner, career waitresses still serve creamy milk shakes in those tall, silvery mixing cups, and the booth-side jukeboxes are stuffed with golden oldies. After refueling, rent a bike next door at **Holland's Bicycles** (977 Orange Ave., 619-435-3153) to continue your exploration of Coronado on two wheels. ∎

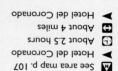

See area map p. 107
Hotel del Coronado
About 4 miles
About 2.5 hours
Hotel del Coronado

NOT TO BE MISSED
- Hotel del Coronado
- Bay Books
- Museum of History and Art
- Clayton's Coffee Shop

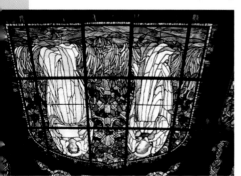

The Tiffany window in Christ Episcopal Church at 1114 9th Street lets there be light.

Silver Strand & the South Bay

Silver Strand & the South Bay

🗺 107 B3

🚊 Blue line trolley; Bus: 29, 901

AS ORANGE AVENUE SLINKS PAST THE HOTEL DEL CORONADO it becomes Silver Strand Boulevard (Calif. 75), a road that stretches the 6-mile length of a narrow spit of land shared by the Naval Amphibious Base, an acclaimed resort, chic bayside housing, and a long, silvery beach. Drive it or ride it—a bike path parallels the road.

Just beyond the Hotel del Coronado, a miniature version of that resort pops up from the east. Now the **Coronado Boat House** restaurant, this former private home—snuggled into Glorietta Bay—was once known as **"Baby Del."** It was constructed in southeast San Diego in 1887, then barged over to Coronado in 1983, where it was restored in the Queen Anne fashion of the parent Del.

About a mile after Orange Avenue merges with Silver Strand Boulevard, the U.S. flag snaps above the **U.S. Naval Amphibious Base,** also to the east. Though separated from the Naval Air Station North Island by the town of Coronado, this important part of the complex—in operation since 1943—hosts most of the U.S. Pacific Fleet's Naval Expeditionary and Naval Special Warfare commands. These include the Special Warfare Combatant Craft Crewmen and the Leap Frogs parachute team. It's not unusual to see military groups—including elite Navy SEALs—training or exercising on nearby beaches.

A bit farther down the Strand (and accessed by Coronado Bay Road) is **Loews Coronado Bay Resort** *(619-424-4000)*. Perched on a secluded 15-acre peninsula jutting into San Diego Bay, this upscale resort is a favorite stay for boaters, who drop anchor at the property's 80-slip marina. Locals frequent the award-winning restaurant, which also has great views.

Next door, Coronado Cays takes

Dribbly castles on the sand are still a seaside ritual at Silver Strand State Beach, four miles south of Coronado.

up the rest of the Strand's eastern side. This exclusive 1,500-unit residential community—a haven for retirees, celebrities, and other seekers of seclusion—occupies the site of Hog Ranch, a dumping ground during Tent City days (see box).

On the west side of the highway, **Silver Strand State Beach** *(5000 Hwy. 75)*—a state park since 1932—is a wild sweep with an RV campground, lifeguards, fire rings, and picnic areas. It's a favorite spot for digging clams and surf fishing.

IMPERIAL BEACH

After passing the Navy's communications post on the right, Calif. 75 enters Imperial Beach, San Diego's southernmost beach community. This oft-overlooked town, popular with surfers since the 1940s, hosts the U.S. Open Sandcastle Competition each July. Professional sculptors and pit their talents against amateurs, creating evanescent masterpieces on either side of the 1,500-foot-long **Imperial Beach Pier**. (After heavy rains, pollution from the Tijuana River prohibits surfing, swimming, or pier fishing.) Locals patronize the cafés and shops of the revamped plaza at the foot of the pier.

South of Imperial Beach, the **Tijuana River National Estu-** **arine Research Reserve** *(301 Caspian Way, 619-575-3613)* is a favorite spot for nature lovers and bird-watchers. Some 370 native and migratory bird species (including the light-footed clapper rail) and many uncommon saltwater plants thrive within the 2,530-acre compound. A **visitor center** at the north edge is open daily; guided nature tours are offered on weekends. ■

Tent city

When John D. Spreckels took over the Hotel del Coronado in 1890, he wooed not just upper-crust types but America's growing middle class. On hotel property to the south, along the Silver Strand, Spreckels erected Camp Coronado (aka Tent City). Its bungalows and striped tents were far less luxurious than those at the nearby Victorian castle, but the reasonably priced lodging was a big hit with visitors of modest means. Other blandishments included a bandstand and dance pavilion, a bowling alley, an indoor pool, a carousel, and a floating casino. Tent City flourished until 1936, when it was abandoned to permit highway straightening. ■

The catch of the day and the view of a lifetime lure diners to the Tin Fish restaurant at the end of Imperial Beach Pier.

Naval aviation takes wing

When businessmen Elisha Babcock, Jr., and Hampton Story purchased and developed Coronado, they left the northern part of the peninsula alone. In fact it was an island named North Coronado, isolated by the narrow (and no longer existent) Spanish Bight. This overlooked sand flat was known primarily as a remote locale for hunting or horseback riding until it entered history as the launching site of U.S. naval aviation.

One other group was partial to North Island: Early aviators had adopted it as a test site some months before the U.S. Navy came to town. Trailblazing aviator Glenn Curtiss, whose flying skills had impressed the Coronado Development Company (CDC) in 1910, made an even bigger splash when he completed the world's first seaplane flight in 1911. Within days of notching that feat, Curtiss had secured a lease from the CDC for North Island.

Brush was cut down and replaced with a 500-foot-long runway, and several proto-hangars were constructed. A few months later, Lt. Theodore G. Ellyson arrived for training under Curtiss, becoming the first U.S. Navy officer to learn to fly. Other students trained by Curtiss included Japanese Lt. C. Yamada, who would assume command of his country's naval aviation with the outbreak of World War II.

In 1914, North Island hosted yet another prewar milestone. An obscure aircraft manufacturer, Glenn Martin, dropped the first parachutist—a 90-pound female civilian named Tiny Broadwick—over San Diego.

In 1917, with the United States embroiled in World War I, Congress appropriated North Island and commissioned the construction of two proper airfields there. On one side of the island, Navy fliers took up residence in a tent city aptly nicknamed "Camp Trouble." On the other side, aviators attached to the Army Signal Corps occupied Rockwell Field.

North Island continued to play a pivotal role after the war. In 1927 it was the launching point for Charles Lindbergh as he headed off

to New York, Paris, and transatlantic immortality. A year later, the Sea Hawks—precursors of the Blue Angels—began thrilling onlookers with stunts and close-formation flying.

By 1937 the Army had shifted its base inland, allowing Navy flight operations to blanket the island. (Later, a 1945 dredging project filled in Spanish Bight, connecting North Island with the Coronado peninsula but leaving the "island" designation intact.)

During World War II, North Island became the principal mainland base supporting the U.S. Navy's combat operations. In addition to supplying and repairing more than a dozen aircraft carriers, it hosted Seabees, Marines, Coast Guardsmen, and a raft of other personnel. Dry docks and shipyards hummed around the clock; hundreds of factory workers and their families made Coronado their home. Acknowledging this role, Congress recognized

Pioneering aeronaut Glenn Curtiss and helpers (above) launch a hydroplane from San Diego's North Island around 1911. They also launched an industry—naval aviation— that would culminate in aircraft carriers such as the flattop shown at right.

the air station as the "Birthplace of Naval Aviation" in 1963.

Curtiss probably wouldn't recognize the small city that is today's Naval Air Station North Island (NASNI). Home to the carriers U.S.S. *Constellation* and U.S.S. *Stennis* as well

as the Navy's only deep submergence rescue vehicles, NASNI has more than 235 aircraft on its field. It is the headquarters for six major military flag staffs and 23 squadrons. The Naval Aviation Depot, meanwhile, is San Diego's largest employer, with 3,800 workers. ■

More places to visit around Coronado

CHULA VISTA NATURE CENTER

These 316 acres at the north edge of Chula Vista shelter one of the Pacific Coast's last remaining salt marshes (in fact, they belong to Sweetwater Marsh National Wildlife Refuge). Inhabitants include approximately 200 bird species; some of these—notably the California least tern—are endangered. Birds can be viewed from a number of vantage points: the nature center's observation deck, inside the aviary, beside the enclosures, or in the course of docent-led or self-guided tours. Rent binoculars from the center's bookstore. 107 C3 Sweetwater Marsh National Wildlife Refuge, 1000 Gunpowder Point Dr., Chula Vista 619-409-5900 Closed Mon. $

A '59 Caddy fin encapsulates Coronado cool.

CORONADO MUSEUM OF HISTORY AND ART

The three well-designed galleries of this museum bring local history to life. One room highlights the Hotel del Coronado and its role in the community's development; a second focuses on local Navy and Army history from World War I to the present; and a third traces the city's history from its Babcock and Story beginnings in the late 1880s to the late 20th century. Displays include archival photos from the Coronado Historical Association's collection of 15,000 images and mementoes contributed by the founder of the Kingston Trio, Coronado resident Nick Reynolds. 107 B4 1100 Orange Ave., Coronado 619-435-7242 Donation Bus: 901

FERRY LANDING MARKETPLACE

Visitors traveling to Coronado via the San Diego Bay-Coronado Ferry are treated to much more than a refreshing ride with dramatic views of the bay bridge; they also alight at this picturesque bay-front enclave, filled with specialty stores, art galleries, cafés, and snack shops. On Tuesday afternoons, a farmer's market beckons locals to load up on fresh flowers, produce, plants, and other items. If you're getting around the San Diego area by bike, you can tote your two-wheeler over on the ferry; if you long to join the two-wheeled throng, you can rent one at Ferry Landing Marketplace, then set out on a leisurely exploration along the designated paths that lead around Coronado and along its beaches. 107 B4 1201 1st St., Coronado 619-435-8895 Bus: 901

U.S. OLYMPIC TRAINING CENTER

A bit farther afield, this state-of-the-art training facility (one of only three in the country) and its near-perfect year-round climate attract athletes hoping to vie in the Olympics. The 150-acre camp offers athletes soccer fields, tennis courts, a cycling course; a 50-lane archery range, an all-weather field-hockey surface, and courses for cycling, canoeing, and kayaking. Free tours leave daily from the Copley Visitor Center, where you can view a short video, then walk through the training areas and athletic dorms via Olympic path. 107 C2 2800 Olympic Park, Chula Vista 619-656-1500 ■

The place where San Diego began has a rich history—Native American, Mexican, and Spanish—still apparent in an original settlement that has retained its colorful character.

Old Town, Mission Valley, & vicinity

A weather vane in Old Town

Old Town, Mission Valley, & vicinity

SITUATED JUST NORTH OF DOWNTOWN AND SLIGHTLY SOUTH OF MISSION Bay, near the intersection of Interstates 5 and 8, San Diego's seemingly modest birthplace ranks at the top of most visitors' must-see lists. Old Town not only reflects the city's beginnings, it also marks the place where California itself came into being. It was just above this enclave that Padre Junípero Serra established Mission San Diego de Alcalá in 1769, creating California's first permanent European settlement.

The mission originally stood atop Presidio Hill, the grassy slope just north of Old Town. Built upon the hill for security measures, the Presidio quickly established itself as a Spanish military outpost, but it proved to be impractical for a larger role: Its scant supplies of food and water could not satisfy the steadily growing population of Spanish soldiers, missionaries, and American Indians. It was decided that the mission should be moved to a neighboring village, where there would be a better water source as well as fertile farmland. In late 1774,

Mission San Diego de Alcalá relocated 6 miles northeast, where it stands today. The Presidio colony stayed in place until the Mexican occupation in 1822, when the residents eventually began to move down the hill, relocating in the flatlands of Old Town.

Once Mexico's Secularization Act of 1833 had been proclaimed, the local land was carved into huge ranchos, and the little settlement at the base of Presidio Hill began to thrive along with the prosperous local landowners. One year later, the area was officially

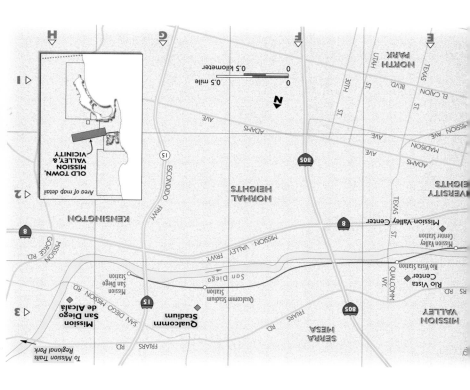

designated a "pueblo," and it became San Diego's first settlement.

Today's visitors can soak up the flavor of the past in Old Town San Diego State Historic Park—a six-block pedestrian-only area where early structures surround the traditional central square, Plaza de las Armas. Many of the original or reconstructed buildings now house tasteful shops or eateries; others, more museum-like, are decorated in keeping with their early uses.

More historic dwellings are located on the streets outside the historic park, an area that is also commonly referred to as Old Town. Art galleries, restaurants, and interesting shops (along with a flavor of Old Mexico) draw plenty of foot traffic. Heritage Park—on a hill just beyond the street-life hubbub of Old Town—is regal with salvaged Victorian buildings. Adjacent to Old Town, Presidio Park is now a grassy expanse topped by the Serra Museum, which features displays of San Diego's early days.

Mission Valley, carved out by the San Diego River, bears few signs of its historic status. The area is now a modern strip with malls, hotels, and a busy freeway running through it.

At Mission Valley's north end stands Qualcomm Stadium, home of the San Diego Chargers football team—and, for now at least, of the Padres baseball team. Mission San Diego de Alcalá looms nearby. Both places are within easy striking distance of Old Town (and downtown) via the clean, sleek San Diego Trolley. ■

Doorway and lintel at the Casa de Estudillo

Old Town San Diego

Old Town San Diego State Historic Park

www.parks.ca.gov

🚗 120 B2

✉️ **Bounded by** Congress, Taylor, Wallace, Calhoun, Juan, & Twiggs Sts.

☎️ 619-220-5422

💲 Donation

🚎 **Blue line trolley;** Coaster train; **Bus:** 5, 5A, 6, 8, 9, 26, 28, 34, 34A, 35, 44, 81

A mariachi band supplies live music for a night out in Old Town.

SAN DIEGO'S ORIGINAL SETTLEMENT HAS BECOME A historic park with thriving business and retail districts, each packed with new discoveries and age-old enticements. True enough, tourists flock here throughout the year, but Old Town remains a favorite attraction for locals, drawn in by the old-fashioned surroundings and the no-hassle Mexican flavor.

Established in 1968, the six-block Old Town San Diego State Historic Park re-creates the city's beginnings within a pedestrian-only area, where restored and rebuilt structures cluster around a large plaza. Although a fire swept through in 1872, seven of the original adobes survived the blaze. Others were painstakingly reconstructed. Just steps from the Old Town trolley stop and public parking lots, visitors can wander about and explore San Diego's earliest buildings and shops—many of them originals still in use, others realistic reproductions. The plaza retains its time-honored position as social hub: Performances and special events are often held here, enticing visitors to watch the crowd or enjoy the festivities. Stop by the park headquarters in **Robinson-Rose House,** at the plaza's northwest end, where both free staff-led tours and self-guided maps are available (see p. 126).

Surrounding the wide-open Plaza de las Armas are the former Wells Fargo Bank, general stores, restaurants, courthouse, school, jail cell, stables, and the first office of the San Diego Union newspaper. Most have been decorated with period furnishings, documents, and artifacts, with doors left open so visitors can roam at leisure.

Other noteworthy structures include the 1851 **Colorado House,** the 1830 **Casa de Machado de Silvas,** and the 1829 **Casa de Estudillo mansion.**

Some of the old adobes house museums and souvenir shops, while others sell clothing, jewelry, and more practical goods. Festive **Bazaar del Mundo,** which spills onto the plaza, is a bustling Mexican-style marketplace filled with shops and restaurants.

OTHER OLD TOWN SIGHTS

Many additional attractions await outside the boundaries of the historic park, along streets next to Old Town. **Whaley House** (2482 San Diego Ave.) claims fame as southern California's oldest two-story brick building. Constructed in 1856 by New York entrepreneur Thomas Whaley (a master brickmaker who purportedly mixed seashells into his plaster and mortar recipe), this seemingly unobtrusive dwelling has served not only as home to generations of the Whaley family, but also as the county courthouse and government seat, saloon, theater, funeral home, and general store. The Whaley House's most intriguing characteristic is undoubtedly the legend that it is haunted. Many people have reportedly seen Thomas Whaley and his wife still "living" in their old abode, along with an assortment of children, pets, and thieves.

Nearby, the circa-1850 **Chapel of the Immaculate Conception** (corner of San Diego Ave. & Twiggs St.), initially built as a private home, was converted by its owner into California's first parish church (with the exception of Mission San Diego de Alcalá). Adobe-walled **El Campo Santo** (San Diego Ave. between Arista & Conde Sts.), established in 1850 as San Diego's first cemetery, harbors the graves of the city's founding fathers as well as those of assorted ne'er-do-wells who met their fate while passing through town. ■

Participants chow down at a Fourth of July pie-eating contest.

Old Town's bold women

Much of San Diego's early history emphasizes its founding fathers. However, at least two women made important contributions as well. In the 1860s, Easterner and suffragist Mary Chase Walker sallied west to become San Diego's first teacher, tackling all eight grades in Old Town's Mason Street School. A cast-iron stove furnished the only heat in the one-room facility, where plumbing was nonexistent.

Tackling a less traditional role, Olive Belle Chambers was appointed deputy sheriff in 1913—California's first woman in that role. Living across the street from the courthouse, Chambers devoted most of her time to caring for the prisoners. She often brought them food from her own home. ■

Heritage Park

Heritage Park

⬛ 120 B2

✉ Bounded by Sunset Rd., Harney St., & Juan St.

☎ 619-291-9784

🚆 Blue line trolley; Coaster; Bus: 5, 5A, 6, 9, 26, 28, 34, 34A, 35, 44, 81

THANKS TO SOHO (SAVE OUR HERITAGE ORGANIZATION), half a dozen fine Victorian treasures that once stood in the way of downtown expansion have been spared demolition, restored to their original beauty, and moved to a place of merit. In Heritage Park they now house offices, retail shops, and a bed-and-breakfast inn.

Located between Old Town and Presidio Park, this 7.8-acre park offers a nostalgic journey through late 19th-century Americana. **Temple Beth Israel,** at the north end of the sloping hill, is one of the most prominent buildings in the park. Constructed in Classic Revival style, this was the first synagogue in Southern California; it opened for Rosh Hashanah celebrations in September 1889.

Eugene Senlis—an employee of horticulturist Kate Session's—lived in the pink 1886 **Senlis Cottage,** next door to the temple. Looming over it is the 20-room **Sherman-Gilbert House.** Built in 1887 in the Stick-Eastlake style, the home displays distinctive stick-, lattice-, and scrollwork in its trim and other

sections. After art-patron sisters Bess and Gertrude Gilbert purchased the home in 1897, it hosted parties honoring such famous performers as Yehudi Menuhin, Artur Rubinstein, and the Trapp Family Singers. Next up is 1887 **Bushyhead House,** an Italianate Victorian once occupied by *San Diego Union* newspaper founder (and town sheriff) Edward Bushyhead.

Atop the hill, the fairy-tale, Queen Anne-style **Christian House** *(619-262-1007),* built in 1889 by merchant Harfield Christian, is now an elegant bed-and-breakfast inn. On the west side of the path are the 1887 **McConaughy House**—once a hospital, now a gift shop—and the 1893 **Burton House,** set up as a tearoom. ■

Temple Beth Israel, southern California's first synagogue, is among the Victorian gems in Heritage Park.

Presidio Park

TOPPED BY THE U.S. FLAG AND OVERLOOKING OLD TOWN, this rolling 40-acre hillside—once trodden by soldiers, missionaries, and Indian neophytes—is now a popular site for weddings, picnics, and informal sports.

Drive or walk up to the top of the 160-foot summit for a view that juxtaposes historical buildings with the new-era commerce of Mission Valley. Within the confines of the park are assorted ruins, the Serra Museum, and the Fort Stockton Memorial. Named for Commodore Robert Stockton in 1846, the now-vanished fort is marked by a cannon, monuments, bronze statues, and a flagpole. The clubhouse at the Presidio Hills Golf Course (on Mason Street) incorporates remnants of circa-1820 **Casa de Cabrillo,** the town's oldest adobe. Towering near the outlined site of the former fortress is the 28-foot-high **Serra Cross;** it was constructed from original mission tiles.

SERRA MUSEUM

Built to commemorate San Diego's original fort and mission, this gleaming, reinforced-concrete museum was designed by architect William Templeton Johnson in homage to the city's Spanish Co-

lonial heritage. Constructed in 1929, the building evokes the city's past with its white stucco arches, red-tile roof, narrow passages, and serene landscaping. It's worth the steep climb to the tower to see how the present-day view compares with the look of the landscape when the museum was built.

The San Diego Historical Society oversees the museum, which is devoted to the city's early days. The building includes many items culled from archaeological excavations at the Presidio. Ceramics displays consist of distinctive wares made by Kumeyaay Indians and Mexicans, as well as European pieces used at the Presidio. A collection of religious artifacts includes both simple and ornate crucifixes, medallions, and ceremonial objects.

Visitors can also view military buttons, men's and women's fine jewelry, and shell trading beads made by the Indians, as well as glass versions used by the Europeans. ■

Presidio Park

🅰 120 B2
✉ Bounded by Hotel Circle South & Mason, Taylor, & Jackson Sts.
🚋 Blue line trolley; Coaster train; Bus: 5, 5A, 6, 8, 9, 26, 28, 34, 34A, 35, 44, 81

Serra Museum

www.sandiegohistory.org
🅰 120 B2
✉ 2727 Presidio Dr.
☎ 619-297-3258
🕐 Closed Mon. in summer; closed Mon.–Thurs. in winter
💲 $
🚋 Blue line trolley; Coaster train; Bus: 5, 5A, 6, 8, 9, 26, 28, 34, 34A, 35, 44, 81

The Serra Museum perches on the flank of Presidio Hill, above Old Town.

An amble through Old Town

Old Town's attractions lie within the six-block Old Town San Diego State Historic Park and along nearby streets. Visitors can sign up for a guided tour or strike out on their own. The area is flat, compact, and easy to navigate, with myriad restaurants and shops close at hand. Presidio Hill, above Old Town, beckons hardier walkers. The festive atmosphere and historic reenactments make this excursion enjoyable for all ages.

Begin this walk at the **Robinson-Rose House** ❶ (*4002 Wallace St., 619-220-5422*), inside Old Town San Diego State Historic Park. This 1853 building was once the family residence of lawyer James W. Robinson; in the 1850s and early 1860s it also housed the *San Diego Herald* and other businesses, making it Old Town's commercial center. The restored home is now the park's **visitor center** and the departure point for organized tours. A diorama on the first floor depicts Old Town as it looked in 1872. Self-guided maps and background reading are available here.

Behind the Robinson-Rose House, seek out the reconstructed wood-frame 1869 **McCoy House** near the corner of San Diego Avenue and Old Beach Street. This building, the former residence of Sheriff James McCoy, will become the park's interpretive center in 2003. Return to the Robinson-Rose House and begin a counterclockwise tour of the main square,

Plaza de las Armas ❷. The first building you reach should be **Wrightington House,** an original adobe formerly used as a clinic for Native Americans and as a U.S. military hospital. Continuing up San Diego Avenue, you'll hit **San Diego House,** a saloon owned and operated by African-American settlers in the mid-1800s. A general store once occupied the two-story prefabricated wooden **U.S. House** next door. The restored **Casa de Machado de Silvas Museum** ❸ (aka the Commercial Restaurant) has served variously as a saloon, art studio, church, boardinghouse, and souvenir shop. Next up, **Racine and Laramie** has been expertly re-created as the cigar, tobacco, and stationery store it once was.

When it opened in 1851, rooms at the two-story **Colorado House** rented out for just 15 dollars a month. Burned in an 1872 fire, the reconstructed building now houses the **Wells, Fargo & Co. Museum.** The Mormon

A waitress prepares to explain yet again the difference between a tostada and an enchilada.

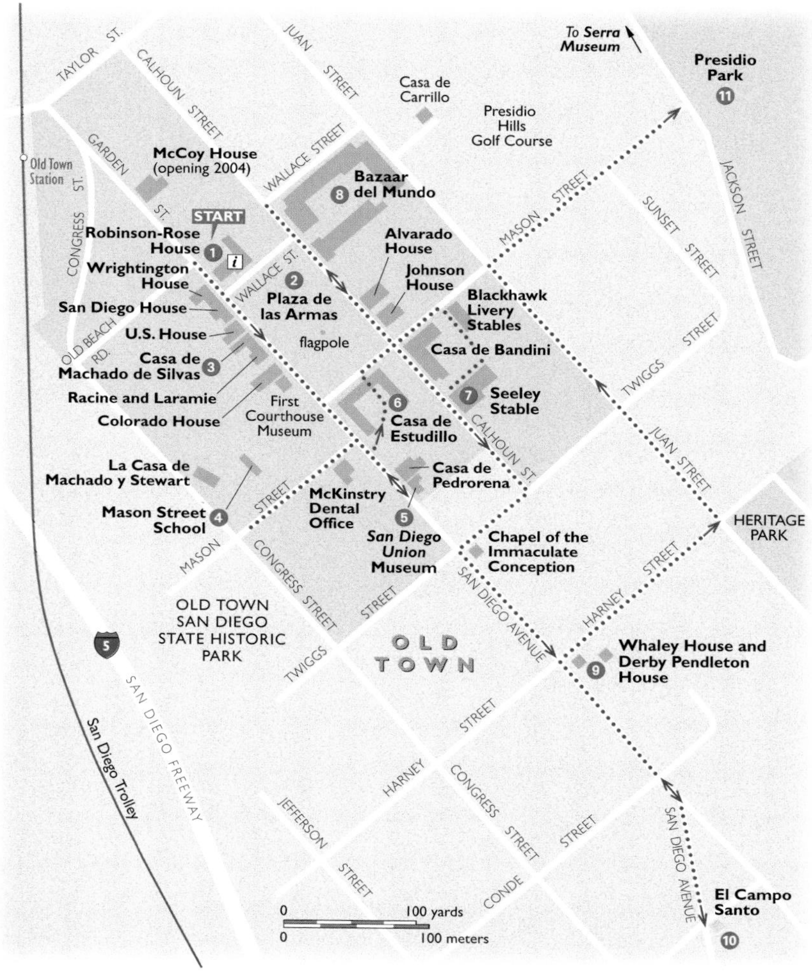

To *Serra Museum*

Presidio Park ⓫

Presidio Hills Golf Course

Casa de Carrillo

TAYLOR ST.

CALHOUN STREET

GARDEN ST.

Old Town Station

CONGRESS ST.

JUAN STREET

WALLACE STREET

MASON STREET

SUNSET STREET

JACKSON STREET

McCoy House (opening 2004)

Bazaar del Mundo ⑧

START

Robinson-Rose House ❶ *i*

Wrightington House

San Diego House

U.S. House

Casa de Machado de Silvas ❸

Racine and Laramie

Colorado House

La Casa de Machado y Stewart

Mason Street School ❹

WALLACE ST.

OLD BEACH RD.

Plaza de las Armas ❷

flagpole

First Courthouse Museum

STREET

MASON

CONGRESS STREET

Alvarado House

Johnson House

Blackhawk Livery Stables

Casa de Bandini

Seeley Stable ⑦

Casa de Estudillo ❻

McKinstry Dental Office

Casa de Pedrorena ❺

San Diego Union Museum

Chapel of the Immaculate Conception

CALHOUN ST.

TWIGGS STREET

JUAN STREET

HARNEY STREET

HERITAGE PARK

SAN DIEGO AVENUE

OLD TOWN SAN DIEGO STATE HISTORIC PARK

5️⃣

SAN DIEGO FREEWAY

San Diego Trolley

TWIGGS STREET

CONGRESS STREET

O L D T O W N

STREET

HARNEY STREET

JEFFERSON STREET

CONGRESS STREET

CONDE STREET

SAN DIEGO AVENUE

Whaley House and Derby Pendleton House ⑨

El Campo Santo ❿

0 ————— 100 yards
0 ————— 100 meters

Battalion helped build San Diego's first **courthouse,** a brick building that served as city hall, sheriff's office, and Anglo-American civic center (the city's first). Across from the courthouse, the flagpole in the plaza marks the spot where the Stars and Stripes were raised on a propped-up ship's mast in 1846—and where fiestas and ceremonies have taken place through the years.

Fifty yards or so behind the courthouse is the reconstructed **Mason Street School** ❹. San Diego's first teacher, Mary Chase Walker, taught eight grades at this one-room school-house (see sidebar p. 123), the only public

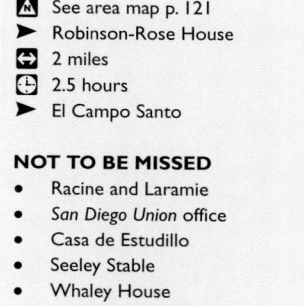

🅰 See area map p. 121
▶ Robinson-Rose House
↔ 2 miles
🕐 2.5 hours
▶ El Campo Santo

NOT TO BE MISSED

- Racine and Laramie
- *San Diego Union* office
- Casa de Estudillo
- Seeley Stable
- Whaley House

school in San Diego County until the late 1860s. Just to the right of the school, **La Casa de Machado y Stewart** has been restored as a house museum with a lovely garden.

Return to the main plaza and turn right to reach the **McKinstry Dental Office** and a dental museum that gives a ghoulish glimpse of the implements and techniques used in bygone days. Diagonally across the street is the first printing office of the *San Diego Union* 5 newspaper. The prefabricated wood-frame edifice was shipped from Maine in 1851. The

exhibit within portrays the newsroom as it looked in 1868, when the first edition of the *Union* (then a four-page weekly) rolled off the press. Reverse direction to **Casa de Pedrorena** next door, the private residence of Spanish immigrant Miguel de Pedrorena.

Continue to walk back toward the square and you'll come to a transomed door recessed in a tile-topped wall. It leads into the courtyard of Old Town's most historic building, **Casa de Estudillo** 6. Constructed between 1827 and 1829, this 12-room adobe

Turquoise and silver jewelry on offer at the Bazaar del Mundo

house was the private residence of Presidio commander José María de Estudillo (his family lived in the house until the 1880s). Its rooms have been authentically restored in period style, with tiled floors and wood-beamed ceilings. Turn right as you leave the residence, then cross Calhoun Street to **Casa de Bandini,** home of Peruvian immigrant Juan Bandini. Such a charmer was Bandini that his home quickly became Old Town's social center in the 1830s. Following the U.S. occupation in 1846, Bandini invited Commodore Stockton to use the property for his headquarters. Albert Seeley purchased the house in 1869, added a second story, and reopened it as the Cosmopolitan Hotel. The **Seeley Stable 7**, next to Casa de Bandini on Calhoun Street, was once a stop on the Yuma–San Diego Stage Line. The reconstructed stable and barn holds a remarkable collection of stagecoaches, branding irons, saddles, and other memorabilia. Walk behind the barn and Casa de Bandini to **Blackhawk Livery Stables,** where you can see vintage blacksmithing equipment.

Exit the stable onto Mason Street and turn left. The modest **Johnson House,** at the corner of Calhoun Street, was built and occupied by Colorado River steamboat operator George Johnson. Neighboring **Alvarado House** was occupied by the sister of Governor Pico (the state's last governor under Mexican rule) as well as by the Alvarado family. In 1854, Francisco Alvarado was charged with illegally selling liquor out of an adobe shed behind the home. It's still there, but now—like so much in Old Town—it's a gift shop, this one selling Native American woven baskets and pottery.

Stroll along Calhoun Street to **Bazaar del Mundo 8**, which opens onto the plaza. This festive open-air marketplace, enlivened by mariachi musicians and other outdoor performers, makes an ideal place to break for Mexican fare and margaritas or pastries and coffee.

Walk back along Calhoun Street or San Diego Avenue, exiting the park boundary at Twiggs Street. The **Chapel of the Immaculate Conception,** at the corner of Twiggs Street and San Diego Avenue, was California's first Roman Catholic church. Buried within is the wealthy rancher who converted this residence into a chapel, then donated it to the city. Continue one block southeast on San Diego

Avenue to **Whaley House 9**, at the corner of Harney Street, San Diego's oldest brick structure—private home and store of the Whaley family, and the first courthouse and county seat—thrills visitors with its reputation as one of the nation's most haunted houses. Behind the Whaley House, **Derby Pendleton House** marks the site where Alonzo Horton purchased downtown San Diego. (Lieutenant George Horatio Derby, who lived here in the 1850s, was known to *San Diego Herald* readers as humor writer "Squibob.") Continue about two blocks south on San Diego Avenue to visit **El Campo Santo 10** (the Holy Field) cemetery, burial spot of San Diego's founding families and various others.

Time and energy permitting, walk back to Whaley House, then turn right and walk one block northeast to the corner of Harney and Juan Streets. This is the entry to **Heritage Park** (see p. 124), a 7.8-acre enclave of restored Victorian homes and buildings. Or walk another block to the corner of Mason and Juan to find the old Presidio Historic Trail. It leads you on a short, steep hike to **Presidio Park 11** and the **Serra Museum** (see p. 125), with a nice view of Old Town. ■

It's in the bag: old-school fun at a sack race

Mission San Diego de Alcalá

Mission San Diego de Alcalá
www.missionsandiego.com

- 121 H3
- 10818 San Diego Mission Rd.
- 619-281-8449
- $
- Blue line trolley; Bus: 13

MISSION SAN DIEGO DE ALCALÁ, THE FIRST OF CALIFORNIA'S 21-mission chain—and the first permanent European settlement—is also considered California's true birthplace. Many historians refer to the mission as the Plymouth Rock of the West Coast. Moved from its original Presidio Hill site, it now sits amid condominiums and busy freeways. Nevertheless, this "Mother of Missions" still invokes the mystique of early San Diego, giving visitors a vicarious feel for mission life through its buildings, sanctuaries, gardens, and shrines.

The **visitor center,** near the mission entrance, provides walking maps. The gift shop sells religious and secular items including books, jewelry, statuary, and souvenirs.

First established atop Presidio Hill on July 16, 1769, by Franciscan Padre Junípero Serra, the fort rapidly grew so crowded that it became clear the mission would fare better in a site with more plentiful water, farmland, and labor. Padre Luis

Jayme (Padre Serra's successor) received permission from the viceroy to move the mission to its present site—a Kumeyaay Indian village named Nipaguay at the time—6 miles northeast of the Presidio. By December 1774 a church, rectory, corral, and 13 residences had been completed under the direction of Padre Jayme and Padre Vincente

Altar

Chapel

In this rendering by Stephen Capsey and Andrew Leck, the mission has been cut away to reveal the chapel, adjoining living quarters, work areas, and various outbuildings, all surrounding a tree-shaded courtyard.

St. Francis Statue in Rose Garden

Rose Garden Gate

Fuster, and San Diego de Alcalá re-opened at the new location.

On November 5, 1775, disgruntled local Indians, accompanied by two Indian neophytes, attacked the mission, setting fire to the church and other buildings and inflicting three casualties—Padre Jayme among them. Padre Serra returned to supervise the mission's reconstruction, this time using fire-retardant adobe walls and tile roofs. A second, larger church was opened in October 1776; other expansions and repairs were completed by 1785. By 1779 the thriving mission had recruited 1,405 converts, and its holdings comprised 50,000 acres of cultivated land, thousands of sheep, cattle, and horses, nearby vineyards, orchards, and vegetable gardens.

Religion dominated the daily lives of both the missionaries and their Indian converts. The neo-phytes' activities included religious, moral, social, and industrial duties. Padres would say Mass at dawn and give instruction in church doctrine, after which a basic breakfast was served. Men spent the days working in the fields and farms, while women focused on domestic work—sewing, spinning, and weaving—as well as making baskets, soap, and other practical items. In the evenings, all would regroup for additional religious instruction and Spanish lessons. After dinner, the Indians were allowed to relax until bedtime—8 p.m. for the women, 9 p.m. for the men. This hardworking schedule varied only during religious celebrations and fiestas, which were usually held in the mission courtyard and formed the center of the neophytes' social life.

The mission continued to face obstacles into the early 1820s. Colonization greatly increased, but it was far less than the missionaries had hoped for. Though an aqueduct system had been constructed in 1795,

Campanario

Casa del
Padre Serra

Choir Loft Window

alternating wet and dry seasons taxed its capabilities. Using native labor, the missionaries expanded on the system: They built a long, tall, and thick stone wall that branched out into ditches throughout the fields.

Other natural events, meanwhile, were likewise taking a toll. An 1803 earthquake slightly damaged the second mission church, and an 1812 temblor razed a mission to the north.

To guard against similar damage at Mission San Diego de Alcalá, the padres incorporated a more earthquake-proof buttress-type structure into a larger church that was under construction at the time. Dedicated in 1813, this new and sturdier church could accommodate the mission's growing population. Mexican occupation reduced the missionaries' powers during the

Padre Junípero Serra is immortalized in bronze at Mission San Diego de Alcala, the city's first church.

1820s, but the Mexican Secularization Act of 1833 wiped them out completely. As a result, San Diego de Alcalá was ultimately deeded to a Mexican man named Santiago Argüello. Though the missionaries were ousted, most of the Indians stayed on in their arduous field jobs. The U.S. Cavalry occupied the mission from 1849 to 1857, making some repairs and structural changes that rendered the long-abandoned buildings habitable.

President Abraham Lincoln ordered the mission restored to the Catholic Church in 1862. By then, a number of the buildings had been stripped or demolished.

After many difficult years, the mission was finally reconstructed and rededicated in 1931. In 1976 Pope Paul VI designated the present mission church a minor basilica; today it continues to serve the local Catholic community as an active parish church.

Though almost the entire original mission has been rebuilt, some of the first structure's remnants have been incorporated in the current building. These include the fachada (front buttress wings), the baptistery arch, and the base of the campanario (bell tower). Other elements—such as hand-hewn beams and hand-wrought hardware—were painstakingly reproduced, resulting in a faithful replica of the early church.

Whitewashed walls, beamed ceilings, handmade tiles, and brick floors—all hallmarks of Mission-style design—complement the simple, uncluttered, 150-foot-long, 35-foot-wide structure. Rising above it all is another masterpiece of Mission architecture: the **campanario,** more than 46 feet tall and holding five bells, some that are original. The church interior follows the simple lines of the mission. Local parishioners still flock to the small wooden chapel for daily Mass. Beneath the cross in the sanctuary are buried five Franciscan fathers, including Padre Jayme.

At the rear of the church building, the **Padre Jayme Museum** is filled with historical information, vestments worn by mission clerics, and a crucifix possibly held by Padre Serra at his death. Also here are exhibits on early California. The **Casa del Padre Serra** next to the visitor center lets you look inside one of California's first rectories; the nearby rose garden marks the final resting place of some who died during the Mission period. The mission grounds are an oasis of sacred statuary and gardens. Prickly cactuses, brilliant bougainvillea, and swaying palms share the courtyard and front entry with a bronze statue of Padre Serra, a Guadalupe Shrine, and a St. Francis wishing well. ∎

Convert this!

When Spanish missionaries first arrived in San Diego and the rest of California, they brought novel items (such as woven cloth) that intrigued and attracted the indigenous populace. Because the missionaries were racked by scurvy, however, their sickly appearance made the Indians suspicious of any gifts of food.

Some Native Americans eventually embraced conversion—but many did not. On November 4, 1775, angry Indians attacked San Diego de Alcalá, the only sizable assault ever launched on any compound in the 21-mission chain.

The mission had already been relocated to the Indian village of Nipaguay and had been up and running for just under a year when the attack occurred. Sometime after midnight, a band of Indians (numbering between 600 and 800, according to varying accounts) swooped into the mission while Padres Luis Jayme and Vincente Fuster and nine other residents were asleep.

At first it seemed like a simple robbery. The attackers broke into vestment cases and handed valuable articles and ornaments to women, who fled to the mountains. But the invaders were far from finished. As their depredations continued, they set fire to the church, guardhouse, and living quarters.

Awakened by the commotion, Padre Fuster and the others had run for cover. Padre Jayme, however, walked straight up to one band of Indians and spoke his usual words of greeting: "Love God, my children."

The Indians may not have understood what he was saying. They turned on the congenial priest, stripped him of his clothes, clubbed him, and riddled his body with arrows. Other mission residents were attacked as well.

When daylight broke, the Indians retreated, leaving the shocked survivors and three casualties amid the wreckage. Padre Jayme's body was eventually found in an arroyo near the mission, so badly maimed that he could be identified only by his hands. A carpenter and the mission blacksmith were killed as well.

No one knows for certain what sparked the attack. According to Padre Francisco Palóu, tribal chiefs in nearby villages may have feared losing their influence once the missionaries began to make spiritual inroads. Whatever the reason, Padre Luis Jayme, dead at 35, was declared California's first martyr. ∎

More places to visit around Old Town

MISSION TRAILS REGIONAL PARK

Northeast of Mission San Diego de Alcalá, this peaceful 5,760-acre area is one of the country's largest urban parks—and possibly its least known. Within its boundaries are Lake Murray, Cowles and Fortuna Mountains, Kumeyaay Lake campground, and the Old Mission Dam (a national historic landmark and part of the first irrigation and engineering project in California). An excellent visitor and interpretive center displays interactive exhibits and sells crafts and books. www.mtrp.org ✉ One Father Junipero Serra Trail, Tierrasanta ☎ 619-668-3275 🕐 Open daily

MISSION VALLEY/HOTEL CIRCLE

Beginning where Interstates 5 and 8 now intersect (just north of Old Town) and running approximately 6 miles north, Mission Valley held the primary water source for San Diego's first settlement. In the 1950s, dams were constructed upstream; commercial development of the area began soon afterward. Today Interstate 8 parallels the San Diego River along roughly the same course that the river once followed.

This is one of San Diego's most commercial strips; both sides of the road are laden with hotels, retail centers, and business districts. An architectural odd couple—Qualcomm Stadium and Mission San Diego de Alcalá—shares the terrain at the valley's northern edge. The main shopping centers along this route are upscale Fashion Valley and less pricey Mission Valley Center, as well as the more prosaic Hazard Center and Rio Vista Shopping Center. Among the four, visitors will find branches of nearly all major department stores and retail chains, as well as multiscreen cinemas and a panoply of dining options.

The San Diego Trolley runs from Old Town to the stadium parking lot, stopping at strategic points along the way. 🅽 Map pp. 120-121 🚋 Blue line trolley; Bus: 13

Right fielder Ryan Klesko commemorates the San Diego Padres' home opener with a high drive to the outfield.

Old Town's Bazaar del Mundo has been enabling shopaholics since 1971.

MORMON BATTALION MEMORIAL VISITOR'S CENTER

Located across from Heritage Park, this center honors the 500 Mormons who began (and the 350 who survived) the longest infantry march in U.S. military history—a 2,000-mile odyssey from Council Bluffs, Iowa, to San Diego. Displays, a video, and on-site volunteers help to clarify the soldiers' 1846 feat; they also furnish insight into the Mormon contributions to early San Diego. 🅽 120 B2 ✉ 2510 Juan St. ☎ 619-298-3317 🕐 Open daily 🚋 Blue line trolley; Coaster train; Bus: 5, 5A, 6, 8, 9, 26, 28, 34, 34A, 35, 44, 81

QUALCOMM STADIUM

Standing within sight of Interstate 8, San Diego's major sports stadium is home to the Chargers football team and (at press time) the Padres baseball team. The San Diego State

University Aztec football team also shares the space, as do crowd-drawing rock groups such as the Rolling Stones.

Called San Diego Stadium when it was built in 1967, the arena was renamed Jack Murphy Stadium in 1980 to honor the recently deceased sportswriter, who had been influential in both the Chargers' move to town and the construction of the major-league facility. In 1997 the stadium was re-renamed Qualcomm after the company agreed to finance a much-needed expan-

Buyers size up the distinctive pottery on display at a Bazaar del Mundo Indian Fair.

sion—a change hotly contested by San Diegans. By the time it hosted 1998's Super Bowl XXXII, the stadium had increased its seating to 75,500 for football games and 65,900 for baseball games, and the San Diego Trolley had extended its line right into the parking lot. On January 26, 2003, the stadium will also be the venue for Super Bowl XXXVII. www.sannet.gov/qualcomm

🗺 121 G3 ✉ 9449 Friars Rd., Mission Valley ☎ 619-641-3100 🚊 Blue line trolley; Bus: 13

SAN DIEGO SHERIFF'S MUSEUM

Opened in 2001, this two-story, 7,000-square-foot museum is the culmination of a three-year project to create a tribute to local law enforcement. Among the displays are a re-creation of San Diego's circa-1850s sheriff's office, a jail cell, an old ball and chain, a bomb-disposal robot, various handcuffs and batons, a veritable arsenal of weaponry, art created by prisoners, and vintage motorcycles. In addition, the museum features a live feed from the modern San Diego sheriff's communications center.

🗺 120 B2 ✉ 2384 San Diego Ave., Old Town ☎ 619-260-1850 🚫 Closed Sun.-Mon. 💲 Donation 🚊 Blue line trolley; Coaster; Bus: 5, 5A, 6, 9, 26, 28, 34, 34A, 35, 44, 81

UNIVERSITY OF SAN DIEGO

Visitors often mistake this university's Spanish Renaissance buildings for San Diego's mission. Built on a mesa overlooking San Diego Bay and Mission Bay, the tallest buildings are visible from Interstates 5 and 8. This independent Catholic university was founded in 1949 as separate colleges for men and women; its design was inspired by the University of Alcalá near Madrid, Spain. Approximately 7,000 students attend the campus, known for its Joan B. Kroc Institute for Peace and Justice and its schools of law, nursing, and business. The campus offers gorgeous gardens and views, but the real standout is the Founder's Chapel with its rose marble floor, white marble altar, stained-glass windows, and gold leaf details. www.acusd.edu

🗺 120 B3 ✉ Alcalá Park (at Linda Vista Rd.) ☎ 619-260-4600 🚌 Bus: 44 ∎

West of downtown San Diego is the finger-shaped peninsula of Point Loma. This spot, where the first Europeans stepped ashore in California, is now a haven for sailors, surfers, and sunseekers.

Point Loma, Shelter Island, & Harbor Island

Inside the lighthouse at Cabrillo National Monument

Point Loma, Shelter Island, & Harbor Island

STANDING LIKE A SENTINEL ABOVE THE HARBOR ENTRANCE, POINT LOMA is one of San Diego's more eclectic areas. It's a medley of posh residential neighborhoods and modest shorefront bungalows, of historic military installations and sprawling parks where southern California's sunshine culture thrives.

Behind its genteel facade, the area has a rich and often gritty history. Point Loma is the place where Spanish explorers came ashore on the California coast in 1542—the first Europeans to meet the local Native Americans. The Spanish largely ignored the peninsula during the next 300 years of their stay in the area, but early American settlers saw potential in its

grassy hills and sheltered coves. Point Loma eventually provided a base for San Diego's own industrial revolution—an economic boom based on whaling and leather tanning. With the establishment of Fort Rosecrans in the 1850s, the U.S. military kicked off a long and mutually beneficial relationship with Point Loma. Many a green recruit was transformed into a first-rate sailor or Marine on the parade grounds and obstacle courses of the peninsula. Cabrillo National Monument, at the tip of Point Loma, is a well-known haven for both history buffs and nature lovers.

North of Point Loma is Ocean Beach, whose wide strand and palm-lined streets make it the archetypal California beach town. Nearby Sunset Cliffs Park lives up to its billing as a perch from which to watch the sun expire into the Pacific. Although they have not escaped gentrification, harborside neighborhoods such as Roseville and La Playa still carry the flavor of the days when they were the home turf of San Diego's closely knit Portuguese fishing community.

Nowadays the peninsula boasts some of the city's best beaches and most desirable waterfront property. The cachet is somewhat nouveau: Point Loma's reputation as an international boating mecca didn't accrue until the early 1950s, when a submerged shoal in San Diego Bay was reclaimed and made into Shelter Island, one of southern California's largest pleasure-boat facilities. Harbor Island, farther east, took shape a decade later. In addition to bustling marinas, both artificial isles boast waterfront restaurants, luxury hotels, and parks with spectacular views of downtown San Diego and the harbor.

A pleasure craft named for its home waters nuzzles a dock in San Diego Bay.

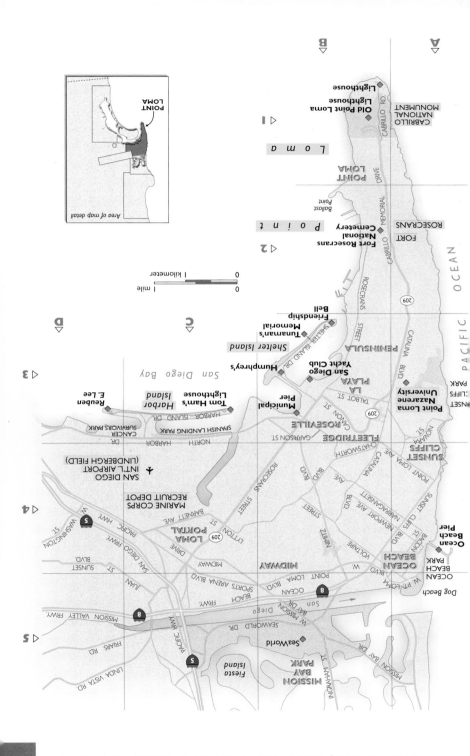

Area of map detail

POINT
LOMA

▷ A

▷ B

CABRILLO
NATIONAL
MONUMENT

Old Point Loma
Lighthouse

Lighthouse

CABRILLO RD.

POINT LOMA

CABRILLO MEMORIAL DRIVE

L o m a

▷ 1

Ballast
Point

FORT
ROSECRANS

Fort Rosecrans
National
Cemetery

P o i n t

▷ 2

CABRILLO MEMORIAL DRIVE

ROSECRANS STREET

(209)

PACIFIC   OCEAN

PENINSULA

CATALINA BLVD

Shelter Island

Tunaman's
Memorial

Friendship
Bell

SHELTER ISLAND DR.

Humphrey's

San Diego
Yacht Club

LA
PLAYA

Point Loma
Nazarene
University

SUNSET
CLIFFS
PARK

▷ C

▷ D

San Diego Bay

▷ 3

Reuben
E. Lee

Harbor
Island

Tom Ham's
Lighthouse

HARBOR ISLAND DR.

CANCER
SURVIVORS PARK

DR

SPANISH LANDING PARK

NORTH   HARBOR

Municipal
Pier

ROSEVILLE

CANON ST.

GARRISON ST.

FLEETRIDGE

CHATSWORTH   ST.

TALBOT ST.

0   1 mile
0   1 kilometer

SAN DIEGO
INT'L. AIRPORT
(LINDBERGH FIELD)

MARINE CORPS
RECRUIT DEPOT

W. WASHINGTON ST.

PACIFIC HWY

SUNSET
BLVD.

▷ 4

5

LOMA
PORTAL

(209)

BARNETT AVE.

LYTTON ST.

MIDWAY

MIDWAY

W. POINT LOMA BLVD

SPORTS ARENA BLVD

ROSECRANS   STREET

SAN DIEGO FRWY

POINT LOMA AVE.

NIMITZ   BLVD

SUNSET   CLIFFS   BLVD

CATALINA   AVE

CHATSWORTH   BLVD

NEWPORT AVE.

NARRAGANSETT   AVE

VOLTAIRE   ST.

BACON   ST.

OCEAN
BEACH
PARK

OCEAN BEACH

W. PT. LOMA BLVD

Ocean
Beach
Pier

Dog Beach

JUAN ST.

BEACH   FRWY

OCEAN   BLVD

W. MISSION BAY DR

San Diego

MISSION VALLEY FRWY.

FRIARS   RD.

LINDA VISTA RD.

PACIFIC HWY.

8

8

5

SeaWorld

Fiesta
Island

SEAWORLD   DR.

INGRAHAM   ST.

MISSION
BAY
PARK

MISSION BAY DR

▷ 5

▷ I

▷ 1

Point Loma

B 139 B1

Point Loma

DON'T LET THE STUNNING VISTAS OR THE MOCK-SPANISH mansions fool you. Long before it became a well-heeled residential area, Point Loma earned its living from some classically rough-and-tumble occupations.

A waterborne view of a seaside mansion

The posh bayside **La Playa** neighborhood near Shelter Island once harbored the largest whaling operation on the West Coast. In the 1850s, when the first whalers arrived from New England, they could harpoon California gray whales in San Diego Bay. La Playa was also a center for leather tanning and tallow production. The hides were shipped around the Horn to New England shoe factories; the gooey tallow went south of the border to Mexican candlemakers. Between the tanneries and the blubber pots, the area must have stunk to high heaven. Nowadays

your nose will be assailed by nothing more noxious than roses and bougainvillea as you explore the narrow lanes at the southern end of La Playa's Rosecrans Street.

Farther east along the peninsula is **Roseville,** named after tanning-and-tallow tycoon Louis Rose. This quaint harborside retreat was a cradle of San Diego's seafood industry. Shortly after statehood, Chinese immigrants established a small fishing village on the shore. By the end of the 19th century, the area was dominated by Portuguese fishermen and their families, working to build a tuna fleet that would eventually be the world's largest.

The local Portuguese influence has waned in recent years, but Roseville's **Municipal Pier,** at the foot of Garrison Street, still bustles with fishing folk. Commercial sportfishing outfits such as **H & M Landing** (619-222-1144) and **Fisherman's Landing** (619-221-8500) use the pier as a staging area for charter trips to the Point Loma kelp beds and the nearby Coronado Islands of Mexico, as well as for winter whale-watching expeditions.

Adorning the slopes above Roseville are the posh homes of **Fleetridge** and **Loma Portal,** where a vacant lot costs more than one million dollars. Beyond is the equally pricey **Sunset Cliffs** neighborhood and its namesake palisades. Vehicle turnoffs and precipitous dirt trails provide fine views of the Pacific, but heed warning signs and don't stray beyond the guardrails—the cliffs can crumble, dashing you onto the rocks.

The waves below Sunset Cliffs are a big draw for surfers.

POINT LOMA NAZARENE UNIVERSITY

Point Loma Nazarene University is a curious footnote in local history. Perched high above the Pacific at the south end of Sunset Cliffs, the facility is a private Christian-based school with more than 60 major areas of study and several graduate programs.

The 90-acre seaside campus got its start in 1897 as something far different: the School for the Revival of the Lost Mysteries of Antiquity, founded by the eccentric Madame Katherine Tingley as the education-al arm of the Theosophical Society of America. This organization op-posed (among other things) sci-ence, materialism, capital punish-ment, violence, and electricity. Tingley selected the spot because she wanted to locate her school on the far western edge of the conti-nent, facing Asia.

Several structures remain from the Theosophical era, including an amphitheater where Tingley staged Shakespearean plays and Greek tragedies, a lovely Victorian man-sion called **Cabrillo Hall**, and flamboyant **Mieras Hall** with its exotic Oriental domes.

FORT ROSECRANS

The southern half of Point Loma is a vast military reservation called Fort Rosecrans that comprises a

number of separate installations. These include the U.S. Fleet Anti-Air Warfare Training Center; the U.S. Navy Electronics Lab; and the U.S. Navy Underwater Center, which maintains a fleet of nuclear submarines. Riddling the hillsides are bunkers, fortified caves, and gun emplacements, some of them dating from the Civil War. Most of the reserve is off-limits to the pub-lic, but you can glimpse its military might from Catalina Boulevard on the drive to the Point Loma lighthouse.

Fort Rosecrans National Cemetery contains the graves of more than 80,000 U.S. veterans and eligible family members. Among the many solemn monuments that grace the cemetery grounds is one honoring the American troops who died at the 1846 Battle of San Pasqual in northern San Di-ego County. Another—an obelisk 75 feet high—pays tribute to the 66 sailors who perished in the 1905 ex-plosion of the U.S.S. *Bennington* in San Diego Bay.

From the graveyard bluffs you can see a rocky spit guarding the entrance to San Diego Bay. This is **Ballast Point**, where Spanish explorer Juan Rodríguez Cabrillo landed in 1542. After naming his discovery Bahía San Miguel, he promptly sailed on in search of more see-worthy sites. ■

Point Loma Nazarene University
🖥 www.pointloma.edu
🅰 139 A3
✉ 3900 Lomaland Dr.
☎ 619-849-2200
🚌 Bus: 23 from downtown San Diego to Catalina Blvd.; transfer to bus 26

Fort Rosecrans National Cemetery
🅰 139 A2
✉ Rosecrans St. (Calif. 209)
☎ 619-553-2084
🚌 Bus: 26 from Old Town Trolley Station in downtown San Diego

Tide-pooling

Tide pools—small, water-filled depressions in coastal rocks and cliffs—teem with marine plants and animals. Incoming waves conceal them at high tide, but low tide cuts them off from the sea and exposes them to view—and exploration—from land.

"Tide-pooling" is a venerable tradition among local beach folk. The Kumeyaay and other Native American groups who originally inhabited this coast harvested the tide pools for their shellfish and other edibles.

In modern times, tide-pooling has become a recreational and educational pastime that entails exploring the pools without disturbing their natural inhabitants. Today's visitors to tide pools should be observers only. Don't damage the delicate creatures by handling them; likewise refrain from destroying their homes by turning over rocks.

Tide pools perform many of the same ecological functions as coral reefs, sheltering a variety of underwater animals. They are part of a rocky intertidal ecosystem that can be divided into several distinct zones. The splash zone—an area above the high-water mark—is the domain of the periwinkle and limpet. Below this is the high intertidal zone, where tides submerge only about ten percent of the surface area. Regular denizens include hermit crabs, acorn barnacles, chitons, and black tegulas with their swirling shells.

The middle intertidal zone is awash in water about half the time. Pools and crevices in this area harbor sea anemones, gooseneck barnacles, tube snails, and red algae. Extreme low tides expose the low intertidal zone; submerged 90 percent of the time, it is the ultimate goal of tide-pooling connoisseurs. Among the curious animals that live here are purple

KEY TO DIAGRAM

1. Rough limpet
2. Sea lettuce
3. Striped shore crab
4. Giant owl limpet
5. Striped sea slug
6. California mussels
7. Pink encrusting coralline algae
8. Volcano barnacles
9. Velvety red sponge
10. Spanish shawl nudibranch
11. Leaf barnacles
12. Common surfgrass
13. Sandcastle worms
14. Rockweeed
15. Giant green anemone
16. Hopkins' rose
17. California sea hare
18. Bat star
19. Panama brittle star
20. Ochre star
21. Warty sea cucumber
22. Sea urchin
23. Rock crab
24. Spiny lobster
25. Black abalone
26. Sargasso weed
27. Coralline red algae
28. Giant keyhole limpet
29. Chestnut cowry
30. Chitons

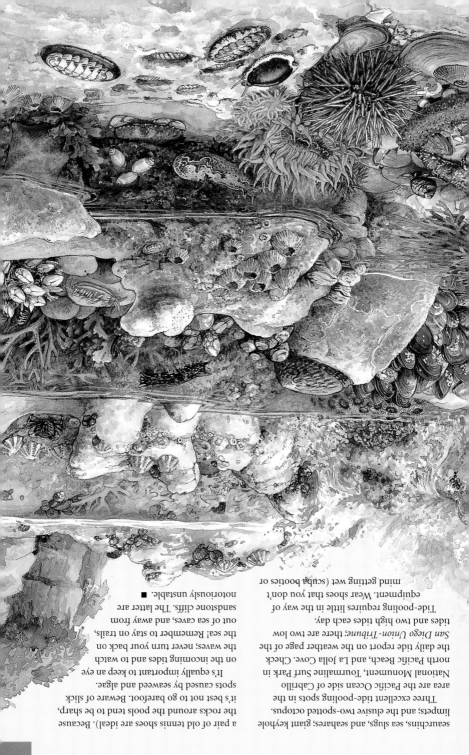

seaurchins, sea slugs, and seahares; giant keyhole limpets; and the elusive two-spotted octopus.

Three excellent tide-pooling spots in the area are the Pacific Ocean side of Cabrillo National Monument, Tourmaline Surf Park in north Pacific Beach, and La Jolla Cove. Check the daily tide report on the weather page of the *San Diego Union-Tribune*; there are two low tides and two high tides each day.

Tide-pooling requires little in the way of equipment. Wear shoes that you don't mind getting wet (scuba booties or a pair of old tennis shoes are ideal). Because the rocks around the pools tend to be sharp, it's best not to go barefoot. Beware of slick spots caused by seaweed and algae.

It's equally important to keep an eye on the incoming tides and to watch the waves; never turn your back on the sea! Remember to stay on trails, out of sea caves, and away from sandstone cliffs. The latter are notoriously unstable. ■

Cabrillo National Monument

GRACING THE TIP OF POINT LOMA IS ONE OF SAN DIEGO'S most beloved spots: Cabrillo National Monument, consistently rated among the National Park Service's top three most visited national monuments. Each year, more than 1.1 million people make the scenic drive to the end of the peninsula to take in the spectacular views, learn a little local history, and explore coastal landscapes that have remained virtually unchanged for hundreds of years.

Cabrillo National Monument

www.nps.gov/cabr

🚹 139 B1

✉ 1800 Cabrillo Memorial Dr.

☎ 619-557-5450

💲 $

🚍 Bus: 26 from the Old Town Trolley Station in downtown San Diego, terminating at the monument entrance

Created in 1913 at the behest of President Woodrow Wilson, the monument is dedicated to the memory of explorer Juan Rodríguez Cabrillo. A veteran of the Spanish campaign to vanquish the Aztecs, Cabrillo was pursuing several goals: He was seeking a trade route to Asia, mapping the uncharted coastline, and searching for a mythical passage between the Atlantic and Pacific that was supposed to lie just north of Mexico. Embarking from Navidad, Mexico, Cabrillo's three ships navigated the west coast of Mexico before cruising into San Diego Bay in September of 1542. They stayed six days before continuing north along the coast; within days of departing San Diego, however, Cabrillo fell and broke a bone. Infection set in and the captain died. Even though historians believe the ships may have reached the Oregon coast, the expedition was deemed a failure; it found neither a trade route, great riches, nor the legendary Strait of Anian.

Inside the **visitor center** is a scale model of Cabrillo's flagship, the *San Salvador*. The center also

has a great bookstore, and an auditorium where you can see slide shows on the monument's human and natural history. The terrace outside affords magnificent views of the city skyline and ships entering and exiting San Diego Bay. Crowning an overlook near the visitor center is a limestone image of Cabrillo; it's a replica of the 1939 statue by Portuguese sculptor Alvaro DeBree that originally stood on the spot but couldn't endure the winds and damp climate.

The park's most recognizable feature is the **Old Point Loma Lighthouse.** Completed in 1855, the Cape Cod-style building and tower looks more like a fairy-tale cottage than a hardworking light station. But for nearly four decades, this was the only lighthouse along the San Diego coast. Unfortunately, it was a bit of a folly: Perched 422 feet above the waterline, the beacon was often shrouded in fog. Not only that, but the architects had neglected to include a foghorn in their

adorable design, rendering the light virtually useless in foul weather. On foggy nights, the light keeper patrolled the rocky shore with a shotgun, firing a blast into the air every so often to warn ships away. By 1891, the old beacon had been retired in favor of a less attractive but much more useful lighthouse at the bottom of the bluff. After two major restoration efforts by the National Park Service, the roof now possesses historically accurate wooden shingles, the interior has been redecorated with Victorian-era wallpaper and furniture, and the correct size and type of third-order Fresnel lens has been installed in the tower. The first two floors are open daily to the public; the tower is open on special occasions only.

East of the old lighthouse you'll find the start of the **Bayside Trail,** a partially paved hiking route that follows an old U.S. Army roadway through typical coastal chaparral and sage scrub. The 2-mile (round-

Cabrillo National Monument, at the tip of Point Loma, was the first coastal meeting site between Europeans and indigenous Californians.

An artist transfers sea and sand to canvas.

trip) trail descends 300 feet toward the water, passing remnants of the elaborate defenses that safeguarded San Diego Bay during World War I and World War II.

Wayside exhibits along the trail provide information on native plants and animals and other aspects of the local ecosystem. Among the flora that thrive in the local sage scrub are buckwheat, Indian paintbrush, prickly pear cactus, lemonade berry, and toyon.

You might also catch a glimpse of local wildlife. Peregrine falcons ride updrafts on the harbor side of Point Loma, while Anna's hummingbirds are found much closer to the ground, flitting among the flowers. The area is also home to the gray fox and the Pacific rattlesnake.

Ambling along the ridge-top walkways south of the lighthouse, you eventually reach the lofty **Whale Overlook,** where it's often possible to spot California gray whales frolicking in the offshore waters during their annual 14,000-mile round-trip migration between Alaska and Baja California. Look for them from late December until early March, when they are on the southward leg of their migration. Bring a good pair of binoculars and watch for their characteristic heart-shaped spouts beyond the kelp beds. Farther north along the ridge, a new exhibit relates the military history of Point Loma during World War II, including data on the 16-inch guns at **Battery Ashburn** that could fire 2,300-pound shells nearly 30 miles into the Pacific.

The only way to reach the national monument's Pacific shore is to exit the park and make a sharp left onto **Cabrillo Road,** which descends steeply toward the ocean. As you turn, notice the historical marker on the grassy slope to the right. Two milestones of sailplane history took place on this spot: the first American glider trip to exceed an hour's duration (a 1929 flight by William H. Bowlus) and a 1930 world-record flight by John C. Barstow of more than 15 hours.

The first thing you meet at the bottom of the hill is the "new" Point Loma Lighthouse, in continuous service since 1891 and now operated by the U.S. Coast Guard. It is not open to the public. Farther along is a parking lot, where signs point the way to short coastal trails and tide pools.

The National Park Service organizes a number of special events during the year, including the annual **Whale Watch Weekend** in January and the anniversary of the first lighting of the Old Point Loma Lighthouse in November. The biggest event of the year is the **Cabrillo Festival** in September, a showcase for Iberian and Native American culture that features everything from Portuguese folk dancing and Spanish cuisine to Kumeyaay basket weaving. The week-long festival also includes a living history camp and a reenactment of Cabrillo's historic landing on San Diego Bay. (Call the monument for a schedule.) ■

Ocean Beach

OCEAN BEACH DOESN'T BEAR QUITE THE HISTORICAL gravitas of its Point Loma neighbors, which may be why it feels comfortable marching to a distinctly different drumbeat. Its sea-view bungalows are now worth small fortunes, yet a blue-collar sensibility prevails along its palm-lined streets.

Ocean Beach
Map p. 139
Bus: 23 from downtown San Diego

Windswept dunes dominated he terrain when the Point Loma Land & Town Company established a seaside subdivision called Ocean Beach in the 1880s. If you didn't have a horse, the only way to reach downtown in those days was to take a stagecoach across the hump of Point Loma, then a steamboat ferry across the bay.

"OB" (as locals fondly call it) slumbered in sunny obscurity until the 1960s, when it became the center of San Diego's psychedelic counterculture. Head shops and tie-dye outlets flourished. The Strand Theater was the coolest place in San Diego to see the film *Easy Rider* because the audience included real bikers. By the end of the 1970s, however, most of the trendies had migrated to Mission and Pacific Beaches, and the neighborhood had inherited a threadbare feel.

Nowadays Ocean Beach moves along at a much slower pace—and with a lot less pretense—than San Diego's other beach 'burbs. Alternative lifestyles continue to be in vogue, and the occasional Jimi Hendrix poster still pops up in the assortment of shops along Newport Avenue.

At the western end of the avenue is the popular **Ocean Beach Pier,** a T-shaped construction that extends half a mile offshore. The pier is a perfect perch for contemplating the sunset or getting a bird's-eye view of surfers chasing waves on the beach adjacent. A bait and tackle shop dispenses anything you need for fishing off the pier.

North of the pier, **Ocean Beach Park** connects the sandy beach to the grassy area behind it. Hard-core beach-volleyball players congregate here on weekends. And with OB throwing up one of the best breaks along the San Diego coast, surfers can be found at just about any time.

Farther north, at the mouth of the San Diego River, the perennially popular **Dog Beach** welcomes canines ecstatic at the chance to frolic leash-free along the strand. ■

Surfing is just one of the lifestyles that Ocean Beach has long embraced.

Shelter Island

Shelter Island

139 B3

Humphrey's Concerts by the Bay
139 B3
2241 Shelter Island Dr.
619-523-1010
$$$$$

Paying homage to the local fishing industry is "Tunaman's Memorial," a bronze sculpture by Franco Vianello.

TOWERING PALM TREES, SLEEK SAILBOATS, FUNKY TROPICAL architecture: In many respects, Shelter Island is quintessential San Diego. But the island is actually a recent creation. It was built between 1932 and 1950, when millions of tons of sand and mud dredged from the bay were heaped onto a shoal off Point Loma.

Standing guard over the narrow spit that connects Shelter Island to the mainland is the 1886 **San Diego Yacht Club.** Over the years, the yacht club has nurtured a number of world-class sailors, including three-time America's Cup winner Dennis Conner. In addition to backing several of Conner's America's Cup campaigns, the club has hosted the prestigious sailing race three times.

Across the yacht basin is another Shelter Island landmark, the waterfront retreat called **Humphrey's,** which stages concerts in a 1,300-seat outdoor amphitheater next to the bay. The concert season runs from May through September, and anyone with a small boat can catch a free show from the water. Artists

who have appeared over the years range from Ray Charles to Willie Nelson to Alice Cooper.

Beyond Humphrey's, a palm-shaded drive winds to the western tip of Shelter Island, passing waterfront resorts, marinas, and picnic areas with stunning views of San Diego Bay. Tucked beneath the palms are two poignant monuments. Inside a small Japanese-style pavilion is the 2.5-ton **Friendship Bell,** a gift from the citizens of Yokohama (San Diego's sister city) and a token of friendship between peoples on opposite sides of the Pacific. The bronze **"Tunaman's Memorial"** near the pier honors the Portuguese, Italian, Japanese, and Slavic immigrants who established the city's tuna fleet. ■

Harbor Island

LIKE ITS SLIGHTLY OLDER SISTER, HARBOR ISLAND WAS born of land scooped from the floor of San Diego Bay and molded into an island. Almost from the moment it was completed in 1969, the little landmass began to bristle with high-rise hotels eager to take advantage of Harbor Island's proximity to both the airport and downtown San Diego. Over the intervening years, more amenities have been added, including boat basins and waterfront parks.

Harbor Island is perhaps best known for its theme restaurants. The **Reuben E. Lee** (619-291-1880) at the island's eastern tip provides a view of downtown San Diego from tables aboard a replica Mississippi River steamboat. At the other end of the island, **Tom Ham's Lighthouse** (619-291-9110) sits beneath a 55-foot-high replica of the original Point Loma beacon. It is said to be the only restaurant in America that doubles as an official U.S. Coast Guard light station. The beam flashes every five seconds.

On the mainland opposite Harbor Island are two small but intriguing green spaces. The new **Cancer Survivors Park** rests in the shadow of the traffic exchange that connects the island to the airport. The two-acre park is dedicated to the millions of living Americans who have been diagnosed with cancer. In addition to a fountain and walkways, the park features sculptures and plaques with inspirational messages and advice on confronting the disease.

Farther west along the waterfront is **Spanish Landing Park,** a place of pleasant waterfront lawns, benches, and walkways. The site commemorates the 1769 meeting between the crews of two Spanish galleons and an expedition led by Padre Junípero Serra and Captain Gaspar de Portolá. Padre Serra stayed behind to found Mission San Diego de Alcalá. ■

The Reuben E. Lee, a paddlewheeler-cum-restaurant, dazzles diners with its down-town views.

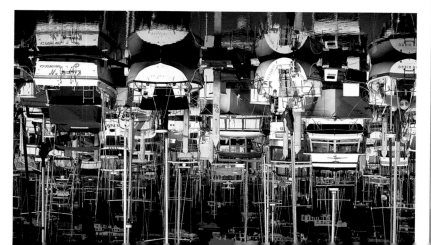

A Shelter Island marina provides landfall for sailors who breeze into town.

More places to visit around Point Loma

LINDBERGH FIELD

San Diego's International Airport at Lindbergh Field holds a special place in history. By the end of the 19th century, the muddy wasteland between downtown and Point Loma had come to be called Dutch Flats. No one could find much use for the area until the dawn of aviation, when local pilots discovered that Dutch Flats provided an ideal place to launch their newfangled flying machines.

One of those pilots was T. Claude Ryan, a retired Army aviator who established a small aircraft factory and passenger airline operation on the edge of the flats. In 1927, Ryan's workshop designed and produced one of the most famous planes in aviation—the *Spirit of St. Louis*. Flight tests were staged over Dutch Flats with a young pilot named Charles Lindbergh at the controls. A month later, Lindbergh and the *Spirit of St. Louis* made their historic transatlantic flight.

Dedicated in 1928, Lindbergh Field soon grew into a hub of West Coast aviation. Not long after, Consolidated Aircraft (later Convair) unveiled a major production facility on the airfield's northern flank. During World War II, the factory was vital to the war effort, churning out more than 6,700 B-24 Liberator bombers and 2,100 Catalina flying boats.

Nowadays Lindbergh Field is also known for its public art; see, for example, the humorous "At the Gate" by Gary Hughes and "In Search of Wilderness" by Les Perhacs. San Diego's port commission organizes free behind-the-scenes tours of some areas of the airport and its artwork. 139 D4 North Harbor Dr. 619-686-6200 Bus: 992 from downtown San Diego

MARINE CORPS RECRUIT DEPOT

The quaint Spanish Colonial ambience of the U.S. Marine Corps Recruit Depot (MCRD) belies the fact that this sprawling facility along Barnett Avenue is the place where aspiring leathernecks have gotten their heads shaved, their boots fitted, and their ears blasted by angry drill sergeants since 1923.

If the arches and tiled roofs remind you of Balboa Park, it's because architect Bertram Goodhue, who designed many park structures, was also responsible for 25 buildings at MCRD. The installation has enjoyed a long partnership with Hollywood dating back to its location for the 1926 blockbuster *Tell It to the Marines*, starring Lon Chaney.

The Command Museum inside the base is open to the public. Exhibits incorporating vehicles, weapons, uniforms, and historic pictures trace the history and traditions of the Marine Corps in southern California. 139 C4 The Command Museum, 1600 Henderson Ave. 619-524-1011 Mon.-Fri. 8-4, Sat. 12-4 Bus: 34 or 34A from downtown San Diego ■

Nestled between the urban scene of downtown San Diego and the cultural attractions of La Jolla are the parks, marinas, and beaches of Mission Bay, where San Diegans come to play.

Mission Bay & beaches

Trophies await the winning eight at Mission Bay's annual San Diego Crew Classic.

Mission Bay & beaches

MISSION BAY, A WATERY PLAYGROUND BETWEEN DOWNTOWN AND LA JOLLA, is one of the primary reasons why San Diegans cherish their laid-back city and its outdoor lifestyle. Sapphire coves and sprawling, emerald-green lawns make this 4,236-acre aquatic park a haven for just about anything you can do beneath a shimmering southern California sun—swimming and fishing, sailing and windsurfing, kayaking and canoeing, cycling and in-line skating, flag football and playground basketball, kite-flying and sand-castle building, or even (heresy!) such less-kinetic pleasures as reading a book beneath the shade of a bayside palm.

When you consider the thousands of people and hundreds of watercraft that throng the waterway each weekend, it's hard to realize that Mission Bay is a relatively new creation. Before the padres showed up in the 1500s, the area was a coastal estuary that served as a breeding ground for aquatic birds and a rich food source for Native American residents. Because it was stippled with treacherous sand-bars and virtually unnavigable, the estuary was dubbed Bahia Falsa (False Bay) by the Spanish.

Not until the late 1940s did local government propose a dramatic transformation of the eight-square-mile swamp. Funded by municipal bonds and spearheaded by the U.S. Army Corps of Engineers, a massive reclamation project—one of the largest public works in California history—was launched. Marshaling expertise gained during the recent war effort, the engineers fashioned artificial islands and bays, shifted millions of tons of sand, and dredged a proper outlet to the Pa-

cific Ocean, transforming the area into a recreational paradise.

Today Mission Bay aims for a balance between public use and private enterprise. Most of the land is reserved for parks, playgrounds, and picnic areas, as well as public boat ramps, aquatic centers, and campgrounds. The remaining parcels are leased to a variety of commercial ventures including waterfront resort hotels, marinas, and SeaWorld of San Diego, the internationally known aquatic theme park. Overall, the park encompasses 27 miles of shoreline and 19 miles of beach.

Settled before Mission Bay's topographical makeover, shoreline communities such as Pacific Beach and Mission Beach boomed in tandem with the park. The former's rowdy bars and music clubs make it a haven for the young and the restless, while Mission Beach is San Diego's highest-density residential area; inside these tightly packed apartments and seafront bungalows, the party never seems to end. ■

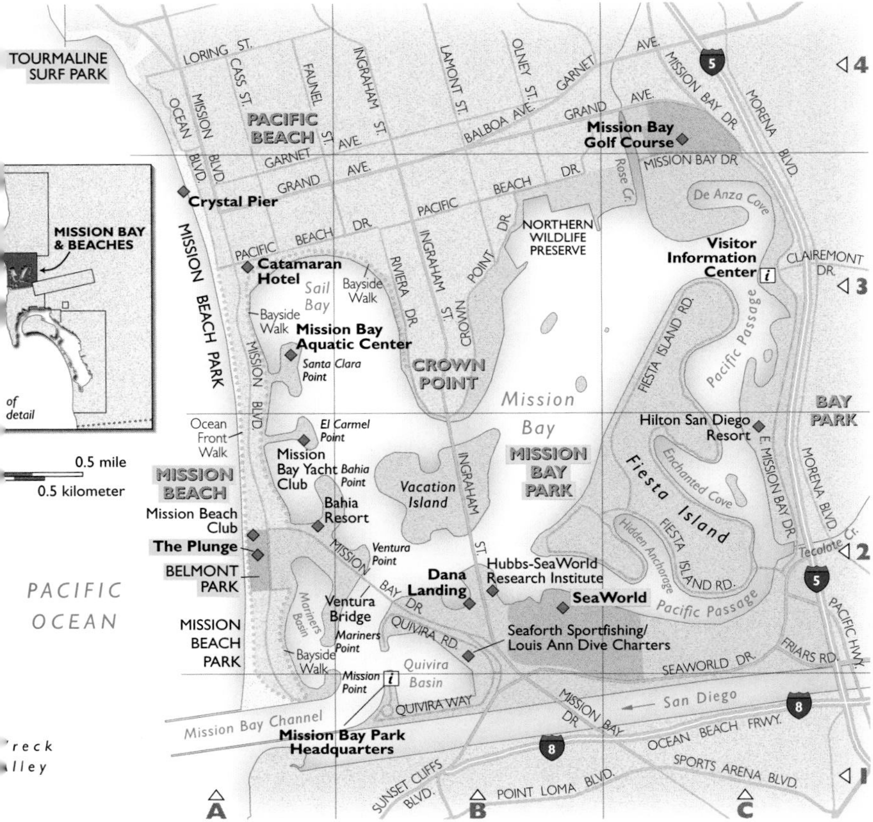

TOURMALINE
SURF PARK

LORING ST.
CASS ST.
FAUNEL ST.
INGRAHAM ST.
LAMONT ST.
OLNEY ST.
GARNET AVE.
MISSION BAY DR.
MORENA BLVD.

OCEAN BLVD.
MISSION BLVD.

PACIFIC BEACH

GARNET AVE.
BALBOA AVE.

GRAND AVE.

Mission Bay Golf Course

MISSION BAY DR.

4

GRAND AVE.

Crystal Pier

PACIFIC BEACH DR.

Rose Cr.

De Anza Cove

MISSION BAY
& BEACHES

PACIFIC BEACH DR.

Catamaran Hotel

RIVIERA DR.

POINT

CROWN DR.

NORTHERN
WILDLIFE
PRESERVE

Visitor Information Center ℹ

CLAIREMONT DR.

3

MISSION BEACH PARK

Sail Bay
Bayside Walk

Bayside Walk

Mission Bay Aquatic Center

Santa Clara Point

CROWN POINT

Mission

FIESTA ISLAND RD.

Pacific Passage

of
detail

Bay

Hilton San Diego
Resort

E. MISSION BAY DR.
MORENA BLVD.

BAY PARK

0.5 mile
0.5 kilometer

Ocean Front Walk

El Carmel Point

Mission Bay Yacht Club

Bahia Point

MISSION BAY PARK

Enchanted Cove

Fiesta Island

MISSION BEACH

Vacation Island

INGRAHAM ST.

FIESTA ISLAND RD.

Hidden Anchorage

Tecolote Cr.

2

Mission Beach Club

Bahia Resort

The Plunge

Ventura Point

Dana Landing

Hubbs-SeaWorld
Research Institute

SeaWorld

Pacific Passage

PACIFIC HWY.

BELMONT PARK

PACIFIC OCEAN

MISSION BLVD.

BAY DR.

Mariners Basin

Ventura Bridge

Mariners Point

QUIVIRA RD.

Seaforth Sportfishing/
Louis Ann Dive Charters

FRIARS RD.

MISSION BEACH PARK

Bayside Walk

Mission Point

Quivira Basin

SEAWORLD DR.

8

*reck
lley*

Mission Bay Channel

QUIVIRA WAY

Mission Bay Park Headquarters

MISSION BAY DR.

San Diego

OCEAN BEACH FRWY.

8

SUNSET CLIFFS BLVD.

POINT LOMA BLVD.

SPORTS ARENA BLVD.

1

A   **B**   **C**

Locals will use anything that rolls to get to Mission Bay beaches.

Mission Bay Park

Mission Bay Park
www.sannet.gov/park-and-recreation/parks/missbay.shtml

🅜 153 B2
✉ 2581 Quivira Ct.
☎ 858-221-8901
🚌 Bus: 34 from downtown San Diego or Pacific Beach

WHERE YOU START IN MISSION BAY—AND WHERE YOU END up—hinges on the sort of recreation you've got in mind. If you want a little of everything, a good jumping-off point is Playa Pacifica Cove on the bay's eastern edge, about halfway between the Claremont Drive and SeaWorld Drive exits off Interstate 5. With its plentiful parking, calm waters, and rambling lawns, the cove is ideal for picnics and swimming; there's even a small "desert island." Overlooking the cove is the posh Hilton San Diego Resort, which offers a waterfront restaurant, bar, and snack shop.

A member of the Navy SEALs' Leap Frogs parachute team heads for a soft landing in Mission Bay.

You don't have to be a hotel guest to hire equipment at **CP Watersports** *(858-275-8945 or 276-4010 ext. 2945)*, where an armada of motorboats, catamarans, sailboards, kayaks, and personal watercraft gathers along the beach. Bicycles and in-line skates are also available.

Breezy waterfront walkways lead north and south from **Playa Pacifica.** These paved trails are popular with joggers, cyclists, skaters, and folks who crave nothing more strenuous than a pleasant stroll at sunset. The northern route passes a **visitor information center** *(800-422-5749 or 619-276-8200)* at the foot of Clairemont Drive. The center offers information about— and admission tickets to—various San Diego attractions.

Another quarter-mile beyond the information center is **De Anza Cove,** where picnic areas, a sheltered beach, and grassy volleyball courts are the main attraction. Nearby is the tiny **Mission Bay Golf Course,** an 18-hole "executive" course where towering floodlights permit evening play. The facility also has a driving range and miniature golf.

Parkland resumes on the south side of the Hilton San Diego Resort, where the waterfront path rambles along Tecolote Shores near a grassy hill that is popular with kite fliers. The San Diego Kite Club meets here for casual flying on the second Saturday of every month; each January the knoll is the site of the New Year's Day Fly.

Farther south, on the other side of Tecolote Creek, a causeway leads to **Fiesta Island,** largest of the bay's sandy castaways. The island remains largely undeveloped—a realm of sand dunes, sagebrush, and beaches where you will often find yourself alone. With its rough edges and wide-open spaces, Fiesta attracts a crowd that's markedly different from the one that visits the bay's better-groomed parklands. The entire island is leash-free, giving dog walkers a place to let their animals scamper through the sand and the surf.

Hidden Anchorage, on Fiesta Island's southern flank, offers a special ramp and course for water-skiers. Along the shores of **Enchanted Cove** is a group campground and aquatic center *(619-221-8901)* where Scouts, Indian Guides, and other adolescent tribes can make as much noise as they like. The island's razor-straight western edge is a gathering place for weekend tailgaters and an excellent spot from which to watch the earsplitting hydroplane races that take place on the bay each fall.

Fiesta Island has two athletic claims to fame. One is Over-the-Line (OTL), an evolved (some would say mutated) form of beach softball invented by San Diegans in the 1950s in which teams of three try to out-hit their opponents. The **Old Mission Bay Beach Athletic Club** *(619-688-0817)* hosts the island's annual World Championship Over-the-Line Tournament. Spanning two weekends in July, the tourney normally draws hundreds of teams and more than 50,000 spectators. The island can also boast of having hosted the world's first triathlon competition, in 1974.

SeaWorld (see pp. 158–159) and its exotic theme-park skyline dominate Mission Bay's southern flank. If you're in the mood for something more organic, amble over to the south side of **Sea-World Drive,** where a quiet waterfront walkway and bike path leads along the banks of the San Diego River. Armored starfish, ghost shrimp, painted limpets, and California halibut are among the species that thrive in this marshy estuary, a wildlife reserve where boating and fishing are prohibited. The serenity makes this quiet stretch prime nesting habitat for the California least tern.

West of SeaWorld, beyond the big traffic interchange, **Quivira Basin** and **Dana Landing** form the twin hubs of Mission Bay's maritime culture. Marinas, boat shops, fishing-equipment stores, and seafood restaurants line the bustling waterfront. This is the place to go if you want to rent a boat, purchase a catamaran, fetch a little bait and tackle, or savor the taste of fresh albacore tuna caught that very day off Baja California. **Seaforth Sportfishing** offers fishing charters to the Point Loma kelp beds and the Coronado Islands off Mexico, as well as whale-watching cruises. **Mission Bay Park Headquarters** *(858-221-8901)* at the end of Quivira Way provides park maps and information on various activities.

The 116-foot **Ventura Bridge**

Mission Bay Golf Course
www.nmwa.org
⚠ 153 C4
✉ 2702 N. Mission Bay Dr.
☎ 858-490-3370
🚌 Bus: 30 from downtown San Diego or Pacific Beach

Seaforth Sportfishing
www.seaforthlanding.com
⚠ 153 B2
✉ 1717 Quivira Rd.
☎ 619-224-3383
🚌 Bus: 34 from downtown San Diego or Pacific Beach

"I didn't know SEALs could fly!"

Mission Bay Aquatic Center

www.mbac.nu

🏠 153 A3

✉ 1001 Santa Clara Pl.

☎ 858-488-1036

🚌 Bus: 34 from downtown San Diego or Pacific Beach

links Quivira Basin and Dana Landing to trendy **Mission Beach**. Half a dozen man-made peninsulas with their own unique personalities preside over the western edge of the bay. **Mission Point** harbors a great playground and wonderful views of boats threading the channel to the open ocean.

The sandy shores of **Mariners Point** are ideal for beach volleyball and Over-the-Line softball; Mariners also hosts major international skateboard competitions. Families flock to **Ventura Point** for its placid picnic and swimming areas. Bahia Resort (800-576-4229 or 858-488-0551), a sprawling bayside complex that was a favorite retreat of Richard Nixon's in the 1960s, dominates **Bahia Point**. Its waterfront walkway is open to the public.

El Carmel Point is home to both the Mission Bay Yacht Club and the sleek sculls of the Cogges-hall Rowing Center. **Santa Clara Point** offers a public boat ramp, a public recreation center (including tennis courts and a weight room), and the **Mission Bay Aquatic Center**, where you can learn to sail, kayak, windsurf, or water-ski. If you already know how, the center rents watercraft and equipment.

Bayside Walk, a scenic path for pedestrians and pedalers, winds all the way up the western edge of Mission Bay from Mission Point to the towering Catamaran Hotel, known for its lush tropical gardens and mock-Polynesian decor. The path continues into Pacific Beach, around the northern edge of Sail Bay, and down the western flank of Crown Point. In addition to leafy picnic areas and playgrounds, the point's fine white strand draws sand-castle aficionados from around the globe.

Tucked into the northwest corner of Crown Point is the **Northern Wildlife Preserve** *(858-221-8901),* a fenced-off area where two endangered bird species—the light-footed clapper rail and the Belding's savanna sparrow—nest among the pickleweed and cordgrass of the marshy estuary at the mouth of Rose Creek. A bridge connects Crown Point to **Vacation Island,** the second largest island in the bay; it's home to a model yacht basin, ski-boat ramps, and (honoring its moniker, perhaps?) yet another waterfront resort hotel. This isle is also the launching site for the bay's annual hydroplane grand prix. ■

Modelmakers prepare to launch their craft at Mission Bay's Model Boat Race, held each year at the San Diego Model Yacht Basin.

Pacific & Mission Beaches

SURFBOARDS AND STRING BIKINIS, HUNKY LIFEGUARDS and party-hearty college kids: Pacific Beach (PB) is about as close as San Diego gets to Miami's gaudy South Beach. The action—both on and off the sand—never seems to stop, especially in the rowdy clubs of Garnet Avenue and on the beachside boardwalk.

This endless-summer image belies a tranquil past: The flatlands between La Jolla and Mission Bay were once cloaked in groves of lemon and orange trees. The community, founded in 1887, was linked to downtown San Diego by a steam train. Victorian hotels and dance pavilions, precursors of today's tourist business, rose along the shore.

Crystal Pier, the neighborhood's most enduring landmark, opened in 1927. Insect-ridden wood pilings condemned the original pier to a watery grave, but it was eventually rebuilt in its present 750-foot form. Besides being an excellent spot for fishing and a great place to watch PB's ever-present surfers, Crystal Pier's quaint clapboard hotel and cottages allow you to sleep atop the waves.

Stretching south from PB is a sandy, 2-mile-long peninsula called **Mission Beach.** Wedged between the Pacific Ocean and Mission Bay, this breezy, waterfront neighborhood is a warren of one-way alleys and narrow "courts" named after other famous beaches. If peace and quiet top your list, stroll along tranquil **Bayside Walk** on the peninsula's leeward edge. Otherwise lose yourself in the perpetual motion machine that is **Ocean Front Walk** on the west side. Bikes, surfboards, and in-line skates can be rented at the Mission Beach Club, north of Belmont Park.

The waters off Mission Beach harbor one of southern California's top scuba attractions—**Wreck Alley.** Several mothballed military vessels were purposely sunk about a mile offshore to create an artificial reef, including the 366-foot Canadian destroyer H.M.C.S. *Yukon* in 2000. Lois Ann Dive Charters is one of several San Diego outfits offering dive trips to Wreck Alley. ∎

Crystal Pier

◪ 153 A3
✉ 4500 Ocean Blvd.
☎ 858-483-6983
(hotel)
🚍 Bus: 30 or 34 from downtown San Diego or La Jolla

Mission Beach Club

◪ 153 A2
✉ 704 Ventura Pl.
☎ 858-488-5050
🚍 Bus: 34 from downtown San Diego or Pacific Beach

Lois Ann Dive Charters

www.loisann.com
◪ 153 B2
☎ 800-201-4381 or 858-780-0130

The thighs have it: Local beaches host many an activity besides sunbathing and water sports.

SeaWorld

SINCE THE EARLY 1960s, SEAWORLD HAS TRANSFORMED itself from a modest attraction with mock mermaids and performing dolphins into an internationally known park sheltering more than 12,000 marine and aquatic animals. More than half a dozen shows and 20 other watery attractions showcase the splendor and infinite variety of the world's oceans, from San Diego's own tide pools to the South Seas and the Arctic wilderness.

Welcoming four million visitors per year, SeaWorld is one of San Diego's (and California's) most popular tourist attractions. It is indisputably a commercial venture, yet the park has also emerged as a local leader in wildlife conservation and public education. From the performing killer whales to the walk-through shark habitat to the hands-on sting-

ray pool, nearly every SeaWorld attraction mixes entertainment with an environmental message. The park's animal rescue and rehabilitation team saves about 100 creatures every year, including beached whales, ailing sea lions, and injured pelicans. After rest and medical treatment, about 70 percent of the creatures are returned to

the wild. Meanwhile, the Hubbs-SeaWorld Research Institute, located just west of the park, has become a center for oceanography and marine mammal research.

SeaWorld's trademark is the killer whale, exemplified by the popular **Shamu Adventure show,** in which the gorgeous black-and-white creatures interact with wet-suited trainers in a massive, seven-million-gallon saltwater habitat. The animals swim faster, leap higher, and pirouette more gracefully than you can imagine. And did we mention their talent for water displacement? Don't sit in the first 14 rows unless you enjoy getting wet.

Another must is the **Dolphin Discovery show,** which high-

lights the remarkable intelligence and acrobatic skills of both bottle-nose dolphins and pilot whales. Nor should you miss the **Clyde and Seamore show,** where a variety of aquatic creatures—California sea lions, river otters, and a huge walrus—prove that animals can rival human comedians.

Not all the shows are animal based. **Cirque de la Mer,** one of the park's newer attractions, features colorfully attired and amazingly flexible humans. This watery summertime circus combines acrobatics, music, lavish costumes, and special effects.

Wild Arctic, an ingenious attraction, presents a chilly Arctic environment that includes polar bears, beluga whales, and walruses. Directly opposite is the **Penguin Encounter,** an Antarctic re-creation where more than 400 penguins strut their stuff in sub-freezing temperatures.

Not to be outdone by other southern California theme parks, SeaWorld has added thrill rides in recent years. Shipwreck Rapids is a simulated white-water raft trip complete with rapids, waterfalls, and caverns. Everyone gets soaked; bring a change of clothes or a typhoon-proof raincoat. If you're traveling with small children, an interlude at Shamu's Happy Harbor playground, with its climbing structure, sand pit, and mock pirate ship, provides a welcome respite from the crowds.

SeaWorld also offers auxiliary programs, including behind-the-scenes tours and a 90-minute dolphin program that allows guests to interact with marine mammals. The cost of these programs is separate from the regular admission; book them in advance. The park also stages evening entertainment during the summer, including fireworks over Mission Bay. ■

SeaWorld
www.seaworld.com
🅼 153 B2
✉ 500 SeaWorld Dr.
☎ 619-226-3901
$ $$$$$
🚍 Bus: 34 or 34A from downtown San Diego; 9 from Pacific Beach

Berths of a nation

learn the ropes of sailing.

Sailing and San Diego have long been synonymous. The city that has hosted three America's Cup regattas and given birth to half a dozen world yachting champions and Olympic medalists is one of the best places in the country to moor your boat or learn the ropes of sailing.

Shelter Island—home to the prestigious San Diego Yacht Club and a handful of other clubs and marinas—is the city's best-known sailing venue, but it is by no means the only place where you can dock, repair, or charter a sailboat. Right outside the airport lie the spiffy marinas and laid-back ambience of Harbor Island. Literally in the shadow of downtown's skyscrapers is the Embarcadero Marina, whose berths are within walking distance of Seaport Village and the Gaslamp Quarter.

Glorietta Bay harbors the Coronado Yacht Club and anchorages next to a bayside golf course. South Bay sailing centers include the Chula Vista Yacht Club and the posh Coronado Cays, Quivira Basin and Dana Landing in Mission Bay and Oceanside Harbor in the North County, meanwhile, support their

own fleets of private pleasure craft. Don't fret if you don't own a boat. Several companies, including **Classic Sailing Adventures** *(800-659-0141 or 619-224-0800)*, organize escorted sails around San Diego Bay and whale-watching cruises off the tip of Point Loma. As an alternative to waterfront hotels, **California Cruisin'** *(800-449-2248 or 619-296-8000)* has designed a "boat & breakfast" program that allows you to bunk down in luxurious yachts berthed at Shelter Island.

Charters are another option. You can rent sailboats by the hour (for a casual jaunt around San Diego Bay or Mission Bay) or by the week (for trips to Catalina, Los Angeles, or Baja California). Skipper the craft yourself or hire an experienced captain and crew. Bareboat charters from outfits such as the **San Diego Sailing Academy** *(800-441-8672 or 619-299-9247)* normally include insurance.

The Ruby Slipper (above) skips across San Diego Bay, while more serious ships vie in the America's Schooner Cup Regatta (below). Opposite: Vintage wheel of wood.

electricity, slip fees, and airport transfers.

If you can't tell the difference between a gunwale and a capstan, a few lessons may be in order. **Learn to Sail San Diego** *(800-792-9726 or 619-925-4778)* on Harbor Island is one of several companies that run week-long, live-aboard sailing courses on San Diego Bay. By the time they complete the course, most students will have learned to handle their own boats, earning an American Sailing Association certificate. ■

More places to visit around Mission Bay

BELMONT PARK

Coney Island meets Hollywood at Belmont Park, a raucous beachfront amusement park in the heart of Mission Beach. Unveiled at the height of the Roaring Twenties, the park offers a mixed bag of fun—thrill rides, arcade games, and carnie food in a setting that evokes bygone days by the shore.

The park's centerpiece is the celebrated Giant Dipper, a wooden roller coaster considered a state-of-the-art thrill ride when it opened in 1925. Derelict and dangerous, the 2,600-foot coaster was scheduled for demolition in the 1980s when a group of local citizens convened a "Save the Coaster" committee. They assumed ownership of the ride and succeeded in having it declared a national historic landmark. The San Diego Coaster Company then renovated the Giant Dipper and now runs the roller coaster itself.

Belmont Park boasts a number of other classic rides including the Liberty Carousel, Tilt-a-Whirl, Vertical Plunge, and bumper cars. For those too young to brave the big rides, the park provides Pirates Cove, a huge indoor play area for younger children.

The Giant Dipper, Belmont Park's 1925 wooden roller coaster, is a national historic landmark.

🗺 153 A2 ⊠ 3190 Mission Blvd. ☎ 858-488-1549 💲 $$ 🚌 Bus: 34 from downtown San Diego or Pacific Beach

THE PLUNGE

Inside the Belmont Park complex is a completely different attraction. Called The Plunge, it was dubbed the world's "largest indoor saltwater pool" when bathers took their first dip in it in 1925. Modeled after the museums in Balboa Park, the Spanish Renaissance design stands in startling contrast to the surrounding carnival rides. The 365,000-gallon pool was renovated in the late 1980s and is no longer saltwater, but it remains a popular spot for swimming lessons and exercise laps in 60-foot lanes. The water is kept at a constant 83°F.

🗺 153 A2 ⊠ 3115 Ocean Front Walk ☎ 858-488-3110 💲 $ 🚌 Bus: 34 from downtown San Diego or Pacific Beach

TOURMALINE SURF PARK

Situated at the north end of Pacific Beach, Tourmaline Surf Park is blessed with some of the region's best conditions for surfing and windsurfing. Waves break about a hundred yards from the beach and tend to be higher than in areas farther south. Swimming and shore fishing are forbidden. Facilities include showers and a free parking lot that often fills on weekends. Tide pools pock the rocky shore north of the park. 🗺 153 A4 🚌 Bus: 30 or 34 from downtown San Diego or La Jolla ■

Fine art, fine beaches, and cutting-edge science make seaside La Jolla and the nearby Golden Triangle two of the city's most fascinating areas.

La Jolla & the Golden Triangle

Colorful character enjoys the view at La Jolla Cove.

La Jolla & the Golden Triangle

WITH ITS SEASIDE VILLAS, STATELY PALMS, AND NARROW STREETS CRAWLING up sun-soaked hillsides, La Jolla looks like a village transplanted from the French Rivier to the southern California coast. The illusion continues amid the chic boutiques and ar galleries of downtown La Jolla and on the golden sands of its beaches, where many a Hollywood icon has strolled.

This most desirable part of San Diego makes no bones about its image as "Beverly Hills by the Sea"; it has gone to great lengths to preserve its privileged ambience and architectural integrity. But don't judge a book by its cover. La Jolla may be gilt-edged at first glance, but local traditions run much deeper than diamonds and dowagers.

As one might expect from the town's location, the Pacific Ocean has always played an important role in local life. La Jolla gave birth to the world's first skin-diving club and has nurtured many oceanographic discoveries. The surf culture endemic to southern California reaches an apex along legendary local strands such as Windansea and the clothing-optional Blacks Beach. And La Jolla Cove serves as a model of how people and na-

ture can thrive around the same body of water. Science is another local stalwart. For nearly a century, La Jolla has cultivated a reputation as one of the globe's intellectual centers, a place where learned men and women could come together, compare notes, and change the world in which we live. The community now harbors one of the nation's greatest concentrations of biotech labs, while the nearby Golden Triangle—the area bounded by Calif. 52 and Interstates 5 and 805—has transformed itself into the Silicon Valley of telecommunications.

They may have christened it with the Spanish word for "jewel" (from the word *joya*), but otherwise the Spanish paid little attention to La Jolla because they used San Diego's anchorage to the south. Late 19th-century developers saw the potential of such a gorgeous area, but ran

A hang glider and pilot take flight from 300-foot-high Torrey Pines Gliderport.

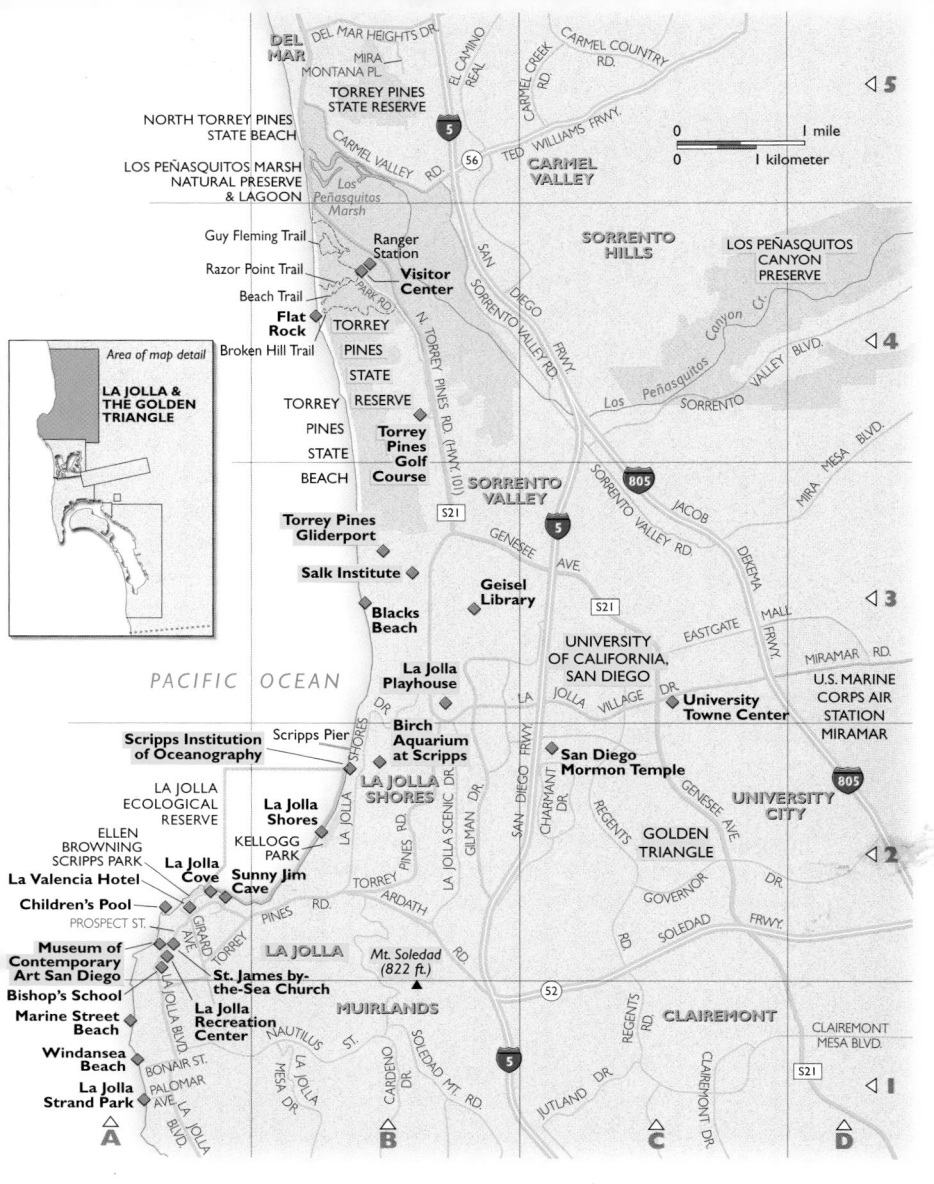

out of money before they could turn their blue-print dreams into reality.

Then, in 1896, newspaper heiress Ellen Browning Scripps came to town. She turned the sleepy seaside village into an architectural showplace and budding scientific hub. From the public library to Torrey Pines to the Scripps Institution of Oceanography, nearly every local landmark has benefited from her philanthropy.

Downtown La Jolla remains the communi-ty's heart and soul. Above the downtown, pala-tial houses surrounding Mount Soledad occu-py the Muirlands. La Jolla Shores describes the broad beach and coastal plain just north of downtown. Inland are the tree-shrouded cam-pus of the University of California, San Diego and the high-tech factories of the Golden Tri-angle. La Jolla's northern extreme is marked by the rugged but hikable 2,000 seaside acres of Torrey Pines State Reserve. ∎

Downtown La Jolla

Window-shopping the ritzy boutiques of downtown La Jolla is not for the faint of plastic.

GRACED BY ART GALLERIES, FASHION BOUTIQUES, AND sidewalk cafés, downtown La Jolla is a great place for a casual stroll or a serious shopping expedition. The "village" covers several dozen blocks inside an area roughly bounded by Torrey Pines Road, Pearl Street, and the sapphire waters of the Pacific Ocean.

The heart of downtown La Jolla is the five-point intersection where Prospect Street, Girard Avenue, and Coast Boulevard converge in a tangle of traffic and crosswalks. Looming over the junction is "the Pink Lady"—the seven-story **La Valencia Hotel**, a masterpiece of California-Mediterranean design that went up in 1926. The hotel's pink stucco walls and domed tower overlook tropical gardens that spill down the hillside toward La Jolla Cove. Among the luminaries drawn to the hotel have been Greta Garbo, Charlie Chaplin, Oprah Winfrey, and Pearl Jam (in fact, lead vocalist Eddie Vedder worked here as a security guard in the early 1990s). Even if you're not staying at La

Valencia, soak up the atmosphere with a stroll through the lobby or a drink in the restored Whaling Bar, where you can take in its famous nautical mural.

East of La Valencia is a bustling three-block stretch of Prospect Street lined with art galleries and fashionable restaurants. The commercial strip ends at Cave Street, which plunges down to La Jolla's famous seafront caverns and cove. Most of the village's historic buildings—eye-catching structures whose function is nearly overwhelmed by their astonishing form—cluster on Prospect. They include **St. James by-the-Sea** church, the **La Jolla Recreation Center** (1915), and the **Bishop's School,** and the

Museum of Contemporary Art San Diego (see p. 170).

Many of these were designed in part or whole by Irving Gill, master of the California-Mediterranean style. From Bishop's School, La Jolla Boulevard shoots downhill toward the sea. **Childrens Pool**—donated in 1931 by philanthropist Ellen Browning Scripps to the youngsters of San Diego—is actually a small, sandy cove shielded by a breakwater. Once a great place for a beach picnic, the pool has been claimed by harbor seals (and their unmistakable aroma). Clamber down the breakwater for a closer view of these sleek squatters basking on the sand or on rocks offshore.

Most pleasant of La Jolla's green spaces is **Ellen Browning Scripps Park,** which stretches between Childrens Pool and La Jolla Cove. Its wide lawns, shaded by Washington palms and Monterey cypress trees, are ideal for kite flying, Frisbee tossing, and aimless relaxing. **La Jolla Cove** itself is one of the more picturesque spots along the San Diego coast, with golden sand and azure water set against wave-splashed cliffs.

The waterfront road and walkway continue east and uphill along the clifftop to the **Cave Store,** an old oceanfront cottage that now houses a small coffee stand, antique shop, and the entrance to **Sunny Jim Cave** *(fee).* The largest of seven wave-cut caverns that pock the La Jolla coast, the cave's small waterfront terrace lies at the bottom of 145 wooden steps. Local legend attributes the cave's name to *Wonderful Wizard of Oz* author L. Frank Baum, who supposedly thought the cave's seaside entrance resembled an early 1900s British cartoon character named Sunny Jim. During Prohibition, the grotto was allegedly a staging point for rumrunners coming up from Mexico.

An unpaved footpath called Coast Walk begins on the waterfront side of Cave Store, winding through a cool pine grove, down into a palm-filled canyon, and across a wooden footbridge before petering out on a clifftop crowded with million-dollar mansions. The paved street that picks up at the end of this footpath takes you back around to Torrey Pines Road and the top of Prospect Street. ■

Mary Star of the Sea Catholic Church, on Girard Avenue

La Jolla beaches

Windansea Beach, La Jolla Strand Park, & Marine Street Beach
- 165 A1
- Bus: 30 (Mon.-Fri.) or 34 from downtown San Diego or downtown La Jolla

La Jolla Cove Beach
- 165 A2
- Bus: 30 or 34 from downtown San Diego; walking distance from downtown La Jolla

La Jolla Shores
- 165 B2
- Bus: 34 from downtown San Diego or downtown La Jolla

Blacks Beach
- 165 B3
- Bus: 34 from downtown San Diego or downtown La Jolla; bus 301 from Del Mar or UTC; walking distance from UCSD

Torrey Pines State Beach
- 165 B4
- Bus: 301 from UTC, UCSD, or Del Mar

La Jolla's beaches welcome both expert surfers and wading children.

THE BEACH BOYS WEREN'T KIDDING WHEN THEY INCLUDED La Jolla in "Surfin' USA," their ode to West Coast beach culture—some of California's most spectacular strands lie along this windswept, wave-scarred coast.

La Jolla's most famous surfing beach is the legendary **Windansea** at the foot of Bonair Street. In the early 1960s author Tom Wolfe featured the beach's motley crew of beach dudes and surfer girls in *The Pump House Gang.* Forty years on, Windansea remains surfer turf, but the beachside rowdies have mellowed into gray-haired vets.

Several enclaves south of Windansea are worth exploring, including the beach of **La Jolla Strand Park** at the foot of Palomar Avenue, where an offshore reef creates a protected swimming area.

North of Windansea are the petite beaches of downtown La Jolla. The offshore reef at **Marine Street Beach** creates some of the highest waves on this coast, ideal for bodysurfing and boogie boarding. **La Jolla Cove** in Ellen Browning Scripps Park offers little shade or sand, but the offshore swimming is almost ideal.

La Jolla Shores, one of the area's largest beaches, extends about a mile near the cove. The Shores differs from other La Jolla strands in that it offers plenty of sand and a big parking lot. Still, it can get crowded on summer weekends. Front and center along the coast is **Kellogg Park** and its playground, fire pits, and lifeguard station. The **La Jolla Ecological Reserve** is just offshore. Established in 1971, the 533-acre park (between Alligator Head and Scripps Pier) is a haven for scuba divers, snorkelers, and kayakers. There's even a special boat-free zone for long-distance swimmers. Current surf, tide, scuba, and swimming conditions are listed on the bulletin board at the La Jolla Cove lifeguard station.

Beyond Scripps Pier, the sand quickly gives way to crashing surf and towering cliffs. If you're really determined, you can walk all the way from La Jolla Shores to **Blacks Beach.** Stretching nearly three miles, this is San Diego's most secluded shore—and, not coincidentally, its only clothing-optional beach. Technically speaking, naked sunbathing is illegal, but the regulation is enforced only on the southern third of the beach. However, Blacks is difficult and dangerous to reach. You can walk from the south or the north only at low tide; otherwise you will be trapped by rising waters. Two trails—Citizen's Trail and the Indian Canyon Trail—lead down to the beach from the gliderport, and both require some athleticism. Avoid other trails, which lead to dead ends.

Anchoring the northern end of La Jolla is the ruggedly handsome **Torrey Pines State Beach.** The strand extends about 3.5 miles south from Los Peñasquitos Marsh. You'll have to walk at low tide to reach the best parts, because most of the beach is tucked beneath 300-foot cliffs. The shoreline varies from tide pools and rocky shelves to slivers of fine sand and secluded coves. You can surf or swim anywhere along Torrey, but only the far northern end has lifeguards. The beach is most easily reached from the twin parking lots at Los Peñasquitos or via paths leading down from the visitor center. ■

Museum of Contemporary Art San Diego (MCASD)

Museum of Contemporary Art San Diego (MCASD)

www.mcasd.org

🅰 165 A2

✉ 700 Prospect St.,
La Jolla

☎ 858-454-3541

🕐 Closed Wed.

💲 $$

🚌 Bus: 30 or 34 from downtown San Diego

FOR MORE THAN HALF A CENTURY, THE MUSEUM OF Contemporary Art San Diego (MCASD) on Prospect Street has stood at the forefront of modern art, with a reputation for staging thought-provoking and sometimes controversial exhibits. Its collections reflect some of the most renowned artists and significant artistic movements of our time.

MCASD's stated mission is to expand the boundaries of contemporary art. It has often been the first museum to recognize artists who went on to become standouts in their fields. Over the years the curators have collected and displayed artwork—such as installations and conceptual art—rarely seen in larger museums. As a result, critics, collectors, and devotees around the globe consider MCASD a harbinger of trends in modern art.

MCASD also focuses on contemporary Latino art. Since the 1980s, the museum has amassed one of the world's most significant collections, representing artists in both the U.S. and numerous Latin American countries.

Through its workshops, seminars, and artist-in-residence programs, the museum functions as a forum and research laboratory for contemporary art and ideas. It also showcases cutting-edge music and film through performances, concerts, and special events such as the annual **Animation Film Festival,** which draws entries and audiences from around the world.

MCASD's permanent collection boasts more than 3,000 paintings, sculptures, drawings, photographs, videos, and multimedia works spanning everything from pop art and minimalism to postmodern architecture and Latin American art. With such a vast assemblage, only a fraction of works is on display at any one time, and the galleries are in constant flux. But that's part of the fun—you never know what you might see.

The museum stages eight to twelve shows each year—the majority of them organized by MCASD curators—and many of them are packaged for travel to other modern-art museums around the world. Among the artists who have featured in MCASD shows are sculptors Robert Mangold and Niki de Saint Phalle; painters Ellsworth Kelly, Francis Bacon, and Frida Kahlo; architects Louis Kahn and Mies van der Rohe; and the wrap artist Christo.

The museum building is a masterpiece itself. Although nowadays it's difficult to tell, the structure started life as a spacious private home (Scripps House), erected in 1916 for heiress Ellen Browning Scripps. Architect Irving Gill designed a startlingly modern house for her, built from stucco and concrete, on a spot overlooking the Pacific Ocean. The unadorned arches and simple lines were a marked contrast to the Edwardian and Spanish Colonial themes prevalent in San Diego at the time.

After Scripps died in 1932, her seaside mansion sat vacant for many years. On the eve of the Second World War, a group of local artists and community leaders banded together to buy the building and transform it into a non-profit center where residents could take art classes and amateur artists could show their work. By the late 1940s, the center was staging ambitious shows that featured Persian artifacts, Southwest Indian paintings, and Ming Dynasty art.

By 1960, the community art center had matured into a proper museum with several wings, and the artistic accent had shifted from eclectic shows to a firm emphasis on contemporary art. The structure had also been enlarged to accommodate bigger shows and a burgeoning permanent collection.

Renowned architects Robert Venturi and Denise Scott Brown were chosen to refurbish and expand the museum in 1986. As devotees of Irving Gill, they made a point of bringing the old Scripps House facade into the new design. Unveiled in 1996, the revamped MCASD was hailed as a triumph of form and function. "This is an exquisite project," raved the architectural critic of the *New York Times*. "The expanded museum is ... woven into the fabric of La Jolla with consummate delicacy and grace." ■

Whimsical creatures by Niki de Saint Phalle frolic in the Garden Gallery.

Scripps Institution of Oceanography

This tide pool overlooking the sea has incubated more than a few marine biologists.

PERCHED ON WOODED BLUFFS AT THE NORTH END OF LA Jolla Shores, the Scripps Institution of Oceanography is one of the world's oldest, largest, and most important centers of ocean science research and teaching.

Scripps Institution of Oceanography

www.scripps.ucsd.edu

165 B2

8602 La Jolla Shores Dr.

858-534-3624

Bus: 34 from downtown San Diego or downtown La Jolla

More than 1,300 scientists, graduate students, and support staff labor at Scripps. The 170-acre campus—situated on some of the most picturesque real estate in southern California—boasts advanced research facilities, including a state-of-the-art hydraulics lab with wind tunnels and wave channels, one of the globe's best marine science libraries, and extensive collections of biological and geological specimens gleaned from oceans around the world.

Scripps is broken down into 18 separate research units, many of them tops in their fields, such as the Center for Marine Biotechnology and Biomedicine, the Interactive Oceanography Division, the Climate Research Division, the Cecil H. and Ida M. Green Institute of Geophysics and Planetary Physics, and the Center for Clouds, Chemistry, and Climate. Scripps supports its own research pier and a fleet of four research vessels, including two ships with sophisticated bathymetric survey systems and a 355-foot marine laboratory called FLIP (FLoating Instrument Platform) that can rotate from horizontal to vertical in 28 minutes.

The institution was born in

1903 as the Marine Biological Association of San Diego. This is turn was the brainchild of UC Berkeley professor William E. Ritter, who wanted to establish a permanent oceanographic research base along the southern California coast. The first "lab" was merely a boathouse at the Hotel del Coronado, but within two years the scientists had moved to a wooden building overlooking La Jolla Cove.

Like so many other local organizations, the research center drew a large part of its early financial aid from Ellen Browning Scripps and her half-brother, newspaper magnate Edward W. Scripps. With their support, the institution purchased a large parcel of vacant land at La Jolla Shores, its home ever since. In 1912, the facility became part of the University of California system and was renamed in honor of the Scripps family.

The first major Scripps research expedition was an ambitious hydrological survey of the Gulf of California, conducted in 1939 aboard a 104-foot schooner donated by the Scripps family. During World War II, most of the staff turned its attention to war-related maritime research, including vital studies on underwater sound detection and submarine warfare that helped the Allies hunt down German U-boats in the Atlantic.

Nowadays the institution's $140-million annual budget derives mostly from federal government contracts and grants—including work for NASA, the National Oceanic and Atmospheric Administration, the Office of Naval Research, and the National Science Foundation—and private support. At any given time, 300 research programs are under way at Scripps. And while the overall emphasis remains on ocean studies, most of these projects are now interdisciplinary—

part of a broad-based effort to determine how sea, air, and land systems work and how they interact with one another.

Among ongoing research activities, Scripps scientists monitor seismic activity in an attempt to pinpoint earthquakes before they happen; develop new technologies

The menacing allure of floating jellyfish

and instruments for underwater research, such as laser-based and sound-imaging devices that can be used to explore the deep oceans; search for organic marine chemicals that can be used to fight disease or dispose of toxic waste; and amass climate records and other evidence to help improve weather forecasting and interpret long-range global climate changes.

When the institution was founded in 1903, the bylaws called for ongoing public interaction, including the development of an aquarium and museum. That commitment has evolved from a couple of glass containers with live fish into the ultramodern **Birch Aquarium at Scripps** (see p. 174), set on the hillside behind the institution. Tens of thousands of schoolchildren visit the aquarium each year. The aquarium's **Planet Earth Express** outreach van carries live aquarium specimens throughout the community. ■

Birch Aquarium at Scripps

ONE OF THE FASTEST AND MOST ENJOYABLE WAYS TO ORIENT yourself to the life that thrives in North America's offshore waters is to visit the Birch Aquarium on the western edge of the University of California, San Diego campus.

The public outreach center for the Scripps Institution of Oceanography, the sprawling complex has more than 60 tanks, an oceanographic museum, a demonstration tide pool, and panoramic views of the coast. Named after New Jersey philanthropists Stephen and Mary Birch, the $14 million facility opened in 1992.

Breaching the forecourt fountain are life-size statues of gray whales. Dead ahead is the expansive **Galleria** entrance hall, where you can pick up a map of the complex. The aquariums are on the right, with the tanks arranged in geographic clusters. The star of the **Pacific Northwest** exhibit is the rarely seen giant octopus. Southern California marine life dominates the next section, culminating in a 70,000-gallon tank that harbors a kelp forest similar to those found off San Diego. The final sections showcase tropical fish as well as the ocean denizens of Baja California.

Across the Galleria is the blue **Planet Museum,** the nation's largest museum featuring ocean exploration and research. Interactive displays help visitors understand everything from currents and tides to earthquakes and plate tectonics. **Ocean Supermarket** shows how many everyday foods and objects contain products derived from the sea. Other exhibits detail Scripps research, the history of oceanography, and global climate change.

The plaza on the ocean side of the Galleria provides sweeping views of the La Jolla coast, plus a discovery station and a simulated tide pool where you can cozy up to a variety of local sea creatures, including sea stars and sea urchins.

Birch offers a number of workshops, lectures, and field trips for the general public. Among the programs are escorted whale-watching trips (December through March), guided tide-pooling trips for children, and family "sleepovers" among the aquarium tanks. ∎

Birch Aquarium at Scripps
www.aquarium.ucsd.edu
- 165 B2
- 2300 Expedition Way, La Jolla
- 858-534-3474
- Bus: 34 from downtown San Diego or downtown La Jolla

Diving, swooping fish, towering kelp beds, and the occasional diver greet visitors just past the main entrance.

La Jolla Playhouse

LAUNCHED SHORTLY AFTER WOLRD WAR II BY GREGORY Peck and several actor friends, the La Jolla Playhouse has evolved into one of the country's premier regional theaters. In addition to staging avant-garde drama, it's the launchpad for many a Broadway hit.

Actors Mel Ferrer, Dorothy McGuire, and Gregory Peck stride from the theater they founded in 1947.

After struggling to establish a legitimate stage in Los Angeles where film actors could hone their craft before a live audience, Peck ventured back to his hometown of La Jolla in 1947. With partners Mel Ferrer and Dorothy McGuire, he founded a repertory group called the Actors' Company and persuaded the school board to let them use the La Jolla High School auditorium during summer vacation.

The Playhouse staged several productions each summer, plays that featured some of the biggest names in Hollywood—Olivia de Havilland, Groucho Marx, Charlton Heston, Joseph Cotten, Vincent Price, and Ginger Rogers, just to name a few. Drawn by the quality of the productions and a chance to relax with their friends beside the sea, the actors worked for peanuts.

The party lasted for 18 summers, but declining attendance and the decay of the Hollywood studio system forced the company to disband in 1964. By then, however, La Jollans had grown so enamored of their local theater that several citizens started a fund drive to resurrect the company and build a permanent home for it on the UCSD campus. Their efforts culminated in the 1982 construction of a state-of-the-art theater that is now shared by the Playhouse and the university drama department.

With Des McAnuff as artistic director, the Playhouse earned a reputation for the quality and audacity of its productions. From Stephen Sondheim to Athol Fugard, many of the world's top playwrights and directors flocked to La Jolla, transforming the theater into an international hub of creative expression and a cradle for Broadway hits.

Among the Tony Award-winning productions that got their start here were *Big River* (1984), Frank Galati's adaptation of *The Grapes of Wrath* (1989), *The Who's Tommy* (1992), and *How to Succeed in Business without Really Trying* with Matthew Broderick (1994). In 1993, the Playhouse snagged a Tony of its own as America's Outstanding Regional Theater. ∎

La Jolla Playhouse
www.lajollaplayhouse.com
- 165 B3
- 2910 La Jolla Village Dr., UCSD, La Jolla
- 858-550-1010
- $$$$$
- Bus: 30 or 34 from downtown La Jolla; 41 from Fashion Valley; 301 from Del Mar

Salk Institute

FOUNDED IN 1960 ON A HILLTOP SITE NEAR UCSD, THE SALK Institute for Biological Studies is both a center for scientific study and a classic example of postmodern American architecture.

Salk Institute
www.salk.edu
📍 10010 N. Torrey Pines Rd.
📞 858-453-4100
🚌 Bus: 301 from UTC or Del Mar
🅿 165 B3

After discovering a vaccine for polio at the University of Pittsburgh Medical School, Dr. Jonas Salk relocated to San Diego to develop his own center for medical and scientific research. This "acropolis of science" was intended to be a space where scientists and scholars from many different fields could brainstorm ideas, then try to turn those concepts into reality in the institute's labs.

Salk hired celebrated architect Louis Kahn to design and build a complex as audacious and breathtaking as the experiments that would be conducted within. The result is a masterpiece of American architecture, often featured in textbooks and touted as an example of how form and function can flow together into a handsome, unified design. Kahn's centerpiece is a

The Salk Institute, designed by Louis Kahn, provides a postmodern milieu for the complex research within.

travertine marble plaza flanked by identical, six-story laboratories fashioned from an offbeat combination of natural wood and prefabricated concrete—structures that seem to hover above the Pacific Ocean.

Salk research is heavily slanted toward fundamental biology and its relationship to medicine and health, with special emphasis on molecular biology, genetics, and neuroscience. More than 900 scientists work within its gray, sharply angled walls, trying to develop cures for the most pressing medical needs of our time, including cancer, autism, multiple sclerosis, diabetes, Alzheimer's, and AIDS. Other scientific nuts that Salk researchers are currently trying to crack include the structure and function of proteins, signaling mechanisms in cells,

Dr. Jonas Salk

From actress Raquel Welch to award-winning running back Rashaan Salaam, all manner of people have claimed La Jolla as their hometown. Yet one of its most beloved residents—Dr. Jonas Salk, who improved the lives of millions of people around the globe—was a transplanted Easterner.

Salk was born in New York City in 1914, the descendant of Russian Jews. The first member of his family to attend college, he eventually earned a spot at New York University Medical School. After his medical internship, he took a research position at the University of Michigan to participate in a project to develop an influenza vaccine—the start of his lifelong love affair with immunology.

In 1947, Salk joined the faculty at the University of Pittsburgh medical school. Using the knowledge that he had gained while studying influenza, Salk took up the daunting task of finding a vaccine for polio. Working with a number of other researchers, including Dr. Thomas Francis, by 1955 Salk had developed a vaccine that was safe and effective.

Salk declined to patent the vaccine, believing that widespread distribution was more important than personal benefit. As a result of both his brilliant science and his unselfish personality, Salk was

widely praised as a hero of modern medical science.

Setting his sights on even loftier medical goals, Salk moved to La Jolla in the early 1960s and founded the Salk Institute for Biological Studies. In subsequent years, he received many honors, including the Presidential Medal of Freedom and the Nehru Award for International Understanding. His final years were devoted to developing an AIDS vaccine. Jonas Salk also had a longstanding interest in finding a "cure" for the world's "cancer of war," which he called the "cancer of the world." The dedicated scientist died in 1995 at the age of 80. ∎

and the secrets of the human brain. Jonas Salk is by no means the only renowned scientist associated with the institute. Dr Jacob Bronowski, a senior fellow at Salk from 1965 until his death in 1974, wrote and narrated *The Ascent of Man*, an acclaimed BBC television series about the history of science.

Every summer, the institute stages a public benefit concert, called "Symphony at Salk," under the stars in the main courtyard. Free 45-minute tours of the complex are also offered twice daily (call ahead for reservations). ∎

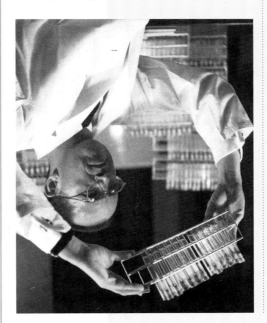

Dr. Jonas Salk discovered the world's first vaccine for polio.

UCSD

UCSD
www.ucsd.edu
🅰 165 C3
✉ 9500 Gilman Dr.,
La Jolla
☎ 858-534-4414
🚌 Bus: 30 or 34 from
downtown La Jolla;
41 from Fashion
Valley; 301 from
Del Mar

**Mandeville
Special
Collections
Library**
http://orpheus.ucsd.edu/spe
ccoll
☎ 858-534-2533

EVEN THOUGH IT IS A RELATIVE NEWCOMER IN THE academic world, the University of California, San Diego (UCSD) has blossomed in only four decades into one of the nation's premier educational institutions. It is a bastion of science and technology and a center for visual and performing arts.

Perched on a wooded mesa above La Jolla Shores, the sprawling campus supports more than 21,000 students and 4,000 faculty members. It was founded in 1960 as the sixth branch of the prestigious University of California system. Rather than merely basking in the San Diego sunshine, UCSD's early administrators set out to make it one of the nation's best universities.

An early emphasis on science attracted a bevy of Nobel Prize winners—among them Linus Pauling, Harold Urey, and Francis Crick—to the research and teaching staff. Soon the University of California, San Diego was producing its own laureates, such as Maria Goeppert-Mayer, who in 1963 became only the second woman (after Marie Curie) to win a Nobel Prize for physics.

Meanwhile, the experimental atmosphere and academic liberalism fostered by chancellor William McGill drew rebellious spirits such as political activist Angela Davis and Marxist philosopher Herbert Marcuse in the late 1960s.

As the home base of the La Jolla Playhouse (see p. 175) and cutting-edge drama and music programs, UCSD has made its mark in the fine arts as well. While affiliated with the university, both Roger Reynolds and Bernard Rands, won Pulitzer Prizes for music.

Taking its cue from the British system rather than the American, the university is divided into six Oxford-type undergraduate colleges with their own academic fortes and curricular focus. This unusual structure provides students with a more personal, intimate academic environment within the context of a large university. Students enrolled at the six colleges may pursue any of UCSD's 100 or so undergraduate majors.

The campus also supports half a dozen graduate programs. These include the Jacobs School of Engineering, the Graduate School of International Relations and Pacific Studies, the Scripps Institution of Oceanography (see pp.172-173), and the School of Medicine. UCSD consistently ranks among the nation's top ten universities in the quality of its doctoral programs and faculty.

UCSD may not have ivy-covered walls or Gothic courtyards, but the 1,200-acre campus exhibits a certain postmodern charm. Broad lawns and eucalyptus groves frame structures of steel and glass. Foremost among university landmarks is the stunning **Geisel Library,** named after the late La Jolla author Theodor Geisel ("Dr. Seuss") and his wife, Audrey. Designed by noted architect William Pereira, the library opened in 1970 to critical acclaim. The diamond-shaped glass-and-concrete structure, which seems to defy the laws of gravity, is often compared to a UFO.

Tucked inside the Geisel building is the **Mandeville Special Collections Library,** which houses many of the university's rare books and historical documents. Within its confines, the Don Cameron Allen Renaissance Collection features more than 5,000 works ranging from a first edition of Sir Walter Raleigh's *History of the World* (1614) to rare collections of British historical documents such as the *Harleian Miscellany* and the *Somers Tracts*.

The library also boasts 1,800 works on Baja California and 8,500 items on Dr. Seuss. Although the archives are open only to academically accredited researchers, the collection mounts regular exhibitions that are free of charge to the general public.

Another UCSD feature is the **Stuart Collection,** an offbeat outdoor art display scattered from one end of campus to the other. Works range from Nam June Paik's "video graveyard" and a 560-foot mosaic snake by Alexis Smith to Bruce Nauman's rooftop neon light

show and a giant fiberglass bird by Niki de Saint Phalle. A walking-tour map of the collection can be downloaded from http://stuart collection.ucsd.edu/map.

UCSD sports teams are called the Tritons after the son of Poseidon, the Greek god of the sea—a nod to the university's association with the Scripps Institution of Oceanography. Although most of the teams didn't exist 30 years ago, the Tritons have made their presence felt in national collegiate sports. Triton teams have earned NCAA Division II and III titles in soccer, volleyball, tennis, golf, and water polo.

The University Communications department offers free public tours of the UCSD campus every Sunday afternoon. Reservations (858-534-4414) are required. ■

So evocative of a UFO is William Pereira's Geisel Library at UCSD that the building has served as the setting for sci-fi TV shows.

Mount Soledad & the Golden Triangle

TOWERING 822 FEET ABOVE LA JOLLA IS A TREELESS PEAK called Mount Soledad, one of the highest points in the city of San Diego and also one of the best vantage points along the entire southern California coast.

As the Spanish name suggests, the windswept crag can be a place of glorious solitude—except on holiday weekends, when parking spaces at the top of the undulating access road are at a premium. The view, which often exceeds 50 miles, takes in the La Jolla coast, San Diego Bay, and the far-off Cuyamaca Mountains. Charles Lindbergh launched a glider from the summit of Soledad in 1930, then piloted the tiny craft

"Stargazer," a 1983 metal sculpture by Alexander Liberman, swirls in front of the Golden Triangle's San Diego Tech Center.

all the way to the Del Mar beach.

A 43-foot-high cross crowns the mountaintop, a bone of contention for many years between groups who advocated the separation of church and state and those championing religious expression and free speech. The city of San Diego ended the controversy in 1998 by selling the cross and a small portion of the summit to a private, non-profit war-memorial organization. Since then, the Mt. Soledad Memorial Association, Inc., has completed the first phase of the **Veterans Memorial Walls,** six walls that will eventually hold more than 3,000 black granite plaques bearing the names, photos, and stories of U.S. military personnel from all branches of the service who served in foreign wars and conflicts.

Spreading below Soledad's eastern slopes is the Golden Triangle, a wedge of ultramodern urbanity bounded by three freeways, I-5, I-805, and Calif. 52. The Triangle took shape in the 1970s as a commercial and residential area serving UCSD and the myriad research institutes on Torrey Mesa. Life in the Triangle revolves around the vast **University Towne Center (UTC)** mall, with its department stores, ice-skating rink, and marine-life fountains.

Despite its reputation as a rather soulless suburb, the Triangle boasts some of San Diego's most impressive modern architecture. The white spires of the **San Diego Temple for the Church of Jesus**

Dr. Seuss

Although he lived near Jonas Salk and moved in the same social circles, La Jolla's other beloved citizen, Dr. Seuss, labored in the arts, not the sciences. His forte was children's literature, and his career spanned seven decades and more than 40 titles.

Born Theodor Seuss Geisel in Springfield, Massachusetts, in 1904, Geisel studied at Dartmouth College and Oxford University. He went on to earn a living writing humorous cartoons and articles for *Life, Vanity Fair,* and other magazines. He didn't venture into children's literature until 1936, when a steamship voyage to Europe inspired him to write *And to Think That I Saw It on Mulberry Street.* Rejected by 43 publishers, the book was eventually published to modest reviews and humble sales.

After the attack on Pearl Harbor, Geisel enlisted in the U.S. Army. Rather than dispatching him to the front line, the brass decided to put his talents into service in Hollywood. As a member of director Frank Capra's legendary Signal Corps Unit, Geisel captured three Oscars for his war-related cartoons and documentary film work. At war's end, he moved south and settled in La Jolla.

Christ of Latter-day Saints on Charmant Drive shoot into the normally cloudless sky like the turrets of some fairy-tale castle. One steeple is surmounted by a golden image of the angel reputed to have spoken to Mormon church founder Joseph Smith.

Farther inland, on the east side of I-805, is the **Marine Corps Air Station Miramar,** home

Writing as "Dr. Seuss," Theodor Seuss Geisel (1904-1991) filled generations of young imaginations with his fantastical creations.

A pivotal moment in Geisel's writing career occurred in 1954, when *Life* magazine published an article claiming that American children did not read as well as they should for the simple reason that kids' books were boring. Geisel's editor at Random House, Bennett Cerf, asked him to write a book that would interest children in reading more.

The result was *The Cat in the Hat*—an instant best-seller, and the book that both established and ignited Geisel's fame. He went on to write many other classics, including *Green Eggs and Ham* and *How The Grinch Stole Christmas.* Dr. Seuss died in 1991 at the age of 87. ■

base of the 3rd Marine Aircraft Wing and its giant helicopters and high-flying F-18 Hornet fighter jets. The airfield was previously home to the Navy's Top Gun Flight School, immortalized in the 1986 Tom Cruise film of the same name. Each October, Miramar opens its gates to the public for the largest military air show in southern California (858-577-1000). ■

**Torrey Pines
State Reserve**

www.torreypine.org

Map p.165 B4

N. Torrey Pines Rd.
(Calif. 101)

858-755-2063

$

Bus: 50 from
downtown San Diego
to UTC (weekdays),
then 301 past the
reserve entrance

Torrey Pines State Reserve

A WILD PIECE OF CALIFORNIA COAST THAT SPRAWLS across beaches, bluffs, and canyons between La Jolla and Del Mar, Torrey Pines State Reserve is San Diego's own "national park."

The 2,500-acre park was established to protect one of the world's rarest trees, the gnarly Torrey pine (*Pinus torreyana*), which grows only on the coastal bluffs of this area and on Santa Rosa Island off Santa Barbara. But in sheltering the pines, the reserve also protects one of the last stretches of pristine nature along the southern California coast.

Among the ecosystems found within the park boundaries are beach, salt marsh, sea cliff, coastal chaparral, and (of course) pine

forest. Native animal species that thrive here include large creatures such as mule deer, coyotes, and bobcats.

Torrey Pines lends itself to recreation. Joggers, walkers, and cyclists have transformed the main entrance road (which rises 300 feet in less than a mile) into one of San Diego's favorite exercise strips. Surfers and sunbathers congregate on the park's popular beaches. Bird-watchers and wildflower enthusiasts flock to the park with bi-noculars and cameras.

Native Americans lived and hunted in what is now Torrey Pines State Reserve for at least 8,000 years before the arrival of Spanish explorers and missionaries. The Portolá expedition of 1769 probably passed along the park's eastern edge, close to present-day Sorrento Valley Road and Interstate 5. The Spanish dubbed the local trees *pinos soledades* (solitary pines) and called the area Punto de Los Arboles (Point of Trees).

This spectacular coastal reserve shelters the rare Torrey pine tree, which grows only here and on Santa Rosa, one of the Channel Islands.

(see p. 168).

Start your visit at the **visitor center,** a small museum at the top of Park Road. Weekends and holidays, the center is the jumping-off point for guided nature tours of the park.

You can also pick up a map and set out on your own along half a dozen trails that wind across Torrey Mesa. One of the most popular walks is the **Guy Fleming Trail,** a short loop that offers pine forest, wildflowers, ruddy sandstone formations, and ocean views.

More challenging is the **Razor Point Trail,** which drops downhill from the main parking lot to several lookout points perched high atop sheer cliffs. Few trees shade this route, but coastal chaparral and wildflowers abound, and the ocean views are unsurpassed. Keep an eye peeled for dolphins, sea lions, and even whales (in the winter) in the reserve's offshore waters.

The **Beach Trail** is the quickest way to reach the shore. It passes through orange and ocher badlands where neither trees nor flowers grow. The path is often steep and slippery, but your reward at the bottom is a sandy patch and **Flat Rock,** with its tiny tide pools. From there you can walk south at low tide along the shore to **Blacks Beach** (and its clothing-optional enclave; see p. 168) or trek north to the entrance station at the mouth of Carmel Valley. Or try this way to reach the beach. Walk south from the visitor center along the pedestrian-only portion of Park Road, then pick up the 1.2-mile **Broken Hill Trail** down to Flat Rock.

Valley, where you will find **Los Peñasquitos Marsh.** A third section of the reserve occupies isolated bluffs and canyons beyond the homes on the north side of the marsh. Finally, several popular beaches run along the shoreline

Entertaining, educational, and free: Tide-pooling at La Jolla Cove

The Torrey pine tree was "discovered" in 1850 by Charles Parry, a geologist with the U.S.–Mexico Border Survey; he identified it as a separate species and named it after Dr. John Torrey, one of America's leading botanists. Despite attempts by Parry and others to protect the area, the land was used for grazing and the pines were cut for firewood until 1899, when it was declared a city park. In 1956, San Diego citizens voted to transfer Torrey Pines to the California state park system. The reserve falls naturally into four geographic areas. The heart of the park is 300-foot-high **Torrey Pines Mesa,** where the visitor center, ranger station, and most of the hiking trails are found. The mesa drops off into **Carmel**

The Carmel Valley sector contains **North Torrey Pines State Beach,** a strand that parallels North Torrey Pines Road (U.S. 101). You can find surfers and beachcombers on this stretch of coast just about any time of year. On summer weekends, it's packed to the rafters. If you can't find free parking along the highway, try the state reserve lots at the south end of the beach (*fee*) and off Carmel Valley Road.

Inland from the beach is the vast **Los Peñasquitos Marsh Natural Preserve and Lagoon** with its tidal lagoon, mudflats, and salpans. Despite the fact that it's bisected by railroad tracks and flanked by an interstate, the marsh remains an important stopover for migratory birds. The best spot to watch them is from the shoulder of Carmel Valley Road, which runs along the marsh's northern edge. You can also explore the area in such nonmotorized watercraft as kayaks and canoes.

Less well known is the reserve's **Northern Extension,** tucked into the bluffs and canyons of Del Mar. A hiking trail leads into the area from behind Del Mar Heights Elementary School on Mira Montana Place (off Del Mar Heights Road). Besides 1,500 Torrey pines, this section contains scarlet larkspur and coastal blue lilac.

Torrey Pines is a day-use only park; there is no overnight camping or lodging. No food or drinks (other than water) are allowed in the "reserve zones" of Torrey Pines Mesa and the Northern Extension. Picnics are permitted only on the beach. There's no place inside the park to buy drinking water, so visitors must bring their own. All smoking and fires are also taboo. And given the fragility of the local environment, it's only natural that you must stick to designated trails. ∎

Sea kayakers enjoy unobstructed views of double-crested cormorants.

More places to visit around La Jolla

TORREY PINES GLIDERPORT

Perched on grassy bluffs 300 feet above Blacks Beach is Torrey Pines Gliderport, a premier site for hang gliding, paragliding, soaring, and remote-control airplane flying.

TPG's first motorless flight took place in 1928, and Charles Lindbergh is among the distinguished aviators who have flown here. The weather is almost perfect for year-round flight—a high percentage of blue-sky days and westerly winds blowing an ideal 10 miles per hour for more than 250 days each year.

The facility offers instruction, certification, repair services, adventure tours, and equipment sales, in addition to tandem hang-glider and sailplane flights with master pilots. Even if you don't yearn to soar, the clifftop views merit a visit to the gliderport. 🌐 www.flytorrey.com 🅰 165 B3 ✉ 2800 Torrey Pines Scenic Dr. ☎ 858-452-9858 🚌 Bus: 301 from UTC or Del Mar; walking distance from UCSD

TORREY PINES GOLF COURSE

Torrey Pines, located atop oceanside bluffs, has been a mecca for southern California golfers since the 1950s. It consistently ranks among the country's top municipal courses. From Jack Nicklaus to Tom Watson, all of golf's modern greats have teed off here. Events include the PGA Invitational in February and the Junior World Golf Championship in July. Tricky winds, long fairways, and precipitous drops make Torrey's twin courses a challenge even for seasoned pros. The par 72 South Course, refurbished in 2001, is considered the tougher of the two (Greg Chalmers shot the course-record 63). Reservations are strongly encouraged; otherwise you may have a long wait, praying for a no-show or a cancellation. 🌐 www.torreypinesgolfcourse.com 🅰 Map p. 165 B4 ✉ 11480 N. Torrey Pines Rd. ☎ 858-552-1784, 619-570-1234 (computer reservations) 🚌 Bus: 301 from UTC, UCSD, or Del Mar

LOS PEÑASQUITOS CANYON PRESERVE

Protected within the meandering boundaries of Los Peñasquitos Canyon Preserve near Torrey Pines State Reserve and the Golden Triangle are these 4,000 acres of open space and natural beauty.

Founded in 1970, the park takes its name from San Diego's first private Mexican land grant—Rancho Santa Maria de los Peñasquitos—a sprawling cattle ranch that once occupied the area. All that remains of those days is a historic adobe dwelling, now open to the public as a small museum.

The preserve is home to more than 500 plant and 150 animal species, including bobcats, mountain lions, and mule deer. Habitats range from riparian woodland and open grassland to chaparral-covered mesas and boulder-strewn waterfalls. Trails in the preserve are ideal for jogging, walking, and mountain biking. Public access points include Sorrento Valley Boulevard in the west and Black Mountain Road in the east. Rangers and the Friends of Los Peñasquitos Canyon Preserve offer interpretive walks and other programs. 🅰 165 C4 ☎ 858-538-8066 🚆 Coaster train from downtown San Diego to Sorrento Valley station ■

Trying to master Torrey Pines Golf Course can leave you feeling squirrelly.

Stretching from the Pacific Ocean to Palomar Mountain, North County is a mixed bag of sleepy beach towns and bustling suburbs veined by river valleys where nature and farming still reign supreme.

North County

Agave plant at Quail Botanical Gardens

Encountering mule deer is a commonplace occurrence at Palomar Mountain State Park.

North County

SAN DIEGO'S NORTH COUNTY—ALSO KNOWN AS SAN DIEGO NORTH—STRETCHES from La Jolla and Torrey Pines all the way to Camp Pendleton and the Orange County border. Although the various coastal towns seem to blend together as you speed along the interstate, each of them has a distinct history and character.

With more than a million residents spread across more than a dozen thriving cities, North County is an economic and cultural force in its own right. And although greatly affected by San Diego proper, the region often marches to the beat of its own drummer. It has its own daily newspaper, mass transit system, school districts, and regional airport. It also has its own attitudes, which can differ dramatically from one city to another.

Seaside Del Mar and inland Rancho Santa Fe are among the most affluent communities on the West Coast, places that aren't afraid to flaunt their wealth. From fashion queen Zandra Rhodes and pop singer to golfer Phil Mickelson and Bill Gates, both places have attracted a steady stream of celebrated homeowners.

Floral shirts and baggy shorts are about as

formal as it gets in Encinitas and Solana Beach, the epitome of laid-back California beach towns. Half a dozen strands and some of the region's best surf breaks lure a steady stream of wave-riding fanatics, who also frequent the taco stalls and taverns along old Highway 101.

Despite its rich history and agricultural heritage, Carlsbad is largely a new creation, refashioned over the past 20 years into one of the county's most important cities after San Diego. High-tech businesses sprout where flower fields and cattle ranches once dominated. New homes stretch inland as far as the eye can see, and the city continues to grow.

Oceanside and Escondido are hard-working cities where a blue-collar sensibility prevails. The local populations here, more diverse than those in some surrounding communities, include large contingents of Latinos and South Pacific Islanders. Their vibrant cultures enrich the mix and enliven the proceedings.

North County has also worked hard to transform itself into an independent tourist destination. The endless beaches and Del Mar's summer Thoroughbred races have been a major draw for years. But two of the San

Diego area's best modern attractions—Lego-land and the San Diego Wild Animal Park—are also to be found here. Spots such as Mission San Luis Rey and San Pasqual Battle-field State Historic Park emphasize local history, while the region's agricultural bounty takes the forefront at the Carlsbad Flower Fields and at Escondido's wineries. ■

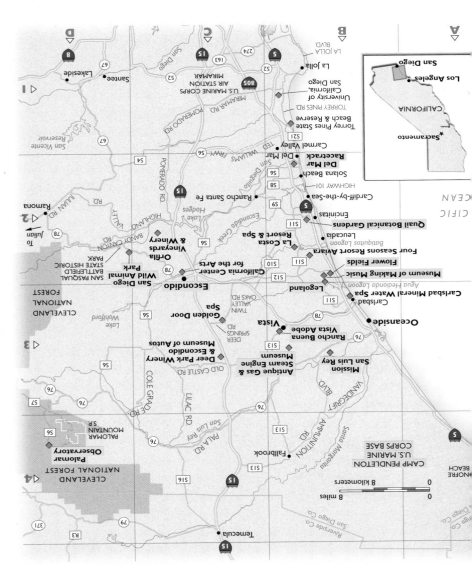

A drive up the coast

Old Highway 101 hugs the coast between Del Mar and Oceanside, cruising through posh seaside communities and fabled surfer enclaves as it passes some of California's most remarkable beaches.

Start at the ocean end of Carmel Valley, where sandstone bluffs offer a sweeping view of Torrey Pines State Beach and Reserve and the La Jolla coast. Driving north along Highway 101, you soon zoom into **Del Mar ❶,** an old-money San Diego beach community. The tony main street is lined with bookstores, boutiques, and outdoor cafés, but the town's hippie past still shines through storefronts promising health food and psychic readings. The best access to Del Mar's fabulous beach is at the bottom of 15th Street, where there's a park, a playground, some seaside restaurants, and the historic **Powerhouse** building, converted into a community center in 2000.

The highway dips into the **San Dieguito**

A surfer reminisces at the shrine to board-dom.

River Valley, the western end of a new greenway known as **San Dieguito River Park.** The new park stretches 55 miles inland along the banks of the San Dieguito River, all the way from the coast to Volcan Mountain just north of Julian. Beyond the railroad tracks on the right side of 101 looms the celebrated **Del Mar Racetrack;** a sandy strand is on the left. Rising above the beach, the **James Scripps Bluff Preserve ❷** safeguards a tiny archaeological site where "Del Mar Man" was discovered in 1929. Dated to 3500 B.C., the bones are the oldest human remains found in San Diego, belonging to a civilization that may predate the tribes who greeted the first Spanish visitors.

Up ahead is **Solana Beach ❸,** a sleepy coastal town where seascapes take a back seat to art and music. The funky Cedros Design District—a three-block stretch of Cedros Avenue south of the glass-walled train station, which was moved here from Del Mar in 1995—contains antique stores, offbeat boutiques, and craft outlets. To reach it, take a right on Via de la Valle, then your first left on Cedros Avenue. The avenue's best-known tenant is the **Belly Up Tavern** (*143 S. Cedros Ave., 858-481-8140*), a premier music venue for more than 20 years. There's a show nearly every night, with the tunage running the gamut from rock and folk to world beat and reggae.

San Elijo Lagoon, one of the county's largest coastal wetlands, separates Solana Beach from much larger Encinitas. Three hundred bird species have been spotted along the six miles of hiking trails in the 900-acre reserve. The San Elijo Lagoon Conservancy (*760-435-5640*) hosts free nature walks on the second Saturday morning of each month along a waterfront trail at the north end of North Rios Avenue in Solana Beach. The stretch of sand north and south of the lagoon mouth is **Cardiff State Beach ❹,** where sailboarders cavort and seafood restaurants overlook (and are sometimes thrashed by) the pounding surf.

With more than 60,000 residents, **Encinitas ❺** is one of the county's largest cities, a

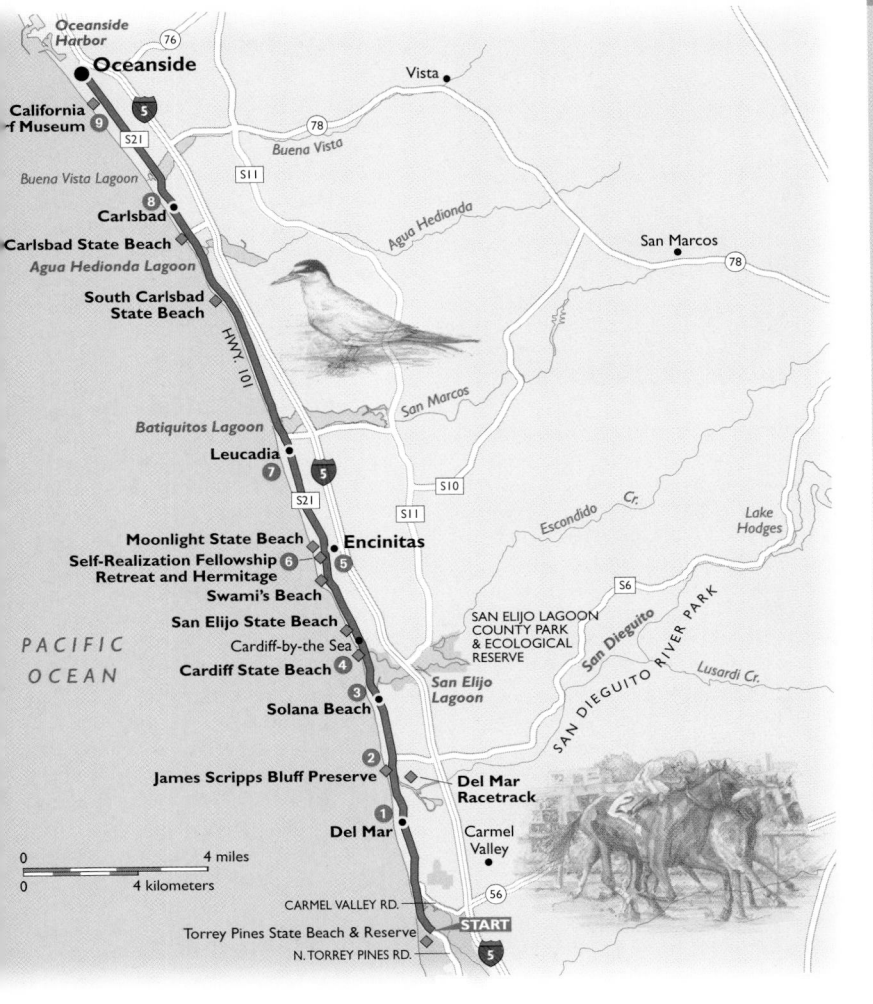

Oceanside Harbor
76
Oceanside
Vista
California f Museum 9
S21 5
78
Buena Vista
S11
Buena Vista Lagoon
8
Carlsbad
San Marcos
Carlsbad State Beach
Agua Hedionda Lagoon
Agua Hedionda
South Carlsbad State Beach
78
San Marcos
Batiquitos Lagoon
Leucadia 7 5
S21
S10
San Marcos
S11
Escondido Cr.
Lake Hodges
Moonlight State Beach **Encinitas**
6 5
Self-Realization Fellowship Retreat and Hermitage
S6
Swami's Beach
San Elijo State Beach
SAN ELIJO LAGOON COUNTY PARK & ECOLOGICAL RESERVE
San Dieguito
SAN DIEGUITO RIVER PARK
Cardiff-by-the Sea
Cardiff State Beach 4
San Elijo Lagoon
Lusardi Cr.
Solana Beach
PACIFIC OCEAN
2
James Scripps Bluff Preserve
Del Mar Racetrack
1
Del Mar
Carmel Valley
0   4 miles
0   4 kilometers
CARMEL VALLEY RD.
56
Torrey Pines State Beach & Reserve
START
N. TORREY PINES RD.
5

sprawling municipality that includes well-known beach communities such as Cardiff-by-the-Sea and Leucadia. Voted one of America's "top ten surf towns" by *Surfer* magazine, Encinitas boasts several nifty strands: **San Elijo State Beach** along the Cardiff shore, the legendary **Swami's Beach** for hard-core surfers, and **Moonlight State Beach,** within walking distance of downtown (to reach it, turn left onto Encinitas Boulevard).

Swami's traces its offbeat name to the **Self-Realization Fellowship Retreat and Hermitage** 6 *(760-753-1811; Sun. 2-5 p.m.),* which perches on bluffs above and just north

of the beach. Founded by Indian yoga master Paramahansa Yogananda in 1937, the center offers meditation and spiritual enlightenment to members as well as the general public. Stroll through the hermitage where the yogi lived, or practice yoga in the meditation gardens next to a waterfall and fishpond.

The stretch of Highway 101 through downtown Encinitas looks much as it did 50 years ago, when it was the main route between Los Angeles and San Diego. Biker bars rub elbows with old-fashioned diners and trendy restaurants. Dominating the streetscape is the Mission-style facade of the old **La Paloma**

Above: Buying flowers at a farmer's market Opposite: Summer, it seems, may never end at Swami's Beach in Encinitas.

Theater (471 S. Coast Hwy, 760-436-7469), a venue for concerts, films, and local plays.

From downtown Encinitas, the highway shoots northward through **Leucadia** 7, the roadway shaded by towering eucalyptus trees. Some of the region's most intriguing food is found along this route: For Thai cuisine, pop into **Siamese Basil** in Encinitas (527 S. Coast Hwy, 760-753-3940); for Iranian, seek out **Noo Shin's Persian Restaurant** in Leucadia (966 N. Coast Hwy, 760-436-5558).

Leucadia ("Isle of Paradise") was founded in 1870 by British spiritualists; they named the streets after Greek and Roman gods and mythological figures (Daphne Street, Neptune Avenue, Athena Street, etc.). One of the few structures that remain from that era is the old railroad station, reborn as trendy **Pannikin Coffee and Tea** (510 N. Coast Hwy, 760-436-0033).

Beyond Leucadia is a largely undeveloped stretch of coast that features estuaries and long stretches of often-empty sand. As an ecological reserve and nesting place for the California least tern, **Batiquitos Lagoon** is off-limits to recreation. (San Marcos Creek, which crosses beneath Highway 101, connects it to the ocean.) No such rules apply at **Agua Hedionda Lagoon**, where you can rent kayaks and paddle-boats at California Water Sports (760-434-3089) on the inland side of Interstate 5. Wedged between the two lagoons is **South Carlsbad State Beach**, with a campground overlooking four miles of uncrowded sand.

The town of **Carlsbad** 8 harbors one of the largest collections of historic buildings in North County. Rising over Highway 101 in the village center is the **Twin Inns**—also known as Neiman's Restaurant (2978 Carlsbad Blvd.)—an immaculately restored Queen Anne mansion with gables and turrets. It was built in 1887 as the home of Gerhard Schutte, who named the town after Karlsbad in Bohemia. (Political boundaries have since been redrawn; the town now sits in the Czech Republic, where it goes by the name Karlovy Vary.)

Just up the street is the **Alt Karlsbad Hanse House** (2802 Carlsbad Blvd.), a replica of a Hanseatic house in Germany; it presently houses the Carlsbad Mineral Water Spa (see p. 198). Nearby is the **Children's Discovery Museum of North County** (300 Carlsbad Village Dr., in Village Faire Shopping Ctr, 760-720-0737, $), where kids can wander through dozens of hands-on exhibits demonstrating various principles of science, history, and ecology.

This coastal drive finally runs its course, appropriately enough, in **Oceanside**—an eclectic seaside town with a large South Pacific émigré presence (Camp Pendleton forms the city's northern border), and another huge contingent of sun seekers. Unlike the affluent beach communities farther south, Oceanside sports a casual, it's-all-good attitude.

The wide beaches on either side of Ocean-side Municipal Pier (the longest wooden pier on the U.S. West Coast) are crowded on weekends. But there's normally a warm patch of sand—and a catchable wave—for everyone.

Devotees of board culture should check out the **California Surf Museum** 9 (760-721-6876; www.surfmuseum.org) on Highway 101, diagonally across from the Oceanside civic center. The collection is packed with surf artifacts and memorabilia from all around the globe, including one of Duke Kahanamoku's redwood longboards.

With a pristine marina and numerous restaurants, **Oceanside Harbor** next to the San Luis Rey River bustles with waterfront activity. **Helgren's** (760-722-2133) organizes sportfishing, whale-watching, and harbor sightseeing cruises. Or you can cap the day by renting your own sailboat or kayak at Oceanside Boat Rentals (760-722-0028). ∎

Del Mar Racetrack

FOR 43 DAYS EACH SUMMER, THE AMERICAN HORSE-RAC-ING cosmos whirls around the Del Mar Racetrack. But the track is more than just a place to throw your money away. When the ponies aren't running, the grounds are given over to a multitude of other activities: concerts, antique shows, holiday pageants, and San Diego's annual county fair—a year-round slate that turns the Thoroughbred Club into a hub of local arts and entertainment.

Del Mar Racetrack

![A] 189 B2

![envelope] 2260 Jimmy Durante Blvd, Del Mar

![phone] 858-755-1141

![$] $$

![S] Coaster train or Amtrak to Solana Beach; free shuttle bus from station to track during race season

www.delmarracing.com

The "Cadillac of racetracks," Del Mar has long been one of the nation's leading racing venues. For more than a decade, it has topped the U.S. in daily average attendance; it also consistently ranks among the top three in daily average handle (betting). The season runs from late July to early September, with races every day of the week but Tuesday. Opening day—with its outrageous costumes and "Truly Fabulous Hats Contest"—normally draws the largest crowd. But the track's signature event is the

million-dollar Pacific Classic, a mile-and-a-quarter challenge that draws some of the world's leading horses. Other top stakes include the Ramona Handicap, the Del Mar Oaks, and the Del Mar Debutante. Born in the Depression and raised on Hollywood chic, the track's history is the stuff of southern California legend. In the 1930s, the state of California and the Work Projects Administration (WPA) allocated money and manpower for the development of a fairground and racetrack in Del Mar. Movie

actors Bing Crosby and Pat O'Brien got involved in the project, then dragooned their Hollywood buddies to join the board of directors and attend the races. Bing even wrote a song to promote the track—"Where the Turf Meets the Surf"—which is still played at the start and finish of every Del Mar race day. With Crosby greeting people at the front gates, a standing-room-only crowd of 15,000 packed the grandstand on opening day (July 3, 1937). The track never looked back.

During the late 1930s and '40s, the silver-screen elite assembled in Del Mar each summer to party at the Thoroughbred Club and splash in the nearby Pacific. Jimmy Durante, W. C. Fields, Hoagy Carmichael, Gloria Swanson, Ava Gardner, Lucille Ball, and Mickey Rooney were all regulars.

Beyond its celebrity renown, Del Mar earned a reputation for excellent racing. Several of the great moments of 20th-century Thoroughbred history occurred here, such as the 1938 match race between legendary Seabiscuit and Argentine champion Ligaroti, which "the Biscuit" won by a nose. That same year, Del Mar became the first track to use photos to determine the winners of close races, employing a special camera developed by a Paramount Studios cinematographer. Johnny Longden and Bill Shoemaker both set world records here for most career wins. In 1996, the track's largest-ever crowd (44,181) saw Cigar fail in his bid to break Citation's record for consecutive victories.

In the old days, the horses were exercised on nearby Del Mar Beach. Nowadays they confine their workout to the track itself. You can watch the early-morning spectacle through the huge picture windows of the track's **Clubhouse Terrace Restaurant**, which is open for breakfast (weekends only) during race season. Other special events include post-race jazz concerts, family fun days, jockey photo days, and a huge party in the paddock after the summer's last race.

The annual San Diego County Fair takes place in late June and early July, when the racetrack stables, and parking lots are transformed into one of California's biggest summer fun zones. Highlights include midway thrill rides, garden pavilions, and animal husbandry stalls. Among the special events are rodeos and grandstand concerts by top-name pop, rock, and country artists.

Another big event on Del Mar Racetrack's sporting calendar is the annual **Del Mar National Horse Show** in April, a major stop on the equestrian circuit since the 1940s. The show attracts many of the country's top riders and horses in the dressage, western, and hunter/jumper categories. ∎

The ponies are off and running at the 1937 Del Mar Racetrack, once the haunt of crooner Bing Crosby and cronies such as Jimmy Durante and Ava Gardner.

Quail Botanical Gardens

TUCKED IN THE ENCINITAS FOOTHILLS, QUAIL BOTANICAL Gardens is dedicated to conserving rare and endangered plant species from around the world. It also aims to raise public awareness about plant diversity while providing an urban oasis for visitors.

Quail Botanical Gardens

www.qbgardens.com

📍 189 B2

✉ 230 Quail Gardens Dr, Encinitas

☎ 760-436-3036

💲 $$

Founded in 1971 on land donated by Encinitas resident Ruth Baird Larabee, the 30-acre gardens display 5,000 different types of plant life, from native southern California species to exotics from as far away as South Africa and the Himalaya. As the name suggests, Quail Botanical Gardens is also a haven for the eponymous quail and other indigenous birds.

The gardens are divided into geographical and climatic sections. Behind the gift shop are desert plants, an expanse of cactuses and other succulents that includes flora from Madagascar. The arid theme continues in a Mediterranean area with plants from Europe, the Middle East, and the Canary Islands. Tropical species flourish beyond the gazebo in leafy sections dedicated to the plants of Central America,

Nearly 4,000 specimens of plant life find sanctuary within the 30-acre Eden of Quail Botanical Gardens.

Africa, the Pacific islands, and the tropical rain forest. A waterfall and stream bisect this area, and one path leads through a lush palm canyon. You can also walk up the hillside for a commanding view of the surroundings.

The gardens' northern region is reserved for semidesert plants from South America and South Africa. Plants from Australia and New Zealand dominate the eastern sector, while the southern sector, with its Kumeyaay Indian homesite, is dedicated to the native plants and peoples of southern California.

Quail offers nature walks, lectures, educational programs, and landscape advice. Guided tours are offered every Saturday at 10 a.m.; children's tours take place the first Tuesday of each month. No reservations are required. ■

Flower Fields

Flower Fields

www.theflowerfields.com

🅰 189 B2

✉ 5704 Paseo del Norte, Carlsbad

☎ 760-431-0352

💲 $$

EVERY SPRING, THE UNDULATING HILLS EAST OF I-5 IN Carlsbad explode with color. This swirling sea of pink, yellow, red, and orange blossoms is called the Flower Fields.

Like strokes from the brush of a giant artist, the flowers roll across the hillsides in giant bands and chevrons. More than 90 percent of the blooms are ranunculus, native to Asia Minor and sometimes called Persian buttercup. As many as 12 million ranunculus bulbs are harvested from the fields each year for sale at nurseries and garden centers around the country.

The business first took root in 1932, when Frank Frazee introduced the ranunculus to his modest horticultural operation in nearby Oceanside. Frazee's son Edwin moved the ranch to a larger spread in Carlsbad, developed a better bulb, and became the country's only commercial ranunculus grower. By the late 1950s, the ranch had become a popular stop on the coastal route between San Diego and Los Angeles.

When Edwin retired in 1975, his sons moved the operation to its present location off Palomar Airport Road, leasing ranch land from the Ecke family, San Diego's poinsettia-growing dynasty. Although ranunculus remained the major crop, gladioli, tritonia, watsonia, babiana, wandflowers, and blooming shamrock were added as secondary crops. Since then, the ranch has evolved into an official tourist attraction that features the fields and several formal gardens.

When you visit, you can wander through the vast ranunculus fields, immersing yourself in an ocean of vibrant blooms. Carlsbad's temperate climate and moist, sandy soil offer near-ideal conditions for growing the plants. Only about 2

percent of the flowers (4 million stems) are cut and sold each year. Once the bulbs are harvested, most of the blooms are plowed back into the soil for reseeding.

Theme gardens include the **Cottage Garden**, **Fragrance Garden**, and **Shade Garden**. In the **All-American Rose Selection Garden and Rose Walk of Fame** are 173 types of award-winning roses; the **Color Project** garden showcases artists whose medium of choice is flowers. ■

Count on vibrant ranunculus blooms to steal the show when the Carlsbad hills burst into color each spring.

North County resorts

WITH A SUNNY CLIMATE AND A HEALTH-CONSCIOUS populace, North County has evolved into a bastion of health spas and fitness resorts. Head here to reshape your body, refresh your face, or revamp your spirit.

The region's health-spa boom was born of both accident and design. After homesteading a patch of coastal bluffs in 1882, sea captain John Frazier discovered that the local well water possessed "curative powers" for rheumatism and other ailments. He found a believer in German-born Gerhard Schutte, who bought Frazier's ranch and named it Carlsbad after the celebrated European spa (now known as Karlovy Vary, in the Czech Republic). One magazine predicted that Carlsbad was "destined to occupy a foremost place among the great sanitariums of the world." Indeed, people flocked from far and wide to sample the seaside spa's bubbling waters.

The resort hotel and bottling works that Schutte developed were long ago replaced by the Alt Karlsbad Hanse House, where you can still find the original well dug by Captain Frazier. The **Carlsbad Mineral Water Spa** is perhaps the only place in North America where you can enjoy body wraps, mud packs, and aromatherapy within the confines of a German-style gingerbread mansion.

From this humble beginning sprouted a variety of health resorts scattered across North County between the coast and the inland mountains. Most renowned is **La Costa Resort & Spa**, one of the nation's premier health and fitness retreats. Sprawled across 400 acres of upcountry Carlsbad, La Costa features just about everything one might expect of a modern health and recreation retreat. Tee off at either of two championship golf courses or swing your racket at the 21-court tennis center, where the likes of Venus Williams, Jennifer Capriati, and Martina Hingis play during La Costa's annual women's tourney. Choose from an extensive menu of massages that includes shiatsu, reflexology, and aromatherapy. Or have your entire body shrouded

La Costa Resort & Spa
www.lacosta.com
🏠 189 B2
✉ 2100 Costa del Mar Rd., Carlsbad
☎ 800-854-5000

Carlsbad Mineral Water Spa
www.carlsbadmineralspa.com
🏠 189 B3
✉ 2802 Carlsbad Blvd., Carlsbad
☎ 760-434-1887

Golden Door
www.goldendoor.com
🏠 189 C3
☎ 800-424-0777
✉ Escondido

Poolside pampering is the order of the day at the Four Seasons Resort Aviara.

pools, tennis courts, a bathhouse, and a state-of-the-art gym, the Golden Door offers myriad spa treatments and private hiking trails in the nearby hills.

Newest of the North County spas is the decadent **Four Seasons Resort Aviara,** perched on lush bluffs overlooking Batiquitos Lagoon in southern Carlsbad. The hub of a planned community called Aviara, the resort offers both an outstanding hotel and a first-class health spa with whirlpools, massage, and wraps. An Arnold Palmer-designed golf course wraps itself around Aviara's graceful Spanish Colonial-style walls. ■

in herb-saturated linen sheets (claustrophobes need not apply). If you can't find a particular spa treatment at La Costa, chances are it hasn't been invented.

Even more exclusive is the **Golden Door** on the outskirts of Escondido. Founded in 1958 by community activist Deborah Szekely, the architecture replicates an ancient Japanese country inn, reflecting the fact that the resort is dedicated to both mental and physical wellness. In order to provide lavish individual service, no more than 40 guests are allowed each week. In addition to swimming

Left: Casita-style guest rooms are typical at California spas.
Below: The enticements on tap at La Costa Resort & Spa

Four Seasons Resort Aviara
www.fourseasons.com/
aviara
🅰 189 B2
✉ 7100 Four Seasons Pt., Carlsbad
☎ 760-603-6800

Legoland

TAKE 30 MILLION PLASTIC BRICKS, SNAP THEM TOGETHER in the rolling hills of Carlsbad, season with show biz, and what do you get? Legoland California, the region's newest theme park.

Monument to plastic: A young visitor admires a 380,000-brick rendering of the U.S. Capitol Building.

Legoland
www.lego.com/legoland /california
189 B2/B3
One Legoland Dr., Carlsbad
760-918-5346
$$$$$
Coaster train or Amtrak to Carlsbad Poinsettia Station; Bus: 344 from station to park entrance

Legoland, the latest venture of the legendary Danish toy-making company, features more than 5,000 different Lego models and more than 50 separate attractions, ranging from shows and thrill rides to hands-on exhibits and landscaped garden areas. Nearly everything is aimed at children aged 2 to 12, although there's plenty to amuse adults with a healthy interest in scale models.

The park is divided into half a dozen theme areas, starting with (of course) **The Beginning,** an orientation near the front gate that includes shopping, snacks, and

other guest services. Beyond is the **Explore Village,** where millions of Lego bricks have been fashioned into fairy-tale characters, African wildlife, and an interactive water-play area. A boat ride takes visitors along Fairy Tale Brook, while magicians and ventriloquists entertain the young ones in your group. Sky Cruiser and Kid Power Towers—two of the park's popular thrill rides—are situated in the middle of Legoland. The park's own village square is **Fun Town,** where kids can pilot Lego helicopters and biplanes, earn their license at the Junior Driving School, or take a mysterious journey through plastic facsimiles of the Arctic, the Amazon rain forest, and ancient Egypt in Adventurers' Club.

Castle Hill replicates medieval English times in the form of a simulated joust and a rustic playground with rope climbs, cargo nets, and slides. Budding architects and engineers can tinker to their heart's content at the Builders' Guild, with its thousands of Lego bricks. Or you can let your hair down on the Dragon or Spellbreaker roller coasters.

The **Imagination Zone** showcases more sophisticated Lego products. Here kids can build and program computerized Mindstorm robots or assemble their own brick race car and test it on a digital track. Nearby is the embarkation point for the Coast Cruise—a grand tour of Miniland, with its incredible miniatures of American cities and landmarks. The park's fastest ride, the Lego Technic Coaster, is not far away. ■

Palomar Observatory

PRESIDING OVER ONE OF THE NORTH COUNTY'S HIGHEST mountains is Palomar Observatory, a major national astronomical facility and the star attraction of a state park that embraces some of San Diego's most scenic wilderness.

The Pasadena-based California Institute of Technology (Caltech) owns and operates the stargazing facility. Astronomers from Cornell University and the Jet Propulsion Laboratory work here as well.

The main building, with its stark white dome, looks out of place amid the surrounding pines. Inside their own domes are four powerful instruments: the 200-inch Hale Telescope, the 60-inch Caltech Reflecting Telescope, the 48-inch Oschin Telescope, and the 18-inch Schmidt Telescope.

The Hale Telescope has been a workhorse of modern astronomy since it was installed in 1947. At that time, the 350-ton scope was the world's largest optical instrument. Modified several times over the years, the huge instrument is equipped with sensitive position sensors, high-speed computers, and electronic devices that can measure infrared light (and detect dim radiation) from far-off celestial bodies.

The observatory is open daily for free self-guided tours, including a close-up look at the Hale Telescope. Occasional nighttime visits —including a glimpse through the 60-inch scope—are organized by the Reuben H. Fleet Science Center *(619-238-1233)* in Balboa Park. If you're in the mood for a hike, the **Observatory Trail** winds 4.5 miles downhill to the Mendenhall Valley Overlook and the Observatory Campground.

Sharing the mountain with the observatory is **Palomar Mountain State Park,** a top nature destination. Its leafy confines include nearly 2,000 acres of often-rugged terrain populated by mountain lions, bobcats, and mule deer. The park has 31 campsites and half a dozen major hiking paths; the **Doane Valley Nature Trail** leads to trout-stocked Doane Pond. Boucher Hill offers the best vantage points; on clear days you can see all the way to the Pacific Ocean and San Diego Bay. ■

Palomar Observatory
www.astro.caltech.edu/observatories/palomar
⚠ 189 D4
☎ 626-395-4033
🕐 Open daily
💲 Free

Palomar Mountain State Park
www.palomar.statepark.org
⚠ 189 D4
☎ 760-742-3462
💲 $

Resembling a celestial object itself, the dome of the Palomar Observatory rises above the surrounding pines.

Mission San Luis Rey

FOR MORE THAN 200 YEARS, MISSION SAN LUIS DE Francia in Oceanside has been a wellspring of local spiritual and secular life. This place of private prayer and lively public celebrations shines a light on the region's rich multicultural past.

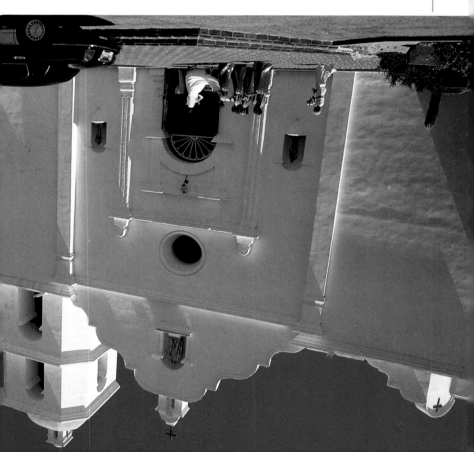

**Mission San
Luis Rey**
www.sanluisrey.org

📍 189 B3

✉ 4050 Mission Ave.,
Oceanside

📞 760-757-3651

💲 $$

🚆 Coaster train or
Amtrak to Ocean-
side; transfer to bus
313

Named after Louis IX, the pious king of France, the mission was established in 1798 as a way station between San Diego de Alcalá and San Juan Capistrano. Although San Luis Rey was one of the last Franciscan outposts developed in California, it became the largest; eventually it was dubbed the "King of Missions" because of its immense size, agricultural production, and large population. Until the mid-19th century, in fact, it was the single largest structure on the west coast of North American.

Like all the California missions, San Luis Rey was secularized in the 1820s after Mexico gained its independence from Spain. The property was broken up into private land grants, and the mission buildings were stripped of any material that might prove useful to local ranchers. The Indian residents dispersed, and San Luis Rey fell into ruin. In 1865, President Abraham

Lincoln signed a proclamation restoring San Luis Rey to the Roman Catholic Church. But the grounds remained vacant until 1892, when a group of Franciscans reoccupied the property with the intent of transforming it into a missionary college. Irish-born Father Jeremiah Joseph O'Keefe led the renovation, gradually nursing the mission back to life. Restoration efforts continued through most of the 20th century. During the Spanish-American War, U.S. troops briefly occupied the mission.

The **Mission Church,** with its understated Spanish Colonial facade and simple bell tower, is the start of any mission visit. Completed in 1815, the nave stretches 165 feet—commodious enough to hold 1,000 worshipers in its early days. The impressive altar, with its gilded statues and blue trim, blends Spanish baroque and Moorish styles. A registered historical landmark, the old mission church is still available for weddings, funerals, and concerts. Mass is celebrated every Saturday evening at 5:30.

Next to the church is the **Convento** building, its facade decorated with 13 of the original 32 whitewashed arches. Inside are a gift shop and the **Mission Museum.** Exhibits cover the Native American, Spanish mission, Mexican, and Spanish-American War periods. Among the artifacts on display are 18th-century vestments and religious artwork.

The hub of mission life, both in olden times and today, is the **Patio of the Quadrangle,** surrounded by a classic Spanish Colonial colonnade. An old Spanish fountain and the first pepper tree planted in California highlight the neatly trimmed lawn and flowerbeds. Rooms flanking the patio provide housing for the current friars and space for a **Franciscan Retreat Center;** here individuals and groups can experience solitude and healing, education and renewal.

East of the church is the **Mission Cemetery,** one of the oldest active burial grounds in California. Early friars, Native Americans who helped build the mission, and pioneers of the San Luis Rey Valley are among those interred here. The grounds also contain the ruined barracks of the mission garrison and the **Sunken Gardens,** or *lavandería,* where mission Indians once bathed and washed their clothes.

San Luis Rey hosts a year-round slate of community events, including a Christmas Faire and a Heritage Ball in August, when the patio becomes an open-air ballroom. ■

Founded in 1798, Mission San Luis Rey—"King of Missions"—continues to serve local parishioners and wedding parties.

Escondido

SAN DIEGO COUNTY'S LARGEST INLAND CITY IS ESCONDIDO, a one-time center of avocado, citrus fruit, and grape growing that has burgeoned into a community of more than 130,000 people.

As the Spanish name (Hidden) suggests, Escondido is secreted within the foothills of the Coast Range, in easy striking distance of Palomar Mountain, Julian, and the Cuyamacas. Surrounded by mountains, the valley has its own dry microclimate. Summer temperatures are always warmer than along the coast; winter nights are cooler.

Although Escondido is a bedroom suburb for greater San Diego, civic leaders have encouraged the community to forge its own identity. Foremost among their projects is the **California Center for the Arts,** a showcase for everything from stand-up comedy and Chinese acrobats to ballet and country-western music. Designed by Charles Moore and opened in 1994, the attractive 12-acre complex includes a museum of 20th-century art, a large concert hall, and a small performing-arts theater.

Escondido's rich soil and arid climate create ideal grape-growing conditions. Southeast of town is **Orfila Vineyards and Winery,** which counts Merlot and Chardonnay among the wines in its stable. Guided tours are offered daily at 2 p.m., but you can tour the winery on your own at any time.

Escondido's other resident vintner is **Deer Park Winery,** about ten minutes north of town via Interstate 15. Similar varieties are grown and bottled here, available for tasting inside the market building. Provision your party from the Deer Park deli and stage an impromptu picnic amid the vines.

The winery also operates the adjacent **Escondido Museum of Autos,** which displays more than 120 vehicles and an array of classic neon garage and dealership signs. Bygone radios, vacuums, and televisions round out the collection. ■

The Buena Vista Social Club heats up the stage at the California Center for the Arts.

San Diego Wild Animal Park

SITUATED ON 1,800 ACRES OF ROLLING GRASSLAND AND rocky canyons near Escondido, the San Diego Wild Animal Park is a haven for endangered species that doubles as a major tourist attraction.

By the end of the 1960s, administrators at the San Diego Zoo had concluded that its Balboa Park location was no longer large enough to accommodate the zoological society's long-term goals—among them captive breeding and behavioral studies. The solution: a second "campus," where animals could roam in large enclosures similar to their natural surroundings. With its wide-open spaces—and its uncanny likeness to the East African savanna—the San Pasqual Valley emerged as a natural choice for the new park, which opened in 1972. Thirty years down the line, the Wild Animal Park now harbors more than 3,200 rare and exotic animals from 400 species. It maintains the country's largest veterinary hospital and has built a worldwide reputation for the propagation of rare and endangered animals. Among the almost extinct

species bred at the park—and later reintroduced into the wild—are the California condor (see p. 206), Arabian oryx, and Przewalski's horse.

The park is divided into two main sections: a more traditional zoo area with smaller animal exhibits that can be explored on foot and a massive "backcountry" area with huge, multispecies enclosures that can be viewed only from hiking trails or an electric tram. Beyond the front entrance gate is **Nairobi Village,** site of most of the park's guest amenities, including restaurants and picnic areas. Near the village center is an Animal Care Center where visitors can view newborns and a petting kraal that gives kids close encounters with several species. Open-air theaters host educational bird and elephant shows several times each day. You can also hand-feed colorful tropical birds at Lorikeet Landing.

How the zebra got its stripes becomes clear in a re-created natural habitat.

San Diego Wild Animal Park

www.wildanimalpark.org

🅰 189 D2

✉ 15500 San Pasqual Valley Rd. (Hwy. 78), Escondido

☎ 760-747-8702

💲 $$$$$

Scattered around the village are a dozen enclosures for smaller animals such as the meerkat, dik-dik, and Red River hog, Mombasa Lagoon is a refuge for exotic birds—the rare Chilean flamingo is one—as well as for feathered creatures migrating along the California coast. On the western edge of the lagoon is one of the park's most popular exhibits, a huge breeding habitat for lowland gorillas.

Condor Ridge, the park's

newest theme area, spreads out north of the village. This hilltop sanctuary protects rare North American animals such as the California condor, desert bighorn sheep, Aplomado falcon, and black-tailed prairie dog. Nearby are the park's rambling **Kupanda Falls Botanical Gardens**, centerpiece of a botanical collection that safeguards more than 3,500 species from all around the globe. There are special areas for native California, Baja, and South African plants,

as well as greenhouses for fuchsia, epiphytes, and bonsai.

Tumbling down a lush hillside south of the village is the **Heart of Africa**, a 32-acre habitat populated by unusual creatures such as the okapi, the giant eland, the bat-eared fox, and the ground hornbill. At the bottom of the safari trail is a lake with flamingos, storks, and other African birds, as well as a large cheetah enclosure and a terrace where you can feed giraffes by hand (see pp. 18-19).

Got time on your hands and a pair of sturdy shoes on your feet? Explore the park's vast hinterland on the **Kilimanjaro Safari Walk**, which rambles for nearly two miles between Heart of Africa and Condor Ridge. Several viewpoints along the route provide sweeping views of the huge East African multispecies enclosure with its herds of giraffe, zebra, antelope, and rhino. You can also gaze down into habitats for Sumatran tigers and African lions.

The only way to see the rest of the park's backcountry is by boarding the **Wgasa Bush Line** at Simba Station in the village. Narrated by knowledgeable (and often humorous) keepers, the train meanders more than five miles through six distinct habitats: Asian Plains, East African Plains, North Africa, Asian Waterhole, South Africa, and Mongolian Steppe. The 50-minute journey seemingly transports you far from southern California suburbia.

The Wild Animal Park hosts special events during the year, including "Park at Dark" nighttime hours during the valley's sultry summer months, a chrysanthemum festival in the fall, and a Festival of Lights during the Christmas holidays. The park also runs "Roar & Snore" sleepovers at a tented camp next to the East African plains. ■

Camp Pendleton

SAN DIEGO IS SEPARATED FROM ORANGE COUNTY AND
L.A.'s urban sprawl by Camp Pendleton, a massive U.S. Marine Corps
base that occupies the coast north of Oceanside. With more than
125,000 fairly pristine acres, the military facility is the largest undeveloped tract along the entire southern California coast and a refuge
for wildlife.

Pendleton is home base for the 1st
Marine Division and the 1st Marine
Expeditionary Force, including
many units that fought in the Gulf
War and Afghanistan. The base's
beaches, valleys, and mountains
provide realistic terrain in which to
train for various types of combat,
from large-scale amphibious landings to highly specialized missions.
You might catch a glimpse of
Marines training in their helicopters and tanks as you drive the
17 miles of Interstate 5 between
Oceanside and San Clemente. Ci-

vilians can observe these military
maneuvers from the vista point on
the freeway's west (southbound)
side, about halfway between the
Basilone Road exit and the Las
Pulgas exit. During full-scale war
games, you may spot aircraft carriers and destroyers anchored offshore and hovercraft zipping
toward the beach carrying troops
and supplies.

Camp Pendleton's history is rich
and varied. The Spanish Portolá
expedition of 1769, which trekked
along this stretch of coast on its

Camp Pendleton

- 🌐 www.cpp.usmc.mil
- 🚗 189 B4
- ☎ 760-725-5569
- 🚌 Bus: North County
  Transit District
  (760-722-6283) bus
  314 or 317

San Onofre
State Beach

- 🚗 189 A4
- ✉ Basilone Rd., San
  Onofre (Basilone Rd.
  exit off I-5)
- ☎ 949-366-8500
- 💲 $

**Military flight
maneuvers can be
witnessed from
the camp view-
point off I-5.**

way from San Diego to Monterey, named the area Santa Margarita. In 1844, after Mexico had gained its independence from Spain, the area became a private land grant called Rancho Santa Margarita. A few years later, English cattle baron John "Don Juan" Forster took control of the ranch by paying off the gambling debts of his brother-in-law, Pio Pico.

The land remained a thriving cattle ranch until the 1940s, when it was purchased by the U.S. Marine Corps and transformed into one of the world's largest Marine training facilities. The camp was named after General Joseph H. Pendleton and officially dedicated by President Franklin D. Roosevelt in June of 1942.

Since that year, Camp Pendleton has filled its primary purpose— molding soldiers—and taken on a secondary one as a sanctuary for wildlife. While the rest of the southern California coast gave way to bulldozers, Camp Pendleton stayed largely untouched, a place where indigenous flora and fauna continue to thrive. To manage these resources, the base has a large natural and cultural resource management staff. It also employs full-time biologists and archaeologists.

Tucked in the northwest corner of the base is **San Onofre State Beach,** one of the wilder stretches of the San Diego coast. The sand extends for nearly four miles, much of it anchoring sandstone bluffs covered in chaparral and wildflowers. Six marked trails lead down to the strand from Old Highway 101, which runs right through the heart of the state beach.

San Onofre is one of the few places along the San Diego coast where you can camp within sight and sound of the waves. As a result, the beach is often packed in summer. During the rest of the year,

Nature at Pendleton

From coastal dune communities and salt marshes to riparian woodlands and chaparral, Camp Pendleton harbors more than a dozen vegetation communities. Within its confines are four major watersheds including the meandering Santa Margarita, one of the last free-flowing (undammed) rivers left in southern California.

Equally staggering is the species count. It includes 18 threatened and endangered species, 818 different plant types, 300 birds, 60 fish, 43 reptiles and amphibians (including the red diamond rattlesnake), and 50 mammals—among them mountain lion, gray fox, and beaver. ■

however—especially on weekdays—you can often find yourself alone on the beach. At the north end is a legendary surfing spot called **Trestles** and a marshy area around the mouth of San Mateo Creek. At the southern extreme are a clothing-optional area and the twin towers of the San Onofre Nuclear Power Plant—about the only artificial structure visible along this stretch of coast.

For a closer look at Camp Pendleton and its human and animal life, take a self-guided tour (8 a.m.-5 p.m. daily), starting from the main gate near the Camp Pendleton exit off Interstate 5 in Oceanside. You'll need your own vehicle, plus a valid driver's license, proof of insurance, and vehicle registration. The tour allows you to explore at your own pace. Although the tours were suspended after the terrorist attacks of September 11, 2001, they are expected to resume in 2003. ■

More places to visit in North County

For some good old-fashioned fun, hit the San Diego County Fair, held each summer in Del Mar.

ANTIQUE GAS & STEAM ENGINE MUSEUM

Rural life in early 1900s southern California comes alive at this facility covering 40 acres of rolling farmland on the outskirts of Vista. The museum continues to operate as a genuine farm: The antique machinery is kept in good working order, and most of the acreage is devoted to raising wheat, sorghum, and oats.

The museum's main focus is the century between 1849 and 1950, when agriculture was California's primary business and way of life. Among the exhibits are blacksmith and wheelwright shops, gristmills and sawmills, steam- and gas-driven power units, and a country kitchen.

Twice each year (June and October) the museum stages a Harvest Fair that includes a threshing bee, hay rides, early American arts and crafts demonstrations, and an antique engine and tractor show. ◪ 189 B3 ✉ 2040 N. Santa Fe Ave., Vista ☎ 760-941-1791 ⏰ 10a.m.-4 p.m. daily ⑤ $ 🚌 Bus: 306 from Vista Transit Center

HOT-AIR BALLOONING

The wicker basket of a hot-air balloon is a unique perch from which to navigate North County. Coastal tours offer a bird's-eye view of the Pacific Ocean, the Del Mar coast, the million-dollar mansions of Rancho Santa Fe, the horse ranches of the lush San Dieguito Valley, and other vistas stretching all the way to Mexico's Coronado Islands on a clear day. Balloons lift off from Encinitas, Del Mar, or Temecula, then follow a southbound course that normally ends in Carmel Valley or Del Mar Mesa. Companies include **California Dreamin'** in Escondido (800-373-3359) and **Skysurfer** in Del Mar (800-660-6809). ◪ 189 B3 ⑤ $$$$$

MUSEUM OF MAKING MUSIC

This new museum offers a visual and auditory journey through the history of music, from the 1890s through the 1980s. More than 450 vintage instruments are on display, plus samples of the top tunes of the 20th century. An interactive area lets visitors make their own music on guitars, pianos, drums, and other instruments. ◪ 189 B2 ✉ 5790 Armada Dr., Carlsbad ☎ 760-438-5996 ⏰ Closed Mon. ⑤ $$

RANCHO BUENA VISTA ADOBE

The best preserved of San Diego's old haciendas is Rancho Buena Vista Adobe in Vista, built in the 1850s and still looking much as it did in Mexican days. The 11 rooms, furnished with late 19th-century antiques and decorative arts, give visitors a glimpse of a bygone way of life on the great California ranchos. ◪ 189 B3 ✉ 651 E. Vista Way, Vista ☎ 760-639-6164 or 6139 ⏰ 10 a.m.-3 p.m. Wed.-Sat. ⑤ $ ■

With the international border and Baja California nearby, exotic getaways lie minutes from downtown San Diego. Also within easy reach: mountain villages, a vast desert, wine trails, and a pristine isle.

Baja, East County, & beyond

A street mural in Rosarito

San Juan Capistrano, founded in 1776, is the crown jewel of the Spanish mission system.

Baja, East County, & beyond

FOR SHEER VARIETY, SAN DIEGO RIVALS ANY CITY IN THE WORLD WHEN IT comes to day trips and longer excursions. After seeing the sights of the city, many visitors indulge their itch to cross the Mexican border for a jaunt into Tijuana. The border crossing at San Ysidro, about 18 miles south of downtown San Diego, is the busiest international ground border crossing in the world.

Entering Mexico is usually expeditious, but your return to the United States will almost invariably involve a long line of cars waiting to be cleared by customs and immigration officers. Though commuters may gripe, it can all be part of the fun for visitors who enjoy souvenir bargaining amid a partylike atmosphere. Those going no farther than Tijuana might consider the painless method of taking San Diego's blue-line trolley to the border, then walking across and catching a taxi ($5 or so) to see the sights.

There's far more to Baja California, of course, than bustling, noisy Tijuana. If time permits, intrepid visitors can sample the popular coastal towns of Rosarito and Ensenada, with a stop at Puerto Nuevo for that village's famed lobster dinners. The inland town of Tecate provides an additional unexpected delight—a peaceful, nontouristy ambience just blocks away from another, more remote border station.

San Diego is indeed a large metropolis, yet small towns lurk within a relatively short distance, and hidden pockets of repose punctuate

the urban area. In the forested mountains northeast of the city, the old mining town of Julian offers even more delights—especially during the fall apple harvest. Over the mountain pass from Julian, the vast Anza-Borrego Desert State Park provides the consummate getaway amid mind-boggling geologic formations and wondrous plant and animal life. The region is spectacular in early spring, when the wildflowers bloom.

Inland, just north of the San Diego County line, Temecula—once nothing more than a stagecoach stopover—is now famed as southern California's only developed wine trail. Beyond the county's coastal stretch, serene San Juan Capistrano lures visitors to its famous mission; it also happens to be convenient to many fine beaches and resort towns. A short boat ride away, Santa Catalina Island captivates with its postcard-perfect village and picturesque setting; it is especially popular with divers, sailors, and other water-sport enthusiasts. Even visitors in a time crunch should be able to pack several of these amazingly varied excursions into a single visit. ■

Tijuana

Tijuana Tourism Board
www.seetijuana.com
ⓐ 213 C2
✉ Ave. Paseo de los Heroes 9365-201, Zona Rio
☎ (011-52) 664-684-2854 or 888-775-2417 (in U.S.)
🚆 Blue line trolley

AT FIRST GLANCE IT'S HARD TO IMAGINE THAT NOISY, crowded, supercommercial Tijuana was once just a peaceful dwelling spot for Kumeyaay Indians and Mexican ranchers.

Americans descended on Tijuana en masse in the 1920s, chasing sun, fun, and rum. Prohibition in the U.S., combined with the opening of the Agua Caliente Spa & Casino in Tijuana, turned the town into a mecca for booze, gambling, and a growing list of other decadent pursuits. All were now minutes from the California border—and just a two-hour drive from Los Angeles.

Tijuana boomed until Prohibition was repealed and Mexico outlawed gambling, leading to Agua Caliente's closure in 1935. Yet servicemen in San Diego continue to be tempted by this nearby city where almost anything goes; for decades they've been joined by southern Californians and others with a fascination for exotica. Food, drink, discos, and shopping are the most popular pursuits, but Tijuana offers a wealth of cultural sights and activities as well.

Getting to Tijuana is a snap. I-5 and I-805 both end right at the San Ysidro border crossing. Unless you plan to continue beyond Tijuana, driving is not recommended. Park in a lot at the border and walk across, or catch the San Diego trolley or a private bus from downtown.

However you enter Mexico, souvenir vendors will besiege you at once. Refrain from buying—there will be plenty of chances ahead, and those bags grow cumbersome.

Most attractions are located in Tijuana's Zona Centro and Zona Río, both easily accessible by taxi (about $5). **Avenida Revolución**—a short walk or drive from the border, and the heart of Zona Centro—is the city's top tourist trap: It's lined with boisterous bars, restaurants, nightclubs, tacky shops, and painted donkeys in the streets. Still, few can (or do) resist this noisy magnet, known as La Revu. Note the landmark **El Palacio Frontón** *(between Calles 7a & 8a),* the Moorish-style former jai alai stadium that now hosts fairs and exhibitions. Tijuana's oldest church, the 1902 **Catedral de Nuestra Senora de Guadalupe** *(Ave. Ninos Héroes & Calle 2a),* topped by yellow and blue domes, is a short walk from La Revu.

Zona Río, east of Zona Centro, is a modern, upscale district, yet many day-trippers never see it. Bisected by Paseo de los Heroes and paralleling the Río Tijuana, this section of town is home to fine hotels, restaurants, shops, and more sophisticated nightlife. The **Centro Cultural de Tijuana** *(Paseo de los Héroes, Zona Río, 687-9600, closed Mon.)* dispels the myth of Tijuana as a shabby party town. This gleaming complex hosts prestigious theatrical events, dance performances, concerts, art exhibits, and films. The exquisite **Museo de las Californias,** added in 2002, leads viewers through exhibits that chronicle Baja California from prehistoric times to the present. **Plaza Río Tijuana,** across from the cultural center, is a large, nontouristy shopping complex with department stores, specialty shops, restaurants, and a cinema. Gated schools have replaced the old **Agua Caliente Spa & Casino** *(Paseo de los Héroes & Blvd. Sánchez Taboada),* but the 200-foot-high minaret is still visible. ∎

A vendor dazzles passers-by with her smile and paper-flower bouquets.

More Baja

MANY VISITORS BEGIN AND END THEIR FORAY INTO MEXICO at Tijuana, gleaning an image of that mega-city as their only memory of this delightful country. That's too bad, for those who continue their journey southward into Baja California will discover sweeter surprises: Rosarito Beach, Puerto Nuevo, and Ensenada all lie within a day of San Diego. If you are driving, Mexico 1 or the parallel Mexico 1D toll road (offering a wider, better-paved surface) will take you from Tijuana to all three towns.

Rosarito Beach Convention & Visitors Bureau
www.rosaritobch.com
▲ 213 C2
✉ Blvd. Juárez at Encino (inside Oceana Plaza commercial center
☎ (011-52) 661-612-0396 or 800-962-2252 (in U.S.)

Ensenada Tourist Office
www.enjoyensenada.com
✉ Blvd. Costero 1477
☎ (011-52) 61-78-3675 or 800-310-9687 (in U.S.)

Situated 18 miles south of Tijuana, Rosarito Beach (Playas de Rosarito) has been a favorite playground for visitors since the 1930s, when Hollywood stars turned the sleepy fishing village into a chic retreat. After the Transpeninsular Highway was completed in 1973, tourism began in earnest; by 1995 Rosarito had been designated a municipality. Now boasting a population of more than 100,000, Rosarito has managed to maintain its aura of an authentic Mexican village amid the throngs of visitors—including San Diego college students—who come to party on weekends and holidays.

Boulevard Juárez, an extension of Mexico 1 (the Transpeninsular Highway), serves as Rosarito's main thoroughfare. As such it is lined with artisan stalls, hotels, and restaurants. The north end of town has a more genuine feel to it, while most of the tourist draws cluster at the south end, near the **Rosarito Beach Hotel** (*Blvd. Juárez 22710, 011-52-612-0144 or 866-767-2748*). Dating from Prohibition and once a haven for big-name movie stars and starlets, this illustrious oceanfront hotel is fraying at the seams. Still, as a nostalgic icon, the property rewards travelers seeking to relive its legend—even if it's just to sip a margarita while watching the sun sink into the sea.

There's not much to see in town. Rosarito is known primarily for its 20 miles of expansive beaches, fishing, horseback riding, seafood dining, and shopping (especially for rustic, handcrafted furnishings and other home accessories). Nightlife can become as raucous as that in Tijuana, with visitors imbibing copious quantities of tequila and beer, grabbing the mike at karaoke bars, or disco dancing until dawn. Much of the action takes place at **Festival Plaza** (*N of Rosarito Beach Hotel*), a colorful hotel and entertainment complex where revelers

wander the various bars or listen to live bands in the courtyard.

About three miles south of Rosarito Beach, off the Transpeninsular Highway at Km 34.5, the obscure fishing village of **Popotla** hit the limelight when Twentieth Century Fox chose it as a shooting locale for *Titanic*. Though Fox Studios Baja was intended to be a temporary set, it has since been used for scenes in *Pearl Harbor* and *Tomorrow Never Dies*, becoming both a permanent facility and a tourist attraction. The studio's **Foxploration** *(866-369-2252 from U.S., closed Tues.-Wed., adm. fee)* ushers visitors through phases of the moviemaking process. It also features *Titanic* sets and props, an open-air amphitheater, fast-food outlets, and a gift shop.

The Km 44 exit off the Transpeninsular Highway leads to **Puerto Nuevo,** a tiny coastal village known for its delicious seafood, notably local lobster. A few dozen other dining establishments have grown up around **Ortega's Patio** *(614-1619),* the town's original lobster restaurant. Mexican arts and crafts are sold at shops along the main street, a pleasant browse that lets you walk off the calories.

Ensenada (population about 350,000), 75 miles south of Tijuana, is a well-developed city and cruise-ship port. Attractions and entertainment abound. Once a hub of ranching and gold-mining, Ensenada now prospers from its fishing fleet and fish-processing industry. It is also the gateway to Baja's **Guadalupe Valley** wine country.

Civic pride swells this traditional Mexican city, where visitors can enjoy the revamped seaside promenade and the numerous pleasant plazas in town. Along the waterfront, the hacienda-style **Riviera del Pacífico**—fashionable with celebrities in the 1930s—was eclipsed by the ban on gambling.

Rescued from oblivion in the 1990s, the complex is now the city's social, civic, and cultural center. Visitors can tour the exquisite gardens, the extravagant public areas (when not in use), and the **Museo de Historia de Ensenada** *(Riviera del Pacífico, 61-77-0594),* where exhibits highlight regional history.

Sportfishing operators organize outings to pursue albacore, bonito, yellowtail, and other local species. Baja's oldest winery, the 1888 **Bodegas de Santo Tomás** *(Ave. Miramar 666, 61-78-3333, Mon.-Fri. & weekends by appt.),* welcomes visitors to taste its popular varietals. Legendary **Hussong's Cantina** *(Ave. Ruíz 113, 61-78-3210)* has been rehydrating customers since 1892. ∎

Chaises longues await poolside loungers at the retro Rosarito Beach Hotel.

Baja California Tourism Information
☎ **800-225-2786**
    (in U.S.)

The little village of Puerto Nuevo is famed for its curios (opposite page) and crustaceans (below).

Julian & vicinity

SAN DIEGO'S GOLD FEVER REACHED A FEVER PITCH HERE in 1869, when cattleman Fred Coleman discovered flecks of the stuff in a creek nearby. Gold was being mined within a year, and the little mountain town of Julian had been established.

Baker Dave Smothers proudly displays the fruit tarts of his labors.

The flames spared Julian (population 1,600) itself, which retains the flavor of a Western mining town. There's a well-preserved Main Street, wooden walkways, and original building facades. Shops and galleries display works turned out by artisans in studio cabins scattered around the neighboring woods. Also near at hand are a number of bed-and-breakfast getaways popular among San Diegans. Right in the middle of town, the

Eagle and High Peak Mine gives one-hour tours of its authentic gold mine, leading visitors through the actual tunnels. An on-site museum explains gold-mining machinery and equipment; a small rock shop on the premises offers samples for sale. Head to the **Julian Pioneer Museum** on Washington Street (one block behind Town Hall) to learn more. The memorabilia here include archival photographs, artifacts, tools, clothing, Indian basketry, and a large collection of antique lace.

NEARBY SIGHTS

Seven miles west of Julian, the tiny town of **Santa Ysabel** (*intersection of Calif. 78 & Calif. 79*) is popular for the high-quality local art at **Santa Ysabel Art Gallery** and the tasty goodies on offer at **Dudley's Bakery.**

Mission Santa Ysabel (*on Calif. 79 about 12 miles N of town*) still serves the local Native American population. You can visit the cemetery or go inside for a tour of the small museum containing photos and other artifacts. ■

Nestled in the mountains about 60 miles northeast of San Diego, Julian can be reached from downtown by following I-8 to Calif. 79, which winds north past scenic Cuyamaca Rancho State Park (see pp. 229–230) and into town. The drive is a visual feast capped by an olfactory one: The green forests, bursts of wildflowers, and dustings of snow you pass en route give way in town to the luscious aroma of apple pie and warm cider.

Indeed, Julian is justifiably famous for its apple-harvesting season (*mid-Sept.–mid-Nov.*). In fall the roads fill with families picking produce, sipping cider, and feasting on hot apple pie from village restaurants and roadside stands.

In the tinder-dry summer of 2002, San Diegans were subjected to scents far more acrid than those of apple pie. Ferreting out marijuana plants, a California National Guard helicopter hit some electric-power lines, triggering a disastrous forest fire. The $20 million inferno scorched more than 61,000 acres, destroyed 37 homes (and 116 bars), and displaced 500 to 1,000 residents.

Julian Chamber of Commerce
www.julianca.com
📍 213 D3
✉ 2129 Main St., Julian
☎ 760-765-1857

Eagle and High Peak Mine
📍 213 D3
✉ C St., Julian
☎ 760-765-0036
🕐 Open daily, weather permitting
💲 $$

Julian Pioneer Museum
📍 213 D3
✉ 2811 Washington St., Julian
☎ 760-765-0227
🕐 Open daily
💲 Donation

Anza-Borrego Desert State Park

THE VAST EXPANSE OF THIS PARK—600,000 ACRES AND change—contains diverse and fascinating landforms. With elevations ranging from near sea level to almost 6,200 feet, the park embraces a dizzying array of geologic formations, archaeological sites, plant and wildlife species, and opportunities for hiking, biking, and camping.

Little is known about the humans who lived in the area for more than 5,000 years. Judging from the pictographs and petroglyphs they left behind, however, anthropologists have concluded that they used neither pottery nor bows and arrows. The region was populated by semi-nomadic Kumeyaay and Cahuilla tribes when Spanish explorer Juan Bautista de Anza and others came through in 1774, blazing an immigrant trail from Sonora, Mexico, to Alta California's port of San Diego. Both the Southern Emigrant Trail and the Butterfield Overland Mail route traversed the park's southern portion.

In the early 1900s, the park's rugged southeast corner was re-shaped to make way for the "Impossible Railroad" of John D. Spreckels, Jr. The tunnels and trestles running through Carrizo Gorge are now considered an engineering marvel.

Today Anza-Borrego is the biggest state park in the lower 48. This huge swatch of the Colorado Desert runs more than 70 miles north to south (from Riverside County nearly to the Mexican border) and 32 miles east to west (from eastern San Diego County's Peninsular Range toward the Salton Sea).

Roughly a two-hour drive from downtown San Diego, the park is easy to access by taking I-8 to Rte. S2. If you approach via Julian, you can take either Calif. 79 or Calif. 78 to Rte. S2 (both connect with Rte. S22 into the visitor center and Borrego Springs). The latter two routes take more time but confer grander views as they wind around forested **Cuyamaca Rancho State Park** (see pp. 229-230), through little Julian (see p. 218),

Visitor Information Center

www.anzaborrego.statepark.org

- 213 D3
- Palm Canyon Dr., Borrego Springs
- 760-767-5311; Wildflower Hotline 760-767-4684
- Park open year-round; visitor center open daily Oct.-May, weekends and holidays other months
- $ day-use permits for vehicles at Borrego Palm Canyon & Tamarisk Grove campgrounds, and at Vern Whitaker Horse Camp

Borrego Springs Chamber of Commerce

- 786 Palm Canyon Dr., Borrego Springs
- 760-767-5555

Soaking in the scenery atop a desert overlook in the Borrego Badlands

A Font's Point sunrise illuminates the Santa Rosa Mountains and the Colorado Desert beyond.

and along stretches of high-desert vegetation. The road then descends more than 3,000 feet and crosses the Pacific Crest National Scenic Trail, revealing a stark valley surrounded by desolate mountains. This juxtaposition of cool greenery and dry, barren terrain leaves visitors giddy. Unless you and your vehicle are prepared for extreme heat (summer temperatures of 105°F and higher are common), visit the park between October and May. (Expect plenty of company from late February through March, though, when the wildflowers come into bloom.)

Thousands of acres of wilderness, 500 miles of primitive and dirt roads, and endless expanses of peaceful desert and brilliant sky

await exploration here. Palm groves, cactuses, wildflowers, mule deer, golden eagles, bighorn sheep, iguanas, and rattlesnakes all share the enchanting setting.

Anza-Borrego is that rare park where you can pitch a tent wherever you like (but it must be at least 100 feet from any water source). There are four developed campgrounds and eight primitive camping areas as well. To preserve the environment, vehicles are not allowed off-road. That won't hang you up, though; more than 500 miles of roadway lead to most of the park's popular sights.

Pick up supplies at tiny **Borrego Springs** (the park's commercial center), whose population fluctuates seasonally between 3,000

known for the cactus wrens, mock-ingbirds, and phainopeplas that are drawn to its natural well. The mile-long **Cactus Loop Nature Trail** skirts all sorts of plant life, while the half-mile loop of the **Narrows Earth Trail** focuses on the park's geology.

The 18-mile **Erosion Road** (S22) driving tour shows the hand of nature at work on the land. Stops en route overlook outstanding views or point out the geologic forces that have created mountains, canyons, and earthquake fault lines.

The 26-mile **S2 drive** follows the Southern Emigrant Trail and the historic route formerly used by the Butterfield Overland Mail, the Mormon Battalion, Spanish explorers, Kit Carson, and gold miners. This road also passes the reconstructed 1857 **Vallecito Stage Station,** once a major stop on the overland route, and **Agua Caliente County Park,** where travelers can soothe their aches in the natural hot springs.

Solitude is the reward for those who venture even farther afield. **Font's Point,** in the Borrego Badlands (off Rte. S22, east of the visitor center and Borrego Springs), affords commanding views over the valley, as well as revealing looks at Pliocene and Pleistocene sediments. Archaeology buffs favor **Blair Valley** (off S2, about 8 miles SE of Scissors Crossing) for its Native American pictographs, grinding rocks (morteros), and other signatures of indigenous life. **Fish Creek** (off Split Mountain Rd., S from Calif. 78 near Ocotillo Wells) boasts oddly shaped caves and canyons caused by eons of erosion, as well as a narrow water-split fault line separated by majestic red walls 600 feet high. Nearby is the **Elephant Trees Discovery Trail,** which leads to an instance of the unusual species. ■

and 9,000. The town sports amenities from RV parks and grocery stores to fine hotels and resorts.

From Borrego Springs, it's a short drive west to the park's visitor center, where you can pick up walking-trail and driving-tour maps. The surrounding garden and pond are home to labeled specimens of the region's unique and bizarre cactuses, wildflowers, and other plants.

From the visitor center, signs point to the **Palm Canyon Trail.** This easy 3-mile round-trip hike leads to an oasis filled with cactuses, seasonal waterfalls, a stream, and palm groves. The Borrego Palm Canyon Campground is located nearby. Other short but worthwhile treks include the **Yaqui Well Nature Trail,** a 2-mile path

Let 1,000 cactuses bloom!

Though hostile to human habitation, the desert nurtures myriad other forms of life. Among the most curious are the many shrubs, cactuses, and wildflowers that seem to thrive on pluvial neglect: They flourish in the near-absence of rain—a desert specialty.

Strange and beautiful things grow in stunning profusion throughout Anza-Borrego Desert State Park. Cactuses can be enjoyed year-round in all their prickly grandeur, but wild-flowers are the more coveted prize by far. Their spring blooming spectacle draws thousands of visitors, who come to watch vivid blossoms transform the customary earth tones of the landscape into fields and pockets laden with brilliantly ethereal shades of magenta, blue, yellow, red, white, and purple.

The prime season is usually a two-week window that opens sometime in late February or early March and hinges on that year's rainfall and temperature fluctuations. Because these influences vary annually, it's difficult to predict what sort of display nature will stage. It all comes down to seeds; a handful of soil is likely to be loaded with dozens of both annual and perennial varieties.

The showiest seasons blanket the terrain with yellow brittlebush, red chuparosa, blue phacelia, pink sand verbena, white dune prim-

rose and chicory, and masses of golden dande-lions and sunflowers. As the season unfolds, this floral carpet migrates from the desert floor to higher elevations; if you miss the spectacle lower down, head to Indian Gorge, Blair Valley, or Culp Valley to catch the late bloomers.

As any wildflower maven will tell you, their beauty stems not from their sheer number (or even the intensity of their hues) but from their evanescence. Study your surroundings careful-ly and you'll make some delightful discoveries. Search desert washes and dry slopes for the brittlebush, a member of the sunflower family; its bright yellow flowers in loosely branched clusters measure about 2 to 3 inches wide. (The fragrant branches were reportedly used as incense in California's earliest churches.) The slender desert sunflower (look for 2-inch

golden heads surrounded by 10 or more ob-long rays) grows along roadsides and sandy flatlands, nourishing birds and bees. Often found nearby is the sweet-scented, saucer-shaped white dune primrose. This diaphanous blossom, about 2 inches wide, opens in early evening and closes up again midmorning.

The sand verbena's brilliant pink clusters of tiny trumpet-shaped flowers, held aloft on sticky stalks with long stems, also fringe road-ways. The subtle white flowers of the desert chicory favor shady spots. Desert washes and rocky slopes harbor the chuparosa's deep-red tubular flowers, which bloom at various times throughout the year and are sought out by

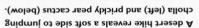

A desert hike reveals a soft side to jumping cholla (left) and prickly pear cactus (below).

hummingbirds and other avian species that sip its sweet nectar. The blue phacelia's pale, bell-shaped blossoms with rounded petals may be seen poking up amid other shrubs along roadsides, hill slopes, and in washes. Anza-Borrego's visitor-center garden (see p. 219) provides glimpses of the park's distinc-tive plants and vegetation. As you wait for the seasonal show to begin, check the wildflower hotline (760-767-4684) for updates. ■

Small towns of San Diego County

▲ 213 C3, C4
🚃 Orange line trolley
to La Mesa

**Ramona
Chamber of
Commerce**
www.ramonachamber.com
✉ 960 Main St.,
Ramona
☎ 760-789-1311

SAN DIEGO MAY SEEM LIKE A BIG CITY FULL OF URBAN neighborhoods and sprawling suburbia, but anyone with time and a car can ferret out a host of hidden surprises.

LA MESA

The city of **La Mesa** is now so large that it appears to be an extension of San Diego. Sitting northeast of downtown, on I-8 near the stadium, it is overlooked by most people traversing this east-west artery. Formerly filled with sheep and cattle ranches, La Mesa is now home to some 55,000 residents.

Drive or take the trolley to the La Mesa Boulevard stop. The 1915 **La Mesa Depot** (*La Mesa Blvd. & Spring St.*), now a part of the San Diego Railroad Museum, once welcomed steam locomotives to town. Enormous malls and shopping centers loom nearby, but most locals ignore them for the Main Street atmosphere of **La Mesa Boulevard.** Stretching for several blocks from the depot, this blissfully noncommercial strip houses a fanciful assortment of low-key mom-and-pop shops. Stores selling antiques, collectibles, and curios predominate, with an intermingling of alfresco restaurants and neighborhood bars. During **Oktoberfest,** beer tents and crafts vendors take to (and take over) the street, drawing thousands of visitors to town for the weekend festivities.

RAMONA

Above the fog line but below the snow line in the foothills of the Cuyamaca Mountains about 36 miles northeast of San Diego, the village of **Ramona** was first inhabited by seminomadic Diegueno Indians. Also known as the Valley of the Sun, this ethnically mixed community of about 15,000 is dotted with horse ranches and farms. Larger businesses have moved in, but the area around Main Street (between 3rd and 10th Streets) has been preserved as **Old Town Ramona;** its antique shops and historic structures (including the original town hall) date from the 1880s.

The **Guy B. Woodward Museum** (*645 Main St., 760-789-7644., Thurs.-Sun., adm. fee*) centers on the Verlaque House—America's only French provincial adobe residence—as well as a complex of historic buildings. Exhibits include wagons, furnishings, artifacts, and documents capturing Ramona in the late 1800s.

Equestrian trails are plentiful; anglers enjoy Sutherland and San Vicente Reservoirs; and two parks cater to hikers and picnickers. Popular annual events are the three-day Ramona Rodeo (held in May) and the four-day Ramona Country Fair (usually in August).

RANCHO SANTA FE

Once a well-kept secret, **Rancho Santa Fe** was spotlighted in tragic fashion by the 1997 mass suicide of Heaven's Gate cult members. Until then, this hideaway 30 miles northeast of San Diego had been a haven for about 4,000 super-affluent residents (including many celebrities) who cherished the privacy and seclusion the area had long afforded them. Fortunately the notoriety proved short-lived, allowing life in this posh community to return to an approximation of normal.

Known by residents as the Ranch, the town was designed in the 1920s by prominent architect Lillian Rice, who patterned it after villages she had visited in Spain. Rice's original 12-room house, constructed in 1922, later became the **Inn at Rancho Santa Fe** *(858-759-1131)*—a pied-à-terre for such luminaries as Errol Flynn, Bing Crosby, and Bette Davis, and still a watering hole with a difference. The village itself evolved around Rice's Spanish Colonial architecture.

Most residents dwell inside magnificent estates secreted among stands of towering eucalyptus trees, fruit orchards, and horse ranches. Park your car near **Paseo Delicias** (the main street) and you can easily negotiate this tiny town on foot. At footing the bill in any village boutique, gallery, or restaurant, however, you're on your own.

FALLBROOK

About 20 miles northwest of Escondido, **Fallbrook**—another town unto itself—takes pride in being "avocado capital of the world." Thousands of acres are planted not only with luscious avocados, but also with oranges, lemons, macadamia trees, and a cornucopia of other subtropical fruits, vegetables, and flowers. Located on the east of Camp Pendleton Marine Base, Fallbrook's 38,000 residents include active service personnel, retirees, and growers and their families.

Head for **Old Main Street** in the village center for browsing and bargains on antiques, collectibles, and handmade crafts. Plenty of old-fashioned eateries offer sustenance nearby. April's annual **Avocado Festival** *(760-728-5845)* honors this heavenly fruit with activities, food, and live entertainment. ∎

Ripe oranges are a frequent treat for the eyes, nose, and tongue in the hill towns northeast of San Diego.

Temecula Valley's wine country

Temecula Chamber of Commerce Visitor Center
www.temecula.org
🅰 213 C4
✉ 28464 Old Town Front St., Temecula
☎ 909-694-0292

Temecula Valley Winegrowers Association
www.temeculawines.org
☎ 909-699-3626

SOUTHERN CALIFORNIA'S ONLY DEVELOPED WINE REGION sits less than 60 miles north of San Diego, just off Interstate 15 near the town of Temecula—a former stop on the Butterfield Overland Mail route. The fragrant vineyards of fifteen prestigious wineries stretch out across rolling hills, backdropped by mountain peaks soaring 10,000 feet high. Even on the warmest summer days, the 1,500-foot elevation assures cool summer breezes.

The Temecula Valley wine trail follows Rancho California Road, with some wineries on adjacent streets *(maps available at visitor center)*. Most wineries offer tastings for a fee and throw in souvenir glasses. There's usually a picnic area; some of the larger operations run restaurants, delis, or shops as well.

Méthode champenoise and premium varietals are the highlights at **Thornton Winery** *(32575 Rancho California Rd.)*, with a gourmet restaurant and well-stocked gift shop. **Callaway Vineyard & Winery** *(32720 Rancho California Rd.)* offers noteworthy California coastal "food-friendly" wines. **Baily Vineyard & Winery** *(33440 La Serena Way)* has a restaurant and deli where you can sample one of their award-winning bottles. A bed-and-breakfast distinguishes the château-style **Churon Winery** *(33233 Rancho California Rd.)*.

The area's newest resident, **Miramonte**, is being planted in Syrah grapes designed to yield a world-class estate wine. **Mount Palomar Winery** *(33820 Rancho California Rd.)* is noted for its fine Mediterranean varietals, gourmet deli, gift shop, concerts, and special events. At **Cilurzo Vineyard & Winery** *(41220 Calle Contento)*, try the Vincheno, a proprietary blend of red and white.

Estate-grown varietals are produced at the hilltop **Falkner Winery** *(40620 Calle Contento)*, while more than 16 different varietals await degustation at **Maurice Car'rie Winery** *(34225 Rancho California Rd.)*, which also owns the neighboring **Van Roekel Vineyards & Winery** *(34567 Rancho California Rd.)*. Almond champagne is just one specialty of the family-owned and operated **Wilson Creek Winery** *(35960 Rancho California Rd.)*. Seven varietals and various champagnes are vinted at **Filsinger Vineyards & Winery** *(39050 De Portola Rd.)*. Misty Key, a blend of Sauvignon Blanc and Johannesburg Riesling, is the proprietary wine at **Keyways Vineyard & Winery** *(37338 De Portola Rd.)*. ■

Just add waiter: A fine white wine awaits tasting in Temecula.

San Juan Capistrano

SAN JUAN CAPISTRANO IS BEST KNOWN FOR ITS HISTORIC Mission San Juan Capistrano, but the small city also boasts three structures from the 1780s in the Los Rios neighborhood and a restored 1895 railroad depot (still used by Amtrak trains making their run up the coast). Architectural walking tours leave from the station platform on Saturdays, heading for all the sights—including the mission.

MISSION SAN JUAN CAPISTRANO

Founded on November 1, 1776, by Franciscan Father Junípero Serra and a missionary band, Mission San Juan Capistrano ranks seventh (counting north from San Diego) in California's Spanish mission system. (In eye appeal, however, many contend it is first.) Chosen for its rich soil and abundant water, the mission accommodated some 2,000 neophytes at its peak. They toiled in neighboring fields, tanned hides, made soap, and undertook any other task required to keep the mission self-sufficient.

Three churches stood on the original site, which comprised tens of thousands of acres but has since shrunk to ten. Only ruins remain of the earliest stone church, but the white **Serra Chapel,** dedicated in 1778, is California's oldest standing church—as well as the only chapel extant where Padre Serra is known to have said Mass. The mission grounds also contain soldiers' barracks, living quarters for the padres, a Native American cemetery, fountain-filled gardens, and a museum displaying the 1865 document that returned the mission to the Church.

The famous **Fiesta de las Colondrinas,** celebrating the annual return of swallows to San Juan Capistrano, traditionally culminates on St. Joseph's Day (March 19). Since records were first kept in the 1770s, this has been roughly the date when flocks of swallows swoop into the mission to nest (and rest!) after their 6,000-mile flight from Goya, Argentina. Dependable dropins for 200 years, the swallows have been a tad less predictable since their nests were briefly removed during renovations in the 1990s.

San Juan Capistrano Chamber of Commerce
www.sanjuanchamber.com
✉ 31871 Camino Capistrano, Ste. 306, San Juan Capistrano
🗺 213 B4
☎ 949-493-4700

Architectural Walking Tours
☎ 949-489-0736
⏱ Sat., 10 a.m.
💲💲 (includes donation for mission admission)

Mission San Juan Capistrano
www.missionsjc.com
✉ Ortega Hwy. & Camino Capistrano
☎ 949-234-1300
⏱ Open daily, except major holidays
💲💲

Votive candles light the way inside Mission San Juan Capistrano.

Santa Catalina Island

Catalina Island Visitors Bureau
www.visitcatalina.org
✉ 1 Green Pier, Avalon
☎ 310-510-1520

Santa Catalina Island Conservancy
🅰 213 A4
✉ Permits: Claressa & 3rd Sts.
☎ 310-510-2595

Ferries
Catalina Classic Cruises (serves San Pedro), 800-641-1004

Catalina Explorer (serves Long Beach & Dana Pt.), 877-432-6276

Catalina Express (serves San Pedro, Long Beach, & Dana Pt.), 800-995-4386

Catalina Passenger Service (serves Newport Beach), 949-673-5245

Tours
Cape Canyon Tour, 310-510-8687

THOUGH IT LIES JUST 22 MILES OFF THE SOUTHERN California coast, Santa Catalina Island—second largest of the Channel Islands after Santa Cruz—feels like a distant land.

The Catalina story starts as early as 500 B.C., when the island was home to Gabrielino Indians. "Officially" discovered during a 1542 voyage by Juan Rodríguez Cabrillo, Catalina was used variously by pirates, Russian fur trappers, and smugglers.

In 1919 Catalina Island came into the possession of chewing-gum magnate William Wrigley, Jr., who constructed a mansion, modernized the town of Avalon into a resort, and promoted the island as a haven for sportfishing. Though the island has had some close calls with real estate developers and big business interests, in the 1970s the Santa Catalina Island Conservancy acquired more than 86 percent of the land; it continues to zealously guard the fragile environment.

Year-round passenger-ferry services depart from San Pedro, Long Beach, Newport Beach, and Dana Point. After an ocean crossing of 1 to 1.5 hours, the ships dock at the wharf in Avalon. Nonresident cars are not allowed in Avalon, and even most locals get around on gas-powered golf carts or bicycles (both can be rented near the wharf).

No matter. This delightful town, where chain establishments are verboten and the permanent population numbers about 3,500, is easy to navigate on foot. Most of the action centers along the **Crescent Avenue boardwalk,** stretching from the boat dock to the circular (and iconic) 1920s **Casino.** Designed as a social center rather than a gambling hall, today the Casino houses the **Catalina Island Museum** *(310-510-2414)* and the Catalina Art Association Art Gallery.

Available tours include undersea and glass-bottom boat excursions, as well as flying-fish trips (Catalina's claim to fame). The island's crystal-clear seas are ideal for swimming, kayaking, snorkeling, fishing, and diving. Tours and equipment rentals are easy to arrange.

Not to be missed is a trek into the unspoiled interior. With its rugged mountains and canyons, remote beaches and coves, and myriad native plants and wildlife—including wild buffalo left behind from the 1920s filming of *The Vanishing American*—Catalina can be a backcountry delight. Hikers, cyclists, and campers must obtain permits from the Santa Catalina Island Conservancy before venturing beyond Avalon. Bus tours of the interior are also available. ∎

Let's talk tiles

Visitors to Santa Catalina Island will be captivated by its profusion of exquisite decorative tiles. Often called the "jewels of Avalon," the vivid glazed squares are products of the Catalina Clay Products Tile and Pottery Plant, which operated at Pebbly Beach from 1927 to 1937.

To see an expansive collection of historic tiles, look along Avalon's waterfront between the ferry landing and the Casino. Here you'll find a distinctive array of brightly colored tiles installed in pathways, fountains, benches, and buildings. Many have been grouped together to form designs and murals. ∎

More places to visit in Baja, East County, & beyond

CARRIZO GORGE RAILWAY

No rail fan can resist the fascination of an excursion on the Carrizo Gorge Railway. Operated in cooperation with the San Diego Railroad Museum, refurbished Pullmans and other vintage railway cars take visitors on a variety of unusual ventures. Many of the trips depart from the historic **Campo Depot** in the high desert, about an hour's drive from downtown San Diego along I-8. The Buckman Springs turnoff leads to Cameron Corners, a tiny community with a trading post and an authentic circa-1950s fast-food outlet. The road then crosses the railway tracks to the Campo Depot, the primary facility for the San Diego Railroad Museum and the site of its railyard and restoration complex.

A popular and unique trip is the daylong excursion to **Tecate, Mexico**—the only tourist railway journey from the United States across an international border. A diesel or steam locomotive pulls vintage passenger coaches and baggage cars over the bridges and through the tunnels of rugged east San Diego County to reach the heart of Tecate. Passengers are offered a tour of the nearby Tecate Brewery, then allowed free time to explore before boarding the train for its return to Campo. An extra-special experience is the first-class option: Passengers enjoy brunch and afternoon snacks, champagne, and pampered service aboard restored Pullman cars.

Another extraordinary journey is the 3.5-hour trek from **Ocotillo** through **Carrizo Gorge** and into Anza-Borrego State Desert Park aboard a historic speeder car or a rail bus powered by a 1932 Model A. Following the little-known (and even less-traveled) "Impossible Railroad" line that dates from the early 1900s, passengers are treated to stunning vistas of the desert, mountains, plants, and wildlife. Once you reach the canyon, the **Goat Canyon Trestle** is just a short walk away. More than 633 feet long and 185 feet high, this is North America's highest operational wooden rail trestle.

Other scheduled adventures include brunch and dinner trains, 1.5-hour backcountry expeditions into scenic **Miller Creek**, an all-day bus-and-train combination from

Papier-mâché peppers attract buyers to a Tijuana store.

downtown's **Santa Fe Depot** (1050 Kettner Blvd, 619-595-3030) to northern Baja's **Guadalupe Valley** wine country, occasional rail jaunts between Tijuana and Tecate, and monthly 35-minute ecotours via rail motor car from the remodeled National City depot into the **South Bay Marshland.**

Passengers undertaking trips into Mexico must clear customs and immigration; they will also need to show proof of U.S. citizenship or legal residency.

✉ 8929 Gardena Way, Lakeside ☎ 619-938-1943 🚆 $-$$$$

CUYAMACA RANCHO STATE PARK

Located 40 miles east of San Diego, this 25,000-acre park within the Peninsular mountain range was once a seasonal home for local Kumeyaay Indians, as well as part of a Mexican land grant. Just an hour away from downtown San Diego, the state park attracts locals who

More places to visit in Baja, East County, & beyond

Entente cordial at the Rosarito Beach Hotel

come for day trips or long weekends. More than 100 miles of hiking, horse, and mountain-biking trails (no rentals available) spiderweb the park, which also includes 6,512-foot **Cuyamaca Peak** and its infinite views. Gentle streams, abundant oak and pine forests, vast meadowlands, 200 bird species, and myriad wildflowers (after a rainy winter, that is) enliven the scenery.

The **Stonewall Mine** site holds the ruins of the mine and a reconstructed miner's cabin housing a historical display. Campgrounds are designated for families and equestrians; there are also two primitive campsites (permits available from park headquarters).

Bordering the state park, **Lake Cuyamaca** (*15027 Hwy. 79, 760-765-0515, www.lakecuyamaca.org*) is a popular boating and fishing spot; it allows RV and tent camping. The 110-acre lake is stocked with more than 44,000 pounds of trout, Florida bass, channel catfish, crappie, bluegill, sturgeon, and other species. Motorboats, paddleboats, and canoes can be rented. Free fishing classes are held Saturdays at 10 a.m.
www.cuyamaca.statepark.org ▲ 213 D3

✉ 12551 Hwy. 79, Descanso ☎ 760-765-0755, reservations 800-444-7275

LA BUFADORA
Situated about 30 miles south of Ensenada (off the Transpeninsular Highway, on BCN-23), this spectacular tidal blowhole set amid the mountainous cliffs at **Punta Banda** performs an incredible show of eruptive, spuming seawater when the surf is high. (When the tide is low, La Bufadora—"the Snort"—issues only a meek harrumph). The blowhole's popularity with both tourists and locals inspired the construction of a fenced-in viewing platform where enthusiasts can watch the phenomenon from safety. Restrooms and parking are nearby; the road to Punta Banda is laden with local growers offering olives, chili peppers, and other colorful tastes of Baja. ▲ 213 C1

TECATE
About an hour's drive east of San Diego, this serene border town offers visitors a refreshing Mexican experience that is the antithesis of Tijuana. Dating from the late-19th century, when ranchers and farmers were drawn to the fertile land, this region has remained a market center practically devoid of tourist trappings. The shady plaza—just a couple of blocks from the U.S. border station—is usually filled with locals who come to stroll and socialize. Musicians take to the bandstand with frequency. Shops and stores cater primarily to residents, though nonaggressive souvenir vendors often ply their trade near the plaza and the border crossing.

Tecate Brewery (*Blvd. Benito Juárez 2009*), established in 1943, produces a well-respected beer and offers tours and tastings.

Rancho La Puerta (*800-443-7565 or 760-744-4222 for reservations*), a chic spa founded by Deborah Szekely (owner of the Golden Door in Escondido, see p. 199), is also located here. Utilizing a combination of body-mind-spirit exercise, the fitness facility is acclaimed for its serene environment, gourmet cuisine, and deluxe Mexican-colonial accommodations. The restorative programs include yoga, meditation, dance, swimming, and other therapies. ▲ 213 C2 ∎

Travelwise

The San Diego trolley rail-ly
gets you around the town.

TRAVELWISE INFORMATION

PLANNING YOUR TRIP

WHEN TO GO

Planning a trip to San Diego is easy, because the weather is usually mild and dry at any time of year. There are generally no discernible "seasons" within the city and coastal areas, where flowers bloom, trees keep their leaves, rain the exception, and frost a rarity. November through March are considered the "rainy" months, though precipitation in most areas hardly amounts to more than a drizzle.

Beachgoers should keep in mind that June, in much of southern California, is often referred to as "June gloom," when the coastal areas become fogged in and the sun rarely makes an appearance. This doesn't usually affect inland areas, however. The fog can be thick along the coast, yet the sun will shine brilliantly just a few miles eastward.

Tijuana and other Baja towns are also "spring-like" most months, though flooding can occur after heavy rains. Unless you're prepared for big crowds, try to avoid Baja over spring break and on popular Mexican holidays such as Cinco de Mayo.

Sports enthusiasts can partake of favorite amusements almost any time of year. Ocean swells attract surfers year-round (wet suits are recommended, even during the summer). Hikers enjoy the mountains during the crisp autumn months, and the desert areas during the winter. The spring wildflower season in the desert is exceptionally delightful; hikers and motorists alike journey inland to witness the strange and beautiful plants at their peak. Summer visitors in Anza-Borrego Desert State Park and high desert areas should be prepared for very high temperatures.

Summer months (June through September), when kids are out of school and families go on vacation, are the most crowded. Del Mar hosts the very popular San Diego County Fair (June-July) and horseracing (July-Sept.), both of which draw huge crowds along most of the coastal strip.

If possible, plan a visit before Memorial Day or after Labor Day, when good deals can be had on everything from airfare to accommodations—even at the ritziest establishments. Beachfront restaurants, open year-round, offer more elbowroom and speedier service—and the crashing surf puts on a show no matter what time of year.

Visitors on a budget will find San Diego can be easy on their wallets. Top attractions such as Balboa Park, the Gaslamp Quarter, Old Town State Historical Park, Mission Bay Park, Anza-Borrego Desert State Park, and the many miles of gorgeous beaches are all free.

CLIMATE

San Diego's Mediterranean climate remains fairly consistent all year. High temperatures range in the mid-60s during winter, the mid to high 70s during summer. Lows average 40-50°F in winter, and 60-65°F in summer. An average of 1.5 inches of rain can fall from November through March. Julian, Mount Palomar, and other mountain areas often have below-freezing temperatures and winter snow, while the Anza-Borrego Desert State Park scorches (expect temperatures to be 105°F and higher) throughout the summer.

WHAT TO TAKE

San Diego's ideal climate and relaxed atmosphere make packing easy. Except for the fancier restaurants and hotels, dress is casual. A coat and tie, for men, and a black cocktail dress for women should suffice for most special-occasion outings. T-shirts, jeans, shorts, a swimsuit, comfortable walking shoes, and beach sandals are the basic necessities, along with sunglasses, sunscreen, and a hat or baseball cap. Evenings can get chilly, even in summer, and at least one sweater as well as a light coat or jacket are advisable. For mountain or desert travel, bring appropriate clothing for the time of year.

Cameras and binoculars are useful items. Virtually any type of sports-related clothing can be purchased or rented once you're here.

INSURANCE

If you become sick or injured, most doctors and hospitals will either require health insurance information or immediate payment (care will be given in dire emergencies, but the bill will be presented without delay). Bring proof of insurance coverage (check to make sure your H.M.O. covers out-of-town incidents), or purchase a supplemental travel insurance policy.

In addition, if you drive to San Diego and/or rent a car, find out if your home policy will cover you and your vehicle. Some credit card companies also cover you and your rental vehicle, if charged on their cards.

For insurance needs in Mexico see pages 238-239.

TRAVELING TO SAN DIEGO

BY AIRPLANE

All major domestic, and some international and regional carriers, fly into San Diego. Many flights are nonstop, while others offer direct or connecting service. British Airways offers nonstop service between San

BY CAR

Interstate 5 is the direct route from Los Angeles, Interstate 15 makes its entrance from Las Vegas, and Interstate 8—the major east-west artery—travels from the Phoenix area into downtown.

Diego and London Gatwick. American Eagle and United Airlines also operate commuter service to McClellan Palomar Airport, in Carlsbad.

Primary airlines serving San Diego include the following:
Alaska Airlines, tel 800-426-0333
Air Canada, tel 888-247-2262
AeroMexico, tel 800-237-6639
American Airlines, tel 800-433-7300
American West, tel 800-235-9292
British Airways, tel 800-247-9297
Continental Airlines, tel 800-231-0856
Delta Air Lines, tel 800-221-1212
Hawaiian Airlines, tel 800-367-5320
Northwest Airlines, tel 800-225-2525
Southwest Airlines, tel 800-435-9792
United Airlines, tel 800-241-6522
US Airways, tel 800-428-4322

AIRPORTS

San Diego International Airport (SAN), 3665 N. Harbor Dr., San Diego, tel 619-231-2100.
McClellan Palomar Airport (CLD), 2198 Palomar Airport Rd., Carlsbad, tel 760-431-4646.

San Diego International Airport (also known as "Lindbergh Field") serves more than a dozen airlines in three terminals: the commuter terminal, Terminal 1, and Terminal 2. The airport continues to undergo expansion and improvements that began in the 1990s.

Passengers will find shuttles, vans, buses, and taxis outside the terminals' baggage claim areas. Follow the signs to the type of transportation desired, and a customer service representative will make sure you get the correct ride to your destination. Airport shuttles charge approximately $7 to downtown hotels, while taxis run about the same (plus tip) for the short ride into town. Shuttles into outlying areas can run from $7 (Old Town) to around $20 (Del Mar).

Many hotels and motels offer complimentary vans for their guests (ask at time of booking, or check with the information area in the baggage claim areas).

Car rental agencies offer free shuttles for customers to the nearby rental sites. The San Diego Metropolitan Transit System bus No. 992 (known as "the Flyer") offers service between all terminals and downtown approximately every 10–15 minutes, from about 5 a.m.–1 a.m. (fare $2.25, exact change).

BY TRAIN

AMTRAK, Santa Fe Depot, 1050 Kettner Blvd., tel 800-872-7245

The Pacific Surfliner travels nine trips daily between San Diego and Los Angeles (including four which travel on to Santa Barbara and San Luis Obispo). The daily Coast Starlight makes the scenic run from San Diego to Seattle, with a short connecting bus ride to San Francisco from Emeryville. Connections can be made to other long distance trains, such as the Southwest Chief and Sunset Limited, in Los Angeles or Fullerton. Double-decker Pacific Surfliner trains offer a café car, laptop computer outlets, and both coach and business class seats; the Coast Starlight features a dining car, lounge, and café.

BY BUS

Greyhound Lines, Inc., 120 W. Broadway, tel 800-231-2222 or 619-239-3266.

Greyhound Lines buses link downtown San Diego with cities nationwide. Buses have reclining seats, lavatory facilities, heating and air conditioning. The depot sits right in the center of downtown near the Gaslamp Quarter.

GETTING AROUND

BY CAR

San Diego's downtown area is relatively compact, and public transportation is somewhat better than that in Los Angeles. Nonetheless, to make the most of a visit and for access to many of the beaches, North County sights, the desert, and mountains—it is almost imperative to have a car.

Be forewarned though: Rain is such a rarity that, when it does happen, the roads become chaotic. Watch for slick conditions: oil in the road comes to the surface when the streets get wet. At the first sign of drizzle, drivers turn on their windshield wipers and headlights. "Storm Watch" is almost invariably the featured story on the evening news, and will most certainly take precedence over war, politics, or crime.

Arm yourself with some good maps and hit the highway. If you avoid weekday rush hours (approximately 7 a.m.–9 a.m. and 4 p.m.–6 p.m.) on the major freeways, it should be smooth sailing. Except for the downtown core, parking is plentiful—some metered, some free. Carry a stack of quarters in case you need to feed a meter. Most shopping malls offer free or validated parking (you can get validated for even buying lemonade or an ice-cream cone).

DRIVING REGULATIONS

Speed limits vary, depending on where you are. The speed limit is

35 mph on most streets, 25 mph in school zones and residential areas. Most freeways have a maximum speed of 65 mph.

In California it is legal to turn right on a red light, but only after coming to a complete stop and if there is nothing approaching from the left (and that includes cyclists, joggers, and skaters). U-turns are also permitted at intersections, unless otherwise indicated. Pedestrians always have the right of way and it is mandatory to stop at a crosswalk until all pedestrians have made it to the other side of the street.

Do not park in red zones or within ten feet of a fire hydrant. Unless your car is appropriately identified, do not park in any of the disable-designated "blue zones." Fines for doing so are quite stiff, and in this politically correct city you might be berated by a local before even climbing out of the car.

Always pull to the right and come to a complete stop when you hear or see an emergency vehicle, whether it is coming up from behind or approaching from ahead. Seat belts are mandatory for all passengers, as are regulation car seats for infants and children (advise car rental agencies if you need this equipment).

Drunk driving is strictly enforced, and the legal alcohol limit is 0.5 percent. Another law that is enforced requires you to turn your tires to the curb if you park on a hill.

CAR BREAKDOWN
Emergency telephones are located at regular intervals along most major freeways. If you belong to an automobile club, it will probably have reciprocal arrangements with the Automobile Club of Southern California. If you are driving a rental car, find out provisions for breakdown and towing beforehand.

CAR RENTALS
Alamo, tel 800-327-9633
Avis, tel 800-831-2847
Budget, tel 800-527-7000
Dollar, tel 800-800-4000
Hertz, tel 800-654-3131
National, tel 800-227-7368
Thrifty, tel 800-847-4389

BY PUBLIC TRANSPORTATION

San Diego Metropolitan Transit System (SDMTS), tel 800-266-6883 or 619-233-3004 (619-685-4900 for 24-hour recorded information).

The SDMTS is the umbrella organization for buses, the San Diego Trolley, and the Coaster. Various components run from Oceanside to the Mexican border. Money-saving passes and multiride tickets, as well as maps and timetables, can be obtained at the organization's Transit Store, conveniently located at 201 Broadway (tel 619-234-1060, www.sdcommute.com), near the Santa Fe Depot, Greyhound bus terminal, and Horton Plaza .

BUSES
Buses operate throughout the metropolitan area, and connect with buses and transportation centers in other parts of the county. Hours of service vary, and many routes offer limited runs on evenings and holidays. Fares range from $1.50-$3.50 each way ($1 for seniors 62 or older, children under 5 are free), and exact change is required. Transfers are free and should be requested upon boarding.

SAN DIEGO TROLLEY
The distinctive red San Diego trolleys offer daily light-rail service on two lines about every 15 minutes 5 a.m.-9 p.m., and every 30 minutes 9 p.m.-1 a.m.

The Orange Line runs from the America Plaza transfer center across from the Santa Fe Depot to Santee in East County, with stops at Seaport Village, the

Gaslamp Quarter, and the Convention Center.

The Blue Line (also accessed from America Plaza) travels between Qualcomm Stadium and Mission San Diego de Alcalá to within 100 feet of the Mexican border. Stops along the way include Little Italy, Old Town, and Mission Valley.

Trolley fares are $1.25-$2.50 each way. Tickets can be purchased at the Transit Store or from trolley station vending machines. Bus and trolley tickets can be used interchangeably when going in one direction, and are good for a period of two hours after validation.

TRAINS
The Coaster commuter rail service runs between the Santa Fe Depot and Oceanside, with stops at Old Town, Sorrento Valley, Solana Beach, Encinitas, and Carlsbad. Eleven trains operate Mon.-Fri., while four trains provide Saturday service.

Fares are based on distance traveled and range from $3.50-$4.75 one way ($1.50-$2.25 for seniors 60 or older), and tickets can be purchased from station vending machines (credit cards are accepted). Tickets can be used to transfer to buses or the trolley within two hours of validation. Bus or trolley tickets can be used in combination with a less expensive "upgrade" when transferring from those modes back to the Coaster.

FERRIES
San Diego Bay-Coronado Ferry, tel 619-234-4111.

This ferry transports passengers between the Broadway Pier on the Embarcadero and Coronado's Ferry Landing Marketplace. Departures are hourly from San Diego (9 a.m.-9 p.m., until 10 p.m. Fri.-Sat.), and on the half hour from Coronado. The one-way fare is $2, with an additional 50-cent charge for bicycles.

BY TAXICAB

Cabs are rarely hailed off San Diego streets, though they can be found outside airport terminals, rail depots, larger hotels, and some attractions and shopping areas. Otherwise order taxis well ahead of departure time. The basic taxi fare is $2.20, plus $2.20 for each additional mile.
Radio-dispatched taxis:
Coronado Cab,
  tel 619-435-6211
La Jolla Cab, tel 858-453-4222
Orange Cab, tel 619-291-3333
San Diego Cab,
  tel 619-226-8294
Yellow Cab, tel 619-234-6161
USA Cab, tel 619-231-1144

BY LIMOUSINE

Limousine service is available for about $50 per hour, and special tour packages can be arranged through most companies.

Avalon Transportation &
  Livery Services, tel 888-440-
  5466 or 619-276-4052
Carey Limousines,
  tel 619-225-9551
La Costa Limousine,
  tel 888-299-5466 or
  858-756-5466
Presidential Limousine & Sedan
  Service, tel 800-708-7009

BY TOUR

For generalized sightseeing, scenic tours, and Mexican excursions, contact San Diego Scenic Tours (tel 858-273-8687) or Contact Tours (tel 619-477-8687).

OLD TOWN TROLLEY TOURS

Two-hour trolley tours depart from various locations for such attractions as Old Town, Balboa Park, the Gaslamp Quarter, the Embarcadero, and Coronado. Passengers can get on and off at leisure. The trolley operates daily 9 a.m.-5 p.m., early June through early October, until 4 p.m. the rest of the year. The

fare is $24, half price for ages 4-12. For more information, call 619-298-8687.

BAY EXCURSIONS

Explore San Diego Bay on various narrated cruises, or aboard evening skyline, brunch, dinner, and other assorted adventure tours. Call San Diego Harbor Excursion (tel 619-234-4111) or Hornblower Cruises (tel 619-686-8715).

For sailing tours and whale-watching excursions call Classic Sailing Adventures (tel 619-224-0800) and Orion Sailing Charters (tel 619-574-7504). All tours depart from the Embarcadero.

HOT AIR BALLOON RIDES

Soar above various North County San Diego areas at sunrise or sunset, in a colorful hot-air balloon. Flights last approximately 45 minutes to one hour and usually include champagne and snacks. Companies include Skysurfer (tel 800-660-6809 or 858-481-6800) and A Balloon & Biplane Adventure by California Dreamin' (tel 800-373-3359).

PRACTICAL ADVICE

COMMUNICATIONS

FAXES, COMPUTERS, & INTERNET ACCESS

Almost every major hotel offers ports for laptop computers, and many have business centers to meet any additional requirements. Kinko's (619-645-3300, www.kinkos.com) has a large downtown facility, and branches in other convenient areas of the city. All offer computer rentals, fax services, internet access, and a plethora of other business requirements—and most are open 24 hours.

NEWSPAPERS

The *San Diego Union-Tribune*, published daily, is the city's major newspaper and provides international, national, and local news. The Thursday edition contains the "Night & Day" entertainment section. The *Los Angeles Times* also publishes a San Diego edition. *USA Today* is widely available, and the *New York Times* and *Wall Street Journal* can be purchased in coin-operated boxes in some parts of town, and at many newsstands.

The free *San Diego Reader* alternative paper, delivered to many convenience stores and cafés, is published each Thursday and contains a comprehensive listing of events and entertainment. *San Diego Magazine*, a glossy monthly, is filled with local interest stories, coverage of society events, restaurant reviews, and entertainment listings. The monthly *San Diego Home and Garden* profiles local residences, architecture, and trends.

POST OFFICES

Main downtown branch:
815 E St., tel 800-275-8777 (general information for all San Diego County post offices).

Post offices are plentiful throughout the area. Regular hours are Mon.-Fri. 8:30 a.m.-5 p.m.; some branches are open Sat. 8:30 a.m.-noon. Stamps can also be purchased from vending machines located in post office foyers.

RADIO

As with television, San Diego's radio stations are also in flux, making almost any list out of date. Again, check newspaper listings for the most current information. KPBS (85.5 FM) is the local National Public Radio affiliate and KSDO (1130 AM) has been a stalwart for local traffic and weather updates.

TELEPHONES

Local information, tel 411
Long-distance information, tel
1 + area code of city + 555-1212
Toll-free directory assistance,
tel 800-555-1212

Public telephones are conveniently located in hotels, restaurants, tourist attractions, shopping malls, service stations, and at many other locations. Local calls cost 35–50 cents (payable in quarters, dimes, or nickels), and some privately owned phones implement time limits. For long distance calls, it's much cheaper to purchase a phone card from the post office or any larger drug stores, or to use your home carrier's telephone calling card. Instructions for collect calls are posted on the telephones. There is no charge to dial "911" for emergency services.

When making calls from hotels or motels, inquire first about charges. Some establishments levy high surcharges for calls placed from guest rooms—even if you're using a calling card. Some accommodations include free local calls.

Area codes: As with many growing cities and the increased lines for computer modems, cell phones, and fax machines, San Diego County now uses three area codes: 619, for downtown and East County; 858, for Pacific Beach, La Jolla, Del Mar, and the Golden Triangle; and 760, for Encinitas, Carlsbad, Oceanside, and inland North County.

When calling from one area code to another—even if it is a local call—it is necessary to dial 1, followed by the area code and seven-digit telephone number. When calling to another number within the same area code, just the seven-digit number will usually suffice.

TELEVISION

San Diego benefits from dozens of cable and noncable stations—including Spanish-language stations—most offering 24-hour programming. Check listings in the daily San Diego Union-Tribune for current listings.

Major network affiliates are channels 6 (FOX), 7 (NBC), 8 (CBS), 10 (ABC), and 15 (PBS). Popular cable stations include CNN, ESPN, American Movie Classics (AMC), Turner Classic Movies (TCM), Arts and Entertainment (A&E), Nickelodeon (NICK), MTV, and BRAVO, HBO, Showtime, and Cinemax are the top premium channels for mainstream films. Almost all accommodations offer free cable television, and many include pay-per-view or complimentary movie channels.

LIQUOR LAWS

The legal drinking age is 21. Bars, restaurants, liquor stores, clubs, supermarkets, and convenience stores are permitted to serve or sell alcohol daily 6 a.m.–2 a.m. Official photo identification (driver's license, passport, or state identification card) is required and must be shown upon request before alcohol can be purchased.

Open containers holding alcohol are not allowed in vehicles, and not even passengers are permitted to drink. It is also illegal to drink on the streets. Some beaches allow consumption of alcohol (not in glass containers); look for posted signs.

MONEY MATTERS

Banks and Automatic Teller Machines (ATMs) are plentiful and conveniently located throughout the city, as well as at shopping centers, and major attractions. Check with your home bank to ascertain which system accepts your card. Some ATMs levy a nominal service charge for some transactions. Credit cards, debit cards, and traveler's checks are accepted almost everywhere, though photo identification is sometimes required. Personal checks from out-of-area banks are not normally accepted for purchases or services.

OPENING TIMES

Banking hours are traditionally Mon.–Thurs. 9 a.m.–3 p.m. Fri. 9 a.m.–6 p.m., though many financial institutions now stay open until 5 or 6 p.m. on weekdays, and some also open Sat. 9 a.m.–noon or 1 p.m. Shops and attractions have variable hours. Department stores are normally open daily 9 a.m.–9 p.m., while some smaller boutiques close around 5 or 6 p.m. Shops in malls usually don't close until 9 p.m. All malls, and most other shops are also open on Sundays. A number of gas stations and large supermarkets stay open for business around the clock. Many museums are closed on Mondays, which is also when most theaters are "dark."

NATIONAL HOLIDAYS

New Year's Day (Jan. 1); Martin Luther King, Jr. Day (3rd Mon. in Jan.); Presidents' Day (3rd Mon. in Feb.); Memorial Day (last Mon. in May); Fourth of July; Labor Day (first Mon. in Sept.); Columbus Day (2nd Mon. in Oct.); Veterans' Day (Nov. 11); Thanksgiving Day (4th Thurs. in Nov.), Christmas Day (Dec. 25).

PLACES OF WORSHIP

Every major faith is represented, with numerous churches, synagogues, temples, and mosques located throughout the county. All are welcome to worship at Mission San Diego de Alcalá's little parish church, while only bona fide Mormons are admitted to the massive, futuristic-looking Church of Latter-Day Saints in the La Jolla/Golden Triangle area. As with much of California, new age and Eastern religions are also quite popular.

TIME DIFFERENCES

San Diego is in the Pacific time zone, which is three hours earlier than New York City, two hours earlier than Chicago, and one hour earlier than Phoenix. Daylight saving time is observed.

TIPPING

Most hotel and wait staff are paid minimum wage and therefore depend upon tips to supplement their income. A 15 percent tip is customary at most restaurants, with 20 percent at more upscale spots. Others who should be tipped: bartenders and café "baristas," 10 percent; taxi drivers, 10-15 percent; hair stylists, 15 percent; valet parking attendants, $2 or more; hotel doormen, $1-$2; porters and bellhops, $1 per bag; hotel

SMOKING

Smoking is definitely frowned upon in this health-conscious city. Smoking is prohibited in all public places, including restaurants and bars, and on all public transportation. In some places, outdoor patios will accommodate smokers, but nonsmokers nearby may complain or frown at the offender(s). Nonsmoking rooms and/or floors are available in almost every hotel and motel.

SALES TAX

Sales tax is not included on store price tags. Expect an additional 7.75 percent to be tacked on to most purchases, including restaurant tabs. A "transient occupancy tax" of 10.5 percent is added to accommodation rates.

Check the Yellow Pages or the Saturday editions of the San Diego Union-Tribune or Los Angeles Times for service listings. Bulletin boards and free newsletters in cafés and new-age shops are a good source for alternative-religion services.

TOILETS

Public restrooms are located at major attractions, shopping malls, department stores, restaurants, cafés, bars, nightclubs, service stations, and at parks and beaches (exercise caution when using the park and beach restrooms, and always make sure that children are accompanied by an adult). Most restaurants and cafés will allow even non-customers to use their facilities.

TRAVELERS WITH DISABILITIES

Access Center of San Diego, 1295 University Ave., #10, San Diego, 92103, tel 619-293-3500.
Accessible San Diego, 1010 2nd Ave., 17th floor, San Diego, 92101, tel 858-279-0724.
Travelers with disabilities will find that San Diego, like most of southern California, is very accessible.

VISITOR INFORMATION

San Diego International Visitor Information Center, 11 Horton Plaza, tel 619-236-1212. Open Mon.-Sat. 8:30 a.m.-5 p.m., daily in summer
La Jolla Visitor Center, 7966 Herschel Ave., tel 619-236-1212. Open Mon.-Sat. 9 a.m.-5 p.m., Sun. 9:30 a.m.-4:30 a.m.
Both locations distribute the "San Diego Official Visitors Pocket Guide," maps, information on hotels and restaurants, helpful tips, and discounts to various attractions.
Downtown Information Center, 225 Broadway, tel 619-235-2222.
International Visitors Information Center, corner of 6th Ave. and L St., tel 619-232-8583.

HELPFUL INTERNET SITES

www.infosandiego.com
www.sandiego.org
www.uniontrib.com

WEATHER

Weather Report, tel 619-289-1212
Beach Report, tel 619-221-8824

EMERGENCIES & HEALTH CARE

CRIME & POLICE

The San Diego Police Department has jurisdiction over the city, while the San Diego Sheriff's Department holds reign on the county. The California Highway Patrol oversees the thoroughfares, and the United States Border Patrol guards the international border with Mexico as well as areas within a 50-mile radius of the U.S. side of the border.
Downtown San Diego and popular visitor areas are relatively crime free. Auto theft and petty theft do occur, so take the proper precautions by keeping cars locked and valuables out of sight.

EMBASSIES & CONSULATES

British Consulate General, 7825 Fay Ave., Suite 200, La Jolla, 92037, tel 858-459-8232.
British Consulate General, 11766 Wilshire Blvd., Suite 1200, Los Angeles, 90025, tel 310-481-0031.
Canadian Consulate General, 550 S. Hope St., 9th Floor, Los Angeles 90071, tel 213-346-2700.

USEFUL NUMBERS & ADDRESSES

• Police, fire, or emergency medical assistance, tel 911 (no coins needed if calling from a public phone)
• Poison Control Center,

TRAVELING TO MEXICO

TRAVEL TO MEXICO

Tijuana and Baja California are part of Mexico, not an extension of California. Special require-ments and precautions need to be taken for anyone anticipating spending a little time south of the border.

PASSPORTS, VISAS, & TOURIST CARDS

U.S. citizens entering Mexico must have either a valid pass-port or official photo identifi-cation (such as a driver's license) as well as an original birth certificate. Citizens of other countries who are permanent U.S. residents must carry a Permanent Resident Alien Card (the "Green Card"), as well as a passport. Visitors from other countries must have a valid passport and a visa that allows re-entry into the United States.

Single parents, or those traveling without their spouse, will need to show a notarized consent form or custody documents before bringing any minor across the border.

For stays exceeding 72 hours, and for journeys south of Ensenada, you must have a tourist card (the "FMT," or Forma Migratoria para Turista), which is btainable at border information booths. This should be kept in your possession until you leave Mexico. The tourist card is not needed for stays of less than 72 hours within the border area.

CAR INSURANCE

It cannot be stressed enough that anyone driving into Baja California or elsewhere in Mexico should obtain a Mexican insurance policy ("seguro") be-fore crossing the border. These are the only policies recognized by Mexican law. Should you be involved in an auto accident

HEALTH

One of San Diego's claims to fame is its sunny, mild climate and healthy lifestyle. Physicians and health care facilities are top-notch, and often accommodate patients from other states who come for cutting-edge treat-ments and therapies. The county is home to numerous health spas and alternative-medicine practitioners.

Prescription drugs, as well as homeopathic medicines are readily available. The city water is generally considered safe to drink, though many prefer bot-tled varieties.

Occasional sewage spills, espe-cially near the Mexican border, sometimes pollute the local waters—watch for posted warning signs at the beaches.

LOST PROPERTY

San Diego International Airport lost property, located on first floor of baggage claim area, tel 619-686-8002.

Report lost, stolen, or rifled baggage immediately to your airline's customer service desk, and the same applies to Amtrak travelers. If something is missing from your hotel room, contact the manager (keep valuables in the hotel safe). If your car is stolen, contact the police department and car rental agency immediately. File a police report for property stolen from inside the vehicle. Even if you don't get the goods back, you'll need the official report for any insurance reimbursement.

LOST CREDIT CARDS

American Express: tel 800-528-4800
Diner's Club: tel 800-234-6377
Discover: tel 800-347-2683
MasterCard: tel 800-307-7309
Visa: tel 800-336-8472

tel 800-876-4766 (CA only)
• American Red Cross, tel 619-542-7400
• California Missing Children Hotline, tel 800-222-3463
• State of California Department of Consumer Affairs, tel 800-952-5210
• San Diego County Medical Society, tel 858-565-8161
• Dental Referral Service, tel 800-511-8663
• Hospitals with 24-hour emergency rooms are:
• Scripps Mercy Hospital, 4077 5th Ave, Hillcrest area, tel 619-294-8111.
• Scripps Hospital, 9888 Genesee Dr, La Jolla area, tel 858-457-4123.
• UCSD Medical Center, 200 W. Arbor Dr, Mission Hills area, tel 619-543-6222.
• Kaiser Foundation Hospital, 4647 Zion Ave, Mission Valley area, tel 619-528-5000.
• Alvarado Hospital Medical Center, 6655 Alvarado Rd, College area, tel 619-287-3270.

24-hour pharmacies:

• Sav-on Drugs, 313 E. Washing-ton St., Hillcrest/Mission Hills area, tel 619-291-7170.
• Sav-on Drugs, 8831 Via La Jolla Dr., La Jolla, tel 858-457-4390.
• Rite Aid, 535 Robinson Ave, Hillcrest area, tel 619-291-3703.

IN CASE OF A CAR ACCIDENT

If anyone is injured, immediately call 911 for ambulance, fire, or police assistance. Often the police only come to the scene of "fender benders" if the damage exceeds $500 or if injuries are involved. All parties are required to exchange names, addresses, telephone numbers, driver's license information, vehicle descriptions, and automobile insurance details. Accidents must be reported to the police department within 24 hours of the incident, retain a copy of the report for your insurance com-pany. If you were driving a rental car, report the incident immedi-ately to the rental company.

(even if you've accidentally run over a rooster), regardless of who is at fault, you could be jailed until all claims are settled —which can be a lengthy time. The Mexican policy guarantees that damages will be paid.

Policies can be obtained at numerous agencies located near the San Ysidro border, through the American Automobile Association, and through some U.S. insurance companies. Some can be purchased via the phone or internet. At least $50,000 worth of liability insurance is the minimum recommendation, with fees ranging about $10 for one day and decreasing for subsequent days. Insurance rates are government regulated and most policies are comparably priced.

If you rent a car in San Diego, make sure to inquire if Baja travel is allowed—many companies will not permit vehicles to cross the border. Citizens of the U.S. and Canada must have a valid national driver's license, and citizens of other countries will need their official driver's license plus an International Driving Permit.

HEALTH INSURANCE
Health insurance is crucial if you plan to travel into Baja. Basic health care is available in Tijuana and other large Mexican cities, but most doctors and hospitals require payment on the spot. Ascertain if your policy covers treatment in Mexico. Also, while many Mexican hospitals can provide adequate care, medical evacuation coverage is usually mandated in cases of critical illness or serious accidents.

CUSTOMS

U.S. residents who have been out of the country for at least 48 hours may return with $400 of duty-free goods. Each family member is allowed the same exemption, and these can be combined. The allowance in-cludes one liter of alcohol (for travelers 21 or older), one bottle of perfume with a U.S. trademark, 200 cigarettes, and 100 non-Cuban cigars.

DRUGS & NARCOTICS

Narcotics and controlled substances are not allowed to be purchased or used in Mexico, or to be brought back into the United States. Myriad pharmacies (farmacias) line the streets and alleys of Tijuana and other Mexican cities and towns. Many have signs offering cheap antidepressants, tranquilizers, and other common medications. Even if you have a legitimate prescription for particular drugs in the United States, you can be arrested for purchasing and transporting these across the border (even if you were simply trying to purchase a refill at bargain prices). Often farmacias work in conjunction with drug agents and police officers, alerting them to the sale.

MEXICAN NATIONAL HOLIDAYS

Mexico (including Tijuana) observes all major national holidays, with government offices, banks, and post offices closed on those days.

New Year's Day (Jan.1); Constitution Day (Feb. 5); Anniversary of Benito Juarez' Birth (Mar. 21); Holy Week (varies, but usually Palm Sunday through Easter Sunday); Labor Day (May 1); Independence Day (Sept. 16); Anniversary of the 1910 Mexican Revolution (Nov. 20); Christmas Day (Dec. 25).

EMERGENCIES

EMBASSIES & CONSULATES
If calling from outside Mexico, you need to dial the country code (52), and Tijuana's city code (644) before the phone number.

United States Consulate, Tapachula 96, Col Hipodromo, Tijuana, tel 622-7400.

British Consulate General, Blvd. Salinas 1500, Fracc Aviación, Tijuana, tel 681-7323.

Canadian Consulate General, German Gedovius 10411, Zona Rio, Tijuana, tel 684-0461.

Mexican Consulate in San Diego, 1549 India St., San Diego, 92101, tel 619-231-8414.

PHONE NUMBERS
Police: 060
Fire: 068
Ambulance (Red Cross): 066

ANNUAL EVENTS

JANUARY
Annual Penguin Day Ski Fest (tel 858-270-0840): Each New Year's Day, water-skiers without wetsuits try to earn the coveted Penguin Patch in the chilly waters of Mission Bay's De Anza Cove.

San Diego Boat Show (tel 858-274-9924): This annual four-day show, held at the San Diego Convention Center and the San Diego Marriott Hotel Marina, features the newest trends in marine industry gear, boat displays, seminars, and international exhibitors.

Martin Luther King, Jr. Day Parade and Festival (tel 619-264-0542): On the Saturday before the third Monday in January, marching bands and floats parade from the County Administration Building to Seaport Village, where an afternoon festival features music, entertainment, an award ceremony, and exhibits.

San Diego Marathon (tel 858-792-2900): San Diego's oldest marathon begins at Plaza Camino Real in Carlsbad on a course that incorporates 14 miles of coastline.

FEBRUARY

Chinese New Year (tel 619-234-4447 or 619-234-7841): Held early in the month at Third Avenue and J Street (downtown); the celebration includes Asian cuisine, martial arts performances, and cultural exhibits.

Kuumba Fest (tel 619-544-1000): African American arts, culture, and history are celebrated throughout the month, with performances held at the Lyceum Theatre in Horton Plaza.

Buick Invitational (tel 800-888-2842 or 619-281-4653): This PGA Tour men's golf tournament draws national and local professionals to La Jolla's Torrey Pines Golf Course.

Mardi Gras (tel 619-233-5227): The Gaslamp Quarter's "Fat Tuesday" celebration includes a parade, a huge block party, and food and drink specialties offered by numerous restaurants and bars.

Wildflowers (tel 760-767-4684): Depending on the rainfall, the desert comes alive with blooms for a two-to-six-week period, between February and April.

MARCH

Ranunculus blooms (tel 760-431-0352): In March and April, the Flower Fields erupt with exquisitely colored ranunculus flowers, which visitors are welcome to tour.

Ocean Beach Kite Festival (tel 619-531-1527): This popular event, held early in March, offers kite-making, decorating, and a flying contest for all ages.

Saint Patrick's Day Parade and Festival (tel 858-268-9111): The annual parade starts at 11 a.m., at Sixth and Juniper Streets; the festival which follows offers vendor booths, Irish food and drink, entertainment, and a beer garden.

Sham Rock (tel 619-233-5008): Billed as the biggest St. Patrick's Day Block Party west of the Mississippi, the Gaslamp Quarter rocks from 4 p.m. until midnight with all things Irish (including green beer).

APRIL

Del Mar National Horse Show (tel 858-792-4252): This prestigious event, held at the Del Mar Fairgrounds through early May, features national and international championship riders, draft horses, and dressage and western hunter-jumper competitions.

Peg Leg Smith Liar's Contest (tel 760-767-5555): Dating from 1916, this is the oldest ongoing storytelling contest in the country. Held in Anza-Borrego Desert State Park on the first Saturday in April, contestants are limited to five-minute lies related to this Wild West legend.

San Diego Crew Classic (tel 858-488-0700): Thousands of rowers from around the world participate in classic competitions at Crown Point Shores in Mission Bay.

Annual Easter Bonnet Parade and Hat Contest (tel 619-239-4287): Hatmaking workshops and the hat contest are followed by a stroll up Fifth Avenue.

Art Walk (tel 619-615-1090): A unique showcase of hundreds of visual and performing artists in downtown's Little Italy.

MAY

Buds 'N' Blooms (tel 619-239-0512): During early May, Balboa Park celebrates spring with floral-themed activities, museum exhibits, outdoor family activities, tours, and performances.

El Cinco de Mayo: This Mexican national holiday (the Fifth of May) is raucously celebrated throughout the county and, of course, in Baja. Old Town

San Diego American Indian Cultural Days (tel 619-281-5964): In late May, traditional Native American entertainment, arts and crafts, and food can be experienced at Balboa Park.

Ethnic Food Fair (tel 619-234-0739): The House of Pacific Relations cottages in Balboa Park celebrate the cuisine and culture of 30 nations, each year in late May.

JUNE

Rock 'n' Roll Marathon (tel 858-450-6510): This exciting marathon in early June runs a course from Balboa Park to the Naval Training Center, with 26 bands playing live music along the way, as well as a post-race concert.

San Diego Blues Festival (tel 619-283-9576): In early June, national and local blues musicians perform at Embarcadero Marina Park South in downtown.

Indian Fair (tel 619-239-2001): Native Americans from around the country gather at Balboa Park's Museum of Man to demonstrate traditional dances and to sell arts, crafts, and traditional food.

San Diego County Fair (tel 858-755-1161 or 858-793-5555): One of the country's largest county fairs is held mid-June through the Fourth of July at the Del Mar Fairgrounds. A midway, exciting carnival rides, food vendors, myriad exhibits, and concerts by top-name performers are among the highlights.

Summer Organ Festival (tel 619-702-8138): Free organ concerts are held Mondays at 7:30 p.m., through the end of

features three days of free entertainment for families, while the Gaslamp Quarter puts on another block party for adults (4–11:30 p.m.) with mariachi music, folk dancing, and plenty of Mexican food and margaritas.

August, at Balboa Park's outdoor Spreckels Organ Pavilion. At the same location, the "Twilight in the Park" series is held Tuesdays, Wednesdays, and Thursdays, 6:15-7:15 p.m. (tel 619-235-0512).

JULY
Fourth of July: Numerous Independence Day celebrations are held throughout San Diego County. Among the most popular are the festivities and fireworks in Coronado, SeaWorld, the Del Mar Fair, and the old-fashioned family-type event at Old Town State Historic Park.

U.S. Open Sandcastle Competition (tel 619-424-6663): The sands around the Imperial Beach pier are transformed into architectural masterpieces by expert sand sculptors in late July.

Over-the-Line Tournament (tel 619-688-0817): Held on two weekends, this sensationally popular San Diego "original" beach softball event—almost 50 years old—takes place on Mission Bay's Fiesta Island, and is not recommended for children or anyone offended by scantily-clad bodies or out-of-control behavior.

Festival of the Bells (tel 619-283-7319): Mid-July celebration of the founding of California's first mission is held on the grounds of Mission San Diego de Alcalá.

San Diego Lesbian, Gay, Bisexual, and Transgender Festival, Parade, and Rally (tel 619-297-7683): Late July. Activities take place in Balboa Park and the Hillcrest area.

AUGUST
America's Finest City Half Marathon (tel 858-792-2900): This well-attended race, held in mid-August, begins at 7 a.m. at the Cabrillo National Monument, winding around San Diego Bay and into downtown, finishing at Balboa Park.

World Body Surfing Championships (tel 760-435-4014): Oceanside is the setting for this late-August competition where international and U.S. body surfers ride the waves equipped only with swim fins.

SEPTEMBER
San Diego Street Scene (tel 619-557-8490): For several days in early September, 25 blocks in the Gaslamp Quarter accommodate this huge urban music festival that hosts major international and national musical performers, as well as local groups.

La Jolla Rough Water Swim (tel 858-456-2100): The country's largest rough water swimming competition, with different age categories, takes place early in the month at La Jolla Cove.

Fiestas Patrías (tel 619-220-5422): Old Town celebrates Mexican Independence Day throughout September.

Cabrillo Festival (tel 619-557-5450): During the last week of the month, 1542 Juan Rodríguez Cabrillo's exploration is commemorated at Cabrillo National Monument, with a festival and reenactment held on the final day.

OCTOBER
Fleet Week (tel 619-524-8727): A city-wide salute to the military begins around mid-month and features a parade of ships, naval ship tours, submarine tours, a golf tournament, and the MCAS Miramar Air Show.

Columbus Day Parade and Festival (tel 619-698-0545): Christopher Columbus is honored with a parade along Pacific Highway, and a fun- and food-filled festival in Little Italy.

Oktoberfest (tel 619-997-2473): This traditional German celebration is lauded for two days in early October in downtown La Mesa, where streets are lined with food and vendor booths and Bavarian bands play.

NOVEMBER
Mother Goose Parade (tel 619-444-8712): More than a half-century old, the Thanksgiving-season East County parade with floats, clowns, bands, and equestrians, begins at 12:30 p.m. at West Main and Chambers Streets, in El Cajon.

Del Mar Fairgrounds Holiday of Lights (tel 858-793-5555): From Thanksgiving until New Year's Day, the Del Mar racetrack infield is transformed by hundreds of brightly lit holiday displays, viewed by visitors as they drive around the track.

DECEMBER
Port of San Diego Bay Parade of Lights: For two weekends in December, dozens of illuminated and decorated boats create a spectacle from the southwest end of Shelter Island, proceeding around the harbor.

Christmas on El Prado (tel 619-239-0512): On the first weekend in December (5-9 p.m.), San Diegans head for Balboa Park where the celebration includes carolers, entertainment, arts and crafts, ethnic food, and free admission to many museums.

Pacific Life Holiday Bowl Parade (tel 619-283-5808): The colorful post-Christmas parade with floats, balloons, and bands precedes the collegiate football bowl game. Beginning at 10 a.m. at the *Star of India,* the parade takes place along Harbor Drive, ending at Seaport Village.

Whalefest (tel 858-534-3474): During whale-watching season (December through March), the Birch Aquarium at Scripps presents special exhibits, educational activities, and whale-watching opportunities (admission fee to aquarium and for special events).

HOTELS & RESTAURANTS

San Diego's geography allows visitors to stay in one location while still being able to access and enjoy other areas of the county

HOTELS

Accommodation options include high-rise or historic hotels, waterfront properties, chic resorts, and casual motels. Downtown appeals to conventioneers, business travelers, and those wanting to be in the center of action. Mission Bay, Mission Valley, Old Town, and the beach areas offer more family-friendly establishments. La Jolla, Del Mar, Coronado, and North County are geared to an upscale, resort-oriented clientele. An eclectic mix of lodgings is sprinkled throughout the mountains, desert, wine country, and Baja California.

Almost all accommodations offer parking facilities (sometimes for a fee), health clubs or exercise rooms, accessibility for disabled guests, and nonsmoking rooms (often entire floors are so designated).

The room price categories given are rack rates; seasonal and weekend rates might vary. Ask about any special deals or packages, and book well ahead if you're coming for a major event or on a holiday. An additional 10.5 percent "transient occupancy tax" will be added to all room rates.

RESTAURANTS

The vast number of dining choices appeal to all appetites and budgets. Visitors should remember that San Diego is a very health-conscious city, reflected in menus that are laden with fresh seafood, creative salads, and many meatless entrees. Mexican food is popular and inexpensive, and can be sampled in restaurants or at take-out stands all over the county (and, of course, across the border).

Casual dress is the norm, though it's best to inquire about any dress codes when making reservations at fancier establishments.

Unless otherwise noted, all restaurants are air-conditioned and offer nonsmoking seating. All restaurants are open daily unless indicated otherwise.

L=Lunch
D=Dinner

CREDIT CARDS

Almost all hotels and restaurants accept major credit cards as well as traveler's checks. Smaller establishments and cafés may accept only cash.
AE=American Express
DIS=Discover
DC=Diners Club
MC=MasterCard
V=Visa

DINING HOURS

Lunch usually runs from 11:30 a.m. until 2 p.m. Dinner often begins around 5 p.m., with 6:30 p.m.-8 p.m. the most popular dining hours. Most places serve until 10 p.m. Some restaurants are either closed on major holidays (Easter, Thanksgiving Day, Christmas Day, and New Year's Day), or offer traditional feasts available by advance reservation only.

ORGANIZATION

Hotels and restaurants are listed first by chapter area, then by price category, then alphabetically.

To help you find hotels and restaurants easily, the nearest cross street to each establishment has been included. This information follows the letters **NCS** with the symbolized information at the end of each entry.

HOTELS
An indication of the cost of a double room without breakfast, is given by **$** signs.

$$$$$	Over $280
$$$$	$200-$280
$$$	$120-200
$$	$80-120
$	Under $80

RESTAURANTS
An indication of the cost of a three-course dinner without drinks is given by $ signs

$$$$$	Over $60
$$$$	$45-60
$$$	$30-45
$$	$15-30
$	Under $15

DOWNTOWN & VICINITY

HOTELS

⊞ THE WESTGATE HOTEL
$$$$
1055 2ND AVE., 92101
TEL 619-238-1818
FAX 619-557-3737
This "Leading Hotel of the World" may not look like much from the outside but once through the doors, guests are stunned at its near re-creation of Versailles, its pervasive opulence and European-castle atmosphere, and the white glove-service in the formal dining room.
⓵ 223 ⊠ ⊛ AE, MC, V
NCS: Broadway

⊞ EMBASSY SUITES HOTEL SAN DIEGO BAY—DOWNTOWN
$$$-$$$$$
601 PACIFIC HWY., 92101
TEL 619-239-2400
FAX 619-239-1520
Spacious and stylish one- and two-bedroom units, some with whirlpools, and many with harbor views—at the Embarcadero, and close to the convention center and Gaslamp Quarter. Compli-

mentary breakfast is included in the rates.

(i) 337 ☕ 🏊 AE, MC, V
NCS: Market St.

🏨 HORTON GRAND HOTEL
$$$-$$$$$
311 ISLAND AVE., 92101
TEL 619-544-1886
FAX 619-544-0058
A sentimental favorite composed of two 1880s buildings, which were moved brick by brick and put together at the present site. Victorian styling, period furnishings, gas fireplaces, and a breezy atrium lobby all add to the ambience.

(i) 132 🏊 AE, MC, V
NCS: 3rd Ave.

🏨 HILTON SAN DIEGO GASLAMP QUARTER
$$$-$$$$
401 K ST., 92101
TEL 619-231-4040
FAX 619-231-6439
An urban boutique-style hotel offering unfettered elegance and contemporary decor along with plenty of Hilton comforts. Just a short stroll from the convention center and waterfront.

(i) 282 ☕ 🏊 AE, MC, V
NCS: 4th Ave.

🏨 MANCHESTER GRAND HYATT REGENCY
$$$-$$$$
ONE MARKET PL., 92101
TEL 619-232-1234
FAX 619-233-6464
This 40-story, full-service high-rise property sits on the waterfront, near the convention center. Contemporary rooms offer city or harbor views. The rooftop bar and excellent restaurant are popular with locals.

(i) 875 ☕ 🏊 AE, MC, V
NCS: 1st Ave.

🏨 SAN DIEGO MARRIOTT HOTEL & MARINA
$$$-$$$$
333 W. HARBOR DR., 92101
TEL 619-234-1500
FAX 619-234-8678

Located adjacent to the convention center, this hotel's twin 25-story towers hover above San Diego Bay and are a short walk away from the Gaslamp Quarter. Myriad services are available, almost all rooms have striking views, and boats can be rented at the hotel's marina.

(i) 1354 ☕ 🏊 AE, MC, V
NCS: 1st Ave.

🏨 COURTYARD BY MARRIOTT
$$$
530 BROADWAY, 92101
TEL 619-446-3000
FAX 619-446-3010
This 14-story property is housed in a restored circa-1920s bank building, within walking distance to downtown offices and attractions. A cozy bar and lobby evoke feel of earlier era, while the amenities meet modern-day standards..

(i) 245 ☕ 🏊 AE, MC, V
NCS: 5th Ave.

🏨 SAN DIEGO SHERATON SUITES—DOWNTOWN
$$$
701 A ST., 92101
TEL 619-696-9800
FAX 619-696-1555
Sheraton's all-suite property is located adjacent to Copley Symphony Hall, and is popular with visiting musicians and music-lovers. Each of the one-bedroom suites offers quality apartment-style furnishings. A restaurant and bar are located in-house.

(i) 254 ☕ 🏊 🏊 AE, MC, V
NCS: 7th Ave.

🏨 U.S. GRANT HOTEL— 🍴 A WYNDHAM HISTORIC HOTEL
$$$
326 BROADWAY, 92101
TEL 619-232-3121
FAX 619-232-3626
Constructed in 1910 by Ulysses S. Grant, Jr., in honor of his President father, this historic hotel is a bastion of dark woods and fine tradition.

The **Grant Grill** has long been a favored hangout for city movers and shakers, who dine on elegantly prepared continental and French cuisine including turtle soup and the chef's special sweetbreads.

(i) 185 ☕ 🏊 AE, MC, V
NCS: 3rd Ave.

🏨 THE WESTIN HORTON PLAZA
$$$
910 BROADWAY CIRCLE, 92101
TEL 619-239-2200
FAX 619-239-0509
Located practically inside the Horton Plaza shopping and entertainment center, yet offering a far more serene environment, with a relaxing lobby, animated sports bar, popular lounge, and contemporary styling.

(i) 450 ☕ 🏊 🏊 AE, MC, V
NCS: 3rd Ave.

🏨 WYNDHAM SAN DIEGO AT EMERALD PLAZA
$$$
400 W. BROADWAY, 92101
TEL 619-239-4500
FAX 619-239-3274
Architecturally striking high-rise towers, inside the Emerald Shapery Building, with soaring atrium lobby and lounge with dramatic hanging glass and lighting effects, and rooms with upscale decor and amenities.

(i) 436 ☕ 🏊 🏊 AE, MC, V
NCS: Columbia St.

RESTAURANTS

🍴 AUBERGINE GRILL
$$$
500 4TH AVE.
TEL 619-232-8100
A sophisticated setting for eclectic cuisines that incorporate Asian, Caribbean, and European flavors with a bit of attitude. The sleek bar serves fruit-infused vodkas and other libations for a snazzy clientele.

🕐 D only; closed Sun.
🏊 All major cards
NCS: Island Ave.

BAYOU BAR & GRILL
$$$
320 MARKET ST.
TEL 619-696-8747
Authentic Cajun cuisine, served amid Louisiana and Mardi Gras decor, including such favorites as soft-shell crabs, po' boy sandwiches, blackened catfish, Andouille sausage, crawfish étouffée, and pralines for dessert. Jazz piano plays most nights.
D only · All major cards NCS: 4th Ave.

DOBSON'S BAR & RESTAURANT
$$$
956 BROADWAY CIRCLE
TEL 619-231-6771
This early entry into the downtown-dining scene hasn't lost popularity over the years. Business-types and the pre-theater crowd delight on stuffed chicken breast, Chilean sea bass, or the claim-to-fame mussel bisque.
Closed Sat. L & Sun. · AE, DC, MC, V NCS: Broadway

FIO'S
$$$
801 5TH AVE.
TEL 619-234-3467
Superb northern Italian cuisine, with heavy emphasis on seafood specialties such as gorgonzola-crusted filet, in this ever-stylish corner restaurant that always drips with well-dressed people watchers. Dine at the sleek bar if you can't get a prized window table.
D only · All major cards NCS: F St.

RAINWATER'S
$$$
1202 KETTNER BLVD.
TEL 619-233-5757
Semi-formal, highly rated East Coast-style restaurant, where well-trained staff serve sophisticated and hearty preparations of aged prime beef, veal and lamb chops, seafood, and signature black bean soup, accompanied by an exceptional wine list.
Closed Sat. L & Sun. · AE, DC, MC, V NCS: Laurel St.

ANTHONY'S FISH GROTTO & THE STAR OF THE SEA ROOM
$$-$$$
1360 N. HARBOR DR.
TEL 619-232-5103
The **Fish Grotto** offers consistently well-prepared seafood in a bay-front location. The lunch is especially popular for catch-of-the-day specials, and fish 'n chips. (The restaurant does not take lunch-hour reservations.) The fancy **Star of the Sea Room** offers exceptional California-influenced seafood dishes, pampered service, and sunset or night-light views of the bay.
The Star D only · All major cards NCS: Broadway

CHIVE
$$-$$$
558 4TH AVE.
TEL 619-232-4483
Chef A. J. Voytko prepares divine menus that might include such varied dishes as spice-crusted lamb loin and duck prepared two ways.
D only NCS: F St.

ATHENS MARKET TAVERNA
$$
109 W. F ST.
TEL 619-234-1955
Don't be fooled by the name: There's nothing market-like about this long-time establishment. The serene and romantic dining room turns out enticing Mediterranean meals, including heavenly soups and authentic salads.
Closed Sat. L & Sun. · All major cards NCS: 2nd Ave.

BLUE POINT COASTAL CUISINE
$$
565 5TH AVE.
TEL 619-233-6623
Romantic supper club atmosphere, where patrons are seated in comfortable oversize banquettes to dine on seafood delicacies such as Blue Point oysters perpared several different ways.
D only NCS: F St.

THE FISH MARKET & TOP OF THE MARKET
$$
750 N. HARBOR DR.
TEL 619-232-3474
Bustling and busy almost every day of the week—locals and tourists gather for casual dining downstairs and more formal setting upstairs. Fresh seafood, prepared to your liking, is offered from a menu printed twice daily; the oyster and sushi bars add pizzazz.
All major cards NCS: Broadway

KIYO'S JAPANESE RESTAURANT & SUSHI BAR
$$
531 F ST.
TEL 619-238-1726
The sizeable number of Japanese customers is good advertisement for this intimate establishment, personally overseen by chef/owner Kiyo. Dining is offered indoors, outdoors, or at the counter. The "chef's menu" of fresh rolls comes highly recommended, as do all the traditional dishes.
Closed Sat. L & Sun. · AE, DIS, MC, V NCS: 5th Ave.

PANDA INN RESTAURANT
$$
506 HORTON PLAZA
TEL 619-233-7800
Poised at the top of the Horton Plaza complex, yet removed from the madding crowds, this establishment serves fine Szechuan and Mandarin cuisine including pork, seafood, and vegetarian selections.
All major cards NCS: Broadway

BALBOA PARK & AROUND

HOTELS

BALBOA PARK INN
$$-$$$
3402 PARK BLVD., 92103
TEL 619-298-0823
FAX 619-294-8070

Across from Balboa Park, this inn's four Spanish Colonial buildings surround a court-yard. Some suite units feature kitchens and whirlpools, and smokers have a designated area for lighting up.

26 All major cards
NCS: University Ave.

PARK MANOR SUITES
$$-$$$
525 SPRUCE ST., 92103
TEL 619-291-0999

Built in the 1920s, this former residential hotel underwent renovation in the 1990s and now offers spacious home-away-from-home units to a predominantly gay and lesbian clientele. On Friday's, the ho-tel's Top of the Park bar is a favorite watering hole.

All major cards
NCS: 5th Ave.

SOMERSET SUITES HOTEL
$$-$$$
606 WASHINGTON ST., 92103
TEL 619-692-5200
FAX 619-692-5299

Spacious all-suite accommo-dations with fully equipped kitchens in a newer modern facility, close to the Hillcrest and Mission Hills neighbor-hoods. Complimentary con-tinental breakfast and evening social hour are bonuses.

80 All major cards
NCS: 6th Ave.

RESTAURANTS

BERTRAND AT MR. A'S
$$$
2550 5TH AVE.
TEL 619-239-1377

Perched at the top of Fifth Avenue Financial Center, this spectacular site long housed the formal Mr. A's before being taken over by the trendier, more gourmet Bertrand. Chef Sabrice Poigin now presents beef tenderloin and dover sole meunière.

Closed Sat.–Sun. L AE, MC, V NCS: Laurel Ave.

ARRIVEDERCI
$$
3845 4TH AVE.
TEL 619-299-6282

It may be tiny, but that doesn't keep locals from jamming the tables both inside and on the patio. Mouthwatering rustic Italian cuisine includes daily specials and old favorites such as gnocchi and ravioli.

All major cards
NCS: University Ave.

THE GATHERING
$$
902 W. WASHINGTON ST.
TEL 619-260-0400

Popular Mission Hills eatery and local hangout, situated on a prominent people-watching corner, offering casual American fare for breakfast, lunch, dinner, and a full bar for sipping cocktails and nibbling on butter-drizzled brie-and-fruit and other appetizers.

All major cards
NCS: Goldfinch St.

SOMETHING SPECIAL

KEMO SABE

Chef Deborah Scott and staff oversee every dish in this elegant and understated dining room, which offers respite from the outside world. Each meal is artistically prepared, using the freshest ingredients and leaning toward Southwestern flavors. The signature dish is the skirt steak with serrano relish, but the baked Brie and the tahini chicken salad are special as well. The sleek bar pours perfect martinis and other cocktails.

$$
3958 5TH AVE.
TEL 619-220-6802
D only All major cards NCS: University Ave.

PARALLEL 33
$$
741 W. WASHINGTON ST.
TEL 619-260-0033

A sophisticated, minimalist setting for dishes unique to countries along the 33rd parallel. Some of the world-food offerings might include Moroccan pie, duck in Asian five-spice sauce, and shrimp and potato samosas with pomegranate glaze.

D only; closed Sun. All major cards NCS: Goldfinch St.

THE PRADO
$$
1549 EL PRADO,
TEL 619-557-9441

Located in Balboa Park's historic House of Hospitality, the Prado affords dramatic theatrical décor to go with a

THE CHEESE SHOP
$
627 4TH AVE.
TEL 619-232-2303

This downtown deli, poised amid trattorias and bistros, puts together terrific sand-wiches (with cheese or without), as well as omelets, old-fashioned oatmeal, homemade granola, and other tasty, yet simple items.

B & L only AE, MC, V
NCS: G St.

KANSAS CITY BARBEQUE
$
610 W. MARKET ST.
TEL 619-231-9680

American Kansas City-style barbeque meals with all the customary trimmings and side dishes in a casual memora-bilia-filled eatery used as a set for the bar scenes in the film Top Gun. Great people-watching patio.

DIS, MC, V
NCS: Harbor Dr.

menu that leans heavily on Latin and Italian flavors. Try the Portobello mushroom salad, skirt steak tacos, and leave room for the desserts. ⊕ Closed Mon. D ⬛ All major cards **NCS:** 6th Ave.

🍴 SUSHI ITTO
$$
441 WASHINGTON ST.
TEL 619-291-6060
This slicked out branch of the Sushi Itto chain establishment offers sushi items that will enthrall the most jaded diner (or the most anti-sushi patron). On the menu are such specialty rolls as the .com and Conehead, spiced with the signature Tampico sauce. ⬛ AE, MC, V **NCS:** 5th Ave.

🍴 CITY DELICATESSEN
$
535 E. UNIVERSITY AVE.
TEL 619-295-2747
This Hillcrest mainstay dishes out classic deli dishes in a casual, pleasing dining room. Breakfast is served all day, sandwiches are stacked high, and bakery goods are made on premises. ⬛ AE, DIS, MC, V **NCS:** 6th Ave.

🍴 CREST CAFÉ
$
425 ROBINSON AVE.
TEL 619-295-2510
A long-time neighborhood café that has gone slightly upscale without losing its casual ambience and loyal clientele. Terrific burgers, creative salads, and wonderful omelets and homemade desserts; the fried onion loaf steals the show. ⬛ All major cards **NCS:** 5th Ave.

🍴 HOB NOB HILL
$
2271 1ST AVE.
TEL 619-239-8176
Line up as the locals have done since 1944 to sup on hearty American comfort food that appeals to families, seniors, and power brokers. Chicken and dumplings, meatloaf and mashed potatoes, and pies baked on the premises are some of the delights. ⬛ AE, DIS, MC, V **NCS:** Laurel St.

CORONADO & THE SILVER STRAND

HOTELS

SOMETHING SPECIAL

🏨 HOTEL DEL CORONADO
U.S. Presidents, British royalty, and an A-list of celebrities have all stayed under the peaked roof of this landmark Victorian seaside resort, with its gingerbread architecture and its sensationally master-crafted public rooms. The hotel underwent a major restoration in 2001.

The **Crown Room** offers an award-winning Sunday brunch. Rooms have been modernized, yet they still evince an aura of tradition. Many services and amenities are available, including rental boats, three lighted tennis courts, bicycles, boutiques, and a conference center.
$$$$$
1500 ORANGE AVE., 92118
TEL 619-435-6611 OR 800-HOTELDEL
FAX 619-522-8262
ℹ️ 688 🚰 🏊 ⬛ All major cards **NCS:** B Ave.

🏨🍴 LOEWS CORONADO BAY RESORT
$$$$-$$$$$
4000 CORONADO BAY RD., 92118
TEL / FAX 619-424-4000
Low-lying, casual yet elegant resort on the Silver Strand, near the Coronado Cays residential area. Spacious accommodations with balconies, many with waterfront views. The many activities include saunas, whirlpools, rental boats, a putting green,

---

PRICES

HOTELS
An indication of the cost of a double room without breakfast, is given by $ signs.

$$$$$	Over $280
$$$$	$200-$280
$$$	$120-200
$$	$80-120
$	Under $80

RESTAURANTS
An indication of the cost of a three-course dinner without drinks is given by $ signs

$$$$$	Over $60
$$$$	$45-60
$$$	$30-45
$$	$15-30
$	Under $15

---

waterskiing, and two lighted tennis courts. The **Azzura Point** restaurant serves creative California-French cuisine. Try the five-course prix-fixe dinner and save room for the fabulous desserts.
ℹ️ 438 🚰 🏊 ⬛ All major cards **NCS:** Silver Strand Blvd.

🏨 CORONADO BEACH RESORT
$$$$
1415 ORANGE AVE., 92118
TEL 619-522-6000
FAX 619-522-6020
Condominium living for guests preferring home-like privacy and who require fewer business services and amenities. The three-story building's interior corridors afford easy access; a laundry is on the premises and complimentary bicycles are provided.
ℹ️ 53 🚰 ⬛ AE, DIS, MC, V **NCS:** B Ave.

🏨 CORONADO ISLAND MARRIOTT RESORT
$$$$
2000 2ND ST., 92118
TEL 619-435-3000
FAX 619-435-4183
Formerly Le Meridien, this lovely sprawl still retains much of its French styling and

---

sophistication yet offers many leisure facilities including a fine-dining restaurant, six lighted tennis courts, saunas, whirlpools, and a boat dock with rental boats, kayaks, and other equipment.

[i] 300 [health club] [outdoor pool] [credit cards] All major cards NCS: Glorietta Blvd.

GLORIETTA BAY INN—CORONADO
$$$-$$$$
1630 GLORIETTA BLVD., 92118
TEL 619-435-3101
FAX 619-435-6182
The 1908 mansion of John D. Spreckels composes one portion of this inn; it features exquisite Victorian touches, including a horseshoe-shaped music room. Costlier historic suites are available in the former home, while most visitors reside in an adjacent contemporary structure.
[i] 100 [outdoor pool] [credit cards] All major cards NCS: Orange Ave.

VILLA CAPRI BY THE SEA
$$-$$$$$
1417 ORANGE AVE, 92118
TEL 619-435-4137
FAX 619-435-3383
Intimate, circa-1950s motel, with European pension-type atmosphere and service; positioned just across the street from the Hotel del Coronado. Rooms are clustered around a sunny patio, where a complimentary continental breakfast is served daily.
[i] 14 [outdoor pool] [credit cards] All major cards NCS: B Ave.

RESTAURANTS

CHEZ LOMA
$$$
1132 LOMA AVE.
TEL 619-435-0661
This former 1889 home-turned-restaurant affords a romantic dining experience inside, on the porch, or patio. Sample continental-French cuisine including fresh fish, poultry, meat, and pastas. The salmon with horseradish crust is delectable.

[D] D only [credit cards] AE, DC, MC, V
NCS: Orange Ave.

PEOHE'S
$$
1201 1ST ST.
TEL 619-437-4474
Peohe's features exotic tropical decor, outstanding bay views, and Polynesian-style seafood specialties such as halibut mai'a and coconut-crunchy shrimp. At the Ferry Landing Marketplace.
[credit cards] AE, MC, V **NCS:** C Ave.

McP'S IRISH PUB & GRILL
$
1107 ORANGE AVE.
TEL 619-435-5280
The casual alehouse fare provided by an ex-Navy SEAL owner includes standout Mulligan stew and other Irish favorites. A mixture of Navy troops, tourists, and locals share the stools and tables. Live local bands are an added bonus.
[credit cards] AE, DIS, MC, V
NCS: C Ave.

OLD TOWN, MISSION VALLEY & VICINITY

HOTELS

TOWN AND COUNTRY RESORT HOTEL
$$$-$$$$
500 HOTEL CIRCLE N., 92108
TEL 619-291-7131
FAX 619-291-3584
Massive sprawling 40-acre hotel and convention center, with guest rooms located in structures rising 2 to 10 stories. Conference-goers bring their families who occupy themselves at the spa, health club, four swimming pools, five restaurants, and three lounges.
**[i] 966 [health club] [outdoor pool] [credit cards] AE, MC, V
NCS:** I-8

BEST WESTERN HACIENDA HOTEL
$$$
4041 HARNEY ST., 92110
TEL 619-298-4707

FAX 619-298-4771
This lovely Spanish-style complex sprawls across a lush hillside above Old Town. Well-appointed accommodations offer private balconies or shared courtyard patios, microwaves, refrigerators. A restaurant and cantina are on premises, and Old Town is at the doorstep.
**[i] 193 [health club] [outdoor pool] [credit cards] AE, MC, V
NCS:** San Diego Ave.

DOUBLETREE CLUB HOTEL
$$$
1515 HOTEL CIRCLE S., 92108
TEL 619-881-6900
FAX 619-260-0147
Family-oriented property with contemporary, spacious, and cheerfully decorated rooms and suites, a restaurant, lounge, gift shop, and kid's video game room. Money-saving packages include admission to the San Diego Zoo and SeaWorld.
**[i] 217 [health club] [outdoor pool] [credit cards] AE, MC, V
NCS:** I-8

HANDLERY HOTEL & RESORT
$$$
950 HOTEL CIRCLE N., 92108
TEL 619-298-0511
FAX 619-298-9793
Conveniently located, family-owned, and family-geared, with three swimming pools, eight tennis courts, whirlpools, saunas, a dining room, and gift shop. Modernized guest rooms offer refrigerators and high-speed internet access.
**[i] 217 [health club] [outdoor pool] [credit cards] AE, MC, V
NCS:** I-8

HILTON SAN DIEGO MISSION VALLEY
$$$
901 CAMINO DEL RIO S., 92108
TEL 619-543-9000
FAX 619-296-9561
A well-positioned 14-story property, popular with visiting business people, that offers conference facilities, a business center, and other needed services. Contemporary rooms

are well-appointed; a restaurant and lounge are on site.
(i) 350 🚩 🏊 🅢 AE, MC, V
NCS: Mission Center Rd.

HOLIDAY INN HOTEL & SUITES
$$$
2435 JEFFERSON ST., 92110
TEL 619-260-8500
FAX 619-297-2078
Holiday Inn fans will be pleased with this Old Town property, harboring cheerful rooms, a restaurant and lounge, and a short walk to the area's historic and entertainment sights.
(i) 171 🚩 🏊 🅢 AE, MC, V
NCS: Old Town Ave.

RAMADA LIMITED OLD TOWN
$$$
3900 OLD TOWN AVE., 92110
TEL 619-299-7400
FAX 619-299-1619
Three-story motel with inviting lobby and guest rooms that offer microwaves and refrigerators. Swimming pool, spa, and sundeck are located in a peaceful courtyard, and Old Town's amenities are a short stroll away.
(i) 125 🚩 🏊 🅢 AE, MC, V
NCS: I-5

SAN DIEGO MARRIOTT MISSION VALLEY
$$$
8757 RIO SAN DIEGO DR., 92108
TEL 619-692-3800
FAX 619-692-0769
The Marriott's 17-story Mission Valley property, close to Qualcomm Stadium and Mission San Diego de Alcalá, aims for business travelers with its amenities and services including a conference center.
(i) 350 🚩 🏊 🅢 AE, MC, V
NCS: Qualcomm Way

OLD TOWN PLAZA HOTEL
$$
2380 MOORE ST., 92110
TEL 619-291-9100
FAX 619-291-4717

Modern well-kept rooms, with in-room refrigerators, heated pool and spa, and walking distance to Old Town's restaurants and shops. A guest laundry and complimentary continental breakfast are also provided.
(i) 79 🏊 🅢 AE, MC, V
NCS: Old Town Ave.

QUALITY RESORT
$$
875 HOTEL CIRCLE S., 92108
TEL 619-298-8282
FAX 619-295-5610
The Quality brand has turned out a wonderful family-oriented resort, close to major attractions, and one of the best deals in town. Set on 20 landscaped acres, facilities include three swimming pools, privileges to the on-site Frog's health club, a cocktail lounge, and 24-hour restaurant.
(i) 202 🚩 🏊 🅢 AE, MC, V
NCS: I-8

RESTAURANTS

ALBIE'S BEEF INN
$$
1201 HOTEL CIRCLE S.
TEL 619-291-1103
Dating from the 1960s, and still with much of the original decor in place, this steakhouse restaurant housed in the Travelodge is a favorite haven for a now-mature crowd as well as for kitsch-seekers. Dine on meat and potatoes (or similar fare) while sunk deep in a leather banquette.
🕑 Closed Sat. L & Sun.
🅢 AE, MC, V **NCS:** I-8

BERTA'S LATIN AMERICAN RESTAURANT
$$
3928 TWIGGS ST.
TEL 619-295-2343
For something a little different other than Old Town's slew of relatively tame Mexican eateries, try Berta's. It offers beef, chicken, and seafood entrees made with the fiery and spicy flavors of Argentina, Brazil, Peru, and other countries.

🕑 Closed Mon. 🅢 AE, MC, V **NCS:** Congress St.

CASA DE BANDINI
$$
2754 CALHOUN ST.
TEL 619-297-8211
This historic landmark within Old Town State Historic Park features a lovely atmosphere, colorful decor, glorious patio, strolling mariachis, and Mexican specialty dishes such as crab and shrimp enchiladas.
🅢 All major cards
NCS: Juan St.

EL AGAVE
$$
2304 SAN DIEGO AVE.
TEL 619-220-0692
Hundreds of different tequilas (as well as other drinks from the full bar) can be sampled along with the out-of-the-ordinary nouvelle Mexican cuisine fused with tastes from Maya, Aztec, and other native cultures. Four different kinds of mole are a menu mainstay.
🅢 AE, MC, V **NCS:** Old Town Ave.

GORDON BIERSCH
$$
5010 MISSION CENTER RD.
619-688-1120
This brewpub never loses popularity with trendy locals who drink pints of German-style lagers with eclectic menu items such as burgers, potstickers, pan-roasted seafood, and pastas.
🅢 AE, MC, V **NCS:** I-8

JACK & GIULIO'S ITALIAN RESTAURANT
$$
2391 SAN DIEGO AVE.
TEL 619-294-2074
Situated in the heart of Old Town, this Italian eatery offers a change of tastes once the Mexican cravings have died down. Pizzas, pastas, sandwiches, and winning entrees such as shrimp scampi, are all on the menu.
🅢 AE, MC, V **NCS:** Old Town Ave.

🍴 EL INDIO
$
3695 INDIA ST.
TEL 619-299-0333
This simple eatery, almost unknown to visitors, beckons locals with some of the most authentic and inexpensive Mexican fare this side of the border. All the favorites, plus combination plates, and tortilla chips made on the premises, are available to eat in or take out.
🃏 MC, V **NCS:** Washington Ave.

🍴 OLD TOWN MEXICAN CAFÉ
$
2489 SAN DIEGO AVE.
TEL 619-297-4330
Both tourists and locals head to this popular establishment, located outside the historic park's boundaries, to feast on reasonably priced enchiladas, carnitas, and other delights. Tortillas are made fresh behind a showcase window.
🃏 All major cards
NCS: Harney St.

POINT LOMA, HARBOR ISLAND, & SHELTER ISLAND

HOTELS

🏨 SHERATON SAN DIEGO HOTEL & MARINA
$$$$
1380 HARBOR ISLAND DR., 92101
TEL 619-291-2900
FAX 619-692-2337
This enormous property, rising 2 to 12 stories, is close to the airport and garners plenty of business travelers as well as locals who enjoy the hotel's restaurants and entertainment. Plentiful business and leisure services including rental boats, lighted tennis courts, bicycles, and laundry.
🛈 1042 🎽 🏊 🃏 AE, MC, V
NCS: Laurel St.

🏨 BAY CLUB HOTEL & MARINA
$$$
2131 SHELTER ISLAND DR., 92106
TEL 619-224-8888
FAX 619-225-1604
Nonimposing property purveying a light and breezy resort-type ambience. The guest rooms all have balconies with either harbor or marina views. A restaurant and lounge are on premises, and a daily breakfast buffet is included in the rates.
🛈 105 🎽 🏊 🃏 AE, MC, V
NCS: Scott Rd.

🏨 BEST WESTERN ISLAND PALMS HOTEL & MARINA
$$$
2051 SHELTER ISLAND DR., 92106
TEL 619-222-0561
FAX 619-222-9760
Surrounded by San Diego Bay, this palm-fringed property offers soothing waterfront accommodations, a restaurant and lounge, internet access, a whirlpool, game room, and free bicycles.
🛈 97 🎽 🏊 🃏 AE, MC, V
NCS: Scott Rd.

🏨 BEST WESTERN POSADA AT THE YACHT HARBOR
$$$
5005 N. HARBOR DR., 92106
TEL 619-224-3254
FAX 619-224-2186
Most of the guest rooms at this six-story lodging offer balconies, many with views of the adjacent harbor and bay. Complimentary continental breakfast, free local telephone calls, a restaurant and cocktail lounge are added attractions.
🛈 112 🎽 🏊 🃏 AE, MC, V
NCS: Rosecrans St.

🏨 HILTON SAN DIEGO AIRPORT / HARBOR ISLAND
$$$
1960 HARBOR ISLAND DR., 92101

TEL 619-291-6700
FAX 619-293-0694
A smaller option than the nearby Sheraton, yet just as close to the airport and within handy reach of the Sheraton's facilities. Conference rooms and a business center are on hand, as well as a sauna and whirlpool.
🛈 209 🎽 🏊 🃏 AE, MC, V
NCS: Laurel St

🏨 HOLIDAY INN SAN DIEGO BAYSIDE
$$$
4875 N. HARBOR DR., 92106
TEL 619-224-3621
FAX 619-224-3629
This hotel in Point Loma is near naval facilities and convenient to Cabrillo National Monument and many other attractions. Facilities include a business center, nine-hole putting course, and bicycles.
🛈 237 🎽 🏊 🃏 AE, MC, V
NCS: Nimitz Blvd.

🏨 HUMPHREY'S HALF MOON INN & SUITES
$$$
2303 SHELTER ISLAND DR., 92106
TEL 619-224-3411
FAX 619-224-3478
Casual two-story resort, noteworthy for hosting an outdoor summer concert series that draws internationally known performers. Tropical environment, with lush gardens, private marina, a popular waterfront restaurant, lawn games, and bicycle rentals.
🛈 182 🎽 🏊 🃏 AE, MC, V
NCS: Scott Rd.

🏨 SHELTER POINT HOTEL & MARINA
$$$
1551 SHELTER ISLAND DR., 92106
TEL 619-221-8000
FAX 619-221-5953
Low-slung scenic resort facing the bay and marina, and just minutes from the airport. Many guest rooms provide

...views, and there's a marina-view restaurant, children's recreation area, two pools and tennis courts, sand volleyball, and a spa.
🏨 206 💳 AE, MC, V
NCS: Scott Rd.

RESTAURANTS

🍴 JARED'S HARBOR ISLAND
$$$
880 E. HARBOR ISLAND DR.
TEL 619-291-1028
This steakhouse situated inside an old-fashioned riverboat setting continues to delight diners who order from a mainly traditional menu of meat, chicken, chops, and seafood, to go with outstanding views of the harbor and city skyline.
🕐 D only; closed Mon.
NCS: Harbor Dr.
💳 AE, DC, MC, V

🍴 HUMPHREY'S
$$
2241 SHELTER ISLAND DR.
TEL 619-224-3577
A very popular contemporary restaurant and lounge, featuring waterfront and marina views, California-coastal cuisine with Pacific Rim, Mediterranean, and Caribbean flavors, and a nightly roster of live entertainment.
💳 All major cards

🍴 RED SAILS INN
$$
2614 SHELTER ISLAND DR.
TEL 619-223-3030
Tourists with kids join local sailors at this long-time hangout that serves both traditional and contemporary preparations of shellfish and seafood in a relaxed and casual environment. Patio tables afford harbor views.
💳 AE, MC, V NCS: Scott Rd.

🍴 SAM CHOY'S HAWAII AT THE BALI HAI
$$
2230 SHELTER ISLAND DR.
TEL 619-222-1181
Authentic Hawaiian cuisine in a tropical-paradise waterfront setting that appeals to locals and vacationers who yearn for island ambience in a convenient San Diego locale. The Island Sampler and Kona Combo plates both offer selections of the best fare.
💳 AE, DIS, MC, V
NCS: Scott Rd.

SOMETHING SPECIAL

🍴 POINT LOMA SEAFOOD

Few visitors discover this simple, frenzied, no-frills, immensely popular local café. Place your order for the freshest seafood, shrimp cocktails, crab-cake sandwiches, fish and chips—even sushi—then find a table either indoors or outside, where views stretch across the marina to the city skyline. Wait for your number to be called, grab some plastic utensils, and enjoy.
$
2805 EMERSON ST.
TEL 619-223-1109
💳 Cash only NCS: Scott Rd.

🍴 VENETIAN RESTAURANT
$$
3663 VOLTAIRE ST.
TEL 619-223-8197
This Point Loma family-oriented Italian restaurant sits far away from downtown's ubiquitous trattorias. Bring the kids, sit indoors or on the patio, and dine on pizzas or such specialties as veal scallopini and chicken picatta.
🕐 Closed Sat.-Sun. L, 💳 All major cards NCS: Chatsworth Blvd.

MISSION BAY & BEACHES

HOTELS

🏨 CATAMARAN RESORT HOTEL
$$$$
3999 MISSION BLVD., 92109
TEL 858-488-1081
FAX 858-488-1619
Loaded with palms, ponds, and tiki torches, this tropical-style lodging is a favorite with locals who flock to the lounge for dancing and live entertainment. Leisure-oriented property offers rental boats, paddleboats, sailing lessons, windsurfing, bicycle rentals, and a game room.
🏨 313 💳 AE, MC, V
NCS: Garnet Ave.

🏨 HILTON SAN DIEGO RESORT
$$$$
1775 E. MISSION BAY DR., 92109
TEL 619-276-4010
FAX 619-275-7992
Palatial resort with its own aquatic center set on 18 beautiful acres overlooking Mission Bay. Upscale guest rooms have patios or balconies, many with bay views. Offerings include rental boats, putting green, scuba diving, five lighted tennis courts, bicycles, jogging paths, and a full-service spa and fitness center.
🏨 357 💳 AE, MC, V
NCS: Sea World Dr.

PRICES

HOTELS
An indication of the cost of a double room without breakfast, is given by $ signs.
$$$$$ Over $280
$$$$ $200-$280
$$$ $120-200
$$ $80-120
$ Under $80

RESTAURANTS
An indication of the cost of a three-course dinner without drinks is given by $ signs.
$$$$$ Over $60
$$$$ $45-60
$$$ $30-45
$$ $15-30
$ Under $15

KEY 🏨 Hotel 🍴 Restaurant (1) No. of guest rooms 🕐 Closed

🏨 PACIFIC TERRACE HOTEL
$$$$
610 DIAMOND ST., 92109
TEL 858-581-3500
FAX 858-274-3341
Luxurious beachfront accommodations providing a residential feel, yet with hotel services. Lovely rooms have ocean-view balconies or patios, upscale amenities, and a complimentary continental breakfast is included. Surfing lessons and massage therapy are available.
ⓘ 73 🎽 🏊 🚳 AE, MC, V
NCS: Mission Blvd.

SOMETHING SPECIAL

🏨 PARADISE POINT 🍴 RESORT & SPA
Guests of this 44-acre property will feel like they're on some far-off tropical island paradise, when in fact they're just across from SeaWorld and Mission Bay Park. Accommodations are in beautifully redecorated guest rooms or bungalows, and the public areas are exquisite. Facilities include a new spa and fitness center, tennis courts, pools, putting green, a marina, and rental sports equipment. The resort's **Baleen** restaurant (reservations recommended) offers high-quality seafood. For dessert, don't miss the delicious "chocolate hangover."
$$$$
1404 W. VACATION RD., 92109
TEL 858-274-4630
FAX 858-581-5929
ⓘ 462 🎽 🏊 🚳 AE, MC, V
NCS: Ingraham St.

🏨 BEST WESTERN BLUE SEA LODGE
$$$
707 PACIFIC BEACH DR., 92109
TEL 858-488-4700
FAX 858-488-7276
Sitting right on the sands of Pacific Beach, close to local restaurants and nightclubs, SeaWorld and Mission Bay. Many rooms offer sea views, and the swimming pool and spacious sundeck sit right on the beachfront.
ⓘ 130 🏊 🚳 AE, MC, V
NCS: Mission Blvd.

🏨 DANA INN & MARINA
$$$
1710 W. MISSION BAY DR., 92109
TEL 619-222-6440
FAX 619-222-5916
Genteel bayside inn with one-bedroom guest accommodations, a family restaurant, and lounge. Leisure activities include two tennis courts; shuffleboard; and rental boats, canoes, paddleboats, bicycles, and other equipment.
ⓘ 196 🏊 🚳 AE, MC, V
NCS: Ingraham St.

🏨 OCEAN PARK INN
$$$
710 GRAND AVE., 92109
TEL 858-483-5858
FAX 858-274-0823
Three-story newly renovated motel just steps from the beach, bustling boardwalk, shops, and eateries. All rooms feature mini-refrigerators, and patios or balconies. Complimentary continental breakfast served daily.
ⓘ 42 🏊 🚳 AE, MC, V
NCS: Mission Blvd.

RESTAURANTS

🍴 BACI'S
$$
1955 MORENA BLVD.
TEL 619-275-2094
Located in a less than glamorous spot, on the east side of Mission Bay and I-5, this surprisingly sophisticated intimate Italian restaurant has wooed locals since the 1970s. Homemade pastas, veal marsala, and osso buco are some highlights.
🕐 Closed Sat. L & Sun.
🚳 All major cards **NCS:** I-5

🍴 CHATEAU ORLEANS
$$
926 TURQUOISE ST.
TEL 858-488-6744
Louisiana-style decor and delights include large portions of Cajun specialties. "Uncle Bubba's Ribeye" blackened steak is one signature dish, and the "Holy Trinity" offers a sampling of étouffée, jambalaya, and gumbo. Live music most weekends.
🕐 D only; closed Sun.
🚳 AE, MC, V **NCS:** Garnet Ave.

🍴 QWIIGS BAR & GRILL
$$
5083 SANTA MONICA AVE.
TEL 619-222-1101
Upstairs from the more casual Cecil's Café (see p. 252), this second-story location, across from the beach, assures fabulous views to go along with grilled seafood, great burgers and salads, lobster bisque and clam chowder, plus there's a sushi bar.
🕐 Closed Sat. L 🚳 AE, MC, V **NCS:** Abbott St.

SOMETHING SPECIAL

🍴 SUSHI OTA
It's located in a nondescript strip mall next to a convenience store, but locals wouldn't go anywhere else for their sushi fix. Sit at the bar to sample such perfectly crafted items as soft-shell crab or lightly breaded halibut rolls, or perhaps the heavenly "sushi sundae." Book a spot ahead, or prepare yourself for a lengthy—but worthwhile—wait.
$$
4529 MISSION BAY DR.
TEL 858-270-5670
🕐 Closed Sat.-Mon. L
🚳 AE, MC, V **NCS:** Bunker Hill St.

🍴 WORLD FAMOUS
$$
711 PACIFIC BEACH DR.
TEL 858-272-3100
"World famous" may be pushing it, but this casual beachfront eatery on the boardwalk certainly is well-

H O T E L S   &   R E S T A U R A N T S

known by locals who pack the place for hearty breakfasts, business lunches, romantic dinners, and Sunday brunch. Appetizers, steak-and-seafood combos, and weeknight specials are best bets.
🅢 AE, DC, MC, V
NCS: Garnet Ave.

🍴 CECIL'S CAFÉ & FISH MARKET
$
5083 SANTA MONICA AVE.
TEL 619-222-0501
The penultimate beach café, right across from the ocean, where waves whip the nearby pier as diners enjoy fluffy pancakes, puffy omelets, simple seafood, and Mexican specialties.
🕒 Closed Fri.-Sat. D 🅢 AE, MC, V **NCS:** Abbott St.

🍴 LOTSA PASTA
$
1762 GARNET AVE.
TEL 858-581-6777
Choose from more than a dozen different sauces and a variety of pasta types to create a customized dish that will be cooked to your specifications in the exhibition kitchen. Other items are also available, including the meat-and-vegetable layered "timpano."
🅢 AE, MC, V
NCS: Ingraham St.

LA JOLLA & THE GOLDEN TRIANGLE

HOTELS

SOMETHING SPECIAL

🏨 🍴 LA VALENCIA
An icon on a par with the Beverly Hills Hotel, La Valencia has been a haunt of visiting celebrities and royalty since the 1930s. A decorating makeover has further glamorized the European-style guest rooms and public areas in this pink stucco palace, right in the heart of La Jolla's village and just steps from

the sea. Wander into the Whaling Bar to drink cocktails and people-watch, or treat yourself to an exquisite dinner in the intimate, tower-high **Sky Room.** It serves Continental-French cuisine with nonpareil views of the ocean swallowing the sun.
$$$$$
1132 PROSPECT ST., 92037
TEL 858-454-0771
FAX 858-456-3921
ℹ️ 121 📺 🏊 🅢 AE, MC, V
NCS: Torrey Pines Rd.

🏨 B&B INN AT LA JOLLA
$$$$
7753 DRAPER AVE., 92037
TEL 858-456-2066
FAX 858-456-1510
Luxurious individually decorated rooms housed inside an enchanting two-story historic cottage with antiques and reproduction furnishings, modern baths, a garden, library, and rooftop deck. Gourmet breakfast is served daily on the patio, or in the dining room.
ℹ️ 15 🅢 AE, MC, V
NCS: Pearl St.

🏨 EMBASSY SUITES
$$$$
4550 LA JOLLA VILLAGE DR., 92122
TEL 858-453-0400
FAX 858-453-4226
Excellent option for business clientele who need room to spread out in residential-style suites. A gift shop, café, business center, spa, and sauna are on site, and cooked-to-order breakfast is a daily offering.
ℹ️ 335 📺 🏊 🅢 AE, MC, V
NCS: I-5

🏨 EMPRESS HOTEL OF LA JOLLA
$$$$
7766 FAY AVE., 92037
TEL 858-454-3001
FAX 858-454-6387
Sophisticated European styling, just steps from shops, galleries, and the beach. Guest accommodations and public rooms have a traditional am-

bience, and service is diligent. A sauna and whirlpool are indoors, and complimentary continental breakfast is offered daily.
ℹ️ 73 📺 🅢 AE, MC, V
NCS: Torrey Pines Rd.

🏨 THE GRANDE COLONIAL
$$$$
910 PROSPECT ST., 92037
TEL 858-454-2181
FAX 858-454-5679
Historic four-story grande dame in the heart of La Jolla's shopping and dining district, where luxurious rooms look out on either the sea or village. Room service offers the full menu from the property's respected restaurant.
ℹ️ 75 🏊 🅢 AE, MC, V
NCS: Torrey Pines Rd.

🏨 HILTON LA JOLLA / TORREY PINES
$$$$
10950 N. TORREY PINES RD., 92037
TEL 858-558-1500
Serene and sophisticated cliff-top property, overlooking the ocean and close to Torrey Pines Golf Course. Public rooms and guest accommodations are sleek and chic, and other facilities include three lighted tennis courts, putting green, restaurant, and lounge with entertainment.
ℹ️ 394 📺 🏊 🅢 AE, MC, V
NCS: Genesee Ave.

🏨 HYATT REGENCY LA JOLLA
$$$$
3777 LA JOLLA VILLAGE DR., 92122
TEL 858-552-1234
FAX 858-552-6066
Known for its distinctive architecture, sophisticated environment, excellent health club, and fine restaurants, this Hyatt is just off the freeway, close to UCSD and the Golden Triangle, and is a favorite stay for business travelers.
ℹ️ 419 📺 🏊 🅢 AE, MC, V
NCS: I-5

THE LODGE AT TORREY PINES
$$$$
11480 N. TORREY PINES RD., 92037
TEL 858-453-4420
FAX 858-453-0691
After a complete makeover, this stalwart oceanview lodge, adjacent to the famous Torrey Pines Golf Course, reopened in 2002 as an embodiment of California Craftsman-era architecture, furnishings, and ambience.
🛈 175 🛗 🏊 Ⓒ AE, MC, V
NCS: Genesee Ave.

SEA LODGE AT LA JOLLA SHORES
$$$$
8110 CAMINO DEL ORO, 92037
TEL 858-459-8271
FAX 858-456-9346
Wonderful family getaway place, tucked along La Jolla Shores beach, between the village and Torrey Pines bluffs. Accommodations and facilities at this casual seaside resort are geared toward parents with children in tow, yet they still afford a hint of trendiness.
🛈 128 🛗 🏊 Ⓒ AE, MC, V
NCS: Avenida de la Playa

BEST WESTERN INN BY THE SEA
$$$
7830 FAY AVE., 92037
TEL 858-459-4461
FAX 858-456-2578
Located in the heart of town with well-appointed guest rooms, all with balconies and some with ocean views, walking distance to shops and galleries. Complimentary continental breakfast.
🛈 132 🏊 Ⓒ AE, MC, V
NCS: Prospect St.

HOTEL LA JOLLA AT THE SHORES
$$$
7955 LA JOLLA SHORES DR., 92037
TEL 858-459-0261
FAX 858-459-7649
This boutique-style luxury hotel sits close to the beach, Scripps Institution of Oceanography, and UCSD. Rooms with private balconies offer ocean views, a restaurant provides fine cuisine and live entertainment, and a concierge is on hand for other needs.
🛈 108 🛗 🏊 Ⓒ AE, MC, V
NCS: Torrey Pines Rd.

RESTAURANTS

GEORGE'S AT THE COVE
$$$
1250 PROSPECT ST.
TEL 858-454-4244
This oceanview restaurant serves excellent seasonal seafood, including Maine lobster and seared ahi. The upstairs terrace is more casual and less expensive, where specialties such as black bean soup and smoked chicken garner raves. Reservations required.
Ⓒ All major cards
NCS: Torrey Pines Rd.

MARINE ROOM RESTAURANT
$$$
2000 SPINDRIFT DR.
TEL 858-459-7222
This former beach bungalow, where the waves often crash right up to the glass windows, has been a favorite dining spot since the 1940s. Semi-formal wear is required for diners who choose from elegant preparations of rack of lamb and other American mainstays.
🕒 Closed Mon. L
Ⓒ All major cards
NCS: Torrey Pines Rd.

TAPENADE
$$$
7612 FAY AVE.
TEL 858-551-7500
Rich olive tapenade is immediately presented in this 1930s-style bistro specializing in Provençal cuisine that incorporates seasonal seafood and produce to make a variety of dishes, including grilled scallops, luncheon tarts, and other savory delights.
Ⓒ All major cards
NCS: Silverado St.

BROCKTON VILLA
$$
1235 COAST BLVD.
TEL 858-454-7393
Poised above lovely La Jolla Cove, this former cottage offers a romantic seaside setting for fresh preparations of such favorites as French toast, grilled ahi, meatloaf sandwiches, and seasonal specials.
🕒 Closed Mon. D
Ⓒ All major cards
NCS: Girard Ave.

CAFÉ JAPENGO
$$
8960 UNIVERSITY CENTER LN.
TEL 858-450-3355
Extremely stylish and hip eatery, located at the Hyatt Regency complex in the Golden Triangle area. Delectable Pacific Rim fare includes one of the best sushi bars in town, excellent appetizers, roasted duck, and whole striped bass.
🕒 Closed Sat.-Sun. L
Ⓒ AE, MC, V NCS: I-5

P. F. CHANG'S CHINA BISTRO
$$
4540 LA JOLLA VILLAGE DR.
TEL 858-458-9007
A variety of regional Chinese dishes with a California zing is on the menu at this lively eatery, popular with trendy locals. Try some of the eclectic appetizers, ahi tuna salad, or stick to favorite Chinese standards.
Ⓒ AE, DC, MC, V
NCS: Genesee Ave.

THE COTTAGE
$
7702 FAY AVE.
TEL 858-454-8409
A lovely corner cottage where diners, seated either indoors or on the outside patio, are served fresh baked

goods, tasty soups and salads, Mexican specialties, and other light meals.
🕓 B & L only 🚫 AE, DIS, MC, V **NCS:** Silverado St.

🍴 HOPS! BISTRO & BREWERY
$

4353 LA JOLLA VILLAGE DR.
TEL 858-587-6677
The extensive menu of hearty American fare appeals to the crowds who frequent this local microbrewing pioneer. Heaped sandwiches, stuffed chicken, and salmon and shrimp penne are washed down with the excellent beers and ales.
🚫 AE, MC, V
NCS: Genesee Ave.

NORTH COUNTY

DEL MAR

HOTELS

🏨 FOUR SEASONS RESORT AVIARA
$$$$$

7100 FOUR SEASONS PT., 92009
TEL 760-603-6800
FAX 760-603-6801
This sophisticated resort situated on a hilltop overlooks a beautiful lagoon and the ocean beyond. Public areas and guest rooms are sleek and stylish, and three restaurants, six tennis courts, saunas, whirlpools, steam rooms, bicycles, and spa treatments are available. Not to mention the 18-hole championship golf course.
🛏 329 🖥 🏊 🚫 AE, MC, V
NCS: Aviara Pkwy.

🏨 LA COSTA RESORT & SPA
$$$$$

COSTA DEL MAR RD., 92009
TEL 760-438-9111
FAX 760-931-7585
Celebrated 400-acre lushly landscaped resort, with 21 tennis courts, two 18-hole PGA championship golf courses, full-service health spa,

and a plethora of dining options, lounges, guest services, and other activities.
🛏 478 🖥 🏊 🚫 AE, MC, V
NCS: El Camino Real

🏨🍴 L'AUBERGE DEL MAR RESORT & SPA
$$$$$

1540 CAMINO DEL MAR, 92014
TEL 858-259-1515
FAX 858-755-4940
Chic, upscale, European-style hotel located one block from the beach, across from the Del Mar Plaza, and minutes away from the racetrack and fairgrounds. A lounge, full service spa and fitness facility, French bakery, and shops are on the premises. L'Auberge's Upscale **J. Taylor's** restaurant offers fresh regional cuisine that might include free-range chicken and rack of lamb.
🛏 120 🖥 🏊 🚫 All major cards **NCS:** 15th St.

🏨 DEL MAR INN—A CLARION CARRIAGE HOUSE
$$$

720 CAMINO DEL MAR, 92014
TEL 858-755-9765
FAX 858-792-8196
Friendly, residential-style accommodations, close to beach and village. Three-story property offers spacious rooms, many with ocean views, and provides complimentary continental breakfast and afternoon tea.
🛏 80 🏊 🚫 AE, MC, V
NCS: Del Mar Heights Rd.

🏨 HILTON SAN DIEGO DEL MAR
$$$

15575 JIMMY DURANTE BLVD., 92014
TEL 858-259-1515
FAX 858-792-0353
The Hilton San Diego offers modern guest rooms in a prime location, just across the street from the Del Mar fairgrounds and racetrack, adjacent to a golf driving range and eight lighted tennis courts, and a short drive to

the beach, shops, and restaurants.
🛏 245 🖥 🏊 🚫 AE, MC, V
NCS: Via de la Valle

RESTAURANTS

🍴 BULLY'S
$$

1404 CAMINO DEL MAR,
TEL 858-755-1660
Del Mar locals and racetrack fans have been charging into this clubby spot for decades to feast on succulent prime rib dinners, steaks and chops, juicy "Bully's burgers," and thick-cut fries.
🚫 AE, DC, MC, V
NCS: 15th St.

🍴 SBICCA
$$

215 15TH ST.
TEL 858-481-1001
Charming neighborhood gathering spot, with an upper-level oceanview dining patio. Modern American cuisine includes maple-roasted pork, prime rib, baked artichoke and hearts of palm dip, and homemade desserts. Wine and drink discounts are offered throughout the week.
🚫 AE, MC, V **NCS:** Camino Del Mar

PRICES

HOTELS
An indication of the cost of a double room without breakfast, is given by $ signs.

$$$$$	Over $280
$$$$	$200-$280
$$$	$120-200
$$	$80-120
$	Under $80

RESTAURANTS
An indication of the cost of a three-course dinner without drinks is given by $ signs

$$$$$	Over $60
$$$$	$45-60
$$$	$30-45
$$	$15-30
$	Under $15

HOTELS & RESTAURANTS

CARLSBAD

HOTELS

CARLSBAD INN BEACH RESORT
$$$$
3075 CARLSBAD BLVD., 92008
TEL 760-434-7020
FAX 760-729-4853
Popular resort with gabled roofs and Old World ambience, close to village shops, restaurants, and the Amtrak station. Bicycles, volleyball, a playground, sauna, and whirlpool are additional amenities.
[icon] 62 [icons] AE, MC, V
NCS: Carlsbad Village Dr.

HILTON GARDEN INN CARLSBAD BEACH
$$$
6450 CARLSBAD BLVD, 92009
TEL 760-476-0800
FAX 760-476-1080
Across the street from the beach and close to Legoland. Many of the modern guest rooms have ocean views, a pool and spa afford relaxation, and a casual café serves meals throughout the day.
[icon] 162 [icons] AE, MC, V
NCS: Palomar Airport Rd.

PELICAN COVE INN
$$$
320 WALNUT AVE, 92008
TEL 760-434-5995
FAX 760-434-7649
Charming Cape Cod-style B&B inn, located in a residential area near the beach. Individually decorated guest rooms feature antiques and contemporary pieces, and all have fireplaces, sitting areas, and private baths.
[icon] 8 [icons] AE, MC, V
NCS: Carlsbad Blvd.

RESTAURANTS

BELLEFLEUR WINERY & RESTAURANT
$$
5610 PASEO DEL NORTE
TEL 760-603-1919
This Mediterranean-style eatery, with a distinctive European air, seems an unlikely resident among the Carlsbad Company Stores complex. Menu items include lamb, seafood, and organic chicken; five varieties of house wines available. Wednesdays are Wine & Jazz evenings.
[icons] All major cards
NCS: I-5

NEIMAN'S
$$
300 CARLSBAD VILLAGE DR.
TEL 760-729-4131
This cavernous space inside a converted Victorian mansion holds a fine dining room and a more casual section; diners sup on everything from appetizers to prime rib and macadamia salmon. Live entertainment in the bar most nights. Award-winning Sunday brunch.
[icons] AE, DIS, MC, V
NCS: Carlsbad Blvd.

ENCINITAS

RESTAURANTS

101 DINER
$
552 S. COAST HWY. 101
TEL 760-753-2123
Kitschy roadside diner along a quaint stretch of Pacific Coast Highway, offering classic American fare such as biscuits and gravy and roasted turkey sandwiches, as well as some gourmet-type offerings.
[icon] B & L only; closed Tues.
[icon] Cash only
NCS: Encinitas Blvd.

ESCONDIDO

HOTELS

WELK RESORT SAN DIEGO
$$$$
8860 LAWRENCE WELK DR., 92026
TEL 760-749-3000
FAX 760-749-6182
Entertainer Lawrence Welk's resort offers a tranquil setting for two 18-hole golf courses, three lighted tennis courts, spa treatments, children's activities, and acclaimed entertainment by headliners in the on-site theater.
[icon] 142 [icons] AE, MC
NCS: I-15

SOLANA BEACH

RESTAURANTS

PAMPLEMOUSSE GRILLE
$$$$
514 VIA DE LA VALLE
TEL 858-792-9090
Across the street from the Del Mar Racetrack, this establishment does a brisk business with well-heeled patrons who can afford the imaginative California and Continental preparations of grilled fish, steaks, and veal.
[icon] Closed Sat.-Tues. L
[icons] All major cards
NCS: Jimmy Durante Blvd.

CAFÉ ZINC
$
132 S. CEDROS AVE.
TEL 858-793-5436
This casual eatery in the Cedros Design Center offers mostly outside seating, and delectable and creatively prepared soups, salads, and sandwiches with Italian and vegetarian overtones. The desserts are fabulous.
[icons] All major cards
NCS: Lomas Santa Fe Ave.

TONY'S JACAL
$
621 VALLEY AVE.
TEL 858-755-2274
Located in the Eden Gardens section of town, this friendly and atmospheric establishment with an adjoining bar has been family owned and operated since the 1940s. Choose from a lengthy menu of Mexican specialties (turkey is used, in place of the more traditional chicken, in many dishes).
[icon] Closed Sat. L & Tues.
[icons] AE, DIS, MC, V
NCS: Genevieve St.

BAJA, EAST COUNTY & BEYOND

TIJUANA & BAJA

HOTELS

EL CAMINO REAL
$$$
PASEO DE LOS HEROES 10305, TIJUANA
TEL (011-52) 664-633-4000 OR 800-722-6466 IN U.S.
FAX (011-52) 664-633-4001
Tijuana's newest and sleekest operation, in the fashionable area near the Cultural Center. Guest rooms are well decorated, and offer modern amenities. Dining, lounges, and room service are all available.
🛏 235 AE, MC, V

LAS ROSAS HOTEL & SPA
$$$
TRANSPENINSULAR HWY. KM 105.5
TEL (011-52) 646-174-4310 OR 800-522-1516 IN U.S.
FAX (011-52) 646-174-4595
Book ahead for these lovely accommodations housed inside a palatial pink building, north of Ensenada. Public rooms are elegant, and all guest accommodations provide ocean views, some boast fireplaces.
🛏 32 AE, MC, V

ROSARITO BEACH HOTEL
$$$
BLVD. JUAREZ 22710
TEL (011-52) 661-612-0144 OR 800-343-8582 IN U.S.
FAX (011-52) 661-612-1125
A favorite getaway since the Prohibition era, this seaside hotel still retains its golden-era feel in the public rooms, though guest accommodations tend to be a little under the weather.
🛏 186 AE, MC, V

RESTAURANTS

CIEN ANOS
$$
CALLE JOSE MARIA VELAZCO
1407, ZONA RIO, TIJUANA
TEL (011-52) 664-634-3039
Try something a bit different at this lovely establishment that serves Mexican haute cuisine, each delicacy imbued with distinctive spices and flavors such as tamarind, poblano and other extra-ordinary chile peppers. The wine list favors local vineyards. Reservations are advised.
MC, V

EL NIDO
$$
BLVD. JUAREZ 67, ROSARITO BEACH
TEL (011-52) 661-612-1430
One of Rosarito Beach's oldest restaurants continues to turn out well-prepared mesquite-grilled steaks, other meats and game, in a clubby, wood-paneled dining room.
MC, V

LA ESCONDIDA
$$
SANTA MONICA 1, TIJUANA
TEL (011-52) 664-681-4458
Dine in the converted mansion, or on the patio, surrounded by flowers and greenery. Chateaubriand and roasted quail are some of the customary menu items.
MC, V

JULIAN

HOTELS

THE ARTISTS' LOFT
$$$
4811 PINE RIDGE AVE., 92036
TEL 760-765-0765
Wonderfully romantic rustic-chic retreat in the woods with two rooms, and two self-contained cabins, all unique and individually decorated by the artist/owners.
🛏 4 AE, MC, V
NCS: Pine Hills Rd.

ORCHARD HILL COUNTRY INN
$$$
2502 WASHINGTON ST., 92036
TEL 760-765-1700
FAX 760-765-0290
Stay in California Craftsman-style cottages or spacious American country-style guest rooms in the main building; guest-only restaurant and lounge.
🛏 21 AE, MC, V
NCS: Main St.

JULIAN GOLD RUSH HOTEL B&B
$$
2032 MAIN ST., 92036
TEL 760-765-0201
FAX 760-765-0327
Situated in the heart of town, this historic two-story B&B is convenient to local shops, galleries, and attractions.
🛏 15 AE, MC, V
NCS: Hwy. 79

RESTAURANTS

JULIAN GRILLE
$$
2224 MAIN ST.
TEL 760-765-0173
Casual dining on American fare in a charming former home, with outdoor patio seating. A children's menu and Sunday breakfast offer added appeal.
⊕ Closed Mon. D AE, MC, V NCS: Hwy. 79

BORREGO SPRINGS

HOTELS

LA CASA DEL ZORRO DESERT RESORT
$$$$
3845 YAQUI PASS RD., 92004
TEL 760-767-5323
FAX 760-767-5963
This desert oasis offers luxurious yet earthy accommodations and facilities that include a putting green, five swimming pools, whirlpools, six lighted tennis courts, and a business center. The dining room, evokes early California, serves elegant Mexican and continental specialties. The cocktail lounge offers entertainment and patio seating is on hand.
🛏 104 All major cards NCS: Rams Hill Dr.

HOTELS & RESTAURANTS

PALM CANYON RESORT

$$$
221 PALM CANYON DR., 92004
TEL 760-767-5341
FAX 760-767-4073
Resort-like sprawl, close to the Anza-Borrego Desert State Park visitor center with modern rooms, on-site restaurant, and gift shop. Tour packages include golf, spa, off-road excursions.
60 AE, MC, V NCS: 5 Diamonds Rd.

RANCHO SANTA FE

HOTELS

INN AT RANCHO SANTA FE
$$$$
5951 LINEA DEL CIELO, 92067
TEL 858-756-1131
FAX 858-759-1604
Historic and present-day gathering spot for locals and big-name celebrities in a refined country-inn environment, surrounded by citrus groves. Accommodations are in charming guest rooms and cottages, some with kitchenettes and fireplaces.
89 AE, MC, V NCS: La Granada

RESTAURANTS

SOMETHING SPECIAL

MILLE FLEURS
In the heart of Rancho Santa Fe's village, this gorgeous, flower-filled room is the setting for celebrated patrons who enjoy perfectly executed modern French cuisine—and a sensational wine list to accompany it. Reservations are mandatory, as is proper dress for the occasion.
$$$$$
6009 PASEO DELICIAS
TEL 858-756-3085
Closed Sat.-Sun. L All major cards NCS: La Granada

SANTA CATALINA ISLAND

HOTELS

BANNING HOUSE LODGE
$$$
TWO HARBORS, 90704
TEL 310-510-0303
FAX 310-510-0244
Atmospheric accommodations on the little-visited end of the island. Guest rooms are in the main lodge or nearby units are decorated with antiques and contemporary pieces; most rooms offer unobstructed harbor views. Gourmet cuisine is served in the dining room.
11 AE, MC, V

HOTEL VILLA PORTOFINO
$$$
111 CRESCENT AVE, 90704
TEL 310-510-0555
FAX 310-510-0839
This deluxe establishment on Avalon's boardwalk faces the harbor. The Ristorante Villa Portofino is one of the island's finest dining spots. The chef prepares fresh seafood, veal, chicken, and a wide range of pastas. Start off with the crab cake appetizer.
335 Restaurant D only; closed Tues.-Wed., Nov.-March AE, MC, V NCS: Hill Ave.

PAVILION LODGE
$$
513 CRESCENT AVE, 90704
TEL 310-510-1788
FAX 310-510-1433
Within walking distance of the ferry dock, and right in the middle of Avalon, this 1950s LA-style apartment-type property offers friendly service and easy access to all shops and sights.
73 AE, MC, V NCS: Metropole Ave.

RESTAURANT

EL GALLEON
$$$
411 CRESCENT AVE.
TEL 310-510-1188
This nautical-themed restaurant across from Avalon's harbor provides good views both inside or on the patio. Live Maine lobster and fish 'n' chips are house specialties, with plenty of other options such as interesting salads and sandwiches.
AE, MC, V NCS: Metropole Ave.

TEMECULA

HOTELS

LOMA VISTA B&B
$$$
33350 LA SERENA WAY, 92591
TEL 909-676-7047
FAX 909-676-0077
Bed and breakfast retreat on a hillside overlooking vineyards. Rates include a luscious champagne breakfast and evening wine hour.
10 AE, MC, V NCS: Rancho California Rd.

TEMECULA CREEK INN
$$$
44501 RAINBOW CANYON RD., 92592
TEL 909-694-1000
FAX 909-676-8961
Geared mainly toward golfers, this sedate resort offers spacious guest rooms overlooking the 27-hole championship golf course, along with two tennis courts, hiking trails, and close proximity to wineries.
129 AE, MC, V NCS: I-15

RESTAURANTS

CAFÉ CHAMPAGNE
$$$
32575 RANCHO CALIFORNIA RD., 92591
TEL 909-699-0088
Housed inside the Thornton Winery, the hillside perch affords diners pleasant views of the surrounding vineyards while sampling contemporary California cuisine.
All major cards NCS: Butterfield Stage Rd.

SHOPPING IN SAN DIEGO

San Diego's casual ambience and terrific climate merge with almost every shopping experience. Most malls are centered on outdoor plazas, or are near the water's edge—bringing breezes and fresh air into play. Chic boutiques are spread out among the malls. Gaslamp Quarter, Coronado, La Jolla, and Del Mar. Sea-themed goods (be it T-shirts with silk-screened fish or mugs imprinted with whales) are popular and can be found—appropriately—at shops along the bay and beaches. Unique, high-quality books and gift items can be purchased at most museum gift shops, and at other popular attractions. Few visitors depart this area without Mexican-made items, whether bartered for across the border or purchased in Old Town.

Specialty Districts

San Diego's downtown Gaslamp Quarter offers a trove of interesting shops and galleries. Adams Avenue is the city's popular "antique row": Between Park Avenue and the Kensington neighborhood, hounds will be able to scour numerous dealers purveying everything from estate furnishings to rare books. Prospect Street and Girard Avenue, in La Jolla, is the nucleus for shoppers seeking designer wear and pricey art and jewelry. Coronado's Orange Avenue and Ferry Landing Marketplace feature many one-of-a-kind shops. In North County, the Cedros Design District (Cedros Ave. and Lomas Santa Fe Dr. near the Amtrak Station) draws locals who relish the distinctive designer shops, handcrafted furnishings, jewelry, housewares, fine crafts, nurseries, and garden decor. Las Americas, located on the U.S.—Mexico border, is a mall organized around themed plazas.

ARTS & CRAFTS

Art For Wildlife Galleries, 1201 1st St., #101, Ferry Landing Marketplace, Coronado, tel 619-435-4442.
A gallery devoted entirely to celebrating animals through paintings, prints, sculpture, and assorted gift items in all price ranges.

Artes de Mexico, Bazaar del Mundo, tel 619-296-3266.
Excellent range of folk art, crafts, jewelry, silver, clothing, weavings, and other unique merchandise from all parts of Mexico.

Coronado Art Gallery, 1126 Orange Ave., Coronado, tel 619-435-1819.
Fine prints of San Diego landmarks and floral landscapes, miniatures, etchings, paintings, cards, and gift items.

Maidhof Bros., 1891 San Diego Ave., tel 619-574-1891.
Fascinating range of nautical antiques and memorabilia including

ANTIQUES & COLLECTIBLES

The Antique Warehouse, 212 S. Cedros Ave., tel 858-755-5156.
More than 100 dealers exhibit antiques, collectibles, and memorabilia here in the heart of the Cedros Design District in Solana Beach (Closed Tues.)

tiques and memorabilia including

clocks, furnishings, portholes, brass bells, and gift items.

Ocean Beach Antique Mall, 4847 Newport Ave., tel 619-223-6170.
Locals love to prowl the cubbyholes and cases filled with antique and collectible pottery, jewelry, furnishings, housewares, and other goods purveyed by numerous dealers.

The Old Cracker Factory, 448 W. Market St., tel 619-233-1669.
Dealers housed in this Gaslamp Quarter three-story building offer antiques and collectibles.

SHOPPING MALLS & CENTERS

Malls and shopping centers are sprinkled throughout San Diego County. Almost all are anchored by large department stores and offer branches of retail chain stores (including the big-name booksellers), some one-of-a-kind shops, myriad options for dining and snacking, multiscreen movie theaters, and other services such as salons and day spas. Parking is almost always free (or complimentary for a certain number of hours, with validation). All are open daily.

Bazaar Del Mundo, 2754 Calhoun St., tel 619-296-3161.
Festive flower- and fountain-filled complex with fine Mexican restaurants, and 16 international shops selling folkloric items, imported clothing, arts and crafts, and other unique goods. Opens on to Old Town State Historical Park.

Del Mar Plaza, 1555 Camino del Mar, Del Mar, tel 858-792-1555.
Upscale shops, galleries, and dining; an ocean-view patio provides outdoor seating for sipping wine or coffee drinks.

Fashion Valley, 7007 Friars Rd., Mission Valley, tel 619-688-9113.
Lusciously landscaped outdoor mall with high-end department stores, hundreds of chain and specialty shops, dining options, and a multiscreen cinema.

Cottage Gallery, 2523 San Diego Ave., tel 619-296-1893.
This co-op gallery inside an old cottage features the work—including watercolor, pastel, etching, and oil mediums—of 16 local artists.

Four Winds Kiva Gallery, 647 G St., tel 619-702-2214.
Quality pottery, jewelry, basketry, kachinas, weavings, and other crafts created by Native American artisans.

Seaport Village, 849 W. Harbor Dr., tel 619-235-4014. Located on the Embarcadero, this Eastern seaboard-type 14 landscaped acres offers with waterfront dining, one-of-a-kind shops, and entertainment (including a restored Looff carousel).

Ferry Landing Marketplace, 1201 1st St., Coronado, tel 619-435-8895. Small waterfront complex offering low-key specialty shops, eateries, galleries, and bicycle rentals. Located where the San Diego–Coronado ferry drops anchor.

Westfield Shoppingtown, 324 Horton Plaza, tel 619-238-1596. This brightly-colored, architec-turally fascinating shopping center dominates seven blocks downtown. It has more than 140 specialty shops and chain and department stores, as well as myriad dining options, a 14-screen cinema, outdoor eating areas, street performers, and the underground Lyceum Theatre.

Westfield Shoppingtown— Mission Valley, 1640 Camino del Rio N., Mission Valley, tel 619-296-6375. Close to the Fashion Valley center, this mall features more than 100 specialty stores, a 20-screen cinema, and a dozen or so eateries.

Westfield Shoppingtown— University Town Centre, 4545 La Jolla Village Dr., tel 858-546-8858. About 155 specialty and department stores are located in this park-like center, which also harbor's a multi-screen cinema, indoor Olympic-size skating rink and food court.

BOOKS & MUSIC

Bay Books, 1029 Orange Ave., Coronado, tel 619-435-0070. Terrific shop for browsing a marvelous, eclectic selection of fiction and nonfiction.

D. G. Wills, 7461 Girard Ave., La Jolla, tel 858-456-1800. Irresistible shop packed with stacks of mostly-used tomes on every subject imaginable.

John Cole's Book Shop, 780 Prospect St., La Jolla, tel 858-454-4766. In operation for more than a half-century, and located in an historic cottage, the focus is on art, architecture, Baja California, cookbooks, and children's titles (closed Sun.–Mon.).

Le Travel Store, 745 4th Ave., tel 619-544-0005. Expansive selection of travel books, guides, and maps, as well as luggage, accessories, and other needs.

Libros, 2754 Calhoun St., tel 619-299-1139. Located in Bazaar del Mundo, this shop features Spanish-language books as well as English-language titles related to San Diego history.

Lou's Records, 434 N. Coast Hwy. 101, Encinitas, tel 760-753-1382. New and used CDs, cassettes, DVDs, and LPs; Lou's specializes in independent and local labels, imports, and hard-to-find releases.

Nickelodeon Records, 3335 Adams Ave., Normal Heights, tel 619-284-6083. Out-of-print 1950s-70s LPs, including sound tracks, jazz, and rock 'n' roll.

Off The Record, 3849 5th Ave., Hillcrest, tel 619-298-4755. New and used CDs and LPs, with emphasis on alternative music.

Upstart Crow Bookstore & Coffee House, 835 W. Harbor Dr., tel 619-232-4855. The coffee ambience and a fine assortment of fiction, literary titles and art books reel in readers. In Seaport Village.

Warwick's, 7812 Girard Ave., La Jolla, tel 858-454-0347. Open since 1896, this spacious shop offers more than 60,000 titles, including travel books, mysteries, and books on cassette.

The White Rabbit, 7755 Girard Ave., La Jolla, tel 858-454-3518. A delightful store holding thousands of titles geared to children, from infants through teens.

SPORTING GOODS

Adventure 16 Outdoor & Travel Outfitters, 4620 Alvarado Canyon Rd., Mission Valley, tel 858-283-2374. Also located at 143 S. Cedros Ave., Solana Beach, tel 858-755-7662. Outdoor clothing, boots, gear, backpacks, travel luggage, and accessories.

Hansen's, 1105 S. Coast Hwy. 101, Encinitas, tel 760-753-6595. Good North County source for surfboards, bodyboards, wet-suits, swimsuits, and sportswear.

Pacific Beach Surf Shop & Surf School, 4150 Mission Blvd., Pacific Beach, tel 858-373-1138. New and used surfboards, bodyboards, accessories, footwear, wetsuits, and clothing.

REI, 5556 Copley Dr., tel 858-279-4400. One of the city's finest sources for active wear, hiking boots, tents, sleeping bags, packs, bikes, and other sports gear.

South Coast Surfshop, 5023 Newport Ave., Ocean Beach, tel 619-223-7017. Also located at 740 Felspar St., Pacific Beach, tel 858-483-7660. Complete line of quality surf-boards for sale or rent, plus skateboards, wetsuits, and apparel for men, women, and children.

CLOTHING & ACCESSORIES

Armani Exchange, 7802 Girard Ave., La Jolla, tel 858-551-8193. Casual wear for men and women, along with assorted bags, belts, and other accessories.

The Ascot Shop, 7750 Girard Ave., La Jolla, tel 858-454-4222. Traditional clothing for men, including elegant suits, fine knitwear, socks, and ties.

Carizma, 107 S. Cedros Ave., Solana Beach, tel 858-792-2727. Flowing goddess-wear dresses, gowns, separates, constructed from luscious fabrics in rich and eye-catching colors.

Divas on Fifth, 542 5th Ave., tel 619-235-0550. Chic and trendy apparel for women, including cocktail dresses, evening wear, and accessories that make the outfit.

George Carter Jessop Jeweler, 401 W. C St., tel 619-234-4137. Also located at Hotel del Coronado, Coronado, tel 619-437-1707. High-class jewelry with low-key sales pitches, operating in San Diego since 1892.

The Haberdashery, 817 W. Harbor Dr., Seaport Village, tel 619-233-1770. Coordinated casual wear for men, including slacks, jackets, sweaters, shorts, and golf apparel.

Kippy's, 1114 Orange Ave., Coronado, tel 619-435-6218. Sophisticated bodysuits, swimwear, embellished denim and leather clothing, bags, and belts.

Nicole Miller, 1275 Prospect Ave., La Jolla, tel 858-454-3434. Local outlet for this high-end designer's cocktail dresses, evening wear, and colorful signature silk ties.

Panache, 7636 Girard Ave., La Jolla, tel 858-454-4220.

Pilar's Beachwear, 3745 Mission Blvd., Mission Beach, tel 858-488-3056. Excellent selection of women's swimwear, including international imports, in all styles and sizes.

Tiffany & Company, 7007 Friars Rd., Mission Valley, tel 619-297-7200. Located in the Fashion Valley mall, Tiffany offers its long-cherished collection of fine jewelry and other baubles.

Urban Outfitters, 665 5th Ave., tel 619-231-1010. A chain establishment popular with young hipsters, filled with trendy clothing, shoes, accessories, and housewares.

GIFTS & HOUSEWARES

Babette Schwartz, 421 University Ave., Hillcrest, tel 619-220-7048. Mind-boggling array of cards, toys, and kitschy knick-knacks.

Everett Stunz Company, 7624 Girard Ave., La Jolla, tel 858-459-3305. Famed locally for it's exquisite lines of imported hand-woven bed linens and bath towels.

Gepetto's, Fashion Valley mall, tel 619-294-8878. Delightful assortment of toys, games, puzzles, and other playthings for kids of all ages.

Leaping Lotus, 240 S. Cedros Ave., Solana Beach, tel 858-720-8283. In the heart of the Cedros Design District, this sleek two-level building displays the unique wares of about 100 purveyors.

Maison en Provence, 820 Fort Stockton Dr., Mission Hills, tel 619-298-5318. Country-French imports including linens, pottery, crockery, fabrics, and hand-milled soaps.

MARKETS

Fresh produce, flowers, fish, plants, and other food items and handicrafts can be purchased at farmer's markets, held weekly at the following locations: corner of Normal and Cleveland Sts., Hillcrest (Sun. 9 a.m.–noon); Mission Blvd., at the Promenade Mall, Pacific Beach (Sat. 8 a.m.–noon); 4900 block, Newport Ave., Ocean Beach (Wed. 4-8 p.m.); 1st and B Sts., Ferry Landing Marketplace, Coronado (Tues. 2:30-6 p.m.); Girard Ave. and Genter St., La Jolla Elementary School, La Jolla (Sun. 9 a.m.–1 p.m.); 10th St. and Camino del Mar, Del Mar (Sat. 12-4 p.m.); Cedros Street, Amtrak Station, Solana Beach (Sun. 8 a.m.–noon).

Kobey's Swap Meet, 3500 Sports Arena Blvd. (in the Sports Arena's parking lot), tel 619-226-0650. Great deals on used and new items such as furniture, clothing, plants, tools, jewelry, sunglasses, and a plethora of other goods. (Fri.–Sun. 7 a.m.–3 p.m.)

OUTLET MALLS

Carlsbad Company Stores, 5620 Paseo del Norte, Carlsbad, tel 888-790-7467. Located off I-5, near Legoland, this inviting European-style center features about 80 outlet shops, representing numerous prestigious brands; restaurants, cafés, and a winery.

Viejas Outlet Center, 5000 Willows Rd., Alpine, tel 619-659-2070. Located east of San Diego with over 40 stores and a casino.

ENTERTAINMENT & ACTIVITIES

San Diego boasts a renowned opera company, theaters, and a fine symphony orchestra, as well as smaller theater companies, dance troupes, and other musical talents. Due to the city's active nature and waterfront location, spectator and participant sports are also appropriate under the "entertainment" heading. Comprehensive listings of both indoor and outdoor events can be found in Thursday's *San Diego Union-Tribune*'s "Night & Day" section, Sunday's *Los Angeles Times*' "Calendar" section, the free *San Diego Reader* (distributed at shops, cafés, and convenience stores each Thursday), or the monthly *San Diego Magazine*.

ENTERTAINMENT

Purchase tickets for most major events through Ticketmaster (tel 619-220-8497).

Half-price tickets (plus service charge) are available to many plays and concerts on the day of performance at the Art Tix booth, Horton Plaza at Broadway Circle, tel 619-497-5000.

BALLET, OPERA, & CLASSICAL MUSIC

California Ballet Company, tel 858-560-5676. Professional company, in operation for more than 30 years, annually presents several traditional and contemporary works at venues around the county, including the popular Nutcracker at the Civic Theatre during the Christmas holidays.

La Jolla Chamber Music Society, tel 858-459-3728. Year-round concerts include the Celebrity Series at downtown's Civic Theatre, the Revelle Series at La Jolla's Sherwood Auditorium, and an annual SummerFest.

Malashock Dance & Company, tel 619-235-2266. Founder and artistic director John Malashock and his esteemed dance troupe perform modern and contemporary works at Balboa Park's Old Globe Theatre and other locations.

San Diego Chamber Orchestra, tel 888-848-7326. The San Diego Chamber Orchestra features concerts accessible to a wide range of audiences, with series taking place at La Jolla's Sherwood Auditorium, Rancho Santa Fe's Fairbanks Ranch Country Club, and Escondido's California Center for the Arts, and other sites.

San Diego Opera, 202 C St., Civic Theatre, tel 619-570-1100. Under the direction of Ian Campbell, the San Diego Opera presents five grand operas per year at the Civic Theatre, as well as numerous educational programs and performances geared to all audiences and age levels.

San Diego Symphony Orchestra, 1245 7th Ave., tel 619-235-0804. The regular season is played at Copley Symphony Hall, with the popular San Diego Pops program held at Navy Pier.

CINEMA

The Cove, 7730 Girard Ave., La Jolla, tel 858-459-5404. One-screen cinema showing first-run and art films.

Hillcrest Cinemas, 3965 5th Ave., Hillcrest, tel 619-299-2100. Chic five-screen cinema, with first-rate foreign-, independent-, and American releases. Three-hour parking, with validation, in downstairs garage.

The Ken Cinema, 4061 Adams Ave., Kensington, tel 619-283-3909. This favorite with locals has a frequently changing schedule that includes cult-, independent-, and foreign films, director's cuts, classics, and avant-garde offerings.

La Paloma, 471 S. Hwy. 101, Encinitas, tel 760-436-7469. A treasured 1927 one-screen movie house with Spanish facade, screening foreign films and first-run flicks as well as live concerts and theatrical productions.

Pacific Gaslamp Stadium 15, 701 5th Ave., tel 619-232-0400. A plush 15-screen cinema housed in a converted Victorian building in the Gaslamp Quarter; shows first-run films.

PERFORMANCE VENUES

California Center for the Arts, 340 N. Escondido Blvd., Escondido, tel 800-988-4253. A fabulous year-round line-up at inland North County's prestigious and acoustically divine performing arts center includes such diverse talents as the Whirling Dervishes, the Moody Blues, the Buena Vista Social Club, the National Acrobats of Taiwan, and Hal Holbrook who play in the 1,535-seat concert hall or the 408-seat theater.

Civic Theatre, 202 C St., tel 619-570-1100. This plush 3,000-seat venue with state-of-the-art acoustics hosts the San Diego Opera, California Ballet Company, La Jolla Chamber Music Society, and other premier artists.

Diversionary Theatre, 4545 Park Blvd., Hillcrest, tel 619-220-0097. Contemporary gay- and lesbian-oriented productions are staged for a loyal and diverse audience.

East County Performing Arts Center, 210 E. Main St., El Cajon, tel 619-440-2277. Year-round entertainment at this off-the-beaten-path performing arts center includes surprises such as Israel's oldest dance company, Broadway's Tommy

Tune, and Steve Lawrence and Eydie Gorme.

The Globe Theatres, 1363 Old Globe Way, Balboa Park, tel 619-239-2255.
Internationally renowned complex consisting of the Old Globe Theatre, Cassius Carter Centre Stage, and the Lowell Davies Festival Theatre. Classic and contemporary works are presented year-round, with a Shakespeare festival on the schedule each summer.

Humphrey's by the Bay, 2241 Shelter Island Dr., Shelter Island, tel 619-224-3577.
Humphrey's hosts an immensely popular series of outdoor concerts each summer, reeling in a varied bunch of international talents.

La Jolla Playhouse, 2910 La Jolla Village Dr., La Jolla, tel 858-550-1010.
This esteemed playhouse, part of the Mandell Weiss Center for the Performing Arts on the UCSD campus, is composed of two theaters that present classical and contemporary works, as well as musicals— some which have gone on to Broadway.

Lamb's Players Theatre, 1142 Orange Ave., Coronado, tel 619-437-0600.
Well-respected, artist-driven ensemble that presents year-round thought-provoking works that address spirituality and the human condition.

Mystery Café Dinner Theatre, 505 Kalmia St., tel 619-544-1600.
The Imperial House Restaurant sets the scene for murder and intrigue, drawing the audience into the action.

North Coast Repertory Theatre, 987-D Lomas Santa Fe Dr., Solana Beach, tel 858-481-1055.
Contemporary and classical plays, including some West

Coast premieres, are staged in an intimate setting at the edge of a shopping center.

San Diego Repertory Theatre, 79 Horton Plaza, tel 619-544-1000.
The underground Lyceum Theatre is home to this long-established company that performs culturally diverse dramas and comedies on two different stages.

Sledgehammer Theatre, 1620 6th Ave., tel 619-544-1484.
Controversial, edgy, and occasionally angst-ridden American works are performed in a converted funeral chapel.

Spreckels Theatre, 121 Broadway, tel 619-235-9500.
Historic 1,466-seat theater, in the heart of downtown, where stage plays and concerts are held.

Starlight Theatre, 2005 Pan American Plaza, Balboa Park, tel 619-544-7827.
This outdoor amphitheater has been hosting popular musicals each summer since the 1940s. Situated in the airport's flight path, the actors freeze on stage until the planes pass by.

Sushi, 320 11th Ave., tel 619-235-8466.
Located in a whitewashed loft space inside a converted milk factory, Sushi has been presenting provocative, cutting-edge performance art since its 1980 inception.

Theatre in Old Town, 4040 Twiggs St., tel 619-688-2491.
Long-running lightweight musicals please tourist-heavy audiences in this barnlike venue.

NIGHTLIFE

4th & B, 345 B St., tel 619-231-2131.
One of the city's hippest clubs (located in a former bank building) features eight bars, a plush balcony and theater, and an

eclectic roster of musicians that includes top international stars.

Belly Up Tavern, 143 S. Cedros Ave., Solana Beach, tel 858-481-8140.
It's worth the 25-mile drive up the coast from downtown to catch big-name performers like Koko Taylor and Jefferson Starship, as well as hot local groups. Billiards tables, a bar, and a dance floor add to the fun.

Blind Melons, 710 Garnet Ave., Pacific Beach, tel 858-483-7844.
Blues, rock, reggae, ska, and alternative bands hit the stage most nights at this cool and casual bar near the beach and boardwalk.

Brick by Brick, 1130 Buenos Ave., Bay Park, tel 619-275-5483.
All types of bands play at this diehard club, which once focused on alternative music but now offers something for everyone and every age.

The Casbah, 2501 Kettner Blvd., tel 619-232-4355.
It looks nondescript (possibly, decrepit) from the outside, but this down-and-dirty club is San Diego's pulse on the music world showcasing local alternative bands, touring acts, and occasional headliners.

The Comedy Store, 916 Pearl St., La Jolla, tel 858-454-9176.
Headliner comics are featured at this branch of the L.A. club, where David Letterman, Gary Shandling, and Pauly Shore got their start. Sunday is "open mike" night for locals and wanna-bes.

Croce's, 802 5th Ave., tel 619-233-4355.
Ingrid Croce, wife of the late Jim Croce, pays tribute to all music lovers with big jazz greats playing in the Jazz Bar, and jazz and blues bands.

E Street Alley, 919 4th Ave., tel 619-231-9200.
Hot spot in the Gaslamp, where hipsters maneuver underground

bars and lounges, listening to jazz acts, disco dancing, and shooting pool.

The Flame, 3780 Park Blvd., Hillcrest, tel 619-295-4163.
This mainly lesbian bar is a neighborhood old-timer, and features theme nights, a cigar lounge, martini bar, and dancing galore.

Jimmy Love's, 672 5th Ave., tel 619-595-0123.
Poised on a prominent corner in the Gaslamp, this club offers a continuous party atmosphere for locals and tourists who gather at the cherry-wood bar, or on the spacious dance floor.

Karl Strauss Brewery Restaurant, 1157 Columbia St., downtown, tel 619-234-2739.
San Diego's oldest brewpub is a top gathering spot for local professionals, students, and visitors who choose from 10-12 daily microbrews and quality pub fare.

Martini Ranch, 528 F St., tel 619-235-6100.
A casual upscale bar and lounge that pours 30 house martinis and 20 beers on tap. DJ music plays nightly, and two big screens display sports and other action.

Numbers, 3811 Park Blvd., Hillcrest, tel 619-294-9005.
Don't be misled by the unassuming facade of this gay bar; the enormous interior is packed with good-looking single men dancing the night away to high-energy music. Others circumvent the pool tables and outdoor patio.

Ole Madrid, 751 5th Ave., tel. 619-557-0146.
A swinging Euro-style club, with two rooms of dance action for a hip, thin, black-clad crowd. (Closed Mon.)

Patrick's II, 428 F St., tel 619-233-3077.
A small, classy, almost unnoticeable bar in the heart of the Gaslamp, where live blues

acts play most nights to an appreciative older crowd.

Top of the Hyatt, One Market Pl., tel 619-232-1234.
Sophisticated setting at the top of the Manchester Hyatt Regency Hotel, where cocktails and other libations play second fiddle to the mesmerizing city and harbor views.

Waterfront Bar, 2044 Kettner Blvd., tel 619-232-9656.
Historic waterfront bar, dating from the 1930s, that still serves booze and grub to local characters at the bar or on the sidewalk patio.

Whaling Bar, 1132 Prospect St., La Jolla, tel 858-454-0771.
Inside the distinctive pink stucco La Valencia Hotel, this clubby bar has long been the haunt of Hollywood celebrities, visiting royalty, and sophisticated locals.

Winston's, 1921 Bacon St., Ocean Beach, tel 619-222-6822.
This landmark unpretentious beach bar dishes up live blues, rock, reggae, and other sounds seven nights a week.

ACTIVITIES

OUTFITTERS

BOATING AND FISHING
H&M Landing, 2803 Emerson St., tel 619-222-1144.
Wide range of half-day, whole-day, and overnight fishing trips.

La Jolla Kayak & Company, 2199 Avenida de la Playa, La Jolla, tel 858-459-1114.
Rent kayaks to explore La Jolla's caves and sea cliffs. Paddle and picnic tours are also available.

Marina Sailing of San Diego, 2240 Shelter Island Dr., Shelter Island, tel 619-221-8286.
Learn-to-sail trips, as well as sailboat rentals with or without crew.

Seaforth Boat Rental, 1641 Quivera Rd. Mission Bay, tel 619-223-1681.
Numerous rental boats for fishing, skiing, sailing, jet skiing, and other pursuits, with instruction available.

Seaforth Sportfishing, 1717 Quivera Rd., Mission Bay, tel 619-224-3383.
Half-day and longer fishing trips, near and afar.

CYCLING AND SKATING
Bikes & Beyond, 1201 1st St. #122, Coronado, tel 619-435-7180.
Cycles and skates can be rented at the Ferry Landing Marketplace, where the San Diego ferry docks.

DIVING
Dive Connections, 1500 Quivera Way, Mission Bay, tel 619-523-9282.
Daily dive and snorkel trips to local spots, and down to Mexico.

Diving Locker, 1020 Grand Ave., Pacific Beach, tel 858-272-1120.
Private or group classes for both novices and experts, along with escorted dive trips, equipment, and dive and snorkeling maps.

GOLF
San Diego boasts more than 80 golf courses with opportunities for year-round play. The following are open to the public, and offer at least 18 holes:

Balboa Park Municipal Golf Course, 2600 Golf Course Dr., Balboa Park, tel 619-235-1184.

Coronado Municipal Golf Course, 2000 Visalia Row, Coronado, tel 619-435-3121.

Mission Bay Golf Course, 2702 N. Mission Bay Dr., Mission Bay, tel 858-490-3370.

Torrey Pines Municipal Golf Course, 11480 N. Torrey Pines Rd., La Jolla, tel 858-452-3226.

HANG GLIDING

Torrey Pines Gliderport,
2800 Torrey Pines Scenic Dr., La
Jolla, tel. 858-452-9858.
Near Torrey Pines State
Reserve, parasailers and hang
gliders take off from the cliffs
above the Pacific Ocean. Tandem
flights are available for beginners.

HORSEBACK RIDING

Sandy's Rental Stable, 2060
Hollister St., Imperial Beach, tel
619-424-3124.
Year-round beach and nature
trail rides for all skill levels.

SURFING

San Diego Surfing Academy,
6335 Camirito Telmo, San Diego,
tel 858-565-6892.
Personalized instruction for all
ages, as well as surf camps, Baja
trips, and any necessary
equipment.

SWIMMING

Nearly every hotel and motel
has a heated swimming pool,
with other pools available at
local parks (San Diego City
Parks and Recreation Department, tel 619-685-1322).

Mission Bay Plunge, 3115
Ocean Front Walk, Mission
Beach 858-488-3110.
In operation since the 1920s,
this 175-foot long enclosed pool
offers sectioned-off areas as well
as numerous swimming lanes.

Kearns Memorial Pool, 2229
Morley Field Dr., Balboa Park, tel
619-692-4920.
Swimming and classes are
available to the public.

TENNIS

Many hotels and resorts provide
tennis facilities for guests, as do
the swanky country clubs and
spas. Public parks are also a
good source for free play (San
Diego City Parks and Recreation
Department, tel 619-685-1322).

Balboa Tennis Club, 2221
Morley Field Dr., Balboa Park, tel
619-295-9278.
About half of the Morely Field

RECREATION CENTERS

**Mission Bay Park
Headquarters, 2581** Quivira
Ct., Mission Bay, tel 619-221-
1081.
One of the city's favorite
recreational areas offering 4,600
acres parklands and beaches for
swimming, boating, fishing, golf,
tennis, cycling, and other sports.
Several facilities available.

**Morley Field Sports
Complex, 2221** Morley Field
Dr., Balboa Park, tel 619-692-
4919.
Across from Balboa Park, this
sports complex offers swimming, golf, tennis, Frisbee golf,
and myriad other facilities.

La Jolla Recreation Center,
615 Prospect Ave., La Jolla, tel
858-552-1658.
Nine free courts (five lighted)
are available for public use.

tennis complex's 25 courts are
lighted, and nonmembers can
play for a nominal charge.

SPECTATOR SPORT VENUES

BASEBALL

San Diego Padres, Qualcomm
Stadium, tel 619-374-2784.
The two-time National League
West Division champs go to bat
April through September, playing
home games at Qualcomm
Stadium (until the new stadium
is constructed downtown).

BASKETBALL

**San Diego State University
Aztecs,** Cox Arena, SDSU, tel
619-594-0429.
The men's and women's Aztec
teams play home games at the
campus's Cox Arena, mid-
November to early March.

FOOTBALL

San Diego Chargers,
Qualcomm Stadium, tel 619-280-
2121.
Throughout the fall, San Diego's
NFL team plays home games to

loyal audiences at its renovated
stadium—also shared by the
Aztecs (San Diego State
University) college football team.

HOCKEY

The San Diego Gulls, San
Diego Sports Arena, tel 619-
224-4171.
The West Coast Hockey
League's San Diego Gulls play
the Sports Arena, October to
March.

HORSE RACING

Del Mar Racetrack, 2260
Jimmy Durante Blvd., Del Mar tel
858-755-1141.
Dating from 1937 when celebrities began flocking here, the
Del Mar Racetrack—adjacent to
the beach—still attracts a classy
crowd for its annual Thorough-
bred-racing season, mid-July
through early September. Off-
season wagering is available,
year-round, at the 8,600-square-
foot Surfside Race Place (tel
858-755-1167).

ILLUSTRATIONS CREDITS

Cover: Michael Melford

Interior: All photographs by Michael Melford except for the following:
20, San Diego Historical Society; 22, San Diego Historical Society; 30-31,
San Diego Historical Society; 33, San Diego Historical Society; 40-41,
MPTV; 44 (LE), Bettmann/CORBIS; 44 (RT), Bettmann/CORBIS; 96
(UP), San Diego Historical Society; 116-117, San Diego Historical
Society; 175, Courtesy La Jolla Playhouse; 177, Bettmann/CORBIS; 181
(LE), James L. Amos/CORBIS

Artwork by Maltings Partnership, Derby, England

One of the world's largest non-profit scientific and educational organizations, the National Geographic Society was founded in 1888 "for the increase and diffusion of geographic knowledge." Fulfilling this mission, the Society educates and inspires millions every day through its magazines, books, television programs, videos, maps and atlases, research grants, the National Geographic Bee, teacher workshops, and innovative classroom materials. The Society is supported through membership dues, charitable gifts, and income from the sale of its educational products. This support is vital to National Geographic's mission to increase global understanding and promote conservation of our planet through exploration, research, and education.

For more information, please call 1-800-NGS LINE (647-5463) or write to the following address:

National Geographic Society
1145 17th Street N.W.
Washington, D.C. 20036-4688
U.S.A.

Visit the Society's Web site at www.nationalgeographic.com.

Published by the National Geographic Society

John M. Fahey, Jr., *President and Chief Executive Officer*
Gilbert M. Grosvenor, *Chairman of the Board*
Nina D. Hoffman, *Executive Vice President,*
        President, Books and School Publishing
Kevin Mulroy, *Vice President and Editor-in-Chief*
Elizabeth L. Newhouse, *Director of Travel Publishing*
Charles Kogod, *Director of Photography*
Marianne Koszorus, *Design Director*
Cinda Rose, *Art Director*
Carl Mehler, *Director of Maps*
Barbara A. Noe, *Series Director*

Staff for this book:

Allan Fallow, *Senior Editor and Project Manager*
Marilyn Mofford Gibbons, *Illustrations Editor*
Kay Hankins, *Designer*
Pat Daniels, *Text Editor*
Caroline Hickey, *Senior Researcher*
Victoria Garrett Jones, Michelle Harris,
        Jane Sunderland, *Editorial Researchers*
Matt Chwastyk, Joseph F. Ochlak, Nicholas P. Rosenbach,
        XNR Productions, *Map Edit, Research, and Production*
R. Gary Colbert, *Production Director*
Richard S. Wain, *Production Project Manager*
Sharon Kocsis Berry, *Illustrations Assistant*
Lawrence Porges, *Editorial Specialist*
James Enzinna, *Indexer*
Sallie Greenwood, *Copy Editor*

Map art drawn by ChrisOrr.com, Southampton, England

ISBN 0-7922-6933-0

ISSN 1541-5295

Printed and bound by R.R. Donnelley & Sons, Willard, Ohio
Color separations by Quad Graphics, Alexandria, Virginia
Cover printed by Miken Inc., Cheektowaga, New York

NATIONAL GEOGRAPHIC
TRAVELER

A Century of Travel Expertise in Every Guide

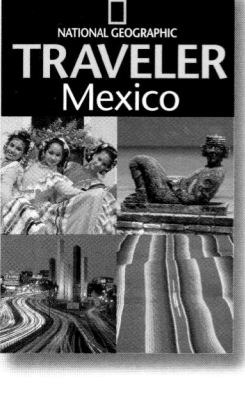

- **Amsterdam** ISBN: 0-7922-7900-X
- **Arizona** ISBN: 0-7922-7899-2
- **Australia** ISBN: 0-7922-7431-8
- **Barcelona** ISBN: 0-7922-7902-6
- **Boston & Environs** ISBN: 0-7922-7926-3
- **California** ISBN: 0-7922-7564-0
- **Canada** ISBN: 0-7922-7427-X
- **The Caribbean** ISBN: 0-7922-7434-2
- **China** ISBN: 0-7922-7921-2
- **Costa Rica** ISBN: 0-7922-7946-8
- **Cuba** ISBN: 0-7922-6931-4
- **Egypt** ISBN: 0-7922-7896-8
- **Florence & Tuscany** ISBN: 0-7922-7924-7
- **Florida** ISBN: 0-7922-7432-6
- **France** ISBN: 0-7922-7426-1
- **Great Britain** ISBN: 0-7922-7425-3
- **Greece** ISBN: 0-7922-7923-9
- **Hawaii** ISBN: 0-7922-7944-1
- **Hong Kong** ISBN: 0-7922-7901-8

- **India** ISBN: 0-7922-7898-4
- **Italy** ISBN: 0-7922-7562-4
- **Japan** ISBN: 0-7922-7563-2
- **London** ISBN: 0-7922-7428-8
- **Los Angeles** ISBN: 0-7922-7947-6
- **Mexico** ISBN: 0-7922-7897-6
- **Miami and the Keys** ISBN: 0-7922-7433-4
- **New Orleans** ISBN: 0-7922-7948-4
- **New York** ISBN: 0-7922-7430-X
- **Paris** ISBN: 0-7922-7429-6
- **Rome** ISBN: 0-7922-7566-7
- **San Diego** ISBN: 0-7922-6933-0
- **San Francisco** ISBN: 0-7922-7565-9
- **Spain** ISBN: 0-7922-7922-0
- **Sydney** ISBN: 0-7922-7435-0
- **Thailand** ISBN: 0-7922-7943-3
- **Venice** ISBN: 0-7922-7917-4
- **Washington, D.C.** ISBN: 0-7922-7903-4

AVAILABLE WHEREVER BOOKS ARE SOLD